Praise for *Losing Your Mind*

Our brains have taken a beating. The trauma of a pandemic and the daily assault of cell phones has damaged our ability to think deeply. In this fascinating study of how the health of the mind impacts our ability to spiritually mature, Dr. Pete Bellini offers hope and rescue of what we thought was lost for good -- our capacity to have the mind of Christ. If you struggle with focus when it comes to spiritual discipline, or long for the healing power of truth, or just want to love the Lord better with your mind, this read is for you.

–**Bishop Carolyn Moore**, Global Methodist Church

The psalmist declares '...I am fearfully and wonderfully made...' (Psalm 139:14). I must confess I usually think of the intricacies of the human body when reading those words, but Dr. Pete Bellini's most recent work, *Losing Your Mind (And Gaining the Mind of Christ): How to Overhaul Your Brain for Faith, Focus, and Flourishing* has greatly expanded my thinking. I've often wondered why some folks have such a difficult time having the mind of Christ, and this book has given me a glimpse of how changing the way we think is the key to the transformation Jesus offers.

Using the best of theology, biblical study, neuroscience, and cognitive behavioral therapy, he has expanded my understanding to include not only the body—but also the mind. In fact, I believe this groundbreaking work will become an incredible resource to help followers of Jesus experience the sanctifying grace of God that comes through the renewing of our minds.

–**Bishop Jeffrey E. Greenway**, Global Methodist Church

I am so grateful to Dr. Pete Bellini for writing *Losing Your Mind (And Gaining the Mind of Christ): How to Overhaul Your Brain for Faith, Focus, and Flourishing* This book is extremely timely and important to the work of the church. American mental health decline is often featured in various media as well as articles that feature the decline in the number of actively practicing Christians. This book explains the neuroscience and how the brain is affected by the act of faithful discipleship. It explains how our minds are literally renewed in Christ Jesus. Pastors seeking to shepherd and disciple congregations will find this book prepares them on a different level to offer discipleship to the world.

–**Bishop Leah Hidde-Gregory**, Global Methodist Church

Dr. Pete Bellini offers us an exciting ground-breaking insight connecting the Christ-commissioned and consecrated work of making disciples (Matthew 28:16-20) with the latest neuroscience research on the brain and human learning. *Losing Your Mind* yokes insight and application together with biblical integrity. Here is a deep intensely practical tool which will enhance both our faithfulness and fruitfulness. I enthusiastically commend this groundbreaking work to all who are serious about making disciples of Jesus Christ!

–Bishop Emeritus Mike Lowry, Global Methodist Church

Dr. Pete Bellini has produced a fascinating study on how our minds work, how to live with the Mind of Christ and how to train our brains for making new disciples of Jesus Christ using wise insights from the science of the mind and how we think of the Biblical truths about salvation through Jesus Christ. *Losing Your Mind* provides practical pastoral illustrations on how to apply Paul's admonition in Romans 12:2: "Do not be conformed to this world, but be transformed by the renewing of your minds so that you may discern what is the will of God--what is good and acceptable and perfect." I highly recommend it for Christian leaders who are committed to making new disciples of Jesus Christ.

–Dr. Kent Millard, President of United Theological Seminary

Losing Your Mind is one of a kind! In this book, Dr. Pete Bellini brings together the latest insights from cognitive neuroscience, the experience of a master of discipleship, and Holy Ghost fire. This book is not only *about* how your brain impacts discipleship. This book shows you how to, in Pete's own words, "lose our mind and gain the mind of Christ."

–Kevin M. Watson, Director of Academic Growth & Formation at Asbury Theological Seminary and Scholar in Residence at Asbury Church, Tulsa, OK

Christian discipleship is designed to bring life transformation. Transformation takes place by God's grace through the renewing of the mind (Romans 12:2). As Dr. Peter Bellini writes in *Losing Your Mind (And Gaining the Mind of Christ): How to Overhaul Your Brain for Faith, Focus, and Flourishing*, "The [Holy] Spirit's work of renewing our minds is fundamental to our discipleship."

Dr. Bellini takes us on an awe-inspiring tour of God's creation, and a mind-expanding exploration of the neurological functioning of the human brain/mind. He demonstrates how our brain has been hardwired for religion in general and for faithful Christian discipleship in particular. *Losing Your Mind* unfolds the remarkable capabilities God has given our brains to enhance our growth in faith and holiness.

Losing Your Mind provides us with an insightful view of the connections between neurology and faith, as well as a practical resource for all who desire to grow as disciples and disciple others. The reader will find a solid foundation in Wesleyan theology, illuminating examples of the transforming power of the Holy Spirit, and helpful charts, outlines, and principles for making/teaching disciples. Dr. Bellini offers passionate invitation for the church to experience the power of the Holy Spirit to renew our minds in Christ and experience the supernatural power of God for witness and service. I am grateful for this gift Dr. Bellini has given the church.

–**Rev. Gregory D. Stover**, Director Global Methodist House of Study, United Theological Seminary, Dean of Presiding Elders, Allegheny West Annual Conference of the Global Methodist Church

This book is precisely what the title suggests, a detailed way to nurture our brains as Christian disciples so we might have the mind of Christ. Dr. Peter Bellini's unusual personal journey and exceptional capacity to weave Scripture, neuroscience, story, boxing, and Wesleyan theology into a cohesive training manual for passionate spiritual discipleship is itself *masterful*. May its fruit be truly abundant to the glory of God.

–**Ron Crandall**, Professor Emeritus, Asbury Theological Seminary

Pete Bellini's newest work combines the heart of a disciple-making pastor with deep scholarly study and the wisdom of a spiritual father. In it, Bellini weaves together practical discipleship, insights from modern neuroscience, images from the world of boxing, and ancient spiritual practices such as deliverance, hearing the voice of God, and other spiritual gifts. When it comes to a holistic understanding of what it really takes to make disciples, Bellini is no mere theoretician. Instead, this book is the work of a man who has actively molded disciples of Jesus Christ for many decades, and the reader gets to reap the fruit. This book will be a gift to anyone seeking to better understand Christian discipleship while experiencing the transformed life made available through Jesus Christ.

–**Matt Judkins**, Lead Pastor, Renewal Church, McAlester, OK

Losing Your Mind (And Gaining the Mind of Christ): How to Overhaul Your Brain for Faith, Focus, and Flourishing is a ground-breaking book connecting discipleship and the human brain while providing a practical guide drawing from Scripture, theology, cognitive neuroscience, and psychology. Bellini's work highlights and delivers a unique perspective into how our minds and faith are in an intricately connected relationship and how the Holy Spirit can use the human brain to transform us into the image of Christ. *Losing Your Mind* is for anyone who wants to grow as a wholehearted disciple of Jesus Christ that can live out faith, wisdom, and victory.

–**Rev. Dr. Rosario Picardo**, church planter, pastor, author, and consultant

Dr. Pete Bellini's book, *Losing Your Mind*, offers a one-two punch in helping the reader understand discipleship using current brain science research to understand the process of how one's mind functions to grow into Christlikeness. This text contains the essentials of discipleship, basic theory and practice of brain science, while utilizing stories and experiences in sports regarding the training process, as he applies it to how one learns and grows as a disciple of Jesus.

Dr. Bellini helps the reader understand the process of repatterning our neural connections as a part of discipleship. He writes in chapter 3, "Discipleship structures and restructures the brain through synaptic plasticity (new or modified neural connections). When we learn and make "connections" between two concepts, we are literally making synaptic connections in the brain."

Dr. Bellini defines a disciple as *"a disciplined learner and follower of Jesus Christ"*, and discipleship as *"the process of learning and following Jesus."* As Romans 12:1 speaks to being transformed or changed by changing and renewing our minds is the beginning of discipleship, and growing as a disciple is the process of one's brains being rewired to Christlikeness.

This is a very helpful book that helps the reader connect the goal and process of discipleship with how one's brain functions and helps the reader identify and apply brain science to the discipleship process. A very practical read, it connects a lot of current brain research and science to the process of becoming a disciple of Jesus.

–**G. Scott Pattison**, Conference Superintendent, Great Lakes Conference, Global Methodist Church

LOSING
YOUR
MIND

PETER BELLINI

LOSING YOUR MIND

(AND GAINING
THE MIND OF CHRIST)

**HOW TO
OVERHAUL YOUR BRAIN
FOR FAITH, FOCUS,
AND FLOURISHING**

invite
PRESS

Plano, Texas

CONTENTS

CHAPTER 3

DISCIPLESHIP 101: DISCIPLING THE MIND

CHAPTER 4

REPENTANCE: CHANGING THE MIND

CHAPTER 5

THE WAR FOR THE MIND

INTRODUCTION

It is common knowledge but uncommonly practiced, that what you think is what you are. A fighter is the sum of his thoughts that occupy his mind on a daily basis. If a fighter decides to actively allow negative thoughts to run rampant in his mind, he will be operating from a negative mental zone."

—Cus D'Amato, boxing sage, coach, and trainer[1]

I am a professor at a denominational seminary and an ordained Elder in my denomination. I am also the founder, owner, and head coach of a boxing club. The club is a free outreach ministry to young men and women that teaches the fundamentals of boxing and uses the metaphor of boxing to teach about life. We are there to not only build good fighters, but to build good people. One of my old coaches used to say, "We build a fighter from the ground up, beginning with their footwork." Contrastingly, with discipleship, God builds a Christian from the brain down. He begins by changing our minds. As the mind goes, so goes the person. Scripture echoes this adage. We are transformed or changed by changing and renewing our minds (Rom. 12:1–2). The apostle Paul used the metaphors of boxing (1 Cor. 9:27), wrestling (Eph. 6:12), running (Phil. 2:16), the Games (1 Cor. 9:24–25; 2 Tim. 2:5), and soldiering (2 Tim. 2:3–4) to explain the rigorous training needed to live a victorious life. This book will not only use sports metaphors to illuminate our understanding of the battle in our minds, but it will also employ elements of cognitive neuroscience to assist us to better comprehend how God hardwires us for discipleship and victory in Christ.

Many of us were not pleased with the state of our minds before we came to Christ. Numerous thoughts then, and even now, were confused, sinful, unwanted, embarrassing, outlandish, and not pleasing to us or God. The vast space between our ears seems to give us more problems than anything else. At times when our minds go haywire, we feel like we are losing our minds, or we would like to lose our minds, meaning to get rid of them. Well, we can! Through salvation, we can lose our mind and gain the mind of Christ (1 Cor. 2:16)! By faith, we do indeed give Christ our old life, including our mind, and receive a new life—the mind of Christ.

---

1. Reemus Baily, *The Cus D'Amato Mind*, 71. (Reemus Boxing, 2017)

However, when we receive our new mind in Christ, it is not fully programmed. The coding of our new software is minimal. Our incipient knowledge of God is just a seed of what is to come. Our new mind is not developed or fully grown. We are newborns in Christ. The seed needs to be watered and nurtured by the Word and Spirit of God. Although we are given a new mind, unfortunately, we actually retain the same old body and the same brain. Yes, the brain that produced all of those unwanted, sinful thoughts and patterns is still in our head, even after accepting Christ as Lord. Thus, the job of the Holy Spirit is to help us to unlearn those old sinful patterns (repentance) and learn new patterns (righteous thinking) that are aligned with God's word.

When I first came to Christ, I did not realize that my mind would need an entire overhaul. Yes, we do lose our minds and gain the mind of Christ, which is the work of the Spirit. The Spirit's work of renewing our minds is fundamental to our discipleship. His sanctifying work begins in our brain. The brain and the mind are central to operating not just our body but our entire being. I will repeat this mantra often: "As the mind goes, so goes the person." Proverbs 23:7 similarly reads, "For as he thinks in his heart, so is he" (NKJV). Our thought life can greatly determine our feelings, actions, and overall being for better or for worse. Not morbidly so, but we need to pay attention to our thinking. The brain is the control center of all that we are in our embodied being. All inputs to Petey Bellini must go through my brain first. The brain-mind apparatus is, hence, strategic in defining who we are (our being) and what we do (our doing). It follows then, that discipleship should begin there as well. The Holy Spirit, the Spirit of Truth, our primary disciplemaker, uses truth as a tool to craft our minds into the image of God in Christ. He forms our new identity in Christ by renewing our minds with God's word. The word "reshapes our brains" (neuroplasticity and synaptogenesis) as we hear and obey it. We will learn more about those fancy words and that process throughout the book.

Losing Your Mind (And Gaining the Mind of Christ): How to Overhaul Your Brain for Faith, Focus, and Flourishing is basically a book about discipleship and its relationship to the brain and mind. Along with Scripture and theology, our study will be resourced by basic cognitive neuroscience and psychology to help make the connection deeper between the discipleship process and our brain. This text contains the essentials of discipleship, basic theory, and practice. We begin in the first chapter with the mind of God revealed in the order of creation. We will study the universe and God's greatest creation in the universe, the human brain. We will walk through a cursory examination of the marvel and wonder of the brain, including basic brain anatomy, which will assist us in understanding how God transforms us by working through the systems, structures, and functions of the brain. In Chapter 2, we target our goal: the mind of Christ. Christ is our holy example, and his thoughts are our pattern to emulate since Jesus Christ is the perfect and full image of God. We are being molded into his image to look like him. The mind of Christ is our model. What does that look like? What is the mind of Christ?

In Chapter 3, we will receive a crash course in discipleship. What is discipleship? What are the goals and outcomes? What does Scripture state about discipleship? What are the key practices of a disciple? How does the Spirit disciple us? How does discipleship relate to our brains? In Chapter 4, we will unpack a forgotten but key ancient practice: repentance. Scripture study will lead us to better understand what this often-misunderstood word and practice mean. We will assess repentance in light of the brain through neuroscience and cognitive science. Chapter 5 lays out the impact of spiritual warfare in the process of discipleship. We desire to grow in the image of God, but the enemy of our soul (the voice of temptation) has other plans: to steal, kill, and destroy (John 10:9). However, God equips us with his armor and various spiritual weapons to fight and win the battle. What are those weapons? How do we fight the devil and the flesh (our sinful self)? How can neuroscience and cognitive science help us fight and win the battle?

Chapter 6 is about renewing our minds with the truth, the word of God. We will use a particular method for renewing the mind that I designed years ago called Truth Therapy. Truth Therapy integrates Scripture with adjacent principles in cognitive behavioral therapy (CBT) to offer a strategy for recognizing and resisting lies and reframing and restructuring our thought life with the truth. The basic premise in Truth Therapy is the truth will set us free. If that is true, and Scripture says that it is, then the opposite is true. Lies will bind or imprison us. What are the lies that we have believed about ourselves, our past, others, God, and the world? And what does the truth claim about each of these areas? Knowing the truth will deliver and set us free.

The final chapter is about the person and work of the Holy Spirit and his relationship with discipleship and the brain. How does the Spirit work? Is the power of the Spirit available to us today? How do trauma and hurt affect the brain? How does the Spirit heal us? How can we hear God's voice and be transformed? *Losing Your Mind* is a practical, unique book that investigates how the Holy Spirit disciples us, using the power of God, Scripture, others, and our brain, and how we can participate in the discipleship process by receiving the work of the Spirit in our lives and discipling others.

THE FATHER: THE MIND OF THE FATHER

And this final reason of things is called God.

—Gottfried Leibniz[1]

The Mind of the Father

All of creation reflects the majestic mind of God. God our Father created this wonderful blue planet that we call Earth. On the final day of creation, he crafted the marvel known as man and woman. He created them in his glorious image. God endowed them with a portion of himself. In his image, they were made righteous and good. As icons, they reflect God's character. They were gifted with reason and would function as his representatives in creation. As an image or copy is related to the original, so humanity is in relationship with the Triune God, reflecting his truth, goodness, and beauty. Although Scripture explicitly states that we are made in God's image, early theologians of the church recognized that in some unique way, the entire creation is crafted in the image of God.[2] The vast, spectacular cosmos in all of its glory, intricacy, and exquisite order expresses the heart and mind of God (Ps. 19:1–6; Rom. 1:19–20).

As we explore the universe, it allows us to behold the mind of God. The universe is an icon of the living God, a window to heaven. We see God's goodness and power invested in every square inch of the universe. Whichever angle we ponder on any of its striking facets, we are captured by its Divine elegance and intelligence. All of creation reflects the splendor and grandeur of God. The cosmos is a living icon of the eternal God, an organic metaphor of the ineffable One. Its order, intelligibility, telos, precision, complexity, simplicity, and magnificence are evident and abundant. These qualities and traces do not point to but transcend themselves. They are in glorious and eternal excess (abundance). They are inexplicable in themselves as to their origin, cause, and end. Yet, the features of the cosmos unmistakably point to the One who

---

1. Gottfried Leibniz, *Leibniz Selections*, ed. Philip P. Wiener (Charles Scribner's Sons, 1951), 528. (G. Leibniz 1951).

2. Hans Urs von Balthasar, *Cosmic Liturgy: The Universe According to Maximus the Confessor* (Ignatus Press, 2003). (Balthasar 2003)

articulated them into being. The mind of the Father is revealed everywhere in all things great and small. God's thoughtful words and will have imprinted a cosmos of forms on the canvas of nothingness.[3] Reason, intelligibility, and purpose, or the Divine ideas as Augustine and Aquinas viewed them, are in motion from the micro to the macro universe.

And this mirific backdrop is set in place for the grand *theodrama*, God's action. Man and woman enter the stage portraying their Creator and more so anticipating his entrance where he will portray them. He (whom we call Jesus) will be suited in their garb of flesh and blood to play both parts in the incarnation, both his role and theirs. He will clothe himself in creation, in the cosmos as an icon of all, and yet remain the true substance of the Divine, to take on the passion of our woefulness. Image and substance, attaching himself to us, mixing and entangling himself in our sordid affair, he will perform the unimaginable. He will take our state as his own and give us his own. The Divine man will elevate humanity to their Divine purpose. Humanity through faith's gaze will contemplate the flesh and blood icon and see the invisible One, who transfigures and transports from glory to glory. Penned from the Divine mind, this holy performance will end in eternal encore and *epektasis* (unceasing growth in grace) as it was in the beginning, now, and ever shall be, world without end. Amen!

What a Wonderful World!

As we begin our quest to gain the mind of Christ, let us first zero in on and consider one of God's most august works, the human brain (brain-mind).[4] The human mind is an icon or reflection of the mind of the Father. It has been crafted with the capacity to house and mirror the magnificence of the Divine. Indeed, the Lord waxed eloquently when he enunciated the human mind, even flexing and flaunting. Of all that God has created, the human brain is at the center of God's exquisite, mysterious, marvelous cosmic masterpiece. The brain is as vast, complex, and stunning as the universe itself. In fact, it is a microcosm of the universe, an inner universe or world unto itself. As an object of knowledge, the universe is housed in the thoughts of the mind. And, likewise, the mind, as part of creation, is situated in the universe. The mind is our inner universe, a universe within a universe.

Indeed, how fearfully and wonderfully made is this cognitive, emotional, and behavioral processing organ. God created the human brain with the capacity to understand both the universe and the Divine. The mind is capable of understanding,

---

3. What St. Maximus the Confessor calls the *logoi*.

4. There are many views about the nature of the human mind. Is it a separate substance from the body? Does it emerge from the brain? Is it reduced to the brain? Is the mind an illusion or simulation? Is the mind the cognitive experience of the brain? In this text, at times I will use the term *brain-mind* to refer to the existence and complex relationship between the two, for the two clearly work together. Context will dictate the specific sense of the term *brain-mind*. For more on this discussion, see my book *Artificial General Intelligence (AGI) and the Image of God* (Wipf and Stock, 2023).

though in part, the universe and how it operates. More so, it is capable of understanding God, again in part, and how he operates. Both the universe and God are intelligible to the human mind. We are made capable of understanding God's ways and the ways of the universe. Mutual understanding is possible because we are made in God's image as *God capacitors*. In one sense of the term, the image of God signifies that we were hardwired to know God and enjoy a relationship with him. We have the capacity to understand the Lord and his ways. God can share his thoughts with us, and we can, in a limited way, comprehend them. The mind that God created enables us to discover the universe and the Divine and to interact with both.

The Lord God has created a dazzling, elegant cosmic tabernacle to house his glory. The first chapter of Genesis portrays a rich liturgical picture depicting all of creation as God's holy temple that he comes to inhabit. And within God's vast creation is the microcosm of humanity. Humanity (*adam*) represents the Holy Place, and our mind represents the Holy of Holies, or the center of God's habitation. All of creation was made to worship the Lord, and worship begins in our hearts and minds. Let us contemplate the magnificence of God's handiwork by reviewing some basic scientific facts about God's creation.

Some astrophysicists arguably claim that the universe is 13.7 billon years old, while the Earth is 4.5 billion years old. Others claim a much younger universe. Although the universe was birthed ages ago, it is not stagnant but is still expanding and accelerating. The universe is immense in size. The width of the observable universe is approximately 92 billion light years, while the unobservable and observable universe is 7 trillion light years across. A light year is the distance something travels going 186,000 miles per second for a year or 6 trillion miles, which is 6 with 12 zeroes. Within its immense space are numerous galaxies, black holes, solar systems, planets, and other cosmic phenomena in the universe. Though the universe is full of all sundry galactic, stellar, and planetary wonder, over 95 percent of the universe is invisible, consisting of dark energy and matter we cannot see because these do not respond to light. Much mystery still remains in God's creation.

The universe contains an estimated 200,000,000,000,000,000,000,000. (200 billion trillion) stars, more than all of the grains of sand on all of the beaches in the world. There are around 275 million new stars birthed every day. There are also around two trillion galaxies in the universe. Of course, our solar system is in the Milky Way galaxy, which, though an average sized galaxy, is quite enormous. Our sun takes 225 million years to orbit the Milky Way galaxy. Think of the lights that we see in the heavens at night. When we see the light of a star, we are looking into the past. The light that we see is old and has traveled many light years to get to our eyes. For example, the sun is 93 million miles away. The light of the sun takes eight minutes to arrive at our eyes. We always see the light of the sun as it was eight minutes ago. Time varies throughout the universe relative to one's reference point. A day on Venus is longer than one year on Earth. And strangely, one day on Mercury is twice as long as one year on Mercury. In terms of planets, there are approximately 700 quintillion planets in the universe (7 followed by 20 zeroes). However, it is thought that none are quite like Earth, and most are likely uninhabited. But earth is teeming with life.[5]

Fearfully and Wonderfully Made

There are 8.75 million known living species on Earth, though that number can vary.[6] As if the universe and the earth were not remarkable enough, God created another magnificent wonder, the human body. The average human body is made up of 28 to 36 trillion cells. Every second we produce 25 million cells. The human body is made up of 7 octillion atoms, which is 7 with 27 zeroes following. In fact, "most of a human body's mass is made up of just the 4 trillion cells that compose our musculoskeletal system, connective tissue, and internal organs. Another 40 trillion cells are simply blood cells flowing through our body and 50 trillion are bacterial cells that live in our digestive tracts. There are nearly 10^{28} atoms in a human body and close to 10^{29} subatomic particles that make each of us up. Those numbers are 10 to 100 million times the total number of stars in the universe."[7] Allegedly, according to big bang cosmologists, almost all of our hydrogen atoms were formed in the big bang, about 13.7 billion years ago.[8] It is said that we are dust made of atoms that in turn were made from a star that exploded billions of years ago.

All of these atoms, cells, vessels, bones, and organs meticulously work together organizing, metabolizing, signaling, responding, moving, reproducing, growing, differentiating, synthesizing, respiring, digesting, and so forth, as a fine-tuned organic machine carrying out thousands upon thousands of functions. There are seventy-eight organs in the body. About 60 percent of our body is made of water. Our body's blood vessels, if stretched, could wrap around the Earth four times. "If you unraveled all of the DNA in your body, it would span 34 billion miles, reaching to Pluto (2.66 billion miles away) and back . . . six times."[9] The average human heart beats around 3 billion times throughout an average life span. The human nose can recognize an estimated one trillion different scents. The human eye can distinguish between one

---

5. Tibi Puiu, "There Are Over 70 Quintillion Planets in the Universe—but There's No Place Like Home," ZME Science, November 28, 2019, https://www.zmescience.com/feature-post/space-astronomy/astronomy-articles/how-many-planets-universe/#:~:text=There%20are%20over%20700%20quintillion%20planets%20in%20the%20universe%20%E2%80%94%20but,universe%20is%20extremely%20mind%2Dboggling.&text=Credit%3A%20Pixabay.,planets%20as%20there%20are%20stars. (Puiu 2019)

6. John J. Wiens, "How Many Species Are There on Earth? Progress and Problems," *PLoS Biology* 21, no. 11 (2023): e3002388. https://doi.org/10.1371/journal.pbio.3002388. (Wiens 2023)

7. Ethan Siegel, "Ask Ethan: How Can We Comprehend the Size of the Universe?," Big Think, accessed November 1, 2024, https://bigthink.com/starts-with-a-bang/comprehend-size-universe/. (E. Siegel 2023)

8. Not everyone agrees with the big bang theory of cosmology. There are many versions of the big bang theory. There are also several cosmological theories that differ from the big bang theory. Some Christians hold to a young universe theory of creation. This author does not hold conclusively to any one scientific theory of the origin of the universe. Some are more plausible than others, but none provides evidence beyond a reasonable doubt. Theologically, we know that God created the heavens and the earth.

9. Siegel, "How Can We Comprehend the Size of the Universe?" (E. Siegel 2023)

million different colors. Our eyes blink over 10 million times a year. In an eighty-year life span, a person will take about 672,768,000 breaths. The average person will sleep around 227,760 hours in a lifetime, for one-third of their entire life.

The Three-Pound Gray and White Wonder

Within the human body resides the greatest wonder of God's creation: the human brain. The brain is the control center of the entire human body. It is "the most complex part of the human body. This three-pound organ is the seat of intelligence, interpreter of the senses, initiator of body movement, and controller of behavior. Lying in its bony shell and washed by protective fluid, the brain is the source of all the qualities that define our humanity. It is the crown jewel of the human body."[10] The brain is the size of two fists and weighs around three pounds. The brain contains both gray and white matter. It is mostly made of water (75 percent) and runs on electricity. Each neuron has a resting voltage of 70 millivolts. Our brain's electricity can indeed light up a low wattage light bulb.

The human brain contains around 100 billion neurons (nerve cells) connected by trillions of synapses (gaps between neurons). There are the same number of neurons in the brain as stars in the Milky Way galaxy. The brain accounts for 2 percent of the body's weight but uses 20 percent of the body's blood and oxygen. There are 100,000 miles of blood vessels in the brain. Brain size will triple throughout one's lifetime and will develop into one's late twenties. Cerebral information can travel up to 268 miles per hour and generate up to 25 watts and power a small light bulb. The size of our memory storage can hold 2.5 million gigabytes of data, while an iPhone 14 only has 512 gigabytes. Yet the average attention span is only twenty minutes, shorter than a goldfish. And our short-term memory can only store seven pieces of data for twenty seconds. Each event or instance of consciousness, a now moment, lasts two to three seconds. The average person may have up to 75,000 thoughts a day, though 96 percent of all decisions are made subconsciously. No two people have the exact brain anatomy. The brain changes and reshapes regularly (neuroplasticity) and can make modified or new connections (synaptogenesis). Also, our brain births new neurons (neurogenesis) throughout its lifetime.[11]

The human brain is one of the preeminent marvels that the Lord God has designed. Look at all of the astounding and manifold achievements it has accomplished throughout human history, including medicine, medical procedures, technological discoveries and advances, forms of transportation and communication, great literary works, humanitarian efforts, the arts, and all of the riches developed by human civilization over time. From Plato, Aristotle, and Archimedes to Locke, Leibniz, and Newton, to Einstein, Turing, and Gödel, and all of the rest in between, human genius and innovation have explored and demonstrated the beauty, ingenuity, creativity, power, and performance of the human mind.

10. "Brain Basics: Know your Brain," NIH: National Institute of Neurological Disorders and Strokes, July 17, 2024, https://www.ninds.nih.gov/health-information/public-education/brain-basics/brain-basics-know-your-brain. (NIH: National Institute of Neurological Disorders and Strokes 2024)

11. "Ten Interesting Facts About the Human Brain," Science First, accessed November 1, 2024, https://www.sciencefirst.com/10-interesting-facts-about-the-human-brain/. (Science First n.d.)

Brain Anatomy 101

For our purposes in this book, it is expedient to have a rudimentary understanding of the anatomy of the brain and the primary functions of each major area. Like a car engine, the brain has many parts, each with a specific function that works together to fire up the engine and drive it to perform. Throughout this text, we will examine areas of the brain and how they affect discipleship. We are fearfully and wonderfully made, including our brain. The brain is a vast, complex, and fascinating universe that reflects the wisdom and love of God. The Lord created the brain and all of its components to serve his perfect purpose in our lives. He has ordered every neuron and synapse to his own specifications to fulfill his greater plan of salvation.

When we pray, read the Scriptures, repent and believe the truth, walk by faith, worship God, minister, reach the lost, serve the poor, or make disciples, we are using the full landscape of the brain. The brain is fully engaged throughout our Christian life and in the entire process of discipleship. Its lobes of gray and white matter and biological neural networks (brain circuitry) function as the chief mechanism of the body that the Holy Spirit employs to disciple and transform us into the holy image of Christ.

When my children turned sixteen and received their driver's licenses, I thought it would be beneficial for them if I opened the hood of the car to show them the essential parts of the car and explain the basic process of how the engine starts and runs. It seemed better to know how the car operates than to not know. If they understood what was going on under the hood, they would understand their car better and take better care of it. We can apply the same principle to the brain. The more we know what is going on under the hood of our head, the better we can understand and care for our body and mind. Knowing the various areas and functions of the brain can also help us to pray more specifically and effectively for ourselves and others.

Knowing what goes on inside of our head may additionally assist and inspire us to understand and participate more effectively in the discipleship process. Psychiatrist Daniel Siegel labels this perspective "mindsight." He states, "Mindsight is a kind of focused attention that allows us to see the internal workings of our own minds. It helps us to be aware of our mental processes" and to be informed, intentional, and involved in our own transformation, as aided by neuroscience and the cognitive sciences.[12] He calls it "our seventh sense." Understanding how the brain works on the inside can assist us in becoming better disciples on the outside. We can take an active role in training our brain, since the brain influences the mind, and the mind influences the brain. Also, we can pray specifically and effectively according to the anatomy and functions of the brain as they relate to our discipleship.

Now, let us take a crash course in brain anatomy. *The brain has several parts and many distinct regions that have specialized functions, just like the parts of an engine.* Although the brain is divided into many components, areas, systems, and functions, it operates as a well-running automobile, a church committee, or a finally tuned, harmonious orchestra with many members playing their distinct parts. The brain functions as a "global workspace" that processes and integrates the various operations

---

12. Daniel J. Siegel, *Mindsight: The New Science of Personal Transformation* (Random House, 2010), xi. (D. J. Siegel 2010)

of all of its systems into one conscious experience. We will identify and examine some of the major parts, regions, and systems of the brain, as it relates to discipling the mind. (Refer to Diagrams 1 and 2)

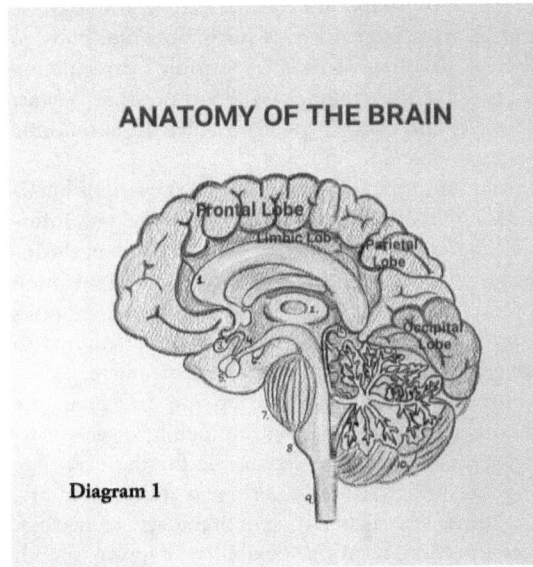

ANATOMY OF THE BRAIN

1. Corpus Callosum
2. Thalamus
3. Optic Chiasm
4. Hypothalamus
5. Pituitary Gland
6. Mammillary Body
7. Pons
8. Medulla Oblongata
9. Spinal Cord
10. Cerebellum
11. Pineal Gland

Diagram 1

Drawing Credit: Paola Bellini

1. Neocortex
2. Hypothalamus
3. Amygdala
4. Hippocampus
5. Locus Coeruleus
6. Spinal Cord
7. Cerebellum
8. Thalamus

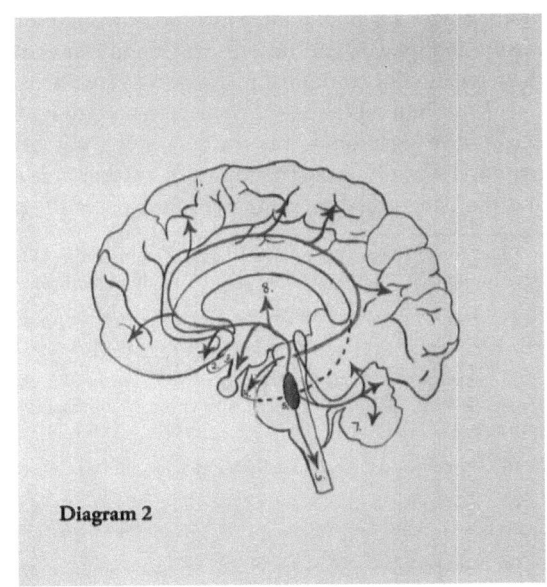

Diagram 2

The brain and the spinal cord make up the central nervous system and make up the main processing and control system of the body (like the engine and the drivetrain of a car). The brain is divided into three major parts: the cerebellum, the brainstem, and the cerebrum. The cerebellum, located in the back of the brain, receives motor information from the body and the cerebral cortex to regulate muscle control, balance, and movement.[13] The brainstem connects the cerebellum and the spinal cord. It relays all signals and information back and forth from the body to the cerebrum and cerebellum and back. The brainstem is responsible for regulating autonomic functions like the heart and breathing rates, and blood pressure.[14] Most of our spiritual practices, including prayer and worship greatly involve the autonomic nervous system, which is related to the brainstem.[15]

The cerebrum, located at the front and top, is divided into left and right hemispheres and is connected in the middle by the corpus callosum, which bridges information from one side to the other. Each hemisphere contains white matter on the inside and gray matter on the outside, known as the cerebral cortex. Although the brain functions as a single processing unit, each hemisphere is responsible for different tasks called lateralization. For example, language and abstract reasoning are attributed to the left, while visual-spatial reasoning is associated with the right hemisphere.

Each hemisphere is divided into four lobes that make up the cerebrum: the frontal, temporal, parietal, and occipital lobes.[16] Regions within each lobe serve various functions. The frontal lobe (prefrontal cortex) is responsible for the executive functions of self-control, reasoning, planning, self-monitoring, working memory, strategizing, organizing, prioritizing, time management, emotional self-regulating, goal setting and achieving, focus and attention, cognitive flexibility, adapting, speech producing (Broca's area), and other functions.[17] The frontal lobe contains the primary motor cortex for bodily movement. The frontal lobe is "active during practices like meditation, prayer, and various rituals and is involved in holding specific beliefs and the regulation of emotional responses to those beliefs."[18]

The temporal lobe constructs representations and abstractions of the world and works with the frontal lobe in developing our belief and behavior systems.[19] The temporal lobe or neocortex houses Wernicke's area responsible for processing written and oral language. The temporal lobe houses the primary auditory cortex (hearing

---

13. Amna Rehman and Yasir Al Khalili, "Neuroanatomy, Occipital Lobe," National Library of Medicine, last updated July 24, 2023, https://www.ncbi.nlm.nih.gov/books/NBK544320/. (Rao, et al. 2009)

14. Hayden Basinger and Jeffrey P. Hogg, "Neuroanatomy, Brainstem," National Library of Medicine, last updated July 4, 2023, https://www.ncbi.nlm.nih.gov/books/NBK544297/ (Basinger and Hogg 2023)

15. Andrew Newberg, *Neurotheology: How Science Can Enlighten Us About Spirituality* (Columbia University Press, 2021), 54–55, 214. (Newberg, Neurotheology: How Science Can Enlighten Us About Spirituality 2021)

16. Some would consider the limbic system and the insula (insular cortex) as lobes.

17. Adele Diamond, "Executive Functions," Annual Review of Psychology 64 (2013): 135–68. Accessed May 1, 2024. https://doi.org/10.1146/annurev-psych-113011-143750. (Diamond 2013)

18. Newberg, *Neurotheology*, 59. (Newberg, Neurotheology: How Science Can Enlighten Us About Spirituality 2021)

19. Newberg, *Neurotheology*, 60. (Newberg, Neurotheology: How Science Can Enlighten Us About Spirituality 2021)

function). The temporal lobe also contains the limbic system (the social-emotional brain), sometimes considered a separate lobe (the limbic lobe), that is responsible for memory, emotions, and behavior. The temporal lobe also processes auditory stimuli as well as encodes memory.[20]

Within the temporal lobe is the hippocampus. The hippocampus is like the RAM and filing system in a computer. It is responsible for categorizing, filing, and memorizing. The hippocampus, which is part of the limbic system, is situated deep within the medial temporal lobe and is also associated with spatial cognition (organization of experience, mental models of reality), processing conflict, learning, and memory (spatial, episodic/autobiographical, short term, and long term). Since discipleship is learning to be like Christ, the hippocampus plays a key role. For cognitive scientists and neuroscientists, memory, the work of the hippocampus, is virtually equated with learning.

In the Old Testament, the Israelites were consistently commanded to "remember" what the Lord accomplished in saving them (Deut. 8–9, 25; Josh. 24; 2 Kings 17:38). In the New Testament, we are promised that the Holy Spirit will help us retrieve the truth from our memory (John 14:26; 1 John 20:27). The Spirit will also teach us the truth in all spiritual matters and reveal Christ to us (John 14:26; 16:13–15). In the Great Commission, Christ commands us to make disciples and to teach them what Christ commanded, and as we have learned (Matthew 28:18–20). All of these spiritual functions operate through the hippocampus.

The almond-shaped amygdala is also located in the temporal lobe and is vital to the limbic system.[21] It is responsible for emotions, emotional modulation, emotional memories, anxiety regulation, decision-making, fight-flight-freeze responses, fear conditioning, social cognition, and more. It acts as our internal alarm system to warn us when there is a perceived threat. The amygdala is also activated when we experience motivation, perhaps after reading Scripture or hearing a convicting sermon.[22] As Augustine claimed that we are creatures motivated by "want" and "desire," the amygdala plays a significant role in these drives. Scripture sums this principle up best: "Where your treasure is, there the desires of your heart will also be (Matthew 6:21 NLT). Neuroscientist Andrew Newberg links intense or ecstatic spiritual practices, such as speaking in tongues, to increased amygdala activity.[23] This practice has also been tested and demonstrated in one study with 1,000 clergy to provide "greater

20. J. A. Kiernan , "Anatomy of the Temporal Lobe," Epilepsy Research Treatment: (2012): 176157. https://doi.org/10.1155/2012/176157. (Kiernan 2012)

21. Qais AbuHasan, Vamsi Reddy, and Waquar Siddiqui, "Neuroanatomy, Amygdala," National Library of Medicine, last updated July 17, 2023, https://www.ncbi.nlm.nih.gov/books/NBK537102/. (Abu-Hasan, Reddy and Siddiqui 2023)

22. Newberg, *Neurotheology*, 62. (Newberg, Neurotheology: How Science Can Enlighten Us About Spirituality 2021)

23. Newberg, *Neurotheology*, 217. (Newberg, Neurotheology: How Science Can Enlighten Us About Spirituality 2021)

emotional stability and less neuroticism."[24] On the other hand, more subdued and decompressing practices, such as meditation, mindfulness, or holy silence, show diminished amygdala activity.[25]

Also, in the limbic system but outside of the lobe is the nucleus accumbens, which is located in the basal forebrain (basal ganglia).[26] The nucleus accumbens is the mediator between our motivation and action.[27] It is significant for positive and negative reinforcement, aversion, incentive, and reward. The nucleus accumbens is where dopamine is rewarded (the reward circuit) for various "goal-directed behaviors."[28] Dopamine is a neuronal hormone and neurotransmitter (chemical messenger) that gives us that elated feeling when we pursue and/or accomplish a task, like pursuing and earning a college degree. Dopamine is also released in the bloodstream upon the activation of our fight, flight, or freeze mechanism. We will also discuss later in the book the connection between the nucleus accumbens, dopamine, attention, and addiction.

In the temporal lobe toward the center of the brain is the thalamus, which is also continuous with the midbrain.[29] The thalamus is a relay and regulating system. It relays sensory and motor signals to the cerebral cortex. The thalamus also regulates consciousness, sleep, and alertness. The hypothalamus is below the thalamus and is part of the limbic system. It is also responsible for relaying and regulating high neuronal traffic. The hypothalamus receives signals from the nervous system and coordinates them with the endocrine system (hormones) to create homeostasis or balance. The hypothalamus regulates our metabolic process, specifically endocrine and nervous systems, in order to create homeostasis.[30]

The hypothalamus is responsible for many bodily functions, including blood pressure, breathing rate, and most of our hormone systems, including the stress hor-

24. Leslie J. Francis and Mandy Robbins, "Personality and Glossolalia: A Study Among Male Evangelical Clergy," *Pastoral Psychology* 51, no. 5 (2003), pp 391-396. (Francis and Robbins 2003)

25. Newberg, *Neurotheology*, 217. (Newberg, Neurotheology: How Science Can Enlighten Us About Spirituality 2021)

26. Yukiori Goto and Anthony A. Grace, "Limbic and Cortical Information Processing in the Nucleus Accumbens," *Trends in Neurosciences* 31, no. 11 (2008): 552–58. https://doi.org/10.1016/j.tins.2008.08.002. (Goto and Grace 2008)

27. E. Fernández-Espejo, "Cómo funciona el nucleus accumbens?" [How Does the Nucleus Accumbens Function?] *Revista de Neurologia* 30, no. (2000): 845–49. Spanish. (Fernandez-Espejo 2000)

28. Goto and Grace, "Limbic and Cortical Information Processing in the Nucleus Accumbens." (Goto and Grace 2008)

29. Tyler J. Torrico and Sunil Munakomi, "Neuroanatomy, Thalamus," National Library of Medicine, last updated July 24, 2023, https://www.ncbi.nlm.nih.gov/books/NBK542184/#:~:text=The%20thalamus%20is%20a%20paired,other%20via%20the%20interthalamic%20adhesion. (Torrico and Munakomi 2023)

30. "Hypothalamus," Cleveland Clinic, last reviewed March 16, 2022, https://my.clevelandclinic.org/health/body/22566-hypothalamus. (Cleveland Clinic 2022)

mone cortisol.[31] The hypothalamus produces releasing hormones that either release or inhibit hormones from the pituitary gland, which is below the hypothalamus. The pituitary gland, part of the endocrine system, produces and secretes a vast variety of hormones into the bloodstream related to growth reproduction, metabolism, stress and trauma response, lactation, childbirth, blood pressure, thyroid control, and more.[32] The hypothalamus manages and controls sex drive, body temperature, hunger, thirst, fullness when eating, attachment, mood, and other functions.[33] The limbic system is associated with our full range of emotions that we experience in our relationship with God, whether they are joy, happiness, sadness, stress, love, or anger.[34] It is also central to emotionally forming connection, attachment, and relationships with others (resonance system), which is essential in discipleship relationships.

Next is the parietal lobe. It is associated with receiving and processing sensory information from the skin, our tactile or touch system (somatosensory cortex). The parietal lobe is responsible for creating an internal map in our minds of the relationship between body awareness, spatial fields, and motion. It is an internal GPS that locates you in relation to other things that your senses detect in the world around you. Self-perception and self-awareness of receptors, such as temperature, pain, pressure, vibration, and other tactile stimuli, are connected with the parietal lobe.[35] The parietal lobe is also associated with language processing, including writing. The parietal lobe most likely plays a significant role in experiencing transcendence or a diminished sense of self before the Holy.[36] In prayer and worship, we can experience oneness or connectedness with God and others due to activity in the parietal lobe.[37]

Finally, there is the occipital lobe, which is the smallest lobe. It is located in the back of the brain. The occipital lobe contains the primary visual cortex. It is responsible for processing visual sensory information via the optic nerves to the visual cortex. The occipital lobe is connected with "visuospatial processing, distance and depth perception, color determination, object and face recognition, and memory

31. Newberg, *Neurotheology*, 61. (Newberg, Neurotheology: How Science Can Enlighten Us About Spirituality 2021)

32. "Pituitary Gland," Cleveland Clinic, last reviewed April 4, 2022, https://my.clevelandclinic.org/health/body/21459-pituitary-gland. (Cleveland Clinic 2022)

33. "Pituitary Gland." (Cleveland Clinic 2022)

34. Newberg, *Neurotheology*, 60. (Newberg, Neurotheology: How Science Can Enlighten Us About Spirituality 2021)

35. "Parietal Lobe," Cleveland Clinic, last updated January 8, 2023, https://my.clevelandclinic.org/health/body/24628-parietal-lobe. (Cleveland Clinic 2023)

36. Newberg, *Neurotheology*, 60, 216. (Newberg, Neurotheology: How Science Can Enlighten Us About Spirituality 2021)

37. Newberg, *Neurotheology*, 216. (Newberg, Neurotheology: How Science Can Enlighten Us About Spirituality 2021)

formation."[38] One neuroscientist discovered that religious symbols, like "the cross," "affect the brain in a primary way," specifically the occipital lobe's visual cortex.[39]

Although we have examined various regions of the brain and have identified the functions associated with each area, no one area is exhaustively responsible for one function. Localization is an oversimplification of the complexity of the brain. All of the roles performed by the brain involve both hemispheres of the brain, many regions, and multiple neural networks performing in harmony. The range of functions of the brain are carried out initially at the brain cell (neuron) level. The neuron is the basic unit within the brain. A neuron is a nerve cell that sends messages throughout your brain and the rest of your body. There are three types: sensory (receive and send sensory signals from sense organs), motor (receive signals to control bodily movement), and interneurons (connecting neurons in the same region).

The brain houses over 100 billion neurons. The neuron carries signals of information from one end of the neuron to the other and across a synapse (a gap) to a receptor neuron. There are over a quadrillion synapses in the brain. Transmission and reception of information occur along vast networks of neurons that operate each area of the brain. Biological neural networks are like sophisticated logistical highway systems, or even mobile cellular networks, that give, transport, and receive signals of sensory and motor information. These signals enable and direct the brain and the body to perform its numerous tasks.

Think of your cell phone when you text. You input a text. It sends an output signal to another phone that receives the signal and gives them the text. Neurons also have inputs and outputs for signaling and messaging from neuron to neuron. Cell phones are connected in a cellular network. Likewise, neurons are connected in a (neural) network for messaging. The more we connect and message someone through our cell phone, the stronger our relational connections become. Similarly, the more we use a particular neural network or pathway, the stronger the neural connection and the brain functions associated with that connection become. Neurons that fire together, or work and signal together, wire together or become more strongly connected. Contrastingly, the less we use that connection, the more we lose that connection. Just like the less we communicate with someone, the more we become disconnected. Fire and wire, and use it or lose it! These neural networks are like a cellular network, or the brain's highway system of connected roads on which information travels.

The neuron has multiple parts. The tentacle-like dendrites receive input signals (neurotransmitters) carrying information from other cells (neurons of sensor cells) to the body of the neuron (soma). These signals are processed in the soma and converted to a charge in the neuron's membrane potential, which generates an action potential. An action potential is a sudden impulse, firing, or spike of electricity that sends the signal down the axon to the terminal. The action potential is a rapid burst of change in voltage across the neuron's membrane that sends the signal of information down

---

38. Rehman and Al Khalili, "Neuroanatomy, Occipital Lobe." (Rehman and Al Khalili 2023)

39. Newberg, *Neurotheology*, 58. (Newberg, Neurotheology: How Science Can Enlighten Us About Spirituality 2021)

the wire-like axon to the terminal or the end of the neuron. The axon connects the soma to the terminal. The action potential is conducted along the axon to the axon terminal; from there a neurotransmitter carries the signal across the synapse (gap between neurons) to the receptor neuron (see Diagrams 3 and 4).

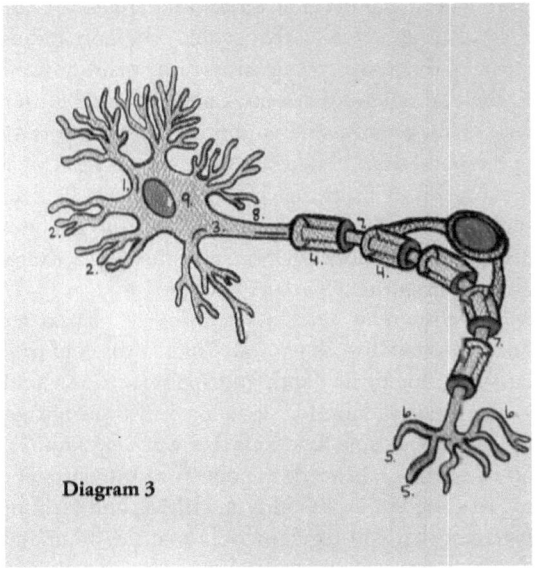

NEURON STRUCTURE

1. **Cell Membrane**
2. **Dendrites**
3. **Axon Hillock**
4. **Myelin Sheath**
5. **Synaptic End Bulbs**
6. **Axon Terminal**
7. **Node of Ranvier**
8. **Axon**
9. **Cell Body**

Diagram 3

Drawing Credit: Paola Bellini

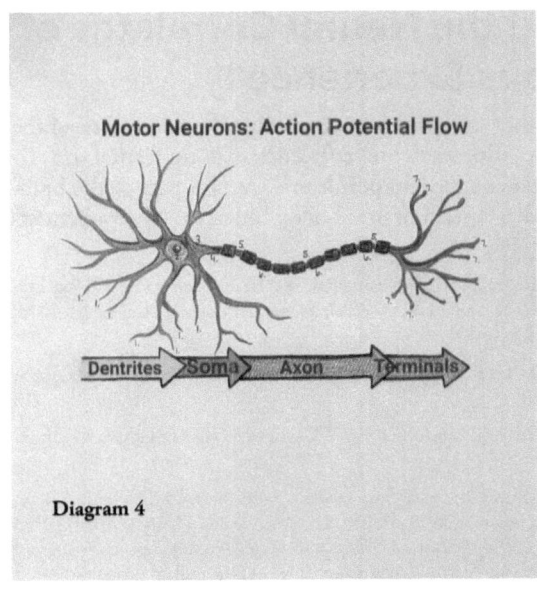

Motor Neurons: Action Potential Flow

Dentrites Soma Axon Terminals

Diagram 4

ACTION POTENTIAL FLOW

1. **Dendrites**
2. **Nucleus**
3. **Hillock**
4. **AP Trigger**
5. **Nodes of Ranvier**
6. **Myelin Sheath**
7. **Synapses**

Neurons communicate with each other at the synapses, which are the junctions or interchanges between the neurons. The neurotransmitter (e.g., dopamine, serotonin, or norepinephrine) is a chemical messenger that transports the information from the sending neuron (presynaptic) to the receiving neuron (postsynaptic). Throughout the brain electrical and chemical signals are transmitted and received across neural networks that enable the brain and the rest of the body to perform its amazing functions.[40] For example, the neurotransmitter dopamine, which is essential to the brain's reward system, can be released during prayer and worship, making us feel joyful, ecstatic, and euphoric.[41] Serotonin is a neurotransmitter that modulates our moods. It is also related to intense emotional responses. Serotonin is greatly involved in our spiritual practices and can be associated with visual experiences,[42] such as visions and revelations. Oxytocin facilitates social bonding that occurs in a discipleship relationship. Norepinephrine is activated when we are vigilant of evil and aroused to spiritual warfare.

The brain, as much as the universe itself, reflects the intricate, miraculous, and marvelous handiwork of God. I like to think of the brain-mind complex as the inner universe, due to its depth and sophistication. Neural highways and networks serve as the infrastructure for signaling and transmitting information that communicate the brain's multiple functions that work for a nobler purpose. All of these remarkable facets of the brain work in concert to present a greater whole, our embodied self, a self that the Spirit of God is sanctifying and forming in the glorious image of Christ. I suggest that you regularly pray that the brain and its various functions align with God's original intention at creation, specifically naming each part and function and pray that they fall into Divine order, performing as the Lord originally intended.

Neuroscience and the Neural Correlates of Religious Experience[43]

Neuroscience is the study of the nervous system, including the brain. One of the chief emphases in neuroscience is to locate neural correlates that are related to various functions and tasks that we experience and perform. A certain part of the brain is said to correlate, or connect with a certain brain or body function. Neuroscientists

---

40. For more on neuroanatomy, neurons, and action potential, see Isaac Chen and Forshing Lui, "Neuroanatomy, Neuron Action Potential," National Library of Medicine, last updated August 14, 2023, https://www.ncbi.nlm.nih.gov/books/NBK546639/ .

41. Newberg, *Neurotheology*, 216. (Newberg, Neurotheology: How Science Can Enlighten Us About Spirituality 2021)

42. Newberg, *Neurotheology*, 218. (Newberg, Neurotheology: How Science Can Enlighten Us About Spirituality 2021)

43. For philosophical analyses on religious experience, one can start with the work of Phillip Wiebe, *Religious Experience: Implications for What is Real* (Cambridge University Press, 2023), *Visions of Jesus* (Oxford University Press, 1997), *God and Other Spirits: Intimations of Transcendence in Christian Experience* (Oxford University Press, 2004), and *Intuitive Knowing as Spiritual Experience* (Palgrave Macmillan, 2015).

seek to extrapolate a correlation between the event and the region(s) of the brain associated with the event, which is called the neural *correlate*. For example, activity in the hippocampus is the neural correlate for memory. Through various methods of brain imaging (fMRI, SPECT, EEG, MEG, PET, and others), neuroscientists are able to observe which areas of the brain light up when certain functions operate, tasks are performed, or phenomena are experienced. In this way, scientists can learn more about how various mechanisms within the brain work and the nature of their relationship to the events correlated with that brain region. So which parts of the brain light up when we pray and experience the Spirit of God? In cognitive science, analyzing religious experience is one aspect of a larger study of altered states of consciousness or what is outside of our normal experiences.

Many neuroscientists, cognitive scientists, and evolutionary psychologists contend that the brain is hardwired for belief in God and that a predisposition for belief is innate to the development of the human species and for the construction and maintenance of a society.[44] These researchers claim that the mechanisms that developed the human brain and its capacity for agency in terms of cognition, emotion, and volition are also responsible for the capacity for belief and ritual, including religious belief. Among the many reasons given for such development, adaptation is the most common and the sturdiest.[45] Religious beliefs, including faith, hope, and love, support human survival, moral practice, societal strength, existential meaning making and coping, and civilization development. The fact has been demonstrated that most societies and civilizations have held religious beliefs and rituals that have been integral to their survival and flourishing.[46] As neuroscientist Andrew Newberg claims, "God won't go away."[47]

For a period of time in neuroscience, there was a movement among scientists to uncover and locate a "god spot" in the brain, the correlate for God in the brain. The hypothesis was that the god spot, or "god module," was the specialized region of the brain responsible for experiencing God. Neuroscientists speculated that the god spot would light up and show activity when one was communicating with God or

---

44. For an example, see Andrew Newberg, Eugene D'Aquilli, and Vince Rause, *Why God Won't Go Away: Brain Science and the Biology of Belief* (Random House, 2022); Andrew Newberg, *Born to Believe: God, Science, and the Origin of Ordinary and Extraordinary Beliefs* (Simon and Schuster, 2008).

45. Newberg, *Neurotheology*, 108–23. (Newberg, Neurotheology: How Science Can Enlighten Us About Spirituality 2021)

46. Newberg, D'Aquilli, and Rause, *Why God Won't Go Away*, 128–41. (Newberg, D'Aquilli and Rause, Why God Won't Go Away: Brain Science and the Biology of Belief 2022)

47. Derived from the title of the book by Newberg, D'Aquilli, and Rause, *Why God Won't Go Away*. (Newberg, D'Aquilli and Rause, Why God Won't Go Away: Brain Science and the Biology of Belief 2022)

15

when God was communicating with the recipient.[48] The quest was to find the neural basis or correlates for religious experience. Ancient medical history up until the late nineteenth century sought to make the connection, postulating that religious experience is tied to a type of epilepsy (temporal lobe epilepsy), what Hippocrates coined the "sacred disease."

Neuroscientist Michael Persinger created the "God helmet" to electromagnetically stimulate the temporal lobe, re-create the sensation of religious experience, and "prove" the connection between epilepsy and spiritual experiences.[49] Subjects who underwent the electrical stimulation attributed the sensation to God categorizing the experience according to the subject's own religious and cultural context. Christians thought it was the Christian God. Muslims experienced it as the God of Islam. However, in other research, subjects, *without* any prior epileptic condition experience activity in the frontal lobe due to their religious practice *without* artificial stimulation, while other religious subjects may experience activity in other regions of the brain apart from the temporal lobe. Thus, the religious experience = epilepsy equation failed.

Neuroscientist Andrew Newberg and anthropologist Eugene D'Aquili used brain imaging (single photon emission computed tomography [SPECT[50]]) to capture neural activity of subjects while meditating. They found diminished activity in the parietal lobe (navigation and spatial orientation) and increased activity in the right frontal cortex (executive function and attention). In a meditative state, the individuals were still and silent and had a lost sense of space and motion. The problem with the measurements was that they needed to pay attention and maintain focus (executive function) on the object of their thought to keep the experiment working, not necessarily because of their "God experience." They found the opposite effect when they studied five women speaking in tongues. Frontal lobe rational activity declined. This region of the brain is responsible for self-control, which is loosened while speaking in an unknown tongue.[51]

48. David Biello, "Searching for God in the Brain," SA Mind 18, no. 5 (October 2007): 38. https://www.scientificamerican.com/article/searching-for-god-in-the-brain/. (Biello 2007) See also Newberg, D'Aquilli, and Rause, *Why God Won't Go Away*; Newberg, *Born to Believe*. Newberg, *Neurotheology*; Carol Rausch Albright and James B. Ashbrook, *Where God Lives in the Brain* (Sourcebooks, 2001); Mario Beauregard and Denyse O'Leary, *The Spiritual Brain: A Neuroscientist's Case for the Existence of the Soul* (HarperCollins, 2008); Mario Beauregard and V. Paquette, "Neural Correlates of a Mystical Experience in Carmelite Nuns," *Neuroscience Letters* 405, no. 3 (September 2006): 186–90; Michael Persinger, *Neuropsychological Bases of God Beliefs* (Praeger, 1987).

49. Biello, "Searching for God in the Brain." (Biello 2007)

50. SPECT is a type of imaging test that uses a radioactive substance to produce an image that is recorded by a special camera in 3D. https://www.mayoclinic.org/tests-procedures/spect-scan/about/pac-20384925. (Mayo Clinic 2024)

51. Biello, "Searching for God in the Brain." (Biello 2007)

One study by Michael Ferguson in 2021[52] discovered that spirituality and religiosity are linked to neural circuits in a region of the brainstem known for fear, pain, altruism, and unconditional love.[53] Despite this conclusion, neuroscientists are hesitant to locate the so-called "god spot" or god module to one area of the brain. They recognize that other areas are at work as well during spiritual or religious experiences.[54]

Canadian neuroscientist Mario Beauregard employed brain imaging (functional magnetic resonance imaging [fMRI]) on fifteen Carmelite nuns during spiritual contemplation. Six brain regions were stirred. The aroused areas are responsible for learning, memory, falling in love, social emotion, and spatial and conscious awareness. Contrary to the hypothesis of a single "god spot" or the just the frontal lobe, multiple areas were engaged. Neural activity was noted in a network that traversed throughout the cerebral scape of the brain.[55] In spite of these fascinating and probing experiments, profound conclusions are challenging to draw. Results only yield general neuroanatomical information, while specific, precise neuronal activity is problematic to isolate.

Each subject is unique and has unique spiritual experiences that are difficult to test against other subjects and their unique experiments. Further, vague and imprecise correlations can lead to diverging and erroneous interpretations by scientists. Ultimately, there is no single localization of Divine experience. Divine experience, like most of our cognitive experiences, engages the "whole brain" in the whole body, which is situated in a social contextual environment. Discovering the neural correlates of religious experience remains an open and perplexing field of investigation.

The Mind and Scriptural Terms

We have concisely examined the brain according to biology. Now we can explore the mind according to the Bible. Scripture frequently references the human mind. It is the seat of our reason. Anthropological terminology is polyphonic and varies throughout Scripture. For example, here are some of the words used to describe faculties and functions of the human person: *nephesh* (Heb: soul, life), *leb* (Heb: heart), *ruach* (Heb: breath, spirit), *basar* (Heb: flesh), *soma* (Gk: body), *psyche* (Gk:

---

52. A lesion network mapping effort in the periaqueductal gray region (PAG) of the brain by Michael A. Ferguson, Frederic L. W. V. J. Schaper, Alexander Cohen, Shan Siddiqi, Sarah M. Merrill, Jared A. Nielsen, Jordan Grafman, Cosimo Urgesi, Franco Fabbro, and Michael D. Fox, "A Neural Circuit for Spirituality and Religiosity Derived from Patients with Brain Lesions," *Biological Psychiatry* 91, no. 4 (2022): 380–88. https://doi.org/10.1016/j.biopsych.2021.06.016. (Ferguson, et al. 2022)

53. Christopher Bergland, "Is the 'God Spot' Rooted Far Below Our Brain's Thinking Cap?," Psychology Today, July 3, 2021, https://www.psychologytoday.com/us/blog/the-athletes-way/202107/is-the-god-spot-rooted-far-below-our-brain-s-thinking-cap. (Bergland 2021)

54. For challenges and future research in seeking the god spot, see W. R. Klemm, "God Spots in the Brain: Nine Categories of Unasked, Unanswered Questions," *Religions* 11, no. 9 (2020): 468. https://doi.org/10.3390/rel11090468.

55. Biello, "Searching for God in the Brain." (Biello 2007)

soul, natural life, self), *kardia* (Gk: heart), *nous* (Gk: mind), *pneuma* (Gk: spirit), *sarx* (Gk: flesh). These terms understood theologically and in context do not seem to point to any form of faculty psychology or a radical partitioning of the human person in terms of our philosophical or scientific notions of substances or properties. Scripture does not intend to present itself in this way, scientifically or philosophically, but theologically.[56]

The nomenclature that we referenced for the human person is to be read theologically, specifically in terms of redemption, and our *entire* redemption. We are to understand the various dimensions of the human person as an integrated whole, "a living soul," "entirely spirit, soul, and body" (Genesis 2:7; 1 Thessalonians 5:23 NIV). Salvation is not only spiritual, nor is it only concerned with the body. But God saves all of us, spirit, soul, and body. According to New Testament scholar Craig Keener, Paul regularly uses the word *soul* to speak to the whole person. However, he employs "soul" only once to identify a part or aspect of a person, and in that usage, the reference is to the entire person (1 Thessalonians 5:23); whether his distinction there between the terms usually rendered "spirit" and "soul" is rhetorical and random or reflects a deeper theological distinction is debated. Paul may make distinctions more for addressing particular issues rather than employing a thoroughgoingly consistent vocabulary.[57] Therefore, we need to ask how the various terms are being used contextually.

Today, in circles of philosophy of mind, cognitive psychology, computer science, and cognitive neuroscience, there is much debate over what is the mind. Is the mind reduced to the brain? Is the mind produced by the brain? Are they two separate realities or substances? Is the mind an illusion or simulation? Is it an aspect of the soul? Is it perhaps an intrinsic part of the brain or matter itself? Is the mind merely cognitive, making us strictly rational creatures? The verdict is still out. We do not have enough evidence to form a valid conclusion.

My strategy is to accept the mind—or, more precisely, consciousness—as basic or fundamental to reality like the laws of physics. It is not derived from anything else in creation but is from God. The mind is the central semantic faculty through which we process reality and come to understand ourselves, others, the world, and God, and is what contributes to making us who we are as individual persons (hypostases). Further, the mind (*nous*) is everything that the Scriptures portray of it, an inner capacity by which we know and love God and neighbor.

---

56. Some would argue that the apostle Paul borrows extensively from Greek philosophical anthropology when using terms such as *flesh, mind, spirit,* and *soul,* while others contend that he borrows the language but gives it new meaning. For a brilliant analysis on Pauline anthropological terminology, see Craig S. Keener, *The Mind of the Spirit: Paul's Approach to Transformed Thinking* (Baker Academic, 2016).

57. Keener, *Mind of the Spirit,* 190–91. (Keener 2016)

Thus, the mind is not solely a cognitive faculty, nor are we as humans defined strictly as rational beings, though we are rational.[58] The Augustinian tradition gets it right. We are creatures of desire and want. The mind is an instrument that is ruled by the desires and wants of the heart (Gen. 6:5; Ps. 24:4; 73:7; Prov. 20:5; Matt. 15:19; Mark 7:21; Acts 8:22; Rom. 2:15). Jesus taught us that evil thoughts proceed from the heart. The heart and mind work together in that the heart is causal to our thinking. The heart determines the content of our thinking. Ultimately, we direct our thoughts and our wills toward what we long and yearn for. The mind is directed by the heart and is ultimately an expression of what is deep inside of us. The writer of Hebrews speaks to this connection with the expression "the thoughts and intents of the heart," signifying that our thinking and our will spring from the depth of our heart's desires (Heb. 4:12 NKJV). Throughout this book, when we use language around the mind and thinking, it is implied that the heart is the source and well-spring from which our minds draw.

"As a person thinks in his or her heart, so is he or she." Our thought life is determining, but it does not act alone. The mind is an instrument of the heart and its passions. The rigorous work of neuroscientists such as Antonio Damasio (b. 1944) surprisingly reveals that we cannot be defined as purely rational beings. We are more emotional beings that think or reason. His book *Descartes' Error* points out that French philosopher René Descartes was incorrect when he defined humans fundamentally as thinking creatures.

Furthermore, we are not beings who exist because we think, but we are beings who exist before we think.[59] A priority is placed on *being* over the thinking. Damasio contends that the center of human activity is in the organism (the body) itself. We are somatic conscious beings.[60] Although we have reason, emotion, and will, we are not strictly any one of those functions; we are whole beings. Each of these domains interacts with the other as an integrated unit. So when we talk about the mind or the mind of Christ, we are referring to reason but much more. Will or volition, physicality, and desire also figure prominently into comprehending the mind of Christ. Christ, as well as you and me, theoretically operate as whole beings and not as segments.

Metaphors of the Mind: God's Home

We can think of our task to develop the mind of Christ through various useful metaphors, like building a house, planting a garden, or programming a computer. The mind does not come fully equipped with good, right, and true ideas. It does not

---

58. Antonio R. Damasio, *Descartes' Error: Emotion, Reason, and the Human Brain* (Avon Books, 1994) (Damasio 1994). The following ideas are adapted from my work, *The Cerulean Soul* (Baylor University Press, 2021), 45–46.

59. (Damasio 1994), 247–52.

60. Damasio, *Descartes' Error*, xii–xii. (Damasio 1994) See also Antonio Damasio, *The Feeling of What Happens: Body and Emotion in the Making of Consciousness* (Harcourt, 1999), for an analysis of the somatic neural ontology of consciousness and how it defines the emerging self.

come fully constructed, but it needs to be built. The mind is like a house that needs to be built. It does not happen haphazardly by doing nothing, by being passive, or through merely wishful thinking. The mind is built intentionally one thought at a time as a house is constructed one stone or brick at a time. Like a house, a mind needs a rock-steady foundation that is made of durable material and is set deeply in the ground, able to uphold the weight that is placed on it. The average house weighs between 80,000 and 160,000 pounds. Indeed, a durable foundation is crucial.

Life can be weighty as well. Thus, wise women and men build their house upon the rock, and the rock of our foundation is Jesus Christ (Matt. 7:24; 1 Cor. 3:11). During COVID-19, there was a wood shortage. I had a porch built during that time. Probably not my best idea. The deck started to crack and warp after a year. I discovered that all of the available yet expensive wood was low quality. Live and learn. Wise people build wisely. Our mind rests on the steadfastness and stability of Jesus Christ.

The word of God is our rock.[61] When all else is shaken, God's word remains firm (Ps. 119:89–91; Matt. 24:25). Every word that proceeds from God's mouth is a stone that we lay one on another so that our mind is a solid structure able to withstand the storms of life. We cannot afford to build on the sinking sand of culture or any other foundation. The uncertainty, incompleteness, insufficiency, inadequacy, inability, approximation and limitation of human philosophy, science, political systems, and even temporal riches are deficient to uphold the weight of life. Life is too much to bear for the soul that is unaided by the one who grounds life itself. God is the ground of all things created. He is the ground of our being and our world.

The Word of God alone provides the substantial building material needed to build a secure life. Christ is our sole foundation. Nothing else can withstand the tornadoes, hurricanes, fires, floods, and earthquakes of this life. We cannot compromise on our building material. The structure of the mind needs to last a lifetime. Do not settle for anything less than the truth. Some materials may look attractive and cost less, but in the end, filling our mind with cognitive candy like internet trash, gossip, lies, social media, political dogma, and the like will only produce a moral rot that will deteriorate the structures of our mind and bring the whole house down. Build surely, slowly, and carefully according to God's blueprint. Build with the highest quality material, the word of God. Create a sturdy and steadfast theological framework of truth that can support a life lived in the Spirit with a roof of worship and, underneath, walls of righteousness. God wants to build every room of our soul so that he may inhabit each of them with his presence.

The Garden of our Mind

My grandfather, who was one of the most industrious workers I knew, was a Master Gardener. He worked day and night in the soil until he died in his eighty-ninth year. Gardening is tough work. I learned that when I assisted him as a youth. Keeping those flower and vegetable beds free from weeds seemed like a never-ending toil.

---

61. Throughout the book, I will use the term "word of God" for Scripture and "Word of God" for the Son of God.

My grandfather served as a landscaper for many prominent people. I best remember keeping Anny Katan's yard with him. Dr. Anny Rosenberg Katan (1898–1992) grew up alongside her best friend Anna Freud (1895–1982), Sigmund Freud's daughter, in Austria. Both Anna and Anny became prominent, pioneer psychoanalysts. Like many Jewish families at that time, the Katans and the Freuds fled Vienna because of the Nazi invasion and persecution. Anna launched the psychoanalytic movement in London, and eventually Dr. Katan and her husband, forerunners in the movement, brought psychoanalysis to the United States. She taught at the School of Medicine of Western Reserve University, now Case Western Reserve, and established the Hannah Perkins School. She also practiced therapy in her office at home. My grandfather and I kept her garden free from weeds outside, while inside, she kept the garden of people's minds free from cognitive weeds. We tended the soil. She tended the soul.

Our mind is like a garden that we must tend. A bounteous garden contains soil that has been broken up and freed from rocks and clumps. Weeds and unwanted growth have been uprooted and cleared away so that seeds can be planted at the right depth and spacing that growth may occur without obstruction. After proper fertilization, watering, and the work of the sun, the plant begins to break through the ground and reach to the sky. In due season it will bear petals, vegetables, or fruit. Like the garden, the fallow ground of our minds needs to be broken up and softened. The mind needs to be open and prepared for the word of God. We break up and prepare the soul through repentance and turning to God. In the parable of the sower (Mark 4), Jesus points out that the soil of our hearts, if left unkept, can become rocky, shallow, and even filled with weeds and thorns that will prevent the plants from growing.

Repentance will remedy this problem. We pray for a broken heart and a contrite spirit (Ps. 51). We pray for the fallow ground of our soul to be broken up and its thorns to be uprooted (Jer. 4:3). "Rend the heart and not the garment," as the prophet directed (Joel 2:13 KJV). The sanctifying Spirit of God will come and create a new heart in us with his law of love inscribed on it (Ezek. 36:26). The seed sown is the word of God (Luke 8:11). Like every seed, the word will reproduce after its own kind (Gen. 1:11–12). It will not return void (Isa. 55:11) but will yield a hundredfold harvest of righteousness, peace, and joy in the Holy Spirit (Mark 4:20; Rom. 14:17; Gal. 5:22). Read and memorize it. Ruminate on God's word throughout the day. Moment by moment, sow words of peace in your soul if you want a harvest of peace. Sow Scriptures of joy in your mind if you want to be filled with joy. Cultivate your mind with the word of God in order to reap the harvest that you desire.

God's word reveals God's nature and his will. It reveals who he is and what he does so that we may be transformed by it into his holy image (Eph. 4:22–24; 1 Pet. 1:23). His word will bring his peace and self-control to our mind. His word will wash us of sin and sanctify us wholly in every way. His word will charge us with his power and commission us with his authority. God's word will change and transform us by renewing our mind. Our mind can become a garden for all of the fruit of the Spirit that will yield acts of mercy and justice. Let others come freely and pick the fruit from our trees and be nourished.

Worldview: Scriptural or Worldly?

As we begin our journey to connect discipleship and the brain-mind, let's start with our mind's unique perspective of the world, the mind's *map* of the world, which we call *worldview*. Worldview is simply how we view the world. It is vital that we are aware of and critique our worldview. Is our worldview formed predominantly by Scripture or other sources? Are we seeing things as God would or as the world would?

Each of our brains makes an updateable operating map of God, self, others, and the world. This map is our working model of reality that helps us understand and navigate life. Our brains are constantly building an inner model of the outer world. And yet, it is more than a model. Our inner universe is not a pure symbol or unrelated representation but is our *real* experience of God, self, others, and the world. Yet this life or reality model is not perfect, because we are not perfect. Our reason is affected negatively by sin, and our understanding as finite beings is fallible and limited. Thus, we are constantly learning, self-correcting, updating, modifying, and reworking our model of reality.

The "we" refers to a particular culture. Each culture differs and does not see the world in the same way. Thus, worldview is basically the unique manner in which a particular people group in a given culture view and understand the big picture of reality. Worldview provides a culture with a pair of glasses or distinct lens to perceive and interpret the world. Cultural anthropologist Paul Hiebert's definition of worldview follows:

> The foundational cognitive, affective, and evaluative assumptions and frameworks a group of people makes about the nature of reality which they use to order their lives. It encompasses people's images or maps of the reality of all things that they use for living their lives. It is the cosmos thought to be true, desirable, and moral by a community of people.[62]

A worldview is assumed. It is the precondition for framing and understanding reality. One is born into a worldview and builds on it along the way through acculturation. Worldview is intuitively picked up, developed, and modified through our interaction with family, friends, school, the community, and other institutions. Acquiring worldview is part of the belief formation and socialization that takes place primarily in the prefrontal cortex, limbic system, amygdala, nucleus accumbens, hippocampus, and brainstem.[63]

---

62. Paul Hiebert, *Transforming Worldviews: An Anthropological Understanding of How People Change* (Baker, 2008), 25–26. (Hiebert 2008)

63. Tamara B. Franklin, Bianca A. Silva, Zinaida Perova, et al., "Prefrontal Cortical Control of a Brainstem Social Behavior Circuit," *Nature Neuroscience* 20 (2017): 260–70. https://doi.org/10.1038/nn.4470 (Franklin, Silva and Perova 2017); Christopher D. Frith, "The Social Brain?," Philosophical Transactions of the Royal Society B 362 (2007): 671–78. https://doi.org/10.1098/rstb.2006.2003 (Frith 2007). R. Adolphs, "The Social Brain: Neural Basis of Social Knowledge," *Annual Review of Psychology* 60 (2009): 693–716. https://doi.org/10.1146/annurev.psych.60.110707.163514 (Adolphs, The Social Brain: The Neural Basis of Social Knowledge 2009); Michael H. Connors and Peter W. Halligan, "Revealing the Cognitive Neuroscience of Belief," *Frontiers in Behavioral Neuroscience* 16 (2022): https://doi.org/10.3389/fnbeh.2022.926742 (Connors and Halligan 2022); T. S. Sathyanarayana Rao, M. R. Asha, K. S. Jagannatha Rao, and P. Vasudevaraju, "The Biochemistry of Belief," *Indian Journal of Psychiatry* 51, no. 4 (2009): 239–41. https://doi.org/10.4103/0019-5545.58285 (Rao, et al. 2009).

At a subjective level, though each of us is different and knows (epistemology), interprets (hermeneutics), and expresses (semiotics) the world uniquely, we exist and interact in *one* literal or real creation, one observable universe. If we claim that each of us or each culture exists in a literally different world, we are mistaken. We may only state that idea figuratively as a metaphor. Each of us does not live in scientifically real, observable, *different* worlds.[64]

Our models of reality are *basically* similar from person to person, or we would not be able to communicate and function. When you see a blue ball, I see a blue ball, though our associations, memories, and meanings may differ. The reason that we both see a blue ball is that there really objectively is a blue ball before us. The reason is that objectively we are looking at the same world (realism), though, subjectively, it can be interpreted and expressed with a low degree of variation or deviation from the norm.

Universally, people *basically* share the same software when viewing the world. However, there are versions of that same software based on people groups. Beyond individual perspectives, a larger grouping of interpretation and expression is categorized as a subculture and even larger as a culture. Cultures are a variant of the universal, and not all cultures see the world exactly the same. Each culture has a unique worldview with its own language, epistemologies, semiotics, hermeneutics, beliefs, values, customs, and cultural artifacts. Each culture has a more or less similar and shared model of the world (worldview) or perspective. We call this type of realism *critical realism.*

Our culture in the United States, though made of many smaller cultures and subcultures, is still primarily Western. We share and operate out of a Western worldview. Our mind models are fundamentally Western, though some of us may be African, Latino, or Asian and can and do function locally out of our smaller culture, which is called *hybridity.* In hybridity, we learn to be bi- or tricultural.

As Westerners, how do we understand ourselves and others? What does our mental map look like? As Western Christians, how do we see our present culture? Is our perspective or worldview informed by Scripture, culture, or both? How does the discipleship of our mind affect our worldview? What are the challenges that believers face today as we engage our cultural milieu? Is spiritual warfare real? If so, how does it affect our mind and our interaction with culture?

Again, within the discipline of cultural anthropology, worldview is the term that simply means how we view the world. The "we" refers to a particular culture. For those in the United States, the worldview of the culture is a Western worldview. The following are elements and characteristics of a Western worldview: rational and empirical (reason and science based); heavy emphasis on personal freedom, individualism (self-reliance, self-preservation, self-interested), private ownership, materialism, free market capitalism, separation of mind or spirit and body (Cartesian dualism), human versus nature (goal of conquering it), either/or black-and-white thinking, pragmatism (metric and results oriented), quantification (measuring, analytics), mechanistic,

---

64. Claims of the potential existence of a multiverse is implying something different than what we are discussing. There may be a different universe, though it has yet to be proven. However, if those hypothetical universes exist as real and observable, that is different than claiming that each person or culture has a distinct view and interpretation of the same real, observable universe.

systematic, tech-based, linear and monochronic in time, youth emphasis (as opposed to elder), and visual among other features.

In his groundbreaking book *Transforming Worldviews*, missionary anthropologist Paul Hiebert identified three levels of culture: *foundational* (worldview), *mediating* (belief and value systems), and *expression* (surface).[65] An iceberg often has a surface level of ice above the water and the bulk of its mass below the water, out of sight. Similarly with culture, the top level, expression, or surface is the level we see and experience daily: clothing, language, music, customs, and so on. The mediating and foundational levels (systems of beliefs and values) are below the surface and are not immediately apparent. We have to dig a bit to perceive the belief and value systems and worldview of another culture.

The surface level reveals the sense apparent (empirical), cultural products, patterns of behavior, signs, rituals, and customs of a people. There we find all of the expressions and artifacts of culture, such as language, food, clothing, art, music, film, sports, and work. These are all above the surface; we experience them regularly. The mediating level is beneath the surface. At this level are our belief and value systems. Our cognitive, affective, and evaluative beliefs and systems are explicit at this level. These beliefs drive what we experience at the expression or surface level. The mediating level also *mediates* our worldview or the foundational level, which is not explicit but implicit. The foundational level of a culture is its worldview that informs our belief and value systems that drive our expressions of culture. In this sense, worldview is similar to a culture's basic philosophy (metaphysics, ontology) about reality.

Hiebert's model of culture was designed to understand levels of conversion in discipleship. For true and lasting change to take place, conversion needs to occur ultimately at the foundational or worldview level and then following at the other two levels. Worldview conversion (a biblical worldview) then will inform conversion at the level of actual beliefs and values that will in turn affect the surface level of expression.[66] Often leadership in the church discovers that many "believers" fall back into sin or fall away once trials and temptations strike.[67] One of the chief causes is that conversion is not taking place at the worldview level.

Frequently, our churches merely target surface level conversion. We push for a change in language. We teach young converts how to speak "Christianese" and use the right buzzwords and phrases. We push for a change in clothing (mostly with women). Dress modestly and not like the world. We push for a change in music. Stop listening to metal, punk, rap, and other forms of music that are worldly. Start to listen to CCM (contemporary Christian Music), which is often like the turkey bacon of real rock and pop music. We push for a surface-level change in every area of appearance, disregarding that God primarily judges the heart (1 Sam. 16:7; Luke 16:15). Hiebert, echoing Scripture, instructs that conversion needs to occur at the deepest level of the human heart, the worldview level.

Surface changes can be important in certain cases to strengthen a believer's understanding of their own identity and commitment to Christ. For example, at one

---

65. Hiebert, *Transforming Worldviews*. (Hiebert 2008)

66. Hiebert, *Transforming Worldviews*, 11–12. (Hiebert 2008)

67. See Mark 4, the parable of the sower. Only one of the four soil types is conducive for true growth.

church that I pastored, we ministered to women who were working in the sex industry, specifically strip clubs. Once they received Christ, they eventually left their line of work. We helped them transition into more godly, gainful employment by helping them get their GED; offering spiritual, mental, and vocational counseling; training in résumé writing and interviewing; and changing their wardrobe. Our women's center, called the Oasis House, had a clothing boutique with free apparel, usually business attire.[68] The new look helped the women confirm that they were a new creation in Christ. It also better suited them for the new line of work that they were pursuing.

We need to note, however, that their new conservative-looking apparel did *not* convert them, nor was it the primary or even secondary sign of their conversion. Conversion occurred at the worldview and mediating level when the Spirit of God convicted and changed their hearts. Further, conversion was evidence by the fruit of the Spirit in their lives that became evident by their subsequent decisions and behavior. The change of clothing merely was a superficial or surface-level decision that reflected much deeper decisions and changes of the heart. Real and lasting change began at the worldview level first, when they repented of sin and surrendered to the Lordship of Jesus Christ.

Following worldview conversion, they changed their beliefs and values about self-identity and expression that was followed by an actual change of clothing, which they came to on their own for the right reasons. Reversing the process becomes either legalistic, superficial, or split-level Christianity, which is Christian on the outside but worldly or unconverted on the inside. We are seeking conversion at the worldview level that will inform conversion at all other levels. Our fundamental perspective about reality needs to be shaped by the Triune God as expressed in Scripture rather than the culture (a Scriptural worldview). Conversion brings us into a new community (culture), the kingdom of God. Conversion and discipleship begin in the mind with worldview transformation. The Spirit leads us from our uncritical cultural worldview to a biblical worldview that reflects the mind of Christ (fruit of the Spirit) and the Kingdom of God (heart attitude reflecting the Sermon on the Mount).

Did God Really Say That? Believing the Lie

Worldview is how our mind sees and processes the world around us. We recognize that not every aspect of our culture and its worldview is aligned with Scripture. A culture's worldview does not necessarily equate with a scriptural worldview. There are incongruencies. For example, Western culture as a whole does not necessarily believe in the God of the Bible. As a culture, we accept certain ideas and perform certain practices that may not be pleasing to God, such as our idolatry of materialism, disregard for life, rampant violence, or racial hatred.

Additionally, our Western worldview has been heavily affected by postmodernism, and some of its influence has been to our detriment. Postmodernism is a philosophical movement that undermines modern Western notions of absolute truth, objectivity, moral absolutes, or realism. Some postmodern circles have come to embrace that there are no metanarratives (Jean Lyotard). A metanarrative is a big story that

---

68. https://oasisforwomen.org/home/ (Oasis House n.d.)

explains all smaller stories, such as the fall of humanity, which describes that we are all by nature in a sinful state. Some contend that knowledge and truth can never be absolute or objective because both are constructs created and controlled by those in power, who create "regimes of truth" (Michel Foucault) to oppress marginalized groups.

In addition, postmodernism claims that there are no ideas, structures, or systems that possess legitimate authority to occupy a metaphysical or central position to supply absolute order, causation, reason, meaning, or purpose, such as God. All such truth claims can be and are to be deconstructed (Jacques Derrida) and shown to be self-contradictory and self-defeating. Thus, we inhabit a culture where truth claims are suspect. There is an open hostility to assertions about absolutes, whether they are metaphysical or moral. The post-truth, post-Christian West will not accept that only Christianity, Christ, or Scripture is *the* purveyor of truth or salvation.

Identifying areas of our Western culture that are misaligned with the word of God is hardly a daunting task. The Spirit longs to redeem culture. He wants to redeem our mental models and worldviews. The Holy Spirit wants to change the way we think about God, ourselves, others, and the world. Biblical change (*metanoia*) begins in the mind with the thoughts of our heart. As we have been reiterating, as the mind goes, so goes the person. The human brain-mind is the major way we process reality. What we think and dwell on affects our lives. If we have thoughts of fear, we become fearful. If we have thoughts of anxiety, we become anxious. If we dwell on the peace of Christ, we will be filled with peace. The mind is the strategic center that influences our lives.

We employ our minds every minute of every day to operate our lives physically, mentally, and emotionally. Our minds also have a sacred function. We use our minds to know, worship, and obey the one true God. Our mind is the throne on which the Spirit of God rests and rules. His presence inhabits our innermost being. The Lord communes with us by revealing himself to our minds. The Spirit communicates his knowledge and will to us through his word. When we meditate and yield to the word of God, we allow his thoughts to transform our thoughts. In essence, his thoughts become our thoughts. And then we are moved to do his will.

The mind was created to be an instrument of righteousness in the world and a vehicle for transformation. The mind was designed to tabernacle the presence of God and be used by God for good and his glory. God built the human brain with immeasurable capacity, power, and influence to receive, know, and share in the Divine. Our minds were created to be inhabited, a holy habitation, enjoyed and used by God. Yet we fill them with everything but God. As the mind goes, so goes the person.

Love or rejection? Peace or torment? Joy or misery? Life or death? Heaven or hell? Whichever you choose, the mind will be the key instrument that will be employed. Influencing and directing the mind will ultimately steer the individual. Thus, the Spirit of God desires to govern the mind (Rom. 8:5–6), but so does the enemy (2 Cor. 4:4; 10:4–5; 1 Pet. 5:8). Satan wants to control our thinking because he knows the mind is strategic. If he is able to establish strongholds in the mind, he will capture us. Christians, there is a war in and for our mind. And we are the spoils!

Satan tempted the thoughts of our primordial parents in the Garden of Eden. He offered them the fruit that God had forbidden: the lust of the flesh and the mind, the pride of life, and the lie to become their own gods. When Eve responded with her interpretation of what God had said, Satan retorted, "Did God really say that . . . ?" (Gen. 3:1). The enemy has been causing humanity to question the word of God ever since that day. He probably has gotten more mileage out of that lie than any other lie that he has spewed in human history. His strategy has not changed since the beginning of time. The reason that he keeps using the same lie is because we keep believing it. Satan steals the seed of God's word from us when it is not planted deeply in our heart (Mark 4:14–15).

When we refuse to trust God's word, St. Peter asserts that we distort and twist Scripture to our own destruction (2 Pet. 3:15–16). If Satan can undermine our trust in Scripture, he can usurp our faith in God concerning all truth related to the nature, promises, and work of God. It is imperative that we perceive the Divine inspiration of Scripture and not reduce it to merely a human concoction. We trust that it is the absolute, saving word of God and that we submit to it. The apostle Paul wrote, "When you received the word of God, which you heard from us, you accepted it not as a human word, but as it actually is, the word of God, which is indeed at work in you who believe" (1 Thess. 2:13). Discipleship begins by believing God's word with all of our heart, mind, and strength.

The enemy of our soul also has his eyes on the same target. He shoots his temptations, suggestions, images, desires, and distorted ideas into our thought life. If we are not vigilant to defend our mind, Satan's thoughts will overthrow our thinking. In essence, the enemy's thoughts then become our thoughts. Throughout time, Satan has used the mind to generate every type of ungodly thought and act against God and unthinkable horrors against humanity. Idolatry, blasphemy, murder, war, genocide, slavery, famine, poverty, oppression, suffering, and the like have littered human history since the beginning of time. The fall of humanity is all too real, and it begins in our minds with our thoughts.

One of the chief ways in which Satan attacks believers is to undermine the word of God, like he in did in the garden with Adam and Eve. If he can get us to doubt the truth of Scripture, we have no defense against deception. Without any standard of truth, we will succumb to the father of lies who doles out false teachers and prophets, doctrines of devils, damnable heresies, works of the flesh, and lying signs and wonders to the deceived. Once trust in the word of God falls, everything falls! Take out Scripture, and you will take out the church.

Satan's First Tactic: Take Away the Bible

Consider the case of so-called progressive New Testament scholar Bart Ehrman. He was raised as an evangelical Christian until he went to Princeton Theological Seminary and studied textual criticism of the Bible. Textual criticism is the science of examining existing manuscripts, understanding the production and transmission of those manuscripts, and reconstructing the text as closely as possible to its original form (the autographs). Many theological institutions teach textual and higher criticism in a way that entices students to doubt the veracity and trustworthiness of the biblical text. During his theological education, Ehrman, though a brilliant man, concluded that the Bible was full of discrepancies and contradictions. This conclusion led him to reject Scripture as a source of truth for Christian faith and doctrine. Worse yet, he has influenced scores of "believers" who have trusted his work and likewise have given up on the veracity, power, and authority of holy Scripture.

Currently, Ehrman considers himself an "agnostic atheist," meaning he does not believe that God exists, but he cannot know it absolutely or in a scientific way. Ehrman's polemical writings, along with those of a host of other progressive scholars, are extremely influential in undermining trust in the Bible among many in the church and the culture. Consider also popular Christian writer and leader Rob Bell, author of *What Is the Bible?*, who claims that the Bible is not a revelation from God but a human invention, a book written solely by humans about humans.[69] For Bell, Scripture is no more inspired than a painter who crafts a work of art or a writer who pens a stirring novel or poem. Why should we then believe absolutely in a book that is not inspired by God but is merely product of imaginative human minds? Well, in fact, most of the church and the culture do not believe Scripture is the word of God.[70]

A recent Gallup poll claims that only 20 percent of Americans believe that the Bible is the actual word of God, while only 25 percent of American Christians take the Bible as the literal word of God.[71] More astoundingly, 16 percent of American Christian believe the Bible is "a book of legends and fables."[72] Sorry, I will not bet my life on the equivalent of *Grimm's Fairy Tales*. If Christians do not believe that Scripture is the actual word of God, what are they putting their trust in for faith and practice? Their own understanding? The culture? An unbelieving pastor? An apostate church?

Over the years, in my own denomination, I have watched trust in Scripture as God's word dwindle down to nothing. In seminary classes, in denominational literature and conferences, in the writings of its leaders, and in regular posts on its largest clergy group pages on social media, leaders claim that the Bible is *not* the word of God but merely a fallible, patriarchal, homophobic, oppressive, human-devised text. On the other hand, our denomination's doctrinal standards confess a high view of Scripture that it is the revelation of God's word, and it "contains all things necessary for salvation"

---

69. Rob Bell, *What Is the Bible? How an Ancient Library of Poems, Letters, and Stories Can Transform the Way You Think and Feel About Everything* (HarperOne, 2019), 4, 81, 116–17, 188, 243–46, 266–67, 286–87, 291, 295–96. (Bell 2019)

70. For an accessible work on the trustworthiness of Scripture, see William Mounce, *Why I Trust the Bible* (Zondervan, 2021).

71. "Gallup: Only 20 Percent of Americans Believe the Bible Is the Actual Word of God," Relevant, July 11, 2022, https://relevantmagazine.com/faith/gallup-only-20-percent-of-americans-believe-the-bible-is-the-actual-word-of-god/. (Relevant 2022)

72. "Gallup: Only 20 Percent of Americans Believe the Bible Is the Actual Word of God." (Relevant 2022)

as our "true rule and guide for faith in practice."[73] Nonetheless, I have witnessed countless times in our seminaries, pulpits, and pews a flat-out denial that Scripture is the true word of God. Once as one of our bishops denied that Scripture is the word of God, he also denied essential Christian doctrines such as Christ's divinity, the Trinity, the incarnation, the atonement, the bodily resurrection, and exclusive salvation in Christ.[74]

Once *trust in Scripture* has been undermined, Satan begins to undermine the *truths of Scripture*, like the divinity, virgin birth, sinless life, saving atonement, exclusive salvation, bodily resurrection, and second coming of Jesus Christ and other important doctrines of the Christian faith. One seems to follow from the other. Remove the foundation and source of truth, and then all of the other proclaimed truths will fall like a house of cards. If the word of God is not the ultimate, absolute, eternal truth, the church and the world have nothing to stand on except the "truth" that is constructed from science, philosophy, other religions, politics, culture, or their own minds. Once Satan steals the word of God from the mind, it is no mystery that he is able to blind and imprison the masses to reject the fundamental truths about God, our world, and ourselves.

Not only do we no longer hold to God's Divine order as revealed in Scripture, but we even challenge what he has revealed in the created order. It becomes no surprise that we believe the absurdities that the enemy peddles today and no longer accept our God-given identifiers, indicators, and relations that are revealed in nature. Satan, the "god of this world," bombards our minds daily through every medium with such lies. He knows what he is doing. His mission has always been to steal, kill, and destroy (John 10:9).

In the Parable of the Sower, Christ instructs his disciples on the preeminence of the word of God (Mark 4:1–20). The seed is the word of God. There are four potential soils in which it can be sown. Only one of them is good soil, a heart that hears, receives, and obeys the word of God. The other soils of the heart are obstructed by thorns, thistles, hardness, superficiality, covetousness, and the worries of this life. The seed will not grow in these types of soil. Explaining the parable, Christ gives us the punchline. If we do not understand *this* parable, we will not be able to understand the *other* parables (Mark 4:13). This teaching about the word of God is key to understanding other parables and teachings of Jesus. A heart that is resolved to hear, receive, and obey the word, and not doubt the veracity of Scripture, will be able to receive truth from God in the future. If the heart does not receive it, the enemy will come and steal it away.

The Mind Is a Warzone

On average, we have around 75,000 thoughts a day. If we have 75,000 thoughts a day, it stands to reason that some of those thoughts are not of God. Let us give the

---

73. The Global Methodist Church. "The Transitional Book of Doctrines and Discipline." April 12, 2022. (The Global Methodist Church 2022)

74. Mark Tooley, "Methodist Bishops and False Doctrine," Juicy Ecumenism, May 19, 2017, https://juicyecumenism.com/2017/05/19/methodist-bishops-false-doctrine/. (Tooley, Methodist Bishops and False Doctrine 2017)

benefit of the doubt that most of the mind's thoughts are probably our own, and a lesser sum are even inspired by God or the devil. Suppose even if 80 percent of our thoughts, or 60,000 of our 75,000 thoughts, originate from us, which is being generous. Then the remaining 20 percent of our thoughts would be divided between God and the enemy. Hypothetically, say the 20 percent is split evenly between the two. That would mean that we would still have minimally 7,500 thoughts a day from the devil. That is quite a sum of evil thoughts. We better know how to defend ourselves. "Well, I don't believe in some evil being with cloven hooves, horns, and a pitchfork," you say. Neither do I. But I do believe in fallen angelic powers that come to us as the voice of temptation, luring us to do evil in God's sight. The devil knows that deceiving the mind is essential to conquering the individual. As a result, most of his work is focused on baiting and trapping the mind with his lies so that he can capture the soul.

We can examine a variety of areas where Satan bombs the mind. One of the most prominent, effective weapons used by the enemy is internet pornography, currently an estimated $97 billion-a-year industry.[75] The following stunning statistics are from *Webroot*, a cybersecurity resource:

Every second

- 28,258 users are watching pornography on the internet,
- $3,075.64 is being spent on pornography on the internet, and
- 372 people are typing the word "adult" into a search engine.

Every day

- 37 pornographic videos are created in the United States,
- 2.5 billion emails containing porn are sent or received,
- 68 million search queries related to pornography—25% of total searches are generated (other sources indicate 30 percent to 37 percent[76]), and
- 116,000 queries related to child pornography are received.

How Online Pornography Affects Americans:

- About 200,000 Americans are classified as "porn addicts."
- Forty million American people regularly visit porn sites.
- 35% of all internet downloads are related to pornography.
- 34% of internet users have experienced unwanted exposure to pornographic content through ads, pop-ups, misdirected links, or emails.

---

75. "How Does the Porn Industry Make Its Money Today?," *Fight the New Drug*, accessed January 9, 2024, https://fightthenewdrug.org/how-does-the-porn-industry-actually-make-money-today/. (Fight the New Drug n.d.)

76. Mark Ward, "Web Porn: Just How Much Is There?," *BBC News*, July 1, 2013, https://www.bbc.com/news/technology-23030090.amp. (Ward 2013)

- 47% of US families report that porn is a problem in their home.
- Porn use increases marital infidelity by more than 300 percent.
- 68% of divorce cases involve one party meeting a new paramour over the internet, while 56% involve one party having an "obsessive interest" in pornographic websites.[77]

These statistics are just the tip of the iceberg of the disaster related to porn use. Pornography, itself a moral pandemic, is strongly related to the following social ills: divorce, rape, addiction (see section below), sex trafficking, child abuse, sexual abuse, pedophilia, violence against women and children, adverse business productivity, depression, anxiety and other mental disorders, healthy sexual development, sexual objectification of others, distorted concept of healthy relationships, and other maladies.[78] The porn pandemic has even spread to the church. An older study from 2015 by Barna Research indicates that "68% of church-going men and more than 50% of pastors regularly view porn."[79]

This plague is even spreading among women. One study indicates that "91.5 percent of men and 60.2 percent of women herein reported having consumed pornography in the last month."[80] This is merely one deadly area where Satan is assaulting the minds of believers and unbelievers alike. Many have been taken captive and cannot escape, while their family and their world around them is being destroyed. Once enslaved, even the thought of liberation to the devastated and defeated soul seems impossible. However, the war did not start out as an insurmountable onslaught. It only began with a simple thought or image shot into the mind from the bow of the enemy.

The devil can come into our mind innocuously while we are unaware, tired, frustrated, bored, or distracted. We let our guard down for a moment, and then he strikes. Or perhaps our curiosity just wants a taste of the forbidden fruit to see what it's like. We are curious to see what all of the rage is about at the party around the tree of the knowledge of good and evil. Just a little sample won't hurt. "I can control myself," we tell ourselves. An old-time Holiness preacher once said that the devil will always take you further than you initially wanted to go. With Satan, a little goes a

---

77.   "Internet Pornography by the Numbers: A Significant Threat to Society," *Webroot*, accessed January 9, 2024, https://www.webroot.com/us/en/resources/tips-articles/internet-pornography-by-the-numbers#:~:text=Internet%20Pornography%20Statistics%20in%20the%20United%20States.the%20word%20%22adult%22%20into%20a%20search%20engine. (WebRoot n.d.)

78.   "How Pornography Impacts Violence Against Women and Child Sex Abuse." Focus for Health Foundation, accessed March 28, 2024, https://www.focusforhealth.org/how-pornography-impacts-violence-against-women-and-child-sex-abuse. (Focus for Health Foundation n.d.)

79.   Porn in the Digital Age: New Research Reveals 10 Trends https://www.barna.com/research/porn-in-the-digital-age-new-research-reveals-10-trends/ https://www.provenmen.org/2014PornSurvey/ accessed January 9, 2024. (Barna Group 2016)

80.   Ingrid Solano, Nicholas R. Eaton, and K. Daniel O'Leary, "Pornography Consumption, Modality and Function in a Large Internet Sample," *Journal of Sex Research* 57, no. 1 (2020): 92–103. https://doi.org/10.1080/00224499.2018.1532488. (Solano, Eaton and O'Leary 2020)

long way. It does take much if its poison. Just a sip of strychnine or a touch of fentanyl, I am sure, will take you out. When the forbidden fruit is toxic it does not take much. If Satan can get you to drop your guard for just a moment, one punch will knock you out. I always tell my fighters that it is the punch that you do not see that takes you out.

Scripture tells us that Satan has come to steal, kill, and destroy (John 10:9). The devil and his fallen angels do not sleep at night. They are up around the clock with a plan to deceive and destroy each one of us. However, our modern mindset thinks Satan is a myth concocted by the church to scare people into conforming to its ways. Many are influenced by the inflated explanatory power of science and struggle to believe that such invisible assassins exist. The demons appreciate our skepticism. It is an effective cover under which they can accomplish much. Scripture is clear about the existence and purpose of the demonic.[81] And those of us who are filled and led by the Spirit are walking in Divine discernment and can detect both demons and their devices. We have realized that when we received Christ as Lord, we were drafted into a long-standing war on the saints. This war is against the rule of God, and the battlefields are in the church, the world, and in the mind. Prior to coming to Christ, when we were blind to the strategies of the enemy, bound and held captive as prisoners of war, we were not aware of our impaired and incarcerated state. We were not aware that a cosmic battle of the ages was raging between the hordes of hell and the soul of humanity.

But once we awakened from our sinful slumber by Christ the Light of the World, we, like the apostle Paul, became aware of the devil's schemes, strategies, and wiles (2 Cor. 2:11; Eph. 6:11). Of course, we do not want to exaggerate the influence of Satan, but we also do not want to underestimate it to our demise either. Those who have been awakened by the Spirit can discern the words of darkness. Our eyes are opened, and like a vigilant boxer, we can see the punches coming before they land. And like a skilled, defensive fighter, we could slip, block, duck, and sidestep them before they hit us.

One of the first lessons learned is that the mind is the battlefield for the spiritual war with the devil. Our thought life is a war zone, and deception is the devil's arsenal. He attacks us with lies and bombs our minds with deceit. Satan's one power, and it is a resourceful one, is the power of deception. All of his tricks and tactics are rooted in deceit. Deception is like a malleable lump of clay that he molds into any form or shape he desires. He is the creator, crafter, author, and inventor of lies. In fact, Scripture calls him the "father of lies" (John 8:44 NIV).

Fighters and war strategists know that "if the enemy leaves a door open, you must rush in."[82] At the moment of the enemy's attack, the victim is often caught off

---

81. For an explanation of the existence and work of the demonic, see Peter Bellini, *Unleashed* (Wipf and Stock, 2018); *The X-Manual: A Comprehensive Handbook on Deliverance and Exorcism* (Wipf and Stock, 2022); and *Thunderstruck! The Deliverance Ministry of John Wesley* (Wipf and Stock, 2023).

82. Sun Tzu, *The Art of War*, trans. Lionel Giles (Allandale Online Publishing, 2000), (Tzu 2000) 18, 85, 98.

guard or in a vulnerable place. "I have hidden your word in my heart that I might not sin against you" (Ps. 119:11 NIV; Prov. 3:1); David the psalmist prepared for battle by buttressing his mind with the word of God. Hiding or storing God's word in his heart is figurative language for treasuring it and committing it to memory, so that he can recall it in the time of battle, use it to defend himself, and hold his ground.[83] Spend quality, extensive time in God's Word reading, meditating, digesting, and memorizing it for future use in time of need.

Memory comes in many forms, including sensory, short-term, working, and long-term. David was most likely working out of his explicit (intentional) long-term, semantic (facts) memory. Memory is formed in three stages: encoding (from senses to brain), storage (one of the four types mentioned), and recall (retrieval). Rehearsing, writing, and perhaps singing Scripture, like David did in Psalm 119, are effective ways to improve memory. We cannot draw our sword against Satan if it is not in the sheath, ready to go.

Has Our Culture Lost Its Mind?

We need to be vigilant of the widespread deception that Satan unleashes at all levels of life. Not only does the enemy tempt the individual into personal sins like pride, lust, anger, jealousy, envy, unbelief, and the like, but he also manufactures sophisticated structures of deception at the level of ideology, systems of belief, collective thinking, worldview, and culture. I believe our culture in many ways has symptoms of a disordered mind. Today, we are being assailed by ungodly ideologies, systems of belief, and practices that undermine the foundation of Western civilization. Erroneous views on sex and gender are usurping fundamental, scientific, tested truths of biology. I call it "political biology"—biological conclusions drawn from one's political perspective or identity politics. I am normally not one drawn to politics, but the staggering onslaught of ideological warfare in our today is unavoidable. We have politicized everything from sex, gender, race, ethnicity, social media, sports, education, counseling, marketing, grammar, math, you name it. We are convinced that politics is the answer to everything and that our political party has all of the answers. Regardless of our political party, everyone deserves humane, equal treatment under the law. We are called to love and not hate one another while consistently upholding the high call of holiness.

Being bombarded every moment with ideologically loaded messages intent on assailing and capturing our minds, we are challenged to remain salt and light. Basic human rights innate to democracy and protected by its founding documents are being assaulted by self-appointed kingdom revolutionaries on the right and so-called social justice warriors on the left. Their ideologies, and even actions, which are often destructive, racist, and violent, are being touted as the only solution to our society's

---

83. Eduardo Camina and Francisco Güell, "The Neuroanatomical, Neurophysiological and Psychological Basis of Memory: Current Models and Their Origins," *Frontiers in Pharmacology* 8 (2017): 438. https://doi.org/10.3389/fphar.2017.00438. (Camina and Güell 2017)

problem. We are witnessing a pandemic of radicalization and indoctrination of our nation, especially the younger generations, by illiberal, uncritical, ill-defined irrational, immoral, ahistorical, pseudo-religious, sociopolitical, corrosive, lethal dogma that has violently seized the minds of the senseless masses on the left and the right, even in the church. Many, including in the church, believe that the culture's answers are found in radical political movements on one side or the other. It is rare to find balanced sociopolitical views and values at the popular level that promote life, health, safety, opportunity, and well-being for all. So when a candidate or a particular group stands for one or two of our espoused values, we feel that we can trust them with greater political power, which is not always the case. Beware of false gospels (cultural dogma) and false messiahs.

More than ever, we need to do our homework in a post-truth age of disinformation and denial. We need to fact-check the fact-checkers who fact-check the fact-checkers. COVID-19 has rightfully inaugurated a wave of skepticism about our institutions. Our once faithful and trusted institutions, such as the sciences, the medical profession, the public educational system, the universities, journalism, media and the press can no longer be counted on to deliver unbiased truth. They have often been politicized, co-opted, and hijacked as vehicles of power to construct and control a new narrative of victimization. Deception has covered the land like a pervasive, thick fog. We fumble to see our way forward, and we cannot vote our way out of it, blue or red. The temptation is to rely on political power and seize control to fix our problems. History shows us that the church and political power were never a good mix. Jesus did not come as that type of leader. He did not seek Herod or Pilate's position to enact change. We need to trust our King, Jesus, who cannot be elected, voted out, or impeached.

Lies Are the Problem. Truth Is the Solution.

Wisdom is calling us to return to the truth and teach it to the generations. A basic principle guiding this text is that *lies blind and bind, but the truth delivers or sets free.* Jesus declared that knowing the truth will set us free (John 8:31–32). That means the opposite is true as well. Lies will enslave us. Satan's main weapon is deception. Our main counter-weapon is the truth. Lies bind. Truth delivers. The lies we believe about self, others, the world, and God will chain and enslave us to sin and death. But the truth of God's word will set us free. Truth breaks the chains that bind us and will deliver us from evil. My hope is that this book will empower the reader to identify the lies that have been believed and have enslaved and, further, to identify the truth in God's word that will set captives free. This simple strategy is the secret to a victorious and fruitful life in Christ. We find deliverance from temptation, sin, and Satan, when we are transformed by renewing our mind with the word of God. When faith and obedience to God's word become a holy habit, we will gain the mind of Christ, one thought at a time.

The mind of Christ is the mind that Christ possesses. It is a mind set on, shaped by, rooted in, desiring, thinking, and acting on the word of God. The mind of Christ, not the mind of culture, thinks the thoughts of God and makes the Father's way its way. It attempts to see life with God's eyes and not with the world's eyes. The mind of Christ values the virtues of God over the vices of the world. In response to God, it obeys rather than rebels. The mind of Christ is sacrificial rather than selfish. It operates by the fruit of the Spirit and not the works of the flesh (Gal. 5). The mind of Christ marks the redemption of our inner life. The mind of Christ is humble and serves. The mind of Christ has the heart of God. The mind of Christ beholds the Father continually and purposes to do his will. Let us seek to have the same mind that was in Christ Jesus (Phil. 2).

Mental Disorders on the Rise

Not all of the warfare or struggles in our mind may be directly related to sin or the demonic. We live in a fallen world. We live in an imperfect world. We live in a world where mental disorders are prevalent, and their origins are not so simply located. Genetic predisposition, environment, nurture, family of origin, culture, stress, and other factors can be involved in the presentation of mental disorders. Psychiatric disorders, which include depression and anxiety, are the leading cause of disability in the United States, followed by cardiovascular and circulatory diseases.[84] For example, depression is the leading cause of disability worldwide in terms of total years lost due to disability.[85]

Psychiatric disorders are also the leading risk factors in suicide.[86] In 2021, suicide was the third leading cause of death for young people ages fifteen to twenty-four.[87] The National Institute of Mental Health reports that an "estimated 43.7 million adults aged 18 or older in the U.S. suffer with Any Mental Illness (AMI) in the past year," representing 18.6 percent of all US adults.[88] Mental disorders are prevalent and on the rise, especially following the COVID-19 pandemic, but possibly an equally disturbing reality is that many disorders are not being treated. For example, the

84. "U.S. Leading Categories of Diseases/Disorders," National Institute of Mental Health, accessed March 9, 2015, http://www.nimh.nih.gov/health/statistics/disability/us-leading-categories-of-diseases-disorders.shtml. (National Institute of Mental Health n.d.)

85. "Depression: A Global Public Health Concern," World Health Organization, accessed January 20, 2016, http://www.who.int/mental_health/management/depression/en. (World Health Organization n.d.)

86. "Suicide in America: Frequently Asked Questions," National Institute of Mental Health, accessed March 9, 2015, http://www.nimh.nih.gov/health/topics/suicide-prevention/index.shtml. (National Institute of Mental Health n.d.)

87. "Suicide," National Institute of Mental Health, accessed November 6, 2024, https://www.nimh.nih (National Institute of Mental Health 2024).gov/health/statistics/suicide. (National Institute of Mental Health 2024)

88. "Mental Illness," National Institute of Mental Health, accessed March 9, 2015, http://www.nimh.nih.gov/health/statistics/prevalence/any-mental-illness-ami-among-adults.shtml. (National Institute of Mental Health 2024)

twelve-month prevalence of any anxiety disorder in the United States among adults is 18.1 percent. Of that 18.1 percent, only 36.9 percent are receiving any treatment, and of that 36.9 percent, only 34.3 percent (or 12.7 percent overall) are receiving minimally adequate treatment.[89]

Contrary to popular belief, these struggles also are prevalent in the church. Lifeway Research claims, Most Protestant senior pastors (66 percent) seldom speak to their congregation about mental illness... About 1 in 6 pastors (16 percent) speak about mental illness once a year. And about a quarter of pastors (22 percent) are reluctant to help those who suffer from acute mental illness because it takes too much time.[90]

> Pastors want to help but do not feel trained and prepared to do so. They often lack human resources and an informed and practical plan of ministry that addresses the complexity of mental health in their congregations. For example, "only a quarter of churches (27 percent) have a plan to assist families affected by mental illness according to pastors. And only 21 percent of family members are aware of a plan in their church."[91] Only 14% of the churches surveyed have a counselor, staff person or leader trained to recognize mental illness.[92] Although the church is ill equipped to minister with persons suffering from mental disorders, "family members (65 percent) and those with mental illness (59 percent) want their church to talk openly about mental illness, so the topic will not be a taboo."[93]

Mental disorders are often underdiagnosed and undertreated because many believers hold to the misconception that because one is a Christian and saved, reads the Bible, goes to church, and/or prays, one should *not* be depressed or have anxiety. Under such misconceptions, a mental disorder is seen as a sign of shame and defeat, and thus the afflicted person hides their struggle and suffers tragically in silence and alone. The fact is that we are human and not God. Additionally, we live in a fallen world that has been wrecked by sin. And some of the sin is our own. Mishap, tragedy, sin, and sickness can befall anyone, even believers. We are not exempt! Like I tell my boxers, "Don't think that you will not get hit when you box. It is like thinking you can go swimming and not get wet. Everyone gets hit who boxes."

---

89. "Any Anxiety Order," National Institute of Health, accessed March 9, 2015, http://www.nimh.nih.gov/health/statistics/prevalence/any-anxiety-disorder-among-adults.shtml. (National Institute of Mental Health n.d.)

90. Bob Smietana, "Mental Illness Remains Taboo Topic for Many Pastors," Lifeway Research, September 22, 2014, http://www.lifewayresearch.com/2014/09/22/mental-illness-remains-taboo-topic-for-many-pastors/. (Smietana 2014)

91. Smietana, "Mental Illness Remains Taboo Topic for Many Pastors." (Smietana 2014)

92. Smietana, "Mental Illness Remains Taboo Topic for Many Pastors." (Smietana 2014)

93. Smietana, "Mental Illness Remains Taboo Topic for Many Pastors." (Smietana 2014)

Although mental disorders are part of living in a fallen, broken world and not demonic in themselves, they may be comorbid with the demonic or create many problems and symptoms that may seem similar to demonic manifestations. They may also open the door to demonic attack. Note that mental disorders are not to be confused with the demonic, though the latter can take advantage of the vulnerability and disorientation brought about by the former. The two, however, are not synonymous. In my ministry I have observed deliverance ministers fail to liberate persons with major depression, only to observe the same persons relieved of the "demonic" symptoms through medication and counseling. The medication did not cast out the demon. The SSRI (selective serotonin reuptake inhibitors) relieved the depression symptoms. If demons were profiting from the mental disorder, treatment closed the door of opportunity by dealing with the depression itself.

A mental disorder is not synonymous with a demon, though demons surely can work through them. Thus, some familiarity with relevant sections of the DSM-5 (*Diagnostic and Statistical Manual of Mental Disorders*), symptomatology and recommendation of professional help when needed, as well as supporting existing diagnoses and prescriptions can be vital. Proper psychiatric or other medical care, including consistent pharmacological, dietary, or other treatment, is essential prior to any clear assessment of demonic activity.

Our God is a healer of spirit, soul, and body. Scripture offers us the hope of a sound mind in that "God has not given us a spirit of fear, but of power and of love and of a sound mind" (2 Tim. 1:7 NKJV). Paul was encouraging Timothy not to be afraid to share his faith. Too often when the enemy sends us thoughts and feelings of fear or worry, we grab a hold of them as if they belong to us or as if God sent them to us. Of course, we all experience fear. Sometimes fear is the amygdala's healthy response to legitimate danger. We can call it "healthy fear." Sometimes fear can be triggered for irrational reasons or for no sound reason at all. We can call that "unhealthy fear." At times, our irrational thinking or even the enemy can stir up unhealthy fear in our minds. Fear to share the gospel, fear of death, fear related to condemnation, and fear of people are examples of unhealthy fear that can come from Satan or our own distorted thinking. Scripture specifically claims that this type of fear is an evil spirit that is *not* from God. God does not give us a spirit of fear. Discern the voice in your head by its fruit and character. Does it breed fear or faith? Satan can send unhealthy fear.[94] Unhealthy fear and faith are polar opposites. You cannot have faith and unhealthy fear at the same time. One cancels out the other.

---

94. Some fear can actually be healthy. The reactor system in our amygdala responds to threats to our safety with either fight, flight, or freeze. This is healthy fear. It corresponds with real danger, and the response of fear is properly measured in proportion to the perceived danger and can be considered a normal response. However, on the other hand our fear can be irrational, unwarranted, unrealistic and not connected to any real threat. An anxious mind houses an alarm system that is constantly triggered whether there is justifiable danger or not. Healthy cognition will weigh out and test the evidence for its probability, reality, and veracity before it makes a logical conclusion regarding the perceived danger. Our thinking elicits emotion. Right thinking elicits right emotions. Distorted thinking releases distorted emotions.

When Moses sent out scouts to survey the promised land, some came back with a fearful report that the enemy was too big and that they were too small to find victory. They did not perceive the land through faith and consider God's promise. Joshua and Caleb surveyed the land and witnessed the same giants but returned with a good report. The difference was that they factored the Almighty God into their assessment. God made the giants look like grasshoppers and not the Israelites. Our working epistemology (theory of knowledge) should always be to "trust in the LORD with all your heart and lean not on your own understanding; in all your ways acknowledge him, and he will make straight your paths. Do not be wise in your own eyes; fear the LORD and shun evil" (Prov. 3:5–7 NIV).

In terms of a "spirit of fear," think of it as F.E.A.R.: False Evidence Appearing Real. Fear knocks at the door. Faith answers. No one is there. A bulk of what we fear never comes to pass. Unhealthy fear is irrational and not from God (2 Tim. 1:7). Instead, perfect love from God casts out all fear. God gives us perfect love, enabling power, and a sound mind of self-control. The Greek word translated "sound mind" is *sōphronismos* (noun), or *sōphroneō* (verb). The semantic range of this powerful word can signify to possess a mind that is sound, sober, moderate, tempered, balanced, and humble. *Sōphroneō* (so-fron-ay-o) is to be in one's right mind, reasoning properly with clear and sober judgment, and exercising self-control over thoughts, passions, and desires. For example, after the Gadarene demoniac was delivered and set free from the Legion of devils by Christ, Mark and Luke describe him as "clothed and in his right mind," or *sōphroneō* (Mark 5:15; Luke 8:35).

We live in a day when *sōphroneō* is a rare commodity. If you need proof, spend an hour on social media and observe the absence of self-control. Self-control is one of the fruits of the Spirit (Gal. 5:23). The Spirit infuses our minds with the power to exercise self-government and discipline. When the world loses its mind, we can keep ours. St. Peter urges, "The end of all things is at hand; therefore, be self-controlled and sober-minded for the sake of your prayers" (1 Pet. 4:7 ESV). During perilous times when everyone else is coming unglued, we can maintain sobriety of mind and rest in the peace of God that works beyond our circumstances and comprehension (Phil. 4:7). The prophet gives us wisdom: "You will keep in perfect peace all who trust in you, all whose thoughts are fixed on you!" (Isa. 26:3 NLT). What consumes our will consumes us for better or for worse.

The Neuroscience and Significance of Attention

A vital function driving effective brain performance and decision-making is attention or focus. Primarily, it is attention that shapes the brain-mind. Attention, located in the executive function in the prefrontal cortex, is the driver of the brain. Attention drives the engine of the train, and the engine pulls the other cars. All of the structures and functions of the brain align with the power and drive of attention. Daniel J. Siegel claims, "One of the key practical lessons of modern neuroscience is that the power to direct our attention has within it the power to shape the brain's firing patterns, as well as the power to shape the architecture of the brain itself," which is called *neuroplasticity*.[95] In fact, "neuroplasticity is activated by attention itself."[96] Needless to say, attention is our human superpower! The neuroscientific rule of thumb says, "Neurons that fire together, wire together." This is called the *Hebbian rule*, named after neuropsychologist Donald Hebb. We will note later how this principle is relevant in addiction and recovery in terms of breaking old patterns and forming new ones.

The brain has many attentional systems. According to the neuroanatomical model of Michael Posner and Steven Petersen, there are three:

- **Reticular Activating System (RAS) or Alert System:** This system is mainly in charge of arousal and sustained attention. It is closely related to the reticular formation and some of its connections, like the frontal areas, limbic systems, the thalamus, and the basal ganglia.
- **Posterior Attentional System (PAS) or Orientation System:** This system is in charge of focused attention and selective attention of visual stimuli. The brain areas related to this system are the posterior parietal cortex, the lateral pulvinar nucleus of the thalamus, and the superior colliculus.
- **Anterior Attentional System (AAS) or Execution System:** This system is in charge of selective attention, sustained attention, and divided attention. It's closely related to the prefrontal dorsolateral cortex, the orbitofrontal cortex, the anterior cingulate cortex, the supplementary motor area, and with the neostriatum (striate nucleus).[97]

Within the three attentional systems, there are six types of attention, according to the McKay Sohlberg and Catherine Mateer's hierarchical model of attention:

- **Arousal:** Refers to our activation level and level of alertness, whether we are tired or energized.
- **Focused attention:** Refers to our ability to focus attention on a stimulus.
- **Sustained attention:** The ability to attend to a stimulus or activity over a long period of time.
- **Selective attention:** The ability to attend to a specific stimulus or activity in the presence of other distracting stimuli.

---

95. Daniel J. Siegel, *Mindsight: The New Science of Personal Transformation* (Random House, 2010), 39. (D. J. Siegel 2010)

96. Siegel, *Mindsight*, 85. (D. J. Siegel 2010)

97. https://www.cognifit.com/attention Accessed May 21, 2024. (Cognifit n.d.) Stephen Grossberg, "The Resonant Brain: How Attentive Conscious Seeing Regulates Action Sequences That Interact with Attentive Cognitive Learning, Recognition, and Prediction," *Attention, Perception, and Psychophysics* 81, no. 7 (2019): 2237–64. https://doi.org/10.3758/s13414-019-01789-2. (Grossberg 2019)

- **Alternating attention:** The ability to change focus attention between two or more stimuli.
- **Divided attention:** The ability to attend different stimuli or attention at the same time.[98]

Let us take a brief look at what goes on in the brain when we focus. When we focus on an object of interest, our attention enables us to filter out distraction and center on our goal. When we focus and give attention to something, we are activating certain functions of the frontal and parietal cortices of the brain and selectively harnessing their power to perform a preferred task. Attention, once activated, drives most of the regions and functions of the brain to carry out its desired outcome. Applied attention over time activates neuroplasticity over certain regions of the brain. Neuroplasticity changes the networks and shape of the brain to perform our desired outcomes. Attention is our God-given, human superpower that drives and shapes our brain. Although we are not aware of the internal process, these activities go on under the hood of our skull, like an engine operates under the hood of the car.

Another key area that assists in controlling the attention process is the "blue spot" (the *locus coeruleus*) at the base of the brain. The blue spot is the main source for the neurotransmitter noradrenaline, a chemical messenger that arouses us to pay attention.[99] Attention (i.e., shutting off distractions and channeling available cerebral resources through focusing) is necessary for mental processing and performance. We have around 100 billion neurons that form over 100 trillion connections, and we think around 75,000 thoughts day.[100] Operating at 20 watts of power and loaded with 34 gigabytes of daily information, the brain needs to regulate (neuromodulation) how it uses its energy and resources to signal, transmit, and process data when activating attention.

When we pay attention, we use and regulate the resources of the mind for a particular task by taking the reins of our own thinking and directing it to a preferred object or goal. When taking the reins, in essence we are taking possession and control of the brain's executive function (prefrontal cortex) through focus and attention.[101] These functions are essential for perceiving, processing, learning, memory, and execution. How we select, which becomes the object of our attention, is determined by our

---

98. Grossberg, "The Resonant Brain." (Grossberg 2019)

99. Max Planck Institute, "How the Brain Helps Us Focus Our Attention," January 7, 2022, https://www.mpg.de/18108721/0106-bild-how-the-brain-s-blue-spot-helps-us-focus-our-attention-149835-x https://www.sciencedaily.com/releases/2022/01/220107121453.htm. (Max Planck Institute 2022)

100. Catherine Caruso, "A New Field of Neuroscience Aims to Map Brain Connections in the Brain." https://hms.harvard.edu/news/new-field-neuroscience-aims-map-connections-brain. Accessed January 2, 2024. (Caruso 2023)

101. See Grace W. Lindsay, "Attention in Psychology, Neuroscience, and Machine Learning," *Frontiers in Computational Neuroscience* 14 (2020): https://doi.org/10.3389/fncom.2020.00029. https://neuroscience-encenews.com/attention-brain-19881/ Accessed January 2, 2024. (Lindsay 2020)

own priorities and preferences.[102] Simply, we focus on what and where we *want* to direct attention. Attention is a matter of desire, intention, reward (dopamine reward and reinforcement circuit), and convenience (neural logistics). These variables are what influence the sifting process when we are faced with an overwhelming saturation of sensual and cognitive stimuli.[103]

Cognitive science also informs us that when we make decisions the brain works through an implicit hierarchy of preferences,[104] a prioritization of what we value and desire. This is often called the AIDA model (the interrelationship between attention, interest, desire, action).[105] Also, what we consistently prefer gets bumped up to the top of the hierarchy and becomes the go-to, or our stable choice.[106] Highest value and consistency or stability are linked and determine choice (value-based decisions). We prefer what we value the highest and the most frequently. Though changing and updating value preferences can occur, changing preferences makes it more difficult for our brain, then, to maintain the status quo. When we invoke and implement attention, our prefrontal cortex is actively prioritizing, selecting, and engaging what will become the content of our memory, learning, and behavior. When you wake up in the morning, your mind is bombarded with a host of things that call for your attention. How will you decide what to do first? We implicitly manage a hierarchy of preferences (from most to least important) that we regularly update with new data and new conclusions. Thus, in the morning, you will choose what is at the top of the hierarchy of preferences.

Attention identifies, shapes, and informs content in our memory, learning, and behaviors, beginning with our decisions. Further, previous selections of preference in-

---

102. Taosheng Liu and Youyang Hou, "A Hierarchy of Attentional Priority Signals in Human Frontoparietal Cortex," *Journal of Neuroscience* 33, no. 42 (2013): 16606–15. https://doi.org/10.1523/JNEUROSCI.1780-13.2013 (Liu and Hou 2013); "Focused Attention," CogniFit, accessed January 2, 2024, https://www.cognifit.com/focused-attention (Cognifit n.d.); also see Sohlberg and Mateer Hierarchical Model, https://www.biamd.org/uploads/8/5/7/7/85779996/peters_-_apt.pdf. Accessed January 2, 2024 (University of Maryland Rehabilitation and Orthopaedic Institute n.d.).

103. Stanlislas Dehaene, "How We Pay Attention Changes the Very Shape of Our Brains," Literary Hub, January 30, 2020, https://lithub.com/how-we-pay-attention-changes-the-very-shape-of-our-brains/. (Dehaene 2020)

104. Alizée Lopez-Persem, Philippe Domenech, and Mathias Pessiglione, "How Prior Preferences Determine Decision-Making Frames and Biases in the Human Brain," *eLife* 19, 5 (2016): e20317. https://doi.org/10.7554/eLife.20317. (Lopez-Persem, Domenech and Pessigione 2016)

105. For an explanation and critique of the AIDA model, see Saba Montazeribarforoushi, Abolfazl Keshavarzsaleh, and Thomas Zoëga Ramsøy, "On the Hierarchy of Choice: An Applied Neuroscience Perspective on the AIDA Model," *Cogent Psychology* 4, no. 1 (2017): https://doi.org/10.1080/23311908.2017.1363343.

106. Katharina Voigt, "Where Do Our Preferences Come From? How Hard Decisions Shape Our Preferences," *Frontiers in Behavioral Neuroscience* 16 (2022): https://doi.org/10.3389/fnbeh.2022.956307. (Voigt 2022)

fluence and facilitate future selections in the brain. The hierarchy is strengthened.[107] The hierarchy of preference is a strong determinant of our choices. The focus of our attention is what will identify, shape, and inform what we worship, what we learn, and what or who we serve. This formidable internal ability to turn off distraction and direct the attention of the powers of our brain to process information for highly effective performance can be employed in our Christian life, specifically in our worship, discipleship, and service. These are all attention dependent.

Primarily, it is attention that shapes the brain. So we must ask ourselves, Where is our attention primarily directed? On God or something else? If it is not God, something else is shaping our brain. If Christ and the things of God are low on our hierarchy of preferences, we will not give them the attention they deserve. The questions are who or what sits at the top of our hierarchy of preference. Is the great I AM at the top of our list day in and day out?

As Christians, we claim, *de jure*, that God uncontestably rests at the top of our desires. Yet, de facto, is this really the case? A few simple metrics can be employed to determine desire or preference, time, passion, and money. Consider our relationship with our cell phones. If we were to log our time spent with Christ versus the time that we are glued to our cell phones, where would the lion's share of our time be spent? Using a simple 1–10 scale, with 10 being the highest degree, in the morning, what is our desire to pray and spend time with God compared with our desire to check our cell phones for emails, texts, social media posts, or responses?

Finally, how much time and money do we spend on a monthly basis on our phone, including cost for the cell phone itself, monthly billing, apps and other expenses related to cell phone use versus how much of our time and finances go to the cause of Christ, including service, tithes, offerings, alms, or however you have been convicted to give? Empirically speaking, our relationship with our cell phones receives the better part of our devotion than the Lord. Most of us could not peel ourselves away from our cell phones for one day if we tried. However, it does not take much effort for some of us to sleep in on Sunday, forget to pray daily, neglect daily Scripture reading, skip financial giving or giving thanksgiving regularly, or disregard serving in some capacity of ministry at least once a month. Ultimately, whatever is enthroned at the top of our hierarchy of preferences is what we will attend to without failure. This rule of thumb seems to be adjacent to the first commandment: "Thou shalt have no other gods besides me!"

When the Mind's Eye Is Single

Scripture also emphasizes the power of attention. The wisdom of Scripture precedes neuroscience by a couple of millennia, and yet it can give us keen insight into the powerful dynamics of focus and attention. In Matthew 6:22–23, Jesus teaches, "The eye is the lamp of the body. So, if your eye is healthy, your whole body will be

---

107. Lopez-Persem, Domenech, and Pessiglione, "How Prior Preferences Determine Decision-Making Frames and Biases in the Human Brain." (Lopez-Persem, Domenech and Pessigione 2016)

full of light, but if your eye is bad, your whole body will be full of darkness. If then the light in you is darkness, how great is the darkness!" (ESV). While most translations use "healthy" or "good" for the Greek word *holon*, the King James Version translates that word as "single." Jesus is teaching us to direct our eye, perhaps physical and mental eye, toward the light and away from the darkness. Focus on him, the Master. And then in verse 24 he warns us that we can only fix our attention and devotion on one master and not two: "No one can serve two masters, for either he will hate the one and love the other, or he will be devoted to the one and despise the other. You cannot serve God and money" (ESV). Christ's throne is a throne fitted for one, not two—there is no passenger seat.

In this passage, the word *eye* refers to our physical eye, but it can also signify the eye of our mind or heart, the inner eyes. At times, we refer to the eyes as the windows of the soul. Perceptions go in and out of the eyes, like light passing through a window. The eye is the aperture of the body and soul that opens us to either light or darkness, depending on which we focus. We will become what we look at for better or for worse. If we focus on fear, we will be filled with fear. If we fix on God's goodness, we will be filled his goodness. The eye (inner and outer) is the faculty of attention that sets the cognitive process in motion.

What has your attention? On which voices and images are you fixing your focus? When we fix our attention on some object, we are opening the window of our soul to its content that will identify, inform, and shape our heart and our Christian discipleship. Our focus will determine our future and the nature of what we will become. For better or for worse, our heart will focus on what it desires or "treasures": "For where your treasure is, there your heart will be also" (Matt. 6:21 ESV). Our heart's true longing and craving are easy to determine. Whatever we find our heart ruminating on and pursuing, that is where we will find what we genuinely treasure. What do we really treasure, God or the things of this world? Attention is the determinant of our true treasure.

Remember that tiny 15-millimeter blue spot at the base of the brain, called the *locus coeruleus?* It is a neuromoculator connected by nerve fibers to most of the brain and is responsible for contributing to control of stress, memory, and attention.[108] Recent research discovered a link between increasing activity of the blue spot, neural oscillations, and pupil size.[109] Noradrenaline is the neurotransmitter responsible for attention. Increase in pupil size is connected with higher noradrenergic activity, regu-

---

108. Max Planck Institute, "How the Brain Helps Us Focus Our Attention." (Max Planck Institute 2022)

109. Max Planck Institute, "How the (Clewett, et al. 2018)Brain Helps Us Focus Our Attention"; David V. Clewett, Ringo Huang, Rico Velasco, Tae-Ho Lee, and Mara Mather, "Locus Coeruleus Activity Strengthens Prioritized Memories Under Arousal," *Journal of Neuroscience* 38, no. 6 (2018): 558–74. https://doi.org/10.1523/JNEUROSCI.2097-17.2017. (Clewett, et al. 2018)

lating neural communication, and higher attention efficacy.[110] Our focused attention then directs us to behavior that is often connected to our reward system, which serves as a motivator to maintain attention and execute the rewarding behavior.[111]

Truly, the eyes are the windows of the soul and the key to attention. If we focus and fix our attention on Christ, the beginning and end (goal) of our faith, we will be filled with the Spirit and will attain our goal of Christlikeness (Heb. 12:1–2). On the other hand, if the work of Satan shifts our attention, we will be filled with darkness and evil. Our focus will fix our future. What we gaze on will transform us one way or another. We can only serve one master, and only one is the Way to salvation and blessing.

The North Star, or Polaris, is the true north that has guided navigators for centuries. The North Star is the one stable reference point in the sky and is perfect for providing faithful direction because it is aligned with the true North Pole, with only a one-degree margin of error. Likewise, Christ is our absolute reference who leads us to the Father because they are perfectly aligned. Christ is our North Star who provides direction through the tumultuous, treacherous, stormy seas of life to our eternal destiny. We need to align and fix our sight on him. Each one of us in our lifetime will face a handful of critical choices that will either make or break our life. Think back. At those times, did we seek Divine direction? Did we follow it? Were our eyes set on our North Star, and are they now?

I remember when I began my academic journey to earn a PhD. The curriculum contained sixty credit hours of courses, competency exams, qualifying exams, writing and defending a proposal, and writing and defending a 250-plus-page dissertation. I drove three hours to school and three hours back for five years and nearly 50,000 miles. I was married with two children, ages eight and ten. I was pastoring a high-conflict church while planting another one. I was stressed as to how I was going to finish this degree with such a full plate. From day one as I drove to school until I received the degree, I kept one image in mind, which the Lord had given me. I would envision myself walking across the graduation stage and receiving that coveted piece of paper. I welded my attention to that image above all, regardless of the insurmountable circumstances. The Lord and attention attained that seemingly unreachable goal.

We are exhorted by James the apostle to be single-minded, focusing on the promises of God (Jas. 1:8; 4:8). A mind that is singly focused on God (the light) and not the world (the darkness) will not be an unstable double-mind. "Doublemindedness" is the unsteady state of having two minds or two contrary perspectives. In one moment, our mind is focused on the things of God, and then in the following moment, it is focused on the things of the world. One mind says yes to God, then only

---

110. "How the Brain's Blue Spot Helps Us Focus Our Attention," Science Daily, January 7, 2022, https://www.sciencedaily.com/releases/2022/01/220107121453.htm. Alpha oscillations at 10 Hertz control sensory input when we are in an inattentive state but are not present when the noradrenaline of the blue spot is present and is active. (Science Daily 2022)

111. Anne Trafton, "How the Brain Responds to Surprising Events," MIT News, June 1, 2022, https://news.mit.edu/2022/noradrenaline-brain-surprise-0601. (Trafton 2022)

a moment later another says no to God and yes to its own way. We flip-flop back and forth like a wet fish out of water. Metaphorically speaking, we have two minds, one focused on the Spirit and the other on the flesh. This state of instability will not last. We will choose one master and will eventually forsake the other.

St. Paul calls us to be intentional and "destroy arguments and every lofty opinion raised against the knowledge of God and take every thought captive to obey Christ" (2 Cor. 10:5 ESV). We need to be intentional to tear down thoughts that oppose the word and will of God. Let us be purposeful to set our eyes on Christ the beginning and end of our faith. Let our eye be single. Let our attention be singular and set on the one true God and have no other gods besides him. Søren Kierkegaard, the Danish existential philosopher, combatted scatterbrained doublemindedness with a directive to attain purity of heart: "To will one thing is, therefore, to will the Good without considering the reward."[112] Purity of heart is to will one thing: God's will.

Such a journey is no walk in the park. The storms and tempests of life will rage. Pleasures and indulgences will surface. Fickleness will sift the unstable soul. Infidelity will seek to seduce the double-minded. It is not an *if* but a *when*. Martin Luther, the great Reformer, exclaimed, "Reason is the Devil's greatest whore."[113] Reason is a gift from God and to be valued But, as Luther implied, it needs to be subject to the Spirit of God. Reason under our own control is a recipe for disaster. Our minds will easily sell out for a price. Satan knows everyone has a price. Our mind is so readily given over to temptation's pleasurable curiosities. We slip and wander into spiritual adultery, which is a path of least resistance against standing in covenant faithfulness with our Lord.

Obviously, I do not condemn wholesale the entire capacity and enterprise of reason. Critical use of reason and science are needed. Reason is an instrument that can be employed for good or evil. It is not irredeemable. The image of God has not been erased from us, but it has been severely defaced. Yet it can still attend to the math, science, logic of this world and even theology. Further, under the regenerating inspiration of the Spirt, reason can comprehend heaven's language of revelation. Nonetheless, the noetic effects of its depravity (sin's residue on the mind) are crippling. If not for the grace of God, we would be crushed under sin's unbearable weight. And even as believers, there are those moments, as the old hymn reflects, "Prone to wander, Lord, I feel it, prone to leave the God I love."[114] Thus, we take seriously Christ's admonition to "Watch and pray that you may not enter into temptation. The spirit indeed is willing, but the flesh is weak" (Matt. 26:41 ESV).

---

112. Søren Kierkegaard, *Purity of Heart is to Will One Thing* (New York: Harper Torchbooks, 1956)., 72, 121–22. (Kierkegaard 1956)

113. Martin Luther, *Church and Ministry II*, Luther's *Works* (Fortress, 1955), 40:175. (Luther 1955)

114. Robert Robinson, "Come, Thou Fount of Every Blessing." (Robinson 1758)

THE MIND OF CHRIST

A man's mind may be likened to a garden, which may be intelligently cultivated or allowed to run wild; but whether cultivated or neglected, it must and will, bring forth.

—James Allen, *The Wisdom of James Allen*

Crazy Days

We live in hectic and crazy times. Our nation, even our world, is sharply divided politically and culturally. It seems like both the left and the right want to rule at all costs. Corruption and chaos tend to be the political and social order of the day. Crime runs rampant in our streets with little consequence. Violence of all modes is commonplace in society. Abuse in all forms is ever-present. Drug use is widespread. Various addictions are hijacking minds at an alarming rate. Mental disorders are on the rise. We are past numb to shocking daily headlines. Violence is happening everywhere without regard. No place is sacred. Churches, synagogues, mosques, schools, parks, concerts, parades, restaurants, drive-thrus, banks, retail stores—you name the place—and violent crimes have taken place there over the past year.

Our children are having to grow up in a world that we never had to face nor could we ever imagine. The type and number of choices they face regarding their identity, gender, sexuality, group identity, social media, drug use, and peer pressure, let alone the usual choices they make in life as they develop and become adults, are incomprehensible and unfair. Their brains are not developed sufficiently to make many of those adult-level choices. From kindergarten through elementary school, my generation never had to face any of these choices, perhaps except peer pressure. I did not have to face bullying on social media. I certainly was not thinking about gender and sex in first grade or what to do if an active shooter was on the premises of our school. Neither were our teachers exposing such content and options to us. The maladies, difficulties, and challenges that we face as a society today are innumerable. It can be overwhelming and dizzying at times. For better or worse, our society is ripe for the radical, either radical destruction or radical restoration. I believe the gates of hell will not prevail against the church. So whatever tomorrow may bring, God, who is the same yesterday, today, and forever, will work his mission through the church.

A Disordered Society

In all of my six decades on this spinning blue planet, I have never experienced the disintegration of societal foundations and norms and ensuing chaos as I do in our current times. Of course, that is my impression. Not all may feel similarly. It seems we are questioning and even overhauling many of the time-tested landmarks that have been used to navigate our way forward as a civilization over the past centuries. The existence of long trusted institutions and practices like democracy, law enforcement, the penal system, marriage, sex and gender, free market capitalism, the sciences, educational systems, and others are being questioned. Are these institutions merely more expressions of oppressive patriarchalism, racism, sexism, and classism? We are questioning if we are better off without them. Thus, we are radically divided by the ism-schism.

Surely, a healthy society should always critique its ideas and practices, past and present, searching for ways to improve as we seek the greatest good for all. Human institutions are fallible. All of the institutions that I mentioned need to be regularly critiqued and improved. But as a former copy machine technician, I learned the mechanic's golden rule: If it ain't broke, don't fix it! This is followed by its silver rule: But if it's almost ready to break, do preventative repair and maintenance so it won't break! Clearly, our society is not perfect and needs continual amelioration of its conditions. However, today it seems like we are taking a basically functional airplane full of passengers and aimlessly dismantling it in midair without a plan to build a better one. This strategy does not seem sound.

Envision a mental health counselor analyzing our society collectively, as if it were one individual person. Imagine if that therapist was specialized in cognitive behavioral therapy (CBT), used its diagnostics to assess our mental health, and employed its therapeutic strategies to treat us.

Allow me to digress briefly and introduce CBT. First, what is CBT? CBT is 'a structured, goal-oriented type of psychotherapy (talk therapy)."[1] More specifically, it is "a form of psychotherapy that focuses on modifying dysfunctional emotions, behaviors, and thoughts by interrogating and uprooting negative or irrational beliefs." CBT has been scientifically proven to treat effectively "depression, anxiety disorders, alcohol and drug use problems, marital problems, eating disorders, and severe mental illness."[2]

Considered a solutions-oriented form of talk therapy, "CBT rests on the idea that thoughts and perceptions influence behavior."[3] CBT recognizes that thoughts shape emotions that shape behavior that shapes thoughts and so on. This is called the "CBT Triangle" and is a helpful framework to understand CBT. Thought, emotion, and behavior are all interrelated and influence each other. However, in CBT, the focus begins with one's thought life, cognition. If we change our thinking, our emotions and behavior will follow.

Thus, this form of therapy attempts to equip the client with the skills to recognize faulty thinking and to learn strategies to change destructive thinking to produc-

---

1. "Cognitive Behavioral Theory (CBT)," Cleveland Clinic, last reviewed August 4, 2022, https://my.clevelandclinic.org/health/treatments/21208-cognitive-behavioral-therapy-cbt. (Cleveland Clinic 2022)

2. "What Is Cognitive Behavioral Therapy?," Clinical Practice Guidelines for the Treatment of Posttraumatic Stress Disorder, accessed April 8, 2024, https://www.apa.org/ptsd-guideline/patients-and-families/cognitive-behavioral. (American Psychological Association 2017)

3. "Cognitive Behavioral Therapy," Psychology Today, accessed April 8, 2024, https://www.psychologytoday.com/us/basics/cognitive-behavioral-therapy. (Psychology Today n.d.)

tive, healthy thinking, that in turn will result in a balanced, mature emotional life and in regulated and healthy behavior. One of the phenomena that CBT attempts to identify is the cognitive distortion in our thinking patterns. Cognitive distortions are thoughts and thought patterns that misrepresent, spin, warp, twist, or alter what is real and true due to some bias, misinformation, or misunderstanding. Wrong, deceptive, or erroneous thinking can lead us to perceive reality or the truth inaccurately. This type of unrealistic thinking is wrapped in negativity and hopelessness. Cognitive distortions can result in feeling anxiety, panic, depression, and paranoia.

So back to our problem. What if our clinical therapist were to analyze and diagnose our society as if it were one person? Many collective mental behaviors and cognitions that have been practiced and even encouraged by society have been discouraged by CBT. For example, take personalizing.[4] In CBT, personalizing simply is a cognitive distortion that occurs when I make things about me when they really are not about me. We live in a world where everything is suited to fit the individual. Almost everything in our market-based culture is created to appeal to our personal preferences. Selfishness sells. We work hard so that we can play hard, and much of our play is around self-gratification. We have our personal preferences about everything.

Personalization is characterized and marketed in our social networks, like Facebook, TikTok, or X (formerly known as Twitter) accounts. Social media is about personalization, the self. Well, really, it's about marketing, money, and control, but the lure is personal preference. Social media is reality TV made for me. Social media is our daily attempt at fifteen minutes of fame with each inflated opinion. And our bank account of opinions has an infinite supply of funds. Each page is all about myself, my likes, my movies, my interest groups, my pics, my personal information, my daily thoughts, my daily events, and everything else you want to know about me, ad nauseum. In the West, we live in millions of autonomous, atomistic cells or prisons of self that occasionally tangentially touch through the prison bars.

Personalization has also become a way in which we perceive the world. We interpret reality personally, which is natural, but at times we over-personalize. I do not merely mean that we live and perceive as persons, but also as subjective, privatized individuals rather than social creatures engaging the world and others. We construe and construct a stifling me-centered world. Everything serves as a means to my personal ends. In terms of mental disorder, personalizing is a type of cognitive distortion that biases how we see reality and truth. When we cannot see past our own partiality and project or interpret self into everything, we may be personalizing.

We make everything about us. Everything becomes directed at us. Everything is against us. Personalizing interprets the self in situations that may not have anything to do with us. People who personalize think everyone is thinking about them, talking about them, involving them, meaning them, and plotting against them in almost every situation. With personalizing, one interprets incoming information as autobiographical even though what is said or occurring may have nothing to do with the person. Things are taken personally when they were not intended to be so.

---

4. Taken in part from my book *Truth Therapy*, where I call cognitive distortions "stinking thinking." Peter Bellini, *Truth Therapy: Renewing Your Mind with the Word of God* Chap. 3 (Wipf and Stock, 2014)

We have seen personalizing take place frequently on social media. Someone posts an article or a general statement about something that is on their hearts. The post reflects their own perspective about their current situation and their reflections on it. Later, they receive sharp, snarky, defensive responses from family, friends, and strangers. They felt the post was directed at them, even though the person posting was not thinking of anyone in particular nor had any intentions of directing the post at anyone. Yet there are always those who will personalize.

Everything is not about us. It rarely is. It is important to be objective in our reasoning and perceptions and to seek after real evidence to test and support our inner claims and conclusions—good old-fashioned thinking. If there is no evidence or not enough evidence, withhold judgment or inference. It is better to err on the side of impersonalizing a situation and being wrong than factoring ourselves and our feelings into everything. We often exercise stinking thinking (cognitive distortion).

Additionally, we often demonize whole groups of people. Demonizing is when we project and conceive of a person or group as irredeemable, incarnate evil because of a flaw or a wrong that we perceive (rightly or wrongly). We refuse to identify and acknowledge any good about that person or group. They are forever irreversibly censured and condemned in our eyes, in spite of any good that they can do or have done. It is irrelevant to mention specific examples. Just fill in the blank: _____ are corrupt. *Those* _____ are evil and deserve punishment. All _____ are stupid and ignorant. Nothing President _____ can say is ever true or right. We allow one or even several mistakes or wrongs to blind us from finding redemption or any good in the object of our condemnation.

Demonizing is a cognitive distortion. Clearly, that person or group is not always wrong and never right. We are all human with agency capable of good and evil, right and wrong. No one is the pure embodiment of evil, except Satan and his angels because redemption is not available to them in this dispensation. A society that demonizes persons and groups is not healthy and collectively exhibits stinking thinking that furthers our collective anxiety, irritability, and rage. The culture on social media and on the streets is a powder keg waiting for the slightest offense to spark an explosion. It does not take much to throw us into a tirade of venomous, vitriolic, verbal assaults or even acts of unwarranted violence. If our current society was being analyzed as a single collective entity, we would be diagnosed with any number of mental disorders. As a people, we do not demonstrate healthy thought lives.

There are a host of cognitive distortions that have become the normative way of thinking in our day, making for a more toxic, hostile, and triggered society.[5] We polarize, a radical either-or or black-and-white thinking regardless of the nuances or the examples of gray in the middle or both-and cases. We overgeneralize. Overgeneralizing is when we make a blanket statement about an individual or a group based on

5. Other cognitive distortions include mind reading, catastrophizing, overgeneralization, all-or-nothing thinking, magnification, minimalization, labeling, emotional reasoning, fortune telling (predictive thinking), unrealistic expectations, "should" statements, arbitrary inference, filtering out the positive and focusing on the negative, and many others. For further exploration, see (Burns 1999) referenced by Arkansas Families First, LLC https://arfamiliesfirst.com/wp-content/uploads/2013/05/Cognitive-Distortions.pdf Accessed April 8, 2024. Olivia Guy-Evans, "13 Cognitive Distortions Identified in CBT," accessed April 8, 2024, Simply Psychology, https://www.simplypsychology.org/cognitive-distortions-in-cbt.html .

one or a few cases. We love to do this with various groups of people with whom we disagree. Those groups, on the right, left, or in the middle, may be delineated based on political view, race, ethnicity, sexuality, socioeconomic status, geographic location, job, career, station in life, and so on. Again, when we overgeneralize, we distort reality. We do not have an accurate picture of the people and world around us. We paint people and situations in such a hopeless light that they are irredeemable in our eyes or inherently flawed or evil. When we view our neighbor as such it is easy to disregard human life and conclude that some have no intrinsic value. Marginalization, oppression, and genocide are not far away.

Healthy, informed critical thinking is becoming rarer in our society. Take the case of the war between Hamas and Israel that began October 7, 2023. Regardless of which side one has taken, it is hoped that one arrived there through compiling and examining admissible evidence from trustworthy, reputable sources, thoroughly researching the long history of tension between the two peoples, and hearing and responding to evidence and arguments from both sides. In response to what was understood to be Israel's colonization of Palestine and an ensuing genocide of its people, masses of students and professional protesters took to the quads of America's elite universities, such as Columbia, Harvard, MIT, Michigan, UCLA, Northwestern, and other schools, and began to protest and occupy those campuses with anti-Zionist (some would say anti-Semitic) chants and intimidation.

One of the most prominent chants was, "From the river to the sea, Palestine will be free." The jaw-dropping revelation came when these presumedly highly educated students were asked by journalists, "Which river and which sea?" half could not answer.[6] In the study, the same students were told that the significance of the chant meant that a one-state solution for Palestine would entail elimination of seven million Israeli Jews and two million Israeli Arabs. The majority of those students then changed their position. The students did not perform their duty to research the facts and examine claims and conclusions. The zeal of frenzied activism and mass psychology inebriated their thinking, preventing them from engaging in calm, sound, critical thinking. Surely, these protesters are not the only ones whose mindless, incendiary fervor ignited the flames of revolution and burned down the foundations of common sense. On the other side of the tracks, we witnessed a few radical groups among the civil protesters on January 6, 2021, storm the US Capitol Building in Washington DC, hoping to keep Donald Trump in power by attempting to prevent the joint session of Congress from counting the votes of the Electoral College, which makes the election results official. Political rage and delirium have become pathological in our country.

---

6. From a study conducted by the Wall Street Journal. Ron E. Hassner, "From Which River to Which Sea?," *Wall Street Journal*, December 5, 2023, https://www.wsj.com/articles/from-which-river-to-which-sea-anti-israel-protests-college-student-ignorance-a682463b. https://www.jpost.com/diaspora/article-776987 (Jerusalem Post Staff 2023) https://reason.com/volokh/2023/12/10/is-support-for-from-the-river-to-the-sea-based-upon-ignorance/ Accessed May 23, 2024 (Adler 2023).

Such stinking thinking exacerbates the already existing volatile, offended, divided, and incensed condition in our society. We need to be aware and not make biased, uninformed conclusions, and to not hear what we want to hear. We need to deny our ego and confirmation bias that wants to hear half the story, the story out of context, ignore the facts, twist and select what proves our point, ignore the rest, and confirm our prejudices and predilections. Our society today is mentally unhealthy. Change and healthy thinking begin with each of us, personally. Jesus Christ is our model.

The Son of God: Jesus Christ—Fully Divine, Fully Human

What kind of mind did Christ have? Was he smart? Was he proficient at math? We may think because Jesus is God that Christ was a genius in human terms. We may imagine that he was the most intelligent person in the world and knew all the facts about math and science. We figure he knew everything about every subject. However, we must remember, Christ was also human. And he chose to be the person that the Father called him to be. He was born into an ordinary family in first-century agrarian Palestine. His father was a carpenter, and most likely he was as well. He was not rich and probably not trained in a classic Hellenistic education. Christ lived before computers; the theory of relativity; calculus; the astronomical discoveries of Copernicus, Galileo, and Kepler; Newton's discovery of the laws of motion. He was born before modern science. Christ, although Divine, was born a man of his times with the knowledge of a man of his day.

He was not a scientist nor was he called to be a scientist, a mathematician, an artist, a politician, or any other vocation of worldly renown. Greater than these, he was called to be the Messiah, the Savior of the world. The aptitudes for quantum dynamics or infinitesimal calculus were not needed to be the Savior of the world. If these qualities were needed to be the Savior, the Father would have sent his Son as a lettered scientist. Instead, what was needed was that God would become like us and carry out his Father's mission to die on the cross for our salvation. He is the Son of God who took humanity upon himself. He is the God-human. He had all of the attributes of divinity, such as omnipotence, omniscience, omnipresence, and absolute holiness. He also had the attributes of a human being, such as finitude, limitation, mortality, freewill, and passibility (i.e., the ability to feel and suffer). He possessed all of the capacities as any other human. He inherited the various idiosyncrasies of genetics from his mother. Christ had his own personality type and every other quality that we deem human. He is fully God and fully human. In theology we call this the Incarnation.

The Incarnation is one of the essentials doctrines of the Christian faith. The church has taught over the centuries that the second person of the Trinity, the Word of God, came in the form of a human to die for our sins. The Son of God became the Son of man. God became human, and yet in becoming human, he also retained his deity. Jesus is both 100 percent God and 100 percent human. The orthodoxy of the church has always taught that Jesus Christ is fully Divine and fully human in one person, At the Council of Chalcedon in 451 CE, the church declared that Christ is "truly God and truly man," one person with two natures (Divine and human), and the two natures are without confusion, change, division, or separation. I do not fully understand the union of two natures in one person (the hypostatic union) in terms of neuroscience or theology. In part, it is a mystery.

For our purposes, it signifies that the mind of Christ was not only Divine but also human. Christ walked the earth as we walk the earth with human understanding. Since he came in human form in a human body, he had a human brain. Since Christ is the Son of God, he had a Divine mind but also a human mind. When we think of Christ's divinity, majesty, and power, we easily forget that he was also a human being. He had to come as a human to live by faith as a human, to be tempted as a human, overcome sin as a human, and suffer and die as a human on our behalf. He took our nature and sin upon himself so that we may become like him, righteous and holy (2 Cor. 5:21; Eph. 4:24–26).

As a human, Jesus lived a life like ours with all of our experiences, except sin. He had thoughts, feelings, actions, joys, disappointment and fulfillment, decisions to be made, conflict, expectations, the full range of human experience. Jesus experienced hunger, thirst, tiredness, peace, anxiety, sorrow, hope, despair (in the garden), pain, happiness—again the full range of human feelings. In this way, he was able to relate to us, identify with us, set the perfect example for us, and overcome on our behalf (Isa. 53:1–8; John 16:33; Heb. 4:14–16). Jesus is our example not only of divinity, but he is the perfect example for our humanity. He demonstrates for us what it looks like to walk by faith as a human and to trust the Father in every step.

Since Christ is both God and human, he has a Divine mind and a human mind. As God, he thinks about life from the perspective of the second person of the Trinity. As a human, he thinks about life from our standpoint, in a limited human body, and susceptible to life's vicissitudes and suffering. As a human, he walks in faith, in the Spirit, and in accordance with Scripture. Living with two natures seems complex to us, but we are not the Son of God. He manages quite easily. God has given us the revelation of the Incarnation (John 1:14), and we know it is true by faith, even though we do not fully understand it with our human limitations. Since Christ is our example of how we are called to live by the Spirit, by faith, and accordance with Scripture, we will examine what it means to have "the mind of Christ" and walk as he walked (1 Cor. 2:16; 1 John 2:6).

What Is the Mind of Christ?

In the first two chapters of 1 Corinthians, the apostle Paul contrasts the wisdom of the world (the Greeks) with the wisdom of God. The wisdom of the world is foolishness in God's eyes because it fails to recognize God's wisdom in Christ (1 Cor. 1:18–31). The wisdom of salvation came in the form of a lowly servant, but the scholars of the world not only did not recognize him as Messiah, but they killed him.

Human wisdom results in death. On the other hand, the wisdom of God, which is true wisdom, is found in Christ, who was crucified on the cross for our sins. The cross, not human philosophy, is God's wisdom and power to save humanity. Thus, the mind of Christ is the mindset or attitude that goes against the grain of worldly knowledge and seeks to do the will of the Father, in this case to suffer and die on the cross. The mind of Christ is fixed on the mission of God. It does not veer off to the left or to the right. Christ is not moved by the agenda of the world, neither the will of Roman politics nor the will of the religious leaders. He is dedicated to accomplishing the Father's will and became for us "wisdom, righteousness, sanctification, and redemption" (1 Cor. 1:30 KJV).

With that type of hyper-focus, we can assume that the Spirit of God worked intensely through Christ's posterior attentional system (PAS), responsible for focused attention, and his anterior attention system (AAS), responsible for sustained attention. Also, his blue spot (locus coeruleus) was quite active in staying the course. He did not do his own will but bypassed any immediate gratification (reward circuit). Instead of playing the short game and receiving an immediate dopamine rush, Christ played the long game and allowed his prefrontal lobe attention to control any short-cuts to the reward circuit. From beginning to end, his mind was passionately and completely focused on the cross: "For the joy set before him he endured the cross' (Heb. 12:2 NIV). The cross and the joy of fulfilling the Father's will were his long-term reward stimuli.

What about the church? What about each of us? Where is our attention being paid? Are we led by the politics and philosophies of the day instead of by the Holy Spirit? Does the culture influence us more than Christ? Have philosophies and ideologies of the world shaped our minds more than Scripture? Christ was led by the Spirit to do the will of the Father that was revealed in the Scriptures (Luke 4:18; 10:21; John 6:38; Rom. 16:25–26; 1 Cor. 15:1–5). Thus, Paul contrasts the mind of the natural man, which is occupied with the knowledge and program of this world, with the mind of Christ, which is occupied with the revelation of God's Spirit,

> That is what the Scriptures mean when they say, "No eye has seen, no ear has heard, and no mind has imagined what God has prepared for those who love him." But it was to us that God revealed these things by his Spirit. For his Spirit searches out everything and shows us God's deep secrets. No one can know a person's thoughts except that person's own spirit, and no one can know God's thoughts except God's own Spirit. And we have received God's Spirit (not the world's spirit), so we can know the wonderful things God has freely given us. When we tell you these things, we do not use words that come from human wisdom. Instead, we speak words given to us by the Spirit, using the Spirit's words to explain spiritual truths. But people who aren't spiritual can't receive these truths from God's Spirit. It all sounds foolish to them and they can't understand it, for only those who are spiritual can understand what the Spirit means. Those who are spiritual can evaluate all things, but they themselves cannot be evaluated by others. For, "Who can know the LORD's thoughts? Who knows enough to teach him?" But we understand these things, for we have the mind of Christ (1 Cor. 2:9–16 NLT).

The mind of Christ is a mind shaped by the Word and Spirit of God, equipped to do the Kingdom work of the Father. The will and work of God through Christ's ministry begin at his birth and culminate at the cross. The mind of Christ is cruciformed, or formed by the cross. Christ's disciples are called to be cross-minded. Cross-mindedness or cruciformity is an attitude of service and sacrifice for God and others. In fact, the cross was on the mind of the Son of God since the beginning of the world (Rev. 13:8). He came into the world with the mission of God emblazoned on his mind. His attention was always set on Jerusalem to die at Golgotha for the sins of the world (Luke 9:21–22, 51; 19:10; 1 Tim. 1:15; Heb. 10:5). Golgotha means "place of the skull." What a fitting place for the Son of Man to die. Truly, he was already crucified in his mind long before he was crucified in his body.

The mind of Christ is a crucified mind, dead to one's own will. Likewise, if we are to walk in the mind of Christ, our minds must also be crucified to the desires and passions of our flesh (Gal 5:24). Additionally, the mind of Christ embodies the fruit of the Spirit: love, joy, peace, longsuffering, gentleness, goodness, meekness, and self-control (Gal. 5:22). It is shaped by the heart attitudes and practices of the Sermon on the Mount (Matthew 5). The mind of Christ thinks about others rather than itself (Phil. 2:1–7). It dwells on the word of God and strategizes ways to love God and neighbor in all situations (Ps.119).

Let us then summarize what is the mind of Christ. First, the mind of Christ knows and does the will of the Father. Second, the mind of Christ is focused, controlled, and led by the Spirit and thus is filled with the Spirit's fruit and power. Finally, the mind of Christ is formed by Scripture and carries it out by faith. Having the mind of Christ first means to know, cherish, and do the will of the Father. When Christ walked in this world as one of us, he was committed to knowing and carrying out the will of his Father. From eternity, he is the only begotten Son who is eternally generated by the Father. The eternal mind of the Father generates his Logos (Word), which is his thought, language, and logic. The Son is the Word (Logos) of the Father personified. If we want to know the heart, mind, and will of the Father, we look to the Son. When we see the Son, we have seen the Father because they are one (John 12:45). Simply, *the mind of Christ is the mind of the Father* expressed through the person and work of Jesus. Christ came to embody and reveal the Father's heart and mind toward us (1 John 4:7–12). He came to glorify the Father and reveal his saving love for the world (John 17:1–5, 21–26; 1 John 4:7–12). Christ came to show us the Father's love for all and calls us to the same.

The Father's love is a supernatural and holy love. The nature of this love cannot be produced by self-interestedness or even the benevolent good will of humanity. It is not the type of love we see spuriously spoken of and dealt out in this world. Lust, pleasure, unconditional tolerance and approval, enjoyment, taste, personal preference, desire, want, even friendship and familial love are all knockoffs of the real thing. God's supernatural holy and perfect love is not natural to us, like growing palm trees in Antarctica. It needs to come from him. We need to receive it through his Spirit. In light of our misinformation and misrepresentation of love, we need to stress love's holy nature. Christ loves righteousness but hates wickedness (Ps. 45:7; Heb. 1:9). Yes, love *hates* some things! Do you love your parents? Do you love your spouse? Do you love your children? Then I am sure you do not love what is wrong, ill, or evil for them. My wife is a miraculous eight-year survivor of stage 4 cancer. I have seen how this plague has ravaged the lives of too many old and young. I hate cancer with a perfect hatred. There are numerous things that I gladly hate, including all types of abuse, bullying, trafficking, murder, and racial hatred, among others. Love does not "love" everything. True love only loves the good. True love is wise.

Thus, love needs boundaries, and God has given them to us in his law. Love is lawful and holy. The apostle Paul put it this way:

> Owe nothing to anyone—except for your obligation to love one another. If you love your neighbor, you will fulfill the requirements of God's law. For the commandments say, "You must not commit adultery. You must not murder. You must not steal. You must not covet." These—and other such commandments—are summed up in this one commandment: "Love your neighbor as yourself." Love does no wrong to others, so love fulfills the requirements of God's law. (Rom 13:8–10 NLT)

Love is wisdom. Love knows that in order to say yes to God, it must say no to evil and sin. Sometimes it is okay for love to say no! Love cannot affirm God and sin at the same time. The church needs to reject the fallacy that in order to love someone or something you must accept everything about that person or thing. Not the case! Christ's love can say, "Neither do I condemn you." But his love also can say, "Go and sin no more." God loves who I am but not all that I do. God loves sinners but not sin!

Second, the mind of Christ is focused, controlled, and led by the Spirit. But does Christ, the Son of God, need to receive and be led by the Spirit? He is God, isn't he? True, Christ who is Divine is already one with the Holy Spirit. However, Christ is also human like us. He came to show us how to live as one of us. He exemplifies a life that does the will of the Father through the power of the Spirit. Even though the second person of the Trinity (the Son of God) is one (in being, nature) with the third person (the Holy Spirit), Christ as a human walked in the Spirit. He was incarnate by the Spirit (Matt. 1:18), baptized in the Spirit (Matt. 3:16), filled with the Spirit (John 3:34), led by the Spirit (Matt. 4:1), ministered by the power of the Spirit (Luke 4:18–19), raised from the dead by the Spirit (Rom. 8:11), and sent the Holy Spirit (John 15:26). Christ's is a Spirit-filled and Spirit-empowered mind. Are we walking in the full fruit and gifts of the Spirit to do the works that Christ did?

Christ, our teacher, has risen and is seated at the right hand of the Father. But he sent the Holy Spirit, the Spirit of Truth, who is our Counselor, to reveal the truth in us. The Spirit of Truth "will teach you all things and will remind you of everything" that Christ had said (John 14:26 NIV). The Holy Spirit is the anointing we receive from the Father who teaches us the truth (1 John 2:20, 27). Furthermore, when "the Spirit of truth, comes, he will guide you into all the truth. He will not speak on his own; he will speak only what he hears, and he will tell you what is yet to come" (John 16:13 NIV). The ascended Christ through the Holy Spirit (the Spirit of Truth) will reveal all that we need to know to live the Christian life. The Spirit will instruct us how to have the mind that was in Jesus. The Spirit will also form us in Christ's image (sanctification).

Third, the mind of Christ is one shaped by God's word. From his youth, Christ was raised in the Jewish tradition. He was circumcised as all Jewish male infants were. He was in the Temple learning Torah, the books of Moses (Luke 2:46–47). Being instructed in the faith, he grew daily in wisdom (Luke 2:39–41). When confronted by the devil, who tempted him in the desert, he responded with Scripture (Matt. 4:1–11). In the four Gospels, Christ also quoted or alluded to the Old Testament in 180 of the 1,800 verses that reference his discourses.[7] Jesus fulfilled, by one estimation, 332 Old Testament prophecies. The odds of one person fulfilling only 48 prophecies is 1 in 10^{157} (which is quite remarkable).[8] As Divine, Christ is the Word. As the Messiah to come, Christ was prophesied by the word of God. And as human, Christ was obedient to Scripture and formed by it. These are the general features of the mind of Christ. He knew and carried out the Father's will. He was filled with the fruit and gifts of the Spirit to fulfill the Father's mission. And he both fulfilled and obeyed the Scriptures as Messiah and our example that we should follow and obey God's word.

The Mind of Christ at Work

As stated earlier, the mind of Christ is a mind directed and shaped by the Word and Spirit of God, equipped to do the Kingdom work of the Father. The will and work of God through Christ's ministry began at his virgin birth and culminated at the cross. Luke 4:18–19, which is a fulfillment of Isaiah 61, captures the heart of Christ's ministry: "The Spirit of the Lord is on me, because he has anointed me to proclaim good news to the poor. He has sent me to proclaim freedom for the prisoners and recovery of sight for the blind, to set the oppressed free, to proclaim the year of the Lord's favor" (Lk. 4:18-19 NIV).

On his way to the cross, Christ ministered the Kingdom. He ministered to everyone, young and old, male and female, Jew and Gentile, free and slave. But he came especially for those who knew that they needed him, for "it is not the healthy who need a doctor, but the sick. I have not come to call the righteous, but sinners" (Mark 2:17 NIV). The Kingdom of God, Paul proclaims, "is righteousness, peace and joy in the Holy Spirit" (Rom. 14:17 NIV). It is not a kingdom or polis of this world. The

---

7. The figures are one person's estimation, but there are others. J. Barton Payne estimated that 574 Old Testament verses point to the Messiah, while Alfred Edersheim cited 456 Old Testament verses. Harold Willmington counted 180 Old Testament verses. "How Many Prophecies Did Jesus Fulfill?," Got Questions, accessed April 9, 2024, https://www.gotquestions.org/prophecies-of-Jesus.html (Got Questions Ministries n.d.). Harold Willmington, "Old Testament Passages Quoted by Jesus Christ," *The Second Person File* (Liberty University, 2017), https://digitalcommons.liberty.edu/cgi/viewcontent.cgi?article=1060&context=second_person. (Willmington November)

8. "The Statistical Probability of Jesus Fulfilling the Messianic Prophecies," Nick Cady, accessed April 9, 2024, https://nickcady.org/2020/02/18/the-statistical-probability-of-jesus-fulfilling-the-messianic-prophecies/. (Cady 2020)

Kingdom, which is spiritual, is in right, peaceful, and joyful relationship with God and others. The God-man purposed in his mind to fulfill this Divine mission and to never get off track. The zeal to do the Father's will consumed him.

Soon after his baptism, the Spirit led him into the wilderness to be tempted by the devil. The mind of Christ was always submitted to the Spirit. Satan attempted to sidetrack Christ three times, all to no avail. Even when offered the kingdoms of the world and all of their contents, Christ resisted the devil using Scripture. Jesus' mind was molded by and fixed on the word of God. No word of demons, angels, man, or woman could usurp his mind. His thoughts were subjected to the word. No agenda could supersede the plan of the Father. He walked in the direction, love, and power of the Spirit.

The Spirit led him to atypical and unconventional people and places, such as tax collectors in trees, prostitutes caught in the act, the demonized in the Decapolis, blind men on the roadside, an adulteress in Samaria, a synagogue ruler whose twelve-year-old daughter died, a woman in the crowd afflicted for twelve years, a man with a thirty-eight-year disability at a pool, a begging leper, and others. As he was directed to ministers to others, his heart was moved with compassion. The healing love of the Father stirred him to touch the untouchable and embrace the unwanted. If we are to have his mind, likewise we must be led by the Spirit to participate in the Father's mission among the poor, the naked, the blind, the hungry, the oppressed, the incarcerated, and the outcast as well as to all people.

Political and religious leaders, family, friends, enemies, convenience, power, provision, reputation, or other opposition would not deter him. In his mind, he was on the cross long before Calvary. "Not my will, but your will be done" rhythmically resonated through his entire being with every step he took toward Jerusalem. The mind of Christ is purposeful and purposed to obey the Father. And as a human, he learned and grew in wisdom and obedience (Luke 2:52; Heb. 5:8). Faithfulness was not automatic, even though Christ is Divine. Christ also has a human will and chose to learn and obey. His servanthood was voluntary, emerging from a pure, devoted heart. If Christ had to learn obedience through opposition and suffering, how much more do we?

The Mind of Christ and Wisdom

We have examined the mind of Christ and noted its various characteristics: Father-pleasing, Spirit-led, mission-directed, Scripture-formed, faith-filled, compassion-moved, humility-oriented, and righteousness-based. Christ personifies in frail flesh the entire gamut of holy virtues attributed to the Divine. The sum of virtues is fully embodied and expressed in Christ as a multifaceted perfectly cut gem that scintillates, and sparkles with radiant light. One ray of light that beams luminously from Christ is wisdom. Scripturally, when we think of wisdom, we think of Solomon. He requested of the Lord to be granted wisdom and knowledge so that he could properly govern his people (1 Chron. 1:10). Because of the purity of his request—he did not ask for wealth or fame—the Lord amply gave Solomon wisdom beyond any king before or after him (1 Chron. 1:12).

Yet one greater than Solomon has come (Matt. 12:42). Many scholars recognize that Christ, the Word of God, came as wisdom personified.[9] Paul proclaimed that Christ is "the power of God and the wisdom of God" (1 Cor. 1:24 NIV). We also find echoes throughout the book of Proverbs that connect Christ with Wisdom, who created the world and instructs the unlearned (Proverbs 1–9). God through Wisdom ordered the universe and orders our hearts and minds. In the book of Proverbs, wisdom is granted for any situation or subject, including faith, life, death, finances, marriage, parenting, relationships, vocation, success, communication, eating, character, integrity, truth, health, virtue and vice, and much more. We are encouraged throughout the book to obtain wisdom and put it into practice. Practically, we observe wisdom in all of its multifaceted splendor in the life of Christ. He is consistently led by the Spirit in word and deed, even under pressure.

The religious leaders would try to trap him with their loaded, passive-aggressive questioning around his identity and lineage, his credentials and authority, the law and the Sabbath, taxes and the temple, marriage and divorce, signs and wonders, and many other contentions. As the personification of wisdom, he demonstrates for us what insight, prudence, and discernment look like in action. Being led by the Spirit, he never missed a beat with the right word and deed at the right moment. After he spoke, there was nothing left to say. The religious leaders were left dumbfounded, while the people were awed by his unprecedented authority, teaching, and wisdom (Matt. 7:29).

However, the ultimate expression of God's power and wisdom is Christ crucified. What appeared to be foolishness and weakness were employed by the Father to destroy sin, death, and the works of the devil, and to secure our salvation. His sagacity did not have the show and appeal of abstract philosophy or political savvy that the leaders of this world desire, "but the wisdom that comes from heaven is first of all pure; then peace-loving, considerate, submissive, full of mercy and good fruit, impartial and sincere" (Jas. 3:17 NIV). Wisdom by definition embraces every virtue and cannot be self-serving. The virtue of true wisdom hides itself from the proud and the vain but is known by its fruit to those who humbly seek it.

There is a categorical difference between wisdom and knowledge. We live in a technological age teeming with knowledge. Everything we desire to know about is a few clicks away. Scientists claim to know the universe inside and out, great and small from the big bang and superstring theories to quantum dynamics. Technology is approaching so-called singularity where AI attains and surpasses human intelligence. We have no shortage of knowledge and information, but often we misuse it. We have a shortage of wisdom. We struggle to channel properly our vast knowledge into prudent choice and usage. Thus, for many an infinite well of knowledge, the internet

---

9. For example, see Ben Witherington III, *Jesus the Sage: The Pilgrimage of Wisdom* (Fortress Press, 2000) and Ben Witherington III, *John's Gospel: A Commentary on the Fourth Gospel* (Westminster John Knox Press, 1999).

becomes a source of vice and the downfall of many. Today we have knowledge, but we do not know how to live. We have knowledge, but we do not know how to use it wisely, virtuously, and productively. Christ models wisdom for us.

The mind of Christ is not only replete with wisdom but is also a reservoir. The mind of Christ is our source for wisdom as well. The Spirit will draw from the mind of Christ and provide the right instruction that we need at the right time and in the right way, which is the nature of wisdom. And like with Christ, wisdom will truly manifest itself when we die with Christ on the cross (Rom. 6:1–7; Gal. 2:20; 5:24). The wisdom of salvation is death to the old way of life and the emergence of the new (2 Cor. 5:21). Wisdom conforms us to the suffering and death of Christ that we may partake of the new life in resurrection (Phil. 3:10). The cross is God's method. It is the apex of his wisdom. Those who have the mind of Christ will deny themselves daily and take up their own cross and follow Jesus to his cross. The Lord comes first.

The sapiential tradition of the Old Testament defines wisdom as the fear of the Lord (Prov. 9:10). Often, we misunderstand the concept "fear of the Lord." We think it means to be terrified of God to the point that we need to keep away from him, lest he destroy us. This is a false concept of God. True fear of the Lord causes us not to avoid or flee from him but to approach him, though in holy reverence. Fear of the Lord recognizes the truth of who God is and responds properly with singular devotion. We worship no gods but the true God, and we prioritize nothing before him. The *shema* calls us to "*Shema Yisrael, Adonai Eloheinu, Adonai echad*," or "Hear O Israel, the Lord your God is One" (Deut. 6:4 NIV). The oneness of God counters our doublemindedness, idolatry, and hypocrisy, demanding singleness of heart and mind. Wisdom means we give God reverence and priority because of who he is. It is the only proper response. Fear of the Lord is to behold the true, raw presence, holiness, righteousness, majesty, power, and authority of the Most High God (the I AM), such that it inspires and commands unconditional and total reverence, awe, terror, humility, urgency, attention, submission, worship, and obedience from all our heart, mind, soul, and strength.

The eminent German theologian Rudolf Otto understood God in this holy light as the "numinous," a *mysterium tremendum et fascinans* (a fearful and fascinating mystery). Language, such as wholly other, transcendent, tremendous, awe-inspiring, overpowering, unapproachable, curious irresistible attractive, and describes the pre-moral, pre-rational experience one undergoes when encountering the numinous, the holy. The numinous is the raw, unadulterated, holy presence of the preeminent I AM that we are aware of before we begin to formulate our theology about him (prerational) and our moral response to him (pre-moral). The parietal lobe lights up when exposed to the numinous transcendent One. A mind marked by wisdom knows and maintains the fear of the Lord as its posture. For a clearer picture of God as a fearful and fascinating mystery, review the burning bush and Mount Sinai narratives in Exodus (Chaps 3, 19–20) and the trisagion of Isaiah (6:1–5). Our God is a consuming fire, and it is a fearful thing to fall into his hands (Heb. 10:31; 12:29). And yet we are fascinated by the mystery of his awe-inspiring presence, and so we take off our sandals and carefully draw near as Moses did.

The Mind of Christ: God's Gift to Us

In 1 Corinthians 2:16, God gives us this amazing promise that believers have been given the mind of Christ. It is a gift given to us by faith. We have the same mind that Jesus had. The problem is that we have to unwrap this gift and begin to use it and develop it. As our brain develops, so our mind also develops and grows. Like every human function, we need to develop our thinking. We do that through learning, which is how we develop as humans. It is how we exercise the muscle of the mind. In fact, learning means brain changing (neuroplasticity).[10] We already have the mind of Christ, but we need to develop it and use it. Just like at birth, we come equipped with the hardware of our physical brain, but we have to use it for it to develop and grow. And if we are to develop the mind of Christ, we need to learn how. It begins with Christ as our Lord. We cannot truly have the mind of Christ until Christ has or controls our minds. As the mind goes, so goes the person!

We are exhorted to "let this mind be in you which was also in Christ Jesus" (Phil. 2:5 NKJV). This passage refers to Christ's humility. He is God, but Scripture claims he did not cling to or take advantage of that position of privilege (Phil. 2:6). Instead, he chose to take on the position of a servant, literally a slave (Phil. 2:7–8). He made himself of no reputation (Phil. 2:7), yet we strive and connive to make our reputation known. Christ has all power and authority, yet he humbled himself. He clothed himself in frail human flesh and offered himself up in death for our life. The mind of Christ is humble, selfless, and sacrificial. Naturally, our minds are not humble, selfless, and sacrificial. We often think of ourselves as better than others and rarely value the other more than ourselves (Phil. 2:3).

Dying to self-centeredness is not our natural predisposition, but it is our primary struggle. Bishop Fenelon pointed out, "The source of our trouble is that we love ourselves with a blind love which reaches the point of idolatry. All that we love outside we love for self alone."[11] Crucifixion begins with the mind. We cannot have the mind of Christ until Christ has (owns) our minds; minds directed by the Spirit (Rom. 8:6). Again, the mind of Christ is a gift, but it needs to be developed. When we surrender, the Spirit will teach us how to think the Father's thoughts; have the Father's heart; and have Christ's attitude, desire, faithfulness, and obedience.

The process of learning and developing the mind of Christ is called discipleship. And discipleship begins in the mind with the process of learning to be like Christ. Additionally, according to neuroscience, discipleship is about the cerebral grunt work of neuroplasticity or brain changing. Discipleship comes from the word disciple (Gk. *mathétēs*) that means a disciplined learner and follower (of Christ).

---

10. Melinda T. Owens and Kimberly D. Tanner, "Teaching as Brain Changing: Exploring Connections Between Neuroscience and Innovative Teaching," *CBE: Life Sciences Education* 16, no. 2: fe2. https://doi.org/10.1187/cbe.17-01-0005. (Summer 2017)

11. François Fénelon, *Christian Perfection* (Bethany Fellowship, 1975), 178. (Fénelon 1975)

Discipleship, then, is the disciplined process of learning and following Christ. Not only is discipleship learning to be like Christ; even more, it is learning Christ (Matt. 11:29; Eph. 4:20). Jesus is our lesson. The object of our study is the person of Christ. Further, he is our teacher or rabbi. Christ our teacher teaches us Christ. "Take my yoke upon you and learn from me," Matthew pens in 11:29 (NIV). Christ is teacher, lesson, and outcome, all in one.

We already have been given the mind of Christ by faith. Now, in order to develop and grow the mind of Christ, we need to learn Christ from Christ so we can be like Christ. Who else can claim to be the teacher, the lesson, and the answer but Christ. Imagine if you had a math teacher who was teaching square roots. The teacher asks, "What is the square root of 7?" The student replies, "2.646, rounded off." The teacher responds, "No. That is not the correct answer. I am the square root of 7." We would not think that teacher was very smart if he or she claimed to be the square root of 7. In fact, we would think he or she had a few screws loose. No good teacher gives him- or herself as an answer, except Christ. Only Jesus has the authority and the grounds to say, "I am the way, the truth, and the life." While other teachers point to the truth, Christ declares, "I am the truth."

The primary source of truth that the Spirit draws from is the holy Scriptures. The Bible is our main source and touchstone for truth. We read in 2 Timothy 3:16 that "All Scripture is inspired by God and is useful to teach us what is true and to make us realize what is wrong in our lives. It corrects us when we are wrong and teaches us to do what is right" (NLT). The Bible is breathed by God, so we can trust it. Scripture informs our doctrine. It gives substance to our worldview and shapes it. The word convicts our souls of what is right and true. And it serves as a rule or instruction for our faith and practice. We need to feed on it daily. Obtain sound theological resources to read and study it daily.[12] Memorize it. Meditate on it. Apply it in your everyday life. It has been said that John Wesley, the founder of Methodism, was so immersed in the Bible as his primary book that it shaped the way he thought and spoke. Wesley's primary spoken language was English, but his primary dialect was Scripture. It was seamlessly woven into his everyday speech and his writings.[13] May the word of God have that degree of influence over us as well.

The Bible is the Spirit's blueprint for building the mind of Christ in us. It provides a striking portrait of Christ, his work, and his life. The Spirit, who is the truth,

---

12. I recommend every disciple to have at least the following study tools: an exhaustive concordance like *Strong's Exhaustive Concordance*; a dictionary or lexicon of Old and New Testament words, such as *Vine's Expository Dictionary* or a Greek–English lexicon like *Thayer's* or *The Analytical Lexicon to the Greek New Testament* (William Mounce) or *A Greek-English Lexicon of the New Testament* (Walter Bauer and Frederick William Danker); a reference on the background of the Bible, such as *The Bible Background Commentary* (NT—Craig Keener); a simple one-volume commentary of the Bible to start with, such as *The Oxford Bible Commentary* (William Barton); a volume on inductive Bible study by either David Bauer or Andreas Kostenberger; and *How to Read the Bible for All It's Worth* (Gordon Fee).

13. In his *Preface to the Standard Sermons*, Wesley called himself a *homo unius libri* ("a man of one book"). In his journal entry for June 2, 1766, Wesley proclaimed boldly, "My ground is the Bible. Yea, I am a Bible-bigot. I follow it in all things, both great and small." Thomas Jackson, ed., *The Works of Rev. John Wesley*, vol. 3 (Wesleyan Methodist Book Room; repr., Baker Books, 1978), 251. (Wesley and Jackson, The Works of Rev. John Wesley 1978)

bears witness to the truth; God's word is truth (John 17:17). The Spirit also bears direct witness to our spirits and reveals wisdom, knowledge, prophecy, and truth (Rom. 8:14–16; 1 Corinthians 12). However, all revelation and illumination that we receive must align with Scripture, which is our touchstone. We are commanded to discern according "to the law and to the testimony! If they do not speak according to this word, *it is* because there is no light in them" (Isa. 8:20 NKJV). If we receive any manifestation or word that does not bear witness with the word and character of God, we need to reject it.

The mind or reason of Christ, which is revealed in the word, must rule over our minds. In neuroscience terms, the impact of the prefrontal cortex in Christ needs to rule over our prefrontal cortex through the work of the Holy Spirit. We need to lose our heads—lose our minds and gain the mind of Christ. The mind of Christ points us to the fact that Christ is the "head." He is the head of the body (of Christ). He is the head or ruler over his body, the church, and over every power and authority (Col. 1:18; 2:10). Christ has supremacy over all because he is the creator and sustainer of all things (Col. 1:16–17), and the fullness of God dwells in his human body (Col. 2:9). The mind of Christ rules over all of creation, and he must rule over our minds as well. Christ's executive function is the chief executive function.

We can think his thoughts, will his will, and feel his feelings when we meditate on Scripture and are filled with the Spirit. These humanly unreachable feats (Isa. 55:8) can only be attained by the Spirit and Word at work in us when we submit to God (Rom. 8:5–6). His mind becomes our mind, and his thoughts become our thoughts when we yield to Christ through the power of the Holy Spirit. Christ's mind becomes our mind, when Christ is received as the head. When he is our head, we see what he sees, hear what he hears, feel what he feels, think what he thinks, and will what he wills. Since it is easy to assume that our thoughts are God's thoughts, we must test the spirits and our thoughts by the Scriptures, lest we be deceived (1 John 4:1). The Spirit guides us through the faithful revelation of God in Scripture. God's word is trustworthy (2 Tim. 3:16). It is our map that guides us. It is our GPS that identifies our location and points us to our destiny in Christ (Ps. 119:105).

Thus, we grow in the mind of Christ when we grow in the truth of God's word that is revealed to us by the Holy Spirit who lives in us. We are led by the Word and the Spirit. Further, Scripture instructs us to "walk by faith, not by sight" (2 Cor. 5:7 ESV). We are exhorted to "fix our eyes not on what is seen, but on what is unseen, since what is seen is temporary, but what is unseen is eternal" (2 Cor. 4:18 NIV). The things of the Spirit and the Kingdom are not seen with our natural eyes but with the eyes of faith (Luke 17:21; John 3:8) We learn and grow in the mind of Christ by walking in faith and trusting God and his Word. Faith is the road that leads to God.

Faith and Reason

Even though faith is the Christian way of knowing, we prefer to be like the Corinthians and the Greeks in general. We love to rely on the power of our minds, the power of reason. We find comfort in the security and certainty of calculation, analysis, logic, and rational argumentation. Reason is clearcut. It solves problems, gives answers, discovers truth, and clarifies issues. Reason empowers us with assurance. The equation 2 + 2 = 4 leaves no room for error, subjectivity, opinion, or doubt. Life would be easy if the world was totally, mathematically rational and everything could be solved neatly and decisively by the power of reason. The fact is that many things are not merely as rational and obvious as 2 + 2 = 4. God is one of those things. The eternal, infinite, all-powerful God transcends the capacity of math or any other subject to comprehend the boundless nature of the Divine. Not only is mere human reason incapable of grasping the ultimate nature of God, but it has also been severely impeded by sin. We call this the *noetic effects of sin.* Sin has damaged, though not eliminated, the image of God within us, including reason. Our minds do not fully function as they were intended to due to the Fall of humanity.

Nevertheless, these impediments do not prevent God from communicating and connecting with us. God chooses to reveal himself freely to us. Revelation is God's principal way of communicating with us. God does not debate or argue with our reason about his existence or nature. He employs demonstration rather than argumentation. He demonstrates or reveals himself by his Spirit through many vehicles. Primarily, God has revealed himself to us through Jesus Christ. He is the fullness of deity in bodily form (Col. 1:19; 2:9). Jesus is God's personified Word spoken to us. We know God in Christ. This knowledge is communicated to us by the Holy Spirit who is the revelator of Jesus Christ (John 14:16, 26; 16:13–15). The work of the Holy Spirit is to bear witness to the person and work of Jesus Christ. Further, the holy Scriptures are the written revelation of God and the Spirit inspired and bears witness to them (2 Tim. 3:16). The tripersonal God (Father, Son, and Holy Spirit) and the Bible are known to us by faith. Faith is our sixth sense (the heart or spirit) that enables us to perceive and know the truth about God.

Although we are primarily led by faith in our relationship with the Lord, it does not mean we throw out our brains. The eminent philosopher Gottfried Leibniz asserted, "The mysteries of God are *above* reason *but not* contrary to reason."[14] We are called to love God with all of our heart, soul, *mind*, and strength (Mark 12:30). God created our brains and expected us to use our minds to their full capacity. We need to use our minds to know and love God. Our heart and our mind work together. Faith and reason work together. However, reason takes a subordinate position to faith. Reason can take us only so far. I believe that we can know that God exists through reason, but we cannot know his specific nature through reason.[15] God must reveal it to us by his Spirit, and we receive his revelation by faith.

The process somewhat works like this: "We know by reason so that we can believe by faith, and we believe by faith so that we can further know by reason."[16] Further,

---

14. Gottfried Wilhelm von Leibniz, *Theodicy* (Open Court Press, 1985), 88. (G. W. Leibniz 1985)

15. There are many "proofs" and arguments for the existence of God. See Petey Bellini, *Through the Threshold: Breaking the Barrier of a Closed Universe* (KDP, 2024); Jerry Walls and Trent Dougherty eds., *Two Dozen (or So) Arguments for God: The Plantinga Project* (Oxford University Press, 2018); Matthew Levering, *Proofs of God: Classical Arguments from Tertullian to Barth* (Baker, 2016), among others.

16. Bellini, *Through the Threshold*, 93.

63

"what reason initiates, faith perfects. Reason though limited assists faith,"[17] but "faith perfects the intellect."[18] To summarize, the tradition following St. Augustine claims, "I believe that I may understand" (*Credo ut intelligam*) and "Faith Seeking Understanding" (*Fides quaerens intellectum*). Thus, in discipling our mind, God wants us to exercise fully both the faculties of faith *and* reason. In other words, studying and engaging truth with your intellect is not of the devil. And neither is being filled with the Holy Spirit and his power emotionalism and meant only for Pentecostals. You surrendered fully to Christ. You paid for your ticket; now, ride all of the rides in his Kingdom!

---

17. Bellini, *Through the Threshold*, 89.

18. Thomas Aquinas, *Summa Theologiae*, sec. par. of part 2, q1, a3. (Kempis 2004)

DISCIPLESHIP 101: DISCIPLING THE MIND

Behold, in the cross is everything, and upon your dying on the cross everything depends. There is no other way to life and to true inward peace than the way of the holy cross and daily mortification. . . . Realize that you must lead a dying life; the more a man dies to himself, the more he begins to live unto God.[1]

—Thomas à Kempis

Definitions

Transforming the mind is the beginning of discipleship. To resist renewing the mind is to remain carnal or immature, as in arrested spiritual development. The work of the Spirit to mold us into Christlikeness begins with our thought life. The Spirit disciples our inner life (thoughts and attitudes of the heart) and then our outer life (behaviors and actions)—from the inside out. The call to discipleship is fundamental to the mission of God that is the ministries of Jesus Christ and the Holy Spirit and to the participation of the church. Before his departure, Jesus commanded his disciples to continue his work to "go and make disciples of all people . . . and teach them to obey everything that I have commanded you." Not only is it the heart of the so-called Great Commission, but discipleship is also exemplified throughout the New Testament and even practiced in the Old Testament (e.g., Matt. 28:18–20; 1 Cor. 4:14–17; 2 Tim. 2:2; 1 Kings 19:19–21; 2 Kings 2). Discipleship has also been a cardinal practice throughout the church age. Intentional discipleship was instrumental to the life of movements such as monasticism, pietism, Moravianism, Methodism, and evangelicalism as a whole.

Today we frequently hear about the need to make disciples. Although discipleship language is common in our churches, it is often vague and impractical. The reason is that many have not *actually* discipled or been discipled. They do not know what it looks like. In my experience as a pastor, missionary, revivalist, and professor, I have discovered that eight out of ten persons have never intentionally discipled or been discipled. At times it is perceived that discipleship happens by osmosis or occasion. Many assume that it occurs automatically. Others recognize occasions when

---

1. Thomas à Kempis, *The Imitation of Christ* (Hendrickson, 2004), 48, 51.

they were edified by someone, but the setting was not an intentional discipleship encounter. I applaud all such occasional experiences. These encounters may happen sporadically and at times frequently, but they are not enough to accomplish the formation and outcomes that New Testament discipleship demands.

Let us lay out a brief overview of discipleship beginning with definitions. The word *disciple* in the Greek New Testament is *mathétés (ma-thay-tays)*.[2] The working definition that I use for *disciple* is based on the word's Scriptural, historical, and etymological contexts: *A disciple is simply a student or a learner.* In ancient learning, seekers or students sought out teachers or masters (e.g., a rabbi) whom they would follow and learn from them by their words and their life. Some teachers would even invite their students to live with them while they were learning (John 1:35–51), embodied learning. The word *disciple* shares the same root as *discipline* and for good reason. Thus, *a disciple is a disciplined learner and follower of Jesus Christ. Discipleship is the process of learning and following Jesus.*

At some point in our lives, we have all been students. We attended primary and secondary school. Others continued on to university and received an undergraduate and even graduate education. We may have taken classes to learn an instrument, a language, a trade, a sport, or some other skill. Regardless of the extent of our educational background, we soon discovered that successful learning involves rigorous, disciplined study. Discipleship begins in the mind. More so, discipleship is the changing and growing of the brain through neuroplasticity, —literally reshaping the brain—by attention (executive system) and motivation (reward system).[3] In other words, discipleship is focusing our attention on Christ, doing what he does, and receiving our temporal and eternal reward of pleasing God and being blessed.

Discipleship, like learning, involves the entire regions and functions of the brain but especially the neocortical regions (sensory, prefrontal, parietal, and motor cortex), the hippocampus (medial temporal lobe), dopaminergic systems (reward circuitry), and the amygdala.[4] Discipleship structures and restructures the brain through synaptic plasticity (new or modified neural connections). When we learn and make connections between two concepts, we are literally making synaptic connections in the brain. Further, synaptic plasticity under the influence of the Holy Spirit and the word of God restructures our neural patterns to begin to look like Christ's (the mind of Christ). We begin to think like Jesus, loving God and others.

Jesus is the object of our learning and following. The journey is not always easy. Discipleship takes intense intentionality, sacrifice, and discipline. Christ gives us a clue to the level of rigor required of a disciple when he exhorts us "to deny [ourselves] and take up [our] cross daily" in order to follow him (Luke 9:23 NIV). Disciples

---

2. For a thorough study of the word *mathétés*, see Michael Wilkins, *The Concept of Disciple in Matthew's Gospel, As Reflected in the Use of the Term "mathétés"* (Brill, 1988).

3. Owens and Tanner, "Teaching as Brain Changing: Exploring Connections Between Neuroscience and Innovative Teaching." (Owens and Tanner 2017)

4. Carol A. Seger and Earl K. Miller, "Category Learning in the Brain," *Annual Review of Neuroscience* 33 (2010): 203–19. https://doi.org/10.1146/annurev.neuro.051508.135546. (Segar and Miller 2010)

carry their own cross. Christ's cross at Calvary is an *atoning* cross. There he died for our sins. We cannot atone for our own sins; we are sinners. Christ is a righteous and spotless lamb offered for our transgressions. The cross of atonement and salvation is *Christ's* cross. Only the Son of God can die for the sins of the world. On the other hand, there is *our* cross (Mark 8:34). Our cross that we are called to carry is a *disciple's cross*. A cross is a place of death. A disciple's cross is where we sacrifice and die to our own will and follow Christ to die with him on his cross (Rom. 6:1–7). At whatever juncture in our Christian journey that we are tempted to go our own way rather than Christ's, we are commanded to say no to our own will (self-denial) and yes to God's will. Self-denial will always involve a sacrifice. Our cross involves self-denial and sacrifice in order to follow Christ.

According to its first-century Roman context, a cross is carried by a malefactor to the place of death, and to the cross one is nailed and dies. It is worth repeating that discipleship is at the heart of Christianity, and the cross and obedience are at the heart of discipleship. Dietrich Bonhoeffer (1906–1945) exclaimed in his classic *The Cost of Discipleship*, "Christianity without the living Christ is inevitably Christianity without discipleship, and Christianity without discipleship is always Christianity without Christ."[5] Bonhoeffer not only wrote about self-denial, he lived it. A Lutheran pastor and Nazi dissident, he took a strong stand for persecuted Jews, opposed Nazification, and refused to participate in the German Christian movement that supported Hitler. Bonhoeffer became a leader in the resistance Confessing Movement. As a result, he was arrested and assigned to the Flossenbürg concentration camp, where he was executed. Bonhoeffer was martyred for being a Christian, a disciple of Jesus Christ, not a super-Christian but a man who simply stood on Scriptural Christianity and refused to renounce Christ.

Thus, being a disciple or participating in the process of discipleship is not detached from being a believer, a Christian, a follower of Christ. No, a disciple is not a super-Christian. Discipleship is not a higher level of Christianity. It is the norm. Discipleship is not the call of elite believers, but it is a call to everyone. Christ preaches the good news of salvation. We respond in faith. This is evangelization, and it is the beginning of discipleship, a lifelong process. We are called to be and make disciples, which is mere Christianity (Matt. 28:18). *Disciple* is a synonym for *believer* or *Christian*. A disciple is a believer. A disciple is a Christian in the fullest, Scriptural sense of the words, believer and Christian. Mere Christianity is "Jesus Christ is Lord." Believe it and live it!

Practical theologians of evangelization and discipleship attempt to define the content of evangelization and discipleship and determine where one ends and the other begins. Some see the two as distinct and separate. Others may see evangelization as the initiation of discipleship or view discipleship as the conclusion of evangelization. Some understand that salvation occurs once one responds faithfully to the invitation from evangelization. Others understand that an initial response is just

---

5.   Dietrich Bonhoeffer, *The Cost of Discipleship* (Macmillan, 1963), 63–64. (Bonhoeffer 1963)

the beginning and needs to bear out in discipleship. I see salvation as involving both evangelization *and* discipleship.

There needs to be a proclamation of the good news (evangelization) followed by a response of repentance for sin and faith in Christ as Lord and Savior from our sins (call). Salvation begins at this point (conversion). The process is not over but has only just begun. Discipleship begins the next phase or development of salvation. Believers are to be catechized further in Christian doctrine (creed) and ethics (code). They are to receive baptism if they haven't already. They should participate in worship, the sacraments, and others means of grace (*cultus*). Disciples are to continue to mature in their faith and be filled with the Spirit. Praying, receiving, identifying, training, and deploying of gifts (*charismata*) for ministry are essential, as we all are given at least one gift and are called to serve and minister in at least one area (commission). Disciples grow in grace in community (*communitas*). One-to-one and small group discipleship facilitate growth along the upward continuum of grace from justifying, regenerating, assuring grace to sanctifying and glorifying grace. Thus, evangelization and discipleship work together to initiate and complete the salvation process. Though there are crisis experiences and levels of growth, a disciple is simply a believer, a Christian, and not a higher order or class of Christian. One can be an immature disciple or a mature one but still be a disciple.

Although there is no disconnect between being a believer and a disciple and no levels of superiority, the nature and goal is the same: no easy believism. The goal is holiness or Christlikeness to experience heaven and heaven on earth. The lifelong call to follow Christ is a call to obey and live under the Lordship of Christ, absolute and total surrender each step of the way. Christ cannot be savior unless he is Lord. He saves us for himself. Thus, it follows that in saving all of us, he *has* all of us. As is often said, "Christ is Lord over all, or he is not Lord at all." Bonhoeffer put it best:

> When Christ calls a man, he bids him come and die. It may be a death like that of the first disciples who had to leave home and work to follow him, or it may be a death like Luther's, who had to leave the monastery and go out into the world. But it is the same death every time—death in Jesus Christ, the death of the old man at his call. . . . In fact every command of Jesus is a call to die . . .[6]

I remember hearing that same distinct, sacred call and responding the same when I came to Christ nearly forty years ago.[7] To a self-proclaimed, self-centered atheist, God expressly revealed himself on the night I was converted. By his grace, I gave myself fully and unreservedly to him. In surrendering my whole self to Christ, I not only parted with my sins, vices, unhealthy relationships, and even my self-serving academic career, but I gave Christ my life with all of its wants, desires, choices, and goals. My radical response was not due to my own strength or holiness. That day I truly learned that Jesus Christ is Lord and tasted his sweeping, all-encompassing

---

6. Bonhoeffer, *The Cost of Discipleship*, 99. (Bonhoeffer 1963)

7. Bellini, *Through the Threshold*. (P. Bellini 2024)

love for me. Following, the Spirit empowered me to give the only right and worthy response, my entire life. When Christ is Lord over our lives, he calls the shots concerning everything in our lives. We rule no more. His throne only has room for one, not two!

The Cross, Self-Denial, Obedience, and Discipleship

As Bonhoeffer said, a disciple is called to die! Yes, the heart of discipleship, the Christian life, *is to deny ourselves, take up our cross daily, and follow Jesus Christ the Lord*. Self-denial is simply to say no to our will when it is contrary to God's will, and to say yes to God's will. Self-denial is virtually unheard of in today's church. When was the last time you heard a sermon on self-denial in our self-indulging culture? No one likes to deny self. We want to affirm self and its wants. However, true disciples renounce their own will, take up their cross of personal sacrifice, and follow the Lord. This command is the *disciple's command*, and the verse is the *disciple's verse* (Matt. 10:38; Mark 8:34; Luke 9:23; John 12:24–25). Jesus himself set the terms. Anything less cannot be Christianity!

Christ's cross was a cross of atonement for our sins. Our cross is a disciples' cross. We carry it not for our salvation but that we may make the sacrifice that says no to ourselves, the world, and anything that would prevent us from following him to his cross, where we are called to be crucified with him (Rom. 6:6). The disciple's life is the cruciform, or cross-shaped, life, the way of the cross (*via crucis*). We walk like Christ walked, dead to our own interests. Self-denial says no to our will and way and yes to God's will and way (Luke 22:42). We cannot follow Christ unless we stop following ourselves. There can only be one leader. We can't serve two masters. One master must hear a no and the other, a yes. The problem with many of today's theologies and sermons is that there is not enough *wood* in them! Though the cross is the center of the gospel, it is not the center of our Sunday sermons. Rarely, amid our saccharine, self-satisfying sermons are we called to take up our cross. Itching ears tend towards messages that offer immediate, worldly gratification. Self-denial and sacrifice don't sell!

Consider what two eminent Christian leaders had to say about self-denial. John Calvin wrote,

> We are not our own; therefore, neither is our own reason or will to rule our acts and counsels. We are not our own; therefore, let us not make it our end to seek what may be agreeable to our carnal nature. We are not our own; therefore, as far as possible, let us forget ourselves and the things that are ours. On the other hand, we are God's; let us, therefore live and die to him (Rom 14:8). We are God's; therefore, let his wisdom and will preside over all our actions. . . . For as the surest source of destruction to men is to obey themselves, so that the only haven of safety is to have no other will, no other wisdom, than to follow the Lord wherever he leads. Let this,

then, be the first step, to abandon ourselves, and devote the whole energy of our minds to the service of God.[8]

Wesley preached,

The "denying" ourselves and the "taking up of our cross," in the full extent of the expression, is not a thing of small concern. It is not expedient only, as are some of the circumstantials of religion; but it is absolutely, indispensably necessary, either to our becoming or continuing his disciples. It is absolutely necessary, in the very nature of the thing, to our "coming after him" and "following him," insomuch that as far as we do not practice [sic] it we are not his disciples. If we do not continually "deny ourselves," we do not learn of him but of other masters. If we do not "take up our cross daily," we do not "come after him," but after the world, or the prince of the world, or our own "fleshly mind." If we are not walking in the way of the cross, we are not following him; we are not treading in his steps, but going back from, or at least wide of, him.[9]

Self-denial is the necessary "no" that we must impress on ourselves when we want to sit on the throne of our own heart. In commanding a holy "no" of ourselves and everything that keeps God from being first in our lives, we are daily taking up the disciple's cross of sacrifice in order to follow him and not ourselves. Crosses signified Roman-style death, crucifixion. God used Christ's cross as the vehicle of our salvation. He also employed the disciple's cross as the vehicle of our self-renunciation that we may obey Christ as Lord. Cross-bearing is the radical call of every disciple. Thus, we must be crucified in our minds (attitudes) first if we are to pick up our cross off the ground and walk with it. It is not a joystick but a rugged cross. You will get splinters!

Taking up the disciple's cross involves sacrifice that often entails suffering. If Christ learned obedience through suffering, how much more do we need it (Acts 9:16; Phil. 1:29; Heb. 5:8; 1 Pet. 5:10)? Supposedly, the immortal heavyweight champ Muhammad Ali stated, "I hated every minute of training, but I said, 'Don't quit. Suffer now and live the rest of your life as a champion.'" Success involves sacrifice and suffering!

Our suffering is not for the forgiveness of sin, like Christ's, but that we may *resist* sin (Acts 9:16; Phil. 1:29; 1 Pet. 5:10). The cross we take up, Scripture states, is our cross. It is personal. The self-denial, sacrifice, and suffering of our personal cross are connected to whatever we personally would put first ahead of God that would prevent us from following him. Bonhoeffer boasts, "Suffering, then, is the badge of true discipleship."[10] He fearlessly continues, "If we refuse to take up our cross and submit to suffering and rejection at the hands of men, we forfeit our fellowship with

8. John Calvin, *Institutes of the Christian Religion*, Henry Beveridge trans. (Hendrickson, 2008), 3:7. (Calvin 2008)

9. John Wesley, Sermon 48, "Self-Denial," in *Works of John Wesley*, vol. 7, *Sermon II*, ed. Thomas Jackson (Wesleyan Conference Office, 1872), 104. (Wesley, Works of John Wesley 1872)

10. Bonhoeffer, *The Cost of Discipleship*, 100. (Bonhoeffer 1963)

Christ and have ceased to follow him."[11] Yes, the cross has splinters, and it is heavy! We need to count its cost. Cruciformity is a daily mindset. The disciple is invited to the cross of Christ to die. We are to remain on the cross, and like St. Paul, we die daily to self-willfulness and our old sinful way of life (1 Cor. 15:31).

Each gospel has its version of the disciple's command of self-denial, followed by an explanation. Luke's Gospel puts it this way:

> Whoever wants to be my disciple must deny themselves and take up their cross daily and follow me. For whoever wants to save their life will lose it, but whoever loses their life for me will save it. What good is it for someone to gain the whole world, and yet lose or forfeit their very self? Whoever is ashamed of me and my words, the Son of Man will be ashamed of them when he comes in his glory and in the glory of the Father and of the holy angels. (Luke 9:23–26 NIV)

The explanation for what it means "to deny oneself, take up one's cross and follow Christ" is that if we do not deny ourselves, we are holding onto or saving our own life. If we save our own life, we are losing it, because we cannot save ourselves. We can only gain or save our life by losing our (sinful) life. In other words, Christ the Savior wants us to surrender our life to him so that he can save us from ourselves. We cannot have salvation if we do not yield fully our lives to Christ. We cannot be his disciple if we follow ourselves. Following ourselves and following Christ are in diametric opposition.

Christ elaborates further. This time he replaces "our life" with "the whole world." Often, holding onto our own life means that we have our own way. We can have what we want. We can take as big a slice of the world as we desire. In this passage, the world means the sum total of everything we could ever want. We all *want* something in this life. And we all *need* something in life. God knows and understands our creaturely status. If we seek God and his righteousness, first, he will provide for the rest (Matt. 6:33). The ultimate question is, What do you want above all else, God or mammon (money)? Where is your allegiance? *Who or what is Lord?*

We can have an elephantine slice of the world, but there is a cost, a high price to pay. The cost for our wants (the world) is our lives. That is the exchange. If we want our way and not Christ's, it will cost us our soul. We may have our own way and have whatever we want, but in the end we will lose everything. We cannot have it both ways. Having our own way (the world) and having God's way are mutually exclusive. If we have everything that we want (gain the world) but we lose our soul, we made a bad deal. Simply, being a disciple will cost us all that we are and all that we have. So count the cost (Luke 14:25–35)!

In neuroscientific terms, when we deny ourselves, we deny playing the short game of instant gratification and play the long game that has the greatest value. Playing the short game, the prefrontal cortex and its reasoning power and will are hijacked in order to pursue hollow pleasures at the expense of the greater good. In

---

11. Bonhoeffer, *The Cost of Discipleship* 101. (Bonhoeffer 1963)

other words, we gain the world and lose our soul. However, when we choose to play the long game, we, under the power of the Spirit (the fruit of self-control) activate the brain's ability to self-regulate. We become aware of our own thoughts and behaviors and are aware that God sees us, which is a medial prefrontal cortex function. We are alerted to the temptation and its consequences of falling (an amygdala function), and thus, by the Spirit, we use our prefrontal cortex executive function to self-regulate and overcome.[12] The Spirit supplies the extra energy to a normally limited prefrontal cortex to attain victory when pressed with temptation. As disciples, we pay the price of self-regulation for long-term gratification.

Once again, we turn to Bonhoeffer to remind us of the cost of discipleship. He makes it plain: There is *cheap* grace and *costly* grace. Cheap grace is "grace without price; grace without cost!"[13] Costly grace "is costly because it cost God the life of his Son, 'ye were bought with a price,' and what has cost God much cannot be cheap for us."[14] Again, Bonhoeffer sums up cheap grace: "Cheap grace means sold on the market like cheapjacks' wares. The sacraments, the forgiveness of sin, and the consolation of religion are thrown away at cut prices. Grace is represented as the Church's inexhaustible treasury, from which she showers blessings with generous hands, without asking questions or fixing limits."[15] And, "Cheap grace is the preaching of forgiveness without requiring repentance, baptism without church discipline, Communion without confession, absolution without personal confession. Cheap grace is grace without discipleship, grace without the cross, grace without Jesus Christ, living and incarnate."[16]

And on costly grace he says, "Costly grace is the treasure hidden in the field; for the sake of it a man will gladly go and sell all that he has. It is the pearl of great price to buy which the merchant will sell all his goods. It is the kingly rule of Christ, for whose sake a man will pluck out the eye which causes him to stumble, it is the call of Christ at which the disciple leaves his nets and follows him."[17] Furthermore, "Such grace is *costly* because it calls us to follow, and it is *grace* because it calls us to follow *Jesus Christ*. It is costly because it costs a man his life, and it is grace because it gives a man the only true life. It is costly because it condemns sin, and grace because it justifies the sinner."[18]

---

12. Todd F. Heatherton, "Neuroscience of Self and Self-Regulation," *Annual Review of Psychology* 62 (2011): 363–90. https://doi.org/10.1146/annurev.psych.121208.131616. The specific self-regulatory functions within the prefrontal cortex are the "ventromedial PFC (vMPFC) including orbitofrontal cortex, lateral PFC, and ACC," the anterior cingulate cortex. (Heatherton, Neuroscience of Self and Self-Regulation 2011)

13. Bonhoeffer, *The Cost of Discipleship*, 45. (Bonhoeffer 1963)

14. Bonhoeffer, *The Cost of Discipleship*, 48. (Bonhoeffer 1963)

15. Bonhoeffer, *The Cost of Discipleship*, 45. (Bonhoeffer 1963)

16. Bonhoeffer, *The Cost of Discipleship*, 47. (Bonhoeffer 1963)

17. Bonhoeffer, *The Cost of Discipleship*, 47. (Bonhoeffer 1963)

18. Bonhoeffer, *The Cost of Discipleship*, 47–48. (Bonhoeffer 1963)

And think about it: Bonhoeffer was describing the church of his day under the yoke of Nazi fascism, three-quarters of a century ago. Today, we are no different, perhaps worse. On one side of the church, we have pursuers of power, peddlers of prosperity, and prophets for profit, proclaiming the health and wealth gospel. Name it and claim it! Blab it and grab it! Whatever you want you can have, but you have to sow a seed (buy a ticket) in order to play God's holy lottery. Christ did not have a house to lay his head, but some believers feel entitled to the world and everything in it. To these "disciples," godliness signifies a way to get rich and gain power (1 Tim. 6:5). Instead, Paul told Timothy that "godliness with contentment is itself great wealth" (1 Tim. 6:6 NLT), and he urged him to run away from the evil temptation and trap of craving money (1 Tim. 6:9–11).

On the other side of the church, we have those who have put Jesus on the discount table. They have cut all costs, marked him down, and are giving him away cheap, even without cost. Much of so-called mainline Christianity (sideline or flatline Christianity) has cut the cost out of the gospel. They have cut out Divine authorship from Scripture. They have cut out teaching and preaching on sin, conviction, repentance, self-denial, sacrifice, the cross, the blood, the absolute truth of Scripture, the deity of Christ, the Incarnation, the virgin birth, the resurrection, exclusive salvation in Christ alone, and other key doctrines of the historic Christian faith. They offer Christ, but he is a marked down or discount version. He is the costless Christ. He is the Christ of convenience and the culture. Whatever the culture wants him to be, the church will re-create him in their image, a Christ of permission and license. Whatever we want we can have, because God is love, and love never says no. Love lets everyone be and do as they please. Love always says yes. These are just a few examples in our day of cheap grace.

Discipleship means choosing Christ over self and the world, God over mammon. We cannot serve two masters. We cannot be doubleminded or have two minds, a mind of the Spirit and a mind of the flesh, or a mind that serves God and a mind that serves self. We were made to serve one God only. There is no other foundation, no other rock on which to build our lives. Either the true God will be the single object of our heart, or something else will be. The heart is the treasure chest of our life. Whatever we truly treasure, or desire, will be locked away in our heart. We can always know what is in our heart. It is the thing we want the most: "Wherever your treasure is, there the desires of your heart will also be" (Matt. 6:21 NLT). What is your treasure? Money, power, sex, status, possessions, or ego? Christ is the treasure of the true disciple. Christ alone. Christ needs to be Lord over our neural hierarchy of preferences and attention. Alignment occurs when the eye of heart and mind is singularly focused on Christ the Light of the world. Singularity of the heart is its purity, as Kierkegaard said.[19] Its focus and desire are for Christ alone. One heart for one God. Bonhoeffer calls it "single-minded obedience."[20]

---

19. Kierkegaard, *Purity of Heart Is to Will One Thing*. (Kierkegaard 1956)

20. Bonhoeffer, *The Cost of Discipleship*, 87–94. (Bonhoeffer 1963)

We choose to follow one master and not two. As wise disciples, we build on the one rock. We pray and seek for his Kingdom and his righteousness before anything else. We pray for a heart that follows Christ's Sermon on the Mount. We ask the Spirit to cultivate Christlikeness in our hearts: humble and poor in spirit, repentant and mournful for sin, meekness or strength under humility, a hunger and thirst for righteousness, merciful, purity, peacemaking, blessed by slander and persecution, salt and light, slow to anger, lustless eyes, to be people of our word, forgiving, loving enemies, giving to the poor, praying and fasting, generous, not covetous, not judgmental, doing to others as we would have done unto us, full of good fruit—being perfect as our heavenly Father is perfect (Matthew 5–7; 5:48).

Let us look at some concrete ways that we can practice self-denial.

Practical Examples of Denying Self

- **Crucify:** The inner life (thoughts and emotions) and the outer life (actions) are aligned with the will and word of God and not the will of self. For example, say no to lustful thoughts and replace them with Matthew 5:27–30.
- **Prayer:** Spend more than 75 percent of your prayer time on others rather than on yourself.
- **Service:** Commit to one or two hands-on ministries at your local church. Even deny yourself the fear of people and share your faith with a stranger once a week.
- **Exercise:** Work out five days a week at least one hour a day. Following, donate your newfound strength and stamina to a church or neighborhood labor project.
- **Diet:** Perhaps quit eating desserts or sugar or eating after dinner. Sponsor someone in need with the money that you save.
- **Finances:** Cut out luxury spending on an item or two and reallocate the amount to help support a missionary, a charity, or a person in need.
- **Listening:** Listen to others to hear, learn, and empathize rather than to strategize for a response.
- **Silence:** Practice periods of fasting from unnecessary talking and even talking in general.
- **Social media:** Fast periodically or totally from social media. Fast from posting on social media for a period or for good. Take the extra time and add it to your devotional life.
- **Self-Importance:** Practice valuing others above yourself through more and better listening, serving, giving, encouraging, thanking, complimenting, attention, and learning.

- **Worship:** Give God more of your time, talent, treasure, trust, desire, focus, leisure, work, and so on. Simply say no to your will when it opposes the will of God and say yes to his will.

Discipleship Is God's Method

This book is about losing our own way of thinking and gaining God's way of thinking. *We lose our mind and gain the mind of Christ.* The Spirit crafts the mind of Christ in us. The Spirit's artisanal work of crafting our minds is essential to discipleship. When the Spirit disciples us, he is also discipling our minds. As described in the previous chapters, the mind takes a central place in our being and the processing of life. Our minds cannot be bypassed in the discipleship process. Repentance (*metanoia*), a change of mind that changes our lives, is the beginning of the call to discipleship. The Spirit appeals to our mind and will with the word of God to turn to Christ. Conversion and discipleship are "more than a feeling," as the old rock band Boston sang. Although discipleship is the work of the Spirit, it involves our full response and cooperation. We must intentionally and actively participate. The Spirit will not drag us to the cross. He prefers to dance as he leads, and we follow.

Most believers are aware that they are called to make disciples. Christ concludes the so-called Great Commission with that very command (Matt. 28:18–20). Making disciples is the feature of many of our church mission and vision statements. It's on our church signs, on our lips, in our Christian books and church philosophies. We all know it, but we do not know how to do it! We look for a book, a manual, or a program on "how to," but discipleship is not a program, though it can involve programs. Discipleship is not about reading a book, though it can involve books.[21] Discipleship is not a formula, though it may involve prescribed instructions, disciplines, and practices. *Discipleship is more than mechanics of "how to."* The number one question I get from students when discussing discipleship is, "What does that look like in practice?" It's the go-to American pragmatic question, and often I ask it as well when trying to apply certain principles. The problem is that we prefer to follow the security and certainty of a well-thought-out plan over the uncertainty of following a person.

When we follow the wind of the Holy Spirit, he blows where he chooses. And walking by faith rarely seems to include detailed instructions before our first step. Dietrich Bonhoeffer comments on following Christ, "Not to know where you are going is the true knowledge."[22] We follow the Spirit. He does not follow us. Discipleship is a relationship. It is a relationship between us and the Triune God. The process is the supernatural socialization of sons and daughters into the family of God by faith, yet using all of our cerebral resources, including our social brain (the limbic system, responsible for social interaction), the medial prefrontal cortex, the anterior cingulate cortex, temporoparietal junction (between temporal and parietal lobes), the medial parietal cortex,

---

21. The Bible, of course, and perhaps other books.

22. Bonhoeffer, *The Cost of Discipleship*, 103. (Bonhoeffer 1963)

the anterior temporal lobes, the resonance system, the dopaminergic reward system, and more.[23] Discipleship is a full-contact sport!

Discipleship is also a life-giving relationship. It is a parent –son or –daughter, teacher–student, doctor–patient, coach–coached, mentor–mentee, leader–led, friend–friend, and lover–loved relationship. These relationships are organic. They can use programs, books, disciplines, strategies, and the like, but relationships consist of more than these elements. A discipleship relationship is spiritual and life changing. It's greater than the sum of its parts. We are talking life-to-life transference that revolutionizes one's existence. Consider Moses and Joshua, Elijah and Elisha, Christ and the Twelve, or Paul and Timothy. Such a relational bond is often more caught than taught. Clearly, discipleship involves teaching as a core practice, but it's more than teaching information and facts. It's life teaching life through modeling. To know some things, they must be seen and experienced first. Initial and even deeper patterns of learning occur through mirror neurons and modeling, which facilitate experiential learning.[24]

The Neuroscience of Learning: Mirror Neurons

The mirror neuron system (MNS) is within the resonance system, which is responsible for emotional bonding. The resonance system is the relational glue that bonds us with others. Resonance circuitry helps us to resonate, vibe, echo, or relate to others. Mirror neurons reflect (mirror) the behavior observed in another. They code what is witnessed and provide an internal simulation of the behavior that could later be executed in terms of repeating the act. On repetition and rehearsal, the connection is strengthened, and effectual learning takes place. As newborns or new Christians, learning begins through imitation.

Mirror neurons were discovered through innovative research in the 1990s. Mirror neurons are a special type of brain cell that enables us to empathize and learn by imitation, one of the fundamental methods of pedagogy. A network of mirror neurons "makes it possible to generate a brain state that matches that of the person being observed, providing an automatic share of their experience."[25] We learn and

23. Tanaz Molapour, Cindy C. Hagan, Brian Silston, Haiyan Wu, Maxwell Ramstead, Karl Friston, and Dean Mobbs, "Seven Computations of the Social Brain," *Social Cognitive and Affective Neuroscience* 16, no. 8 (August 2021): 745–60. https://doi.org/10.1093/scan/nsab024. (Molapour, et al. 2021)

24. Sourya Acharya and Samarth Shukla, "Mirror Neurons: Enigma of the Metaphysical Modular Brain," *Journal of Natural Science, Biology and Medicine* 3, no. 2 (2012): 118–24. https://doi.org/10.4103/0976-9668.101878. (Acharya and Shukla 2012)

25. Julio C. Penagos-Corzo, Michelle Cosio van-Hasselt, Daniela Escobar, Rúben A. Vázquez-Roque, and Gonzalo Flores, "Mirror Neurons and Empathy-Related Regions in Psychopathy: Systematic Review, Meta-Analysis, and a Working Model," *Social Neuroscience* 17, no. 5 (2022): 462–79. Jeremy Sutton, "Mirror Neurons and the Neuroscience of Empathy," Positive Psychology, September 7, 2023, https://positivepsychology.com/mirror-neurons/#:~:text=While%20observing%20such%20emotional%20information,et%20al.%2C%202022. (Sutton 2023)

comprehend through observation and imitation of modeling. When we observe a particular behavior in others our mirror neurons capture and reflect the behavior in our brains in a way that we perceive and interpret the behavior as if we were doing it. Basically, learning often begins by observing and imitating. We learn by what we see, and we do what we see. Human see, human do.

Imitation is followed by experience and interaction with the one modeling and with other students. Studies have illustrated how cognitive development is greatly facilitated by social setting, experience, and interaction with other learners and the instructor.[26] What pedagogy expert David Kolb calls "experiential learning"—that is, people learn best through experience—is the fundamental way we grow in discipleship. This is what I call "life-to-life transference." Though reading and comprehending cognitive propositional truth (doctrine) is foundational, we cannot halt the learning process at that point. Experience needs to move from abstraction to concretization by obeying and putting into practice what Christ has taught and commanded us. Our learning is complete when we are actually performing what has been modeled, and what we have mirrored and experienced, engaging the full senses and a range of brain functions.

As a mediocre guitar player, I cannot tell you how many guitar licks I have learned from YouTube tutorials. They allow one to observe slowly the guitarist's picking and fretting hands repetitively go over and over each note of the guitar part. Before the advent of YouTube, I tried every method of learning complex guitar leads, whether by ear, note, or tablature. None of these modes, for me, works as quickly and efficiently as seeing and imitating. Modeling facilitates imitation and learning. In fact, when I think about many of the skills that I have learned over the years, such as casting out demons, laying hands on the sick, running a board meeting, playing piano or drums, boxing, playing baseball, wrestling, car mechanics, building, fixing, or home improvement, they came easier by observing.

Another consequence of the mirror neuron system working is the learning of empathy. We are actually able to learn to perceive and imitate the emotional states of others, which are essential to being empathic. Siegel states, "In other words this is the way we not only imitate others' behaviors but actually come to resonate with their feelings—the internal flow of their minds."[27] An integral job of mirror neurons is to reflect the feelings of others, which is essential to building empathy, compassion, bonding, and relationships. They help facilitate social learning and our socialization, key dimensions of discipleship and following.

Similarly, *Christ* discipled through modeling, interaction, and experience. He called his disciples to an apprenticeship to walk alongside him and watch him in ministry. As apprentices, they witnessed him teach, preach, heal, cast out demons,

---

26. See Holly J. Inglis, *Sticky Learning: How Neuroscience Supports Teaching That's Remembered* (Fortress, 2014), 14–16, which references the work of Lev Vygotsky, *The Development of Higher Psychological Processes* (Harvard University Press, 1978), 90. Also see David Kolb, *Experiential Learning: Experience as the Source of Learning and Development* (Pearson Education, 2015).

27. Siegel, *Mindsight*, 61. (D. J. Siegel 2010)

care for the poor, and respond to opposition. Christ modeled the ministry that he wanted the disciples to embody and continue after his resurrection and ascension. After modeling, Christ made space in ministry so the disciples could participate, first in a secondary role by following him and then in leadership. Where they once assisted the Master when he ministered to the multitudes, the disciples would themselves teach, preach, heal, cast out demons, care for the poor, and testify before opposition. Finally, once Christ commissioned them to lead and carry out the mission, he sent the Holy Spirit to empower them for the work. The Holy Spirit enabled the disciples to perform the works of Christ and even greater works. With the Spirit indwelling the multitude of believers, more work can be accomplished. The Spirit would not be limited to indwelling one person (Christ), but many (John 14:12).

Jordan (Not Michael) and Building People

Jordan was one of my seminary students. She committed to our school after sitting in on one of my classes, which was open to prospective students. She took many classes with me and heard me share about discipleship. She prayed and asked if I would be willing to disciple her. I usually do not disciple persons of the opposite sex, but it seemed God was giving me the green light on this request. Around eight years ago, we began a fruitful journey together that has involved prayer, counseling, teaching, training, accountability, healing, growing, ministry, and friendship. Jordan, who is also close to my daughter Paola'a age and one of her best friends, became adopted into our Sicilian family, from Jordan to Giordana.

Jordan is a brilliant young woman, a sharp and receptive student, an obedient servant of Christ, and one fully yielded to the Holy Spirit—everything one needs to become a faithful disciple. As her spiritual father, my goal was to model discipleship and bring out of her what Christ purposed in her. She swiftly learned through instruction but more so through our time together in prayer and intercession, in worship, in sessions of counseling and inner healing, ministering together, at our dinner table, at family outings, and even at the batting cages and training at my boxing club. Discipleship happens where life happens. Much was taught, but more was caught. It was our commitment to mutual trust that was developed through modeling and empathy, which became the glue to the discipleship relationship. It enabled her to learn quickly, grow in Christlikeness, and develop ministry skills, like healing, deliverance, counseling, and operating in the gifts of the Spirit. Mirror neurons at work learning and bonding.

Her humility, teachability, and receptivity enabled her to pick up dexterously on my spiritual DNA and gift mix and integrate it into her own. God's leading to take on this discipleship relationship was perfect. He had already given her a similar gift mix and ministry call as my own. She just needed the awareness, jump start, and training to activate, develop, and deploy her gifts and ministry. Currently, Jordan is an associate pastor at her church with a healing and deliverance ministry and is a sought-after conference speaker. Discipleship builds people through people.

When we examine the earthly ministry of Christ, we note that discipleship was Jesus' method of Kingdom build-ng. God is all about people—people over programs, people over bricks and mortar. God builds people, and people (through the Spirit) build the Kingdom.[28] In fact, people are the bricks and mortar or the spiritual stones that build God's holy temple. St. Peter declares, "you also, like living stones, are being built into a spiritual house to be a holy priesthood, offering spiritual sacrifices acceptable to God through Jesus Christ" with Christ as the chief cornerstone (1 Pet. 2:5; Eph. 2:20 NIV). When God builds people, he builds the church. When we participate in building people through discipleship, we are building the church.

The Timothy 222 Principle

Along with the cross, Christ's primary ministry was to make disciples (Matt. 4:19; 10:1; 28:18–20). The primary ministry of Christ was intended to be the primary ministry of his church. Christ by the Spirit chose twelve who would lay the foundation following his ascension. The Twelve were his primary focus. The entire ministry of Christ was immersed in discipleship, and so should ours. He invested his time and energy proportionately in concentric circles of interest. He preached to, taught, and fed the masses (Matt. 14:13–21). After the resurrection, he appeared before the 500 (Luke 22:44–49). He trained and sent out the seventy-two to preach the good news (Luke 10). He called the Twelve to apostleship (Luke 9). And he was transfigured before his inner circle of Peter, James, and John (Matt. 16:28–17:9). Through his investment in those relationships, he was able to disciple the first generations of believers who would disciple the next generation and so on with exponential growth. I call this apprenticeship strategy the Timothy 222 Principle: "And the things you have heard me say in the presence of many witnesses entrust to reliable people who will also be qualified to teach others" (2 Tim. 2:2 NIV).

In this verse, we find four generations of discipleship taking place. Paul, who was discipled by Barnabas, is the first generation mentioned. Timothy, who was discipled by Paul, is the second generation. The third generation is the disciples the verse calls "reliable people who will also be qualified to teach." And the fourth generation is the "others" who will be discipled by the "reliable people." Spiritual sons and daughters will proliferate at the fourth generation—Abraham, Isaac, Jacob, and then the Twelve Tribes. Think: If you successfully *evangelize* one person a day for a year, you will have 365 converts. After two years, 730 After three years, 1,095. After four years, 1,460. After five years, 1,825, and so on. On the other hand, think about if you *disciple* one person a year who also disciples one person a year and so on. The growth starts off slowly year by year: first year is one, second year is two, third year is four, fourth year is eight, fifth year is sixteen, and so on. The disciplemaker will not pass the number of converts of the evangelist until year thirteen. But by year fourteen, the disciplemaker would almost triple the output of the evangelist 16,384 to 5,110. The growth is exponential and long-term (Ssee Diagram 5).

---

28. For an excellent study on the methodology of Jesus in discipleship, see Robert Coleman, *The Master Plan of Evangelism* (Revel , 2006).

This statistic merely shows the quantitative growth, but the qualitative growth is even greater, as we will learn later in this chapter. Evangelism is vital, but a model of evangelism that includes discipleship is even more critical and robust. Simply, transformation is imperative to the evangelism and discipleship process. For many, evangelism usually only involves some type of gospel proclamation. Hopefully, at some point in time, proclamation is followed by a profession of faith and baptism, if needed. However, the work is not complete. Evangelism initiates the process. Discipleship is where training, development, growth, and maturity take place. A robust discipleship process is a rigorous apprenticeship. It should involve at least close mentoring, accountability, extensive creedal catechesis (teaching), moral and ethical training, spiritual disciplines, worship, fellowship, gift identification and deployment, service, and other training and practices.[29] Essentially, learning and following Christ involves learning and practicing *everything* that Jesus has commanded us (Matt. 7:24–29; 11:28–30; 28:18–20). Making disciples involves teaching disciples how to do the same.

Diagram 5

Evangelism vs. Discipleship

Y1 – 365 1		Y9 – 3285 512	
Y2 – 730 2		Y10 – 3650 1024	
Y3 – 1095 4		Y11 – 4015 2048	
Y4 – 1460 16		Y12 – 4380 4096	
Y5 – 1825 32		Y13 – 4745 8192	
Y6 – 2190 64		Y14 – 5110 . . . 16384	
Y7 – 2555 128		Y15 – 5475 . . . 32768	
Y8 – 2920 256			

Brief Scriptural Overview of Discipleship

Moses and Joshua

Though prominent in the New Testament with Jesus, discipleship is a practice we also find in the Old Testament, the ancient Near East, and the classic Greek and Roman worlds.[30] Regardless of the various words employed, the concepts of mentoring and training were prevalent. For example, the book of Proverbs was employed as a discipleship manual for training youth who would become leaders in society. Students would seek out masters and teachers to follow and learn from their lives (mirror neurons). Teachers, such as rabbis or philosophers, would invite students to

---

29. For a robust model of evangelism that includes discipleship, see William Abraham, *The Logic of Evangelism* (Eerdmans, 1989). For one of the most thorough treatments of the subject of discipleship, see Bill Hull, *The Complete Book of Discipleship* (NavPress, 2006).

30. For an excellent study of discipleship throughout the ancient Mediterranean world see part II of Michael Wilkins, *Following the Master: A Biblical Theology of Discipleship* (Zondervan, 1992).

learn from them, follow them, and even live with them. In the ancient Hellenistic world, students would assemble under a gifted philosopher. For example, Socrates trained Plato, Plato trained Aristotle, and Aristotle trained Alexander the Great. A legacy of mentor and mentee was passed on to continue a philosophical tradition like Socrates, and Plato, or to start a new one like Plato and Aristotle and his Lyceum. In the Hebrew world, similarly, priests, teachers, leaders, and prophets were raised through mentoring and discipleship.

On fire since the burning bush, Moses, though, was becoming burned out from wearing so many hats. He was a deliverer, lawgiver, judge, priest, teacher, prophet, husband, and father—sounds like a modern-day pastor's life! All withdrawals and no deposits. Pouring out but little pouring in. Running on empty. Due to chronic stress, most likely, Moses' prefrontal cortex and mental energy were thinning out while his amygdala was enlarging and overreacting. His executive function was overloaded and weakening, while his reactor system (fight, flight, freeze) was in overdrive.[31] As a result of his insane, unmanageable workload, his father-in-law Jethro worried that he would no longer have a son-in-law to take care of his daughter. Jethro advised Moses to multiply himself by division—that is, divide the labor among the leaders that he had been training (The Jethro Principle; Exod. 18:17–27). Moses selected his seventy top leaders whom he trained and imparted unto them the same Spirit that he had so that they could do the same work (Num. 11:16–29). Reproduction! Moses adapted to his stress by reproducing leaders and avoiding burnout while increasing effectiveness.

Additionally, Moses raised up Joshua as his spiritual son to take his mantle and bring the people into the promised land (Deut. 31:7–8, 23). Joshua took an apprentice role and served Moses as his assistant (Exod. 24:13). He followed Moses. From Moses' successes and challenges, Joshua learned how to lead the people through the desert. Moses also observed Joshua's abilities and his call and gave him the responsibility of raising up and leading an army against the Amalekites (Exod. 17:9–10, 13–16). Through battling and overcoming the Amalekites, Joshua was being prepared by the Lord to be the seasoned general who would lead the Israelites over the Canaanites in the Promised Land. As Moses learned that the battle belongs to the Lord, so also Joshua learned that the Lord was his victory banner (Exod. 17:15). Leaders in training, when proven faithful with little, should be given opportunities to work up to higher-level tasks under supervision without competition or jealousy from their mentors.

The overwhelming demands of ministry press on its leaders. Nonetheless, mentors need to be forward thinking and invest their leadership in the next generation. Although the immediate is important, leadership cannot be overburdened by the tyranny and demands of the now. Wise leaders must think about the future and training leadership to carry out God's vision for tomorrow. We must remember not to despise the youth because they may not have the experience and knowledge that the elders possess. Early on Moses identified a courageous and victorious mindset needed for

---

31. For more on the connection between burnout and neurophysiology, see Razia A. G. Khammissa, Simon Nemutandani, Gal Feller, Johan Lemmer, and Liviu Feller, "Burnout Phenomenon: Neurophysiological Factors, Clinical Features, and Aspects of Management," Journal of International Medical Research 50, no. 9 (2022): 3000605221106428. https://doi.org/10.1177/03000605221106428.

leadership in young men like Joshua and Caleb. He trained them up as scouts to go into the promised land to spy and survey it in order to prepare for the coming invasion (Numbers 13).

Joshua demonstrated a durable mind of faith and courage. The Israelites were overwhelmed by the towering size of the inhabitants. Instead of believing the promise that God would give them victory and deliver the land to them, they assessed their chances of conquest based on their own senses and reason. When they gazed on the gigantic Nephilim, they began to drown in their own fears. They exclaimed, "We cannot go up against the people, for they are stronger than we are. . . . We seemed like grasshoppers in our own sight, and we must have seemed the same to them!" (Num. 13:31, 33 BSB). Their fearful mindset blinded them from seeing God's promises. Their faith was suffocated by fear. They judged God's ability based on their own reasoning. Though the Canaanites seemed overwhelming, Caleb countered, "We must go up and take possession of the land, for we can certainly conquer it!" (Num. 13:30 BSB). Joshua and Caleb were trained to cling to the promises of God, trained to reign.

Toward the end of his life, Moses laid his hands on Joshua and anointed him to lead the people. We are told that the anointing was the same authority and Spirit that was on Moses, and it would be imparted to Joshua (Num. 27:18–23; Deut. 34:9). In this way, he could both lead effectively like Moses, and the people would recognize that God was with Joshua as he was with Moses (Josh. 1:1–18). When the person and ministry of a prophet are received, one receives the reward of a prophet, which is their blessing, authority, and anointing (Matt. 10:41). For example, in the case of Elisha, he received a double portion from his spiritual father (2 Kgs. 2:9).

Eli and Samuel

In the Old Testament, we find other examples of discipleship. The tribe of Levi trained their youth for the priesthood. The blessing was passed both naturally and spiritually in this case. The young candidates would be mentored in the tabernacle by an elder priest. They would be trained in the liturgical arts of the tabernacle. They were also trained to hear the voice of God and pray God's will as intercessors for the people. The priesthood perpetuated through parenting spiritual sons.

Due to corruption of leaders like Eli, the Lord could not entrust them with his word and revelations (1 Sam. 3:1). God was ready to raise up a new faithful generation of leaders. Eli, the priest, raised up Samuel, the priest and prophet. Hannah dedicated Samuel for the Lord's service, and he started his training early. The brain is most malleable and trainable at a young age. Ninety percent of the brain develops in the first five years. As a child, he was fitted with a priest's ephod. Day and night he learned the craft of priesthood in the tabernacle under Eli. Although later Eli failed as a spiritual father to his sons Phinehas and Hophni, he successfully taught Samuel how to hear God's voice, which is an indispensable skill for a prophet (1 Samuel 3). Samuel would need that skill to hear from God when he was called to correct Saul and anoint David king (1 Sam. 13:16).[32] Samuel was faithful to the Lord and was successful as a spiritual father to many, including prophets whom he had trained (1 Sam. 10:5).

---

32. In Chapter 7, we discuss hearing the voice of God in more detail.

Elijah and Elisha

Samuel was the first prophet called to anoint the king and hold him accountable. The role of prophet carried high responsibilities. Proper discipleship was needed. Later, the prophet Elijah established a school of the prophets for that purpose. I call the discipleship ministry of Elijah *the order of Elijah.* He trained fledgling prophets one-to-one and in a school with on-the-job training through modeling. Elijah began to disciple young men with a prophetic call. Led by the Spirit, he selected his first candidate, Elisha. Character and fruit were instrumental to his selection. He started with a faithful, humble, teachable, and available farmer. Note, these four qualities are essential for effective discipleship! Holistic learning equals discipleship. Learning comes through teachability, and teachability is the willingness to have the brain trained. Elijah trained up Elisha and the school of the prophets (1 Kgs. 19:19–21; 2 Kgs. 2:16).

Many want to start at the top. Many choose mentees or even leaders based on achievement or accolades and ignore the most imperative qualities, such as humility, faithfulness with little, and teachability. Without these virtues, a disciple in training who relies on their gifts and achievements will fall into temptation. They become top-heavy. They excel in giftedness and ministry, but they are not grounded in the fruit of the Spirit, nor have they been tested by pressure and experience.

Elisha was not from an elite class or upbringing. He came from simple, humble means. He was a faithful farmer. Elijah found him behind the plow with sweat dripping from his brow under the hot sun. Elisha was also teachable. He was accustomed to learning a trade and was disciplined to carry out hard manual labor, like Christ's disciples. On being called, Elisha left everything to follow Elijah. He even burned his plowing equipment for fire to sacrifice his yoke of oxen and cook them for a feast (1 Kgs. 19:21). He died to his old life in order to begin a new one.

Elijah called him by placing his cloak on his shoulders, symbolic of Elijah's covering and mantle (1 Kgs. 19:19). It was a prophetic act declaring that Elisha would be trained to be his successor. First though, Elisha learned to serve Elijah as a humble son. He was faithful in the small things and was then promoted to greater things. Disciples, especially prophets, are forged in humility through simple tasks that carry no glory or reward. Offices should not be given to untrained and untried novices (1 Tim. 3:6). Let them prove themselves faithful through "spiritual latrine duty" where no one is watching. Bypass immediate gratification and develop the long game, which disciplines and develops the brain over time into maturity through the formation of character and virtue.

Former heavyweight champ Larry Holmes, who once defeated Muhammad Ali, started out humbly as Ali's sparring partner. Holmes learned to craft his effective, stinging jab when Ali modeled it on Holmes' face. Sparring with the champ, Holmes was often on the receiving end of Ali's left glove, but he humbly learned from experience. Holmes would go on to develop arguably the best jab in heavyweight history. Don't despise small beginnings. Scripture said that Elisha first functioned as Elijah's servant and ministered to Elijah (1 Kgs. 19:21). In other boxing terms, he was in Elijah's corner with a towel, water, and spit bucket. Most likely, he did menial tasks like cleaning clothes and cooking food as well as praying with Elijah and assisting in his prophetic ministry. He did not start off as bishop or apostle with a large glamourous ministry like we seek today. No two clicks to be a bishop; three clicks and you can be an apostle at rockstarminister.com.

After serving and learning faithfully, it was time for Elisha, the spiritual son, to become the father of that prophetic movement (2 Kings 2–13). Notice the language used throughout Chapter 2. Elisha calls Elijah "father" (2 Kgs. 2:12). Elijah was not his natural father but his spiritual father, who discipled him into a mature prophet. The time had come to release Elisha and give him the blessing of a father, his inheritance. Elisha wanted a double portion of Elijah's anointing to succeed him as the prophet to Israel and to be the father of the school of the prophets. Elijah took his mantle and struck the water of the Jordan, and it split, and they passed through it (2 Kgs. 2:8). Fifty prophets from the school watched and waited back on the other side.

Elijah informed Elisha that God would take him up to heaven in a whirlwind. If Elisha could see Elijah be carried away, he would receive his mantle and prophetic reward. Then, Elijah and Elisha were separated by a chariot of fire. Elijah was taken up. Elisha then cried out, "My father! My father! I see the chariots and charioteers of Israel!" The mantle was released, and Elisha took it on himself. Elisha split the Jordan with his cloak, as Elijah did, and crossed the river to join the company of prophets. They realized that he had acquired the anointing of Elijah because he did the same miracle as Elijah with his mantle, and exclaimed, "Elijah's spirit rests upon Elisha!" (2 Kgs. 2:15 NLT). And it was true. Elijah did eleven miracles in his day, and Elisha performed twenty-two, a double portion. If one reads the entire account of Elisha, one will find many parallels between the two prophets and their ministry. Rounding out the Old Testament tradition, we discover that the school of the prophets' tradition is carried out with other prophets like Isaiah, who had his disciples, and Jeremiah, who raised up his scribe Baruch to be his successor (Isa. 8:16; Jeremiah 36, 45).

Jesus, the Twelve, and the Apostolic Fathers

The story of Elijah and Elisha is echoed in the story of Christ and his disciples. Similarly, Christ called them to leave their lives behind. They followed him, while he trained them on the job. The disciples served and assisted Christ and learned to do ministry. Before his crucifixion, they were also promised a double portion of Christ's anointing, the Holy Spirit. Christ promised them that they would do even greater works because Christ would no longer be limited through one body but would dwell in all of his disciples by the Spirit (John 14:12). Christ told them to wait in Jerusalem after his ascension, and the Holy Spirit would fall on them with tongues of fire and power to be his witnesses (Acts 1:8). At Pentecost, they received Christ's mantle of the Holy Spirit to preach, teach, heal, and cast out demons as he did. The book of Acts is the seamless sequel to the gospel of Luke. The disciples performed the same works as Christ did. And as others recognized that Elisha had Elijah's mantle by the works he performed, so the people recognized that these unlearned disciples had been with Christ because they performed the same signs and wonders as Christ (Acts 4:13). The power of discipleship!

Jesus called and trained the Twelve, who discipled the next generation. For example, John, the beloved of Christ, discipled Polycarp (69–155 CE) and Ignatius (died c. 110), prominent early church fathers. Likewise, Barnabas discipled Paul who discipled Silas, Mark, Timothy, and others. Paul the apostle was a spiritual father to many. He even addressed Timothy as his son (1 Cor. 4:17; 2 Tim. 1:2). Paul wrote to the Corinthians that they had many teachers. The Corinthians did not lack teaching and information. Same with the church today. We have information. We have Christian everything—books, the Bible, seminars, conferences, TV and YouTube programs, schools, and seminaries. What the Corinthian church lacked, and what we lack today, are spiritual fathers. Paul exhorts, "For even if you had ten thousand others to teach you about Christ, you have only one spiritual father. For I became your father in Christ Jesus when I preached the Good News to you" (1 Cor. 4:15 NLT).

Paul birthed (mothered) and fathered the Corinthian church and many others. He understood the function of impartation and reproduction in spiritual parenting so well that he would urge the Corinthians and others to imitate him (1 Cor. 4:16; Phil. 3:17). In other places he would command, "Follow me, as I follow Christ" (1 Cor. 11:1).[33] Further, he sent them Timothy, who bore Paul's spiritual DNA. The Spirit would impart it to the Corinthians through Paul's son, Timothy; "For this reason I have sent to you Timothy, my son whom I love, who is faithful in the Lord. He will remind you of my way of life in Christ Jesus, which agrees with what I teach everywhere in every church" (1 Cor. 4:17 NIV).

Discipleship in the Church Age

The church's legacy of disciplemaking would continue with monasticism in the East (Basil: 330-379 CE), and spiritual parenting in the West (Benedict: 480-547 CE). Following the apostolic, evangelistic work of Patrick (sixth century CE), Celtic monasticism flourished at Iona under Columba (521–597 CE), Columbanus (540–615 CE), and Aidan (d. 651 CE) from the early to the high Middle Ages (500–1200 CE). Iona and its sister monasteries rigorously trained monks in a standard classical education, as well as in the Scriptures, evangelism, and discipleship. They were equipped to plant churches among unreached people groups throughout Europe, following the barbarian invasion of the Roman Empire. Celtic monasticism established a model of academic apostolic missionaries who not only spread the Christian movement but planted other monasteries that educated and trained apostolic missionaries to reproduce the process.[34] Monasticism flourished in the high Middle Ages. At that time, monastic movements led by Dominic (the Dominicans) and Francis of Assisi (the Franciscans) focused on imitating the life of Christ. The Dominicans fol-

---

33. Author's translation.

34. For more on Celtic Christianity, see George Hunter, *The Celtic Way of Evangelism* (Abingdon, 2010).

lowed Christ's model of itinerant evangelism, and the Franciscans followed Christ's model of serving the poor. Instruction and maturity in these monastic orders transpired through apprenticing under a spiritual father, often the abbot of the monastery. Monasteries served as disciplemaking centers to fulfill the Great Commission and the Great Commandment.

We also notice how intentional discipleship was integral to the flourishing of renewal movements, such as Moravianism under Count Zinzendorf (1700–1760) at Herrnhut and Methodism under John Wesley (1703–1791). They effectively employed small group ministry, prayer, training, and deploying the laity for ministry. Methodists administered specialized, small group discipleship for every stage of grace from prevenient and convincing to justifying and sanctifying. From societies, to classes, bands, penitent bands, and select bands, Methodists organized for holiness. Holiness of heart and life was their goal, and they realized that one cannot attain it alone. Methodists called it "social holiness," which meant you could not be a lone-ranger Christian. We need each other for accountability, fellowship, and the means of grace.[35] Methodism became the spiritual parent to the Holiness movement, which became a parent to the Pentecostal movement, which became a parent to the Charismatic movement and other renewalist movements in the two-thirds world. These movements are the fastest growing in the world. Multiplication through impartation!

The Prophet's Reward: Impartation

We noted earlier how Moses imparted to Joshua the Spirit and authority that was on him to lead the people (Num. 27:18–20). Impartation is the blessing and power of being a faithful spiritual son or daughter. It is the prophet's reward for sacrificing and sitting under a prophet or mentor and their ministry (Matt. 10:41). A blessing, a spiritual inheritance is passed on from the fathers and mothers to the children, just as the Holy Spirit was passed on from Christ to his disciples to continue his ministry. There is a law of spiritual reproduction at work. Just think genetically how traits are passed on to our offspring. Sons and daughters receive height, beauty, strength, intelligence, and other proclivities and gifts from their parents. As they are nurtured, those gifts develop and grow with practice until they are fully and successfully functioning. We may say, "I got my mother's intelligence" or "I have my father's strength." Those gifts were given to us and developed by our parents in our lives.

For example, I seemed to have received my father's athleticism. Both of us excelled in a variety of sports. Yet more than receiving the genetic proclivity for sports, I was also trained by him in multiple sports, especially baseball. He imparted to me his knowledge, skills, wisdom, attitude, and mindset that I received and applied to my game. Two roles had to be accepted for this synergy to take place. First, he had to be willing to take the time, have the patience, and make the effort to train me. Second, I had to be willing, humble, and teachable to receive the training. Later, I

---

35. See Kevin Watson's works on discipleship groups within Methodism, including *The Class Meeting*; *The Band Meeting*; *A Blueprint for Discipleship: Wesley's General Rules as a Guide for Christian Living*; and *Pursuing Social Holiness: The Band Meeting in Wesley's Thought and Popular Methodist Practice*.

would receive coaching and training from others who would impart to me various insights and skills.

Thus, I have been given a certain DNA, but I must exercise those raw talents in order to be proficient and not waste them. Further, others will be sent to impart to us, combining our DNA, family nurture, and our own personhood with their contribution. We become a product of nature and nurture. We are an amalgam of all who contribute to us and more because we add our own touch to it all. The whole is more than the sum of the parts. Now, the spiritual method of impartation is not exactly like passing on genes; it is a metaphor.

God through Christ has given us an abundant inheritance of spiritual gifts and fruit that if we do not humbly receive them and be trained in them, we will not walk and operate in them. He also sends us spiritual fathers and mothers into our lives to cross-pollinate their DNA with ours. We help edify and build each other. In the Spirit, I have my own DNA, but it is a product of my own contribution, along with that of countless others who have deposited spiritual riches into my life from multiple streams of the Spirit (Catholic, Orthodox, Methodist, Holiness, Pentecostal). The Spirit has integrated numerous, diverse investments along with my own into my life that comprise my overall gift, ministry, and character mix. Likewise, the same occurs for my spiritual sons and daughters. Many who already have similar personalities and calls are providentially sent my way, like my former student Jordan. The Spirit knows that these spiritual children are called into teaching, prophetic, healing, or deliverance ministries and sends them to spiritual fathers and mothers who are similarly gifted. God equips us to incubate, impart, inspire, and equip the young saints for the work of the ministry through discipleship. Often, he providentially matches us up because each need something from the other, and each has a blessing for the other. Pay attention to those who have been sent into your life. There is a reason!

Sons and Daughters First

Trigger warning! I am about to give you a tough piece of meat to chew. *You cannot disciple someone until you have been discipled—well, at least not effectively. In most cases, you cannot be a spiritual father or mother until you have been a spiritual son or daughter.* This discipleship rule of thumb is one of the most difficult for people to swallow. You will never know the veracity of this fact until you have been intentionally discipled by someone for a period of time. Once you observe Spirit-filled discipleship modeled in your own life from a spiritual father or mother, it becomes apparent what all is involved in the process. You are able to see what discipleship is and what it is not, when discipleship was taking place and when it was not. The experience is the tale of the tape.

As mentioned earlier, discipleship is not a program. It is a relationship, one involving intentional training and learning. Further, discipleship is best learned through modeling in real time. The modeling method is the reason that discipleship cannot be reduced to a program. Remember mirror neurons? The modeling method is also the reason that one needs to be discipled as a prerequisite to discipling others. The process is similar to parenting. We were all parented at some time. Our own upbringing is usually the only class we get on the subject. For better or for worse, parenting was modeled to us.[36] Upon becoming parents ourselves, we intuitively draw from what was modeled by our parents. Of course, we want to carry over the good modeling and critique and correct the poor modeling, but in either case, modeling is the initial source for our parenting (via the social brain and mirror neurons).

I repeat that one cannot be a spiritual father or mother in the fullest sense until one has been a spiritual son or daughter—not only from the topside of spiritual parenting but also from the ground up as a son or daughter. Of course, as a spiritual son or daughter, we are able to witness discipleship modeled before us. We learn spiritual parenting skills from how we were spiritually parented. But we *also* learn how to be a son or a daughter. We learn, like Christ, the obedience of a son or daughter. We learn to submit to righteous caring authority. We learn to be faithful in the small things before we are promoted to greater responsibilities. We learn to be held accountable by gentle yet firm, fair, and consistent spiritual parents. We learn incrementally to trust others who have our best interest in mind. And we learn to trust the process. It is tough to be a good spiritual parent, but it is also challenging to be a good spiritual daughter or son.

My Experience with Discipleship

I grew up in a dysfunctional home. My father was not home much, which was not good. Yet home life was much more peaceful and safer than when he was home. An abusive home environment grows broken people who do not heal quickly or at all. In terms of fathering, I basically had to raise myself and later would come to experience God as my Father and Healer. Along the way, I would gravitate to strong, caring male figures in my life, such as coaches, bosses, and professors. The Lord would use them to deposit what I needed along the way, such as acceptance, affirmation, approval, and other soul-building qualities. The father plays an indispensable role neurologically in the development of children. A father's brain goes through a special neuroplasticity to meet the challenges of fathering:

- A father's ability to empathize and mentalize during pregnancy correlates with later bonding and parenting during infancy.

---

36. Kumar Mehta, "Parenting: Instinctive or Learned? How to Ace Parenting," Forbes, October 31, 2023, https://www.forbes.com/sites/kmehta/2023/10/31/parenting-instinctive-or-learned-how-to-ace-parenting/?sh=540a430773b3. (Mehta 2023) For additional resources on parental modeling, see https://www.theparentpractice.com/blog/80-of-parenting-is-modelling https://scanva.org/parent-resource-post/parents-as-role-models/ https://www.canr.msu.edu/news/monkey_see_monkey_do_model_behavior_in_early_childhood https://www.drchristinahibbert.com/parenting-success-more-about-parent-than-child/parenting-skills/#:~:text=The%20main%20way%20we%20learn,our%20own%20%E2%80%9Cwork%E2%80%9D%20too. And see https://www.theparentpractice.com/blog/80-of-parenting-is-modelling https://scanva.org/parent-resource-post/parents-as-role-models/ https://www.canr.msu.edu/news/monkey_see_monkey_do_model_behavior_in_early_childhood https://www.drchristinahibbert.com/parenting-success-more-about-parent-than-child/parenting-skills/#:~:text=The%20main%20way%20we%20learn,our%20own%20%E2%80%9Cwork%E2%80%9D%20too.

- Specific brain areas in expectant fathers affect social information processing, self-awareness, emotion regulation, and cognitive control.
- Fathers' capacity to mentalize is key for supporting good bonding and effective parenting.[37]

I grew up Roman Catholic from birth but left the church and turned toward atheism and the partying life after my parents finally divorced. Later, I came back to Christ and was radically converted in graduate school. While serving as a prison and campus evangelist, I became part of a campus church that specialized in discipleship. Of course, I had heard of the term *discipleship* and thought I had experienced discipleship but soon learned my experience was paper thin. This particular campus ministry was a plant from Korean missionaries to the United States. The pastor approached students with an opportunity to study the Bible one-to-one. For every positive response, he would meet one-to-one weekly with that student until he had a handful of students. The first five or six students formed a small group. Additionally, each student who was being discipled one-to-one with the pastor was asked to find at least one other student to disciple. In turn, that student was asked to do the same and so on. They were asked to pour into others as they were being poured into. The first generation of the pastor's student disciples were being discipled by the pastor, leading one-to-ones, and leading their small group that was built from one-to-ones. And this process continued to the second, third, fourth generations, and so on.

Hence, no one in the church was not being discipled at least at two levels, one-to-one and in a small group. In most churches, there is no one-to-one discipleship, and small group discipleship is carved out of a church that is already large in attendance. Those churches place in small groups members who have already been attending for some time rather than discipling them from the beginning. Many leaders refuse to disciple one-to-one because they feel it is not the best use of their time. Such a belief cannot be further from the truth. I have been ministering one-to-one discipleship for nearly four decades, and I have found it to be the most powerful, effective, fruitful, and useful practice that God has employed to build his Kingdom.

I teach my students in ministry, like Jordan or my daughter Paola, that if you are a pastor, the second most important thing that you do is pastoring. If you are a music minister, the second most important thing you do relates to the music. If you are the sound technician for the worship service, the second most important thing you do is the sound. What is the most important thing? *Reproduce yourself in someone*

---

37. For more on neuroplasticity in mammalian motherhood and fatherhood, see https://www.psychologytoday.com/us/blog/experimentations/202201/neuroscience-new-fatherhood-empathy-bonding-childcare. Nathan D. Horrell, Melina C. Acosta, and Wendy Saltzman, "Plasticity of the Paternal Brain: Effects of Fatherhood on Neural Structure and Function," *Developmental Psychobiology* 63, no. 5 (2021): 1499–1520. https://doi.org/10.1002/dev.22097; James K. Rilling and Jennifer S. Mascaro, "The Neurobiology of Fatherhood," *Current Opinion in Psychology* 15 (2017): 26–32. https://doi.org/10.1016/j.copsyc.2017.02.013; Eyal Abraham and Ruth Feldman, "The Neural Basis of Human Fatherhood: A Unique Biocultural Perspective on Plasticity of Brain and Behavior," *Clinical Child and Family Psychology Review* 25 (2022): 93–109. https://doi.org/10.1007/s10567-022-00381-9.

else, like Jesus did in the Twelve. People are God's method, so build people in the Spirit. Disciple the next generation of leaders in that particular ministry. Each head of ministry should be mentoring at least one spiritual son or daughter in the Timothy 222 Principle. Everyone be raised up and raise one up.

Personally, I was discipled by the pastor. After evaluating our initial time together, he decided to disciple me. We ended up meeting three times a week for three hours a day for close to two years. Discipleship revolutionized my life like nothing else. More than conferences, seminars, seminary, personal devotional time, or Bible study, one-to-one discipleship enabled me to grow and mature in leaps and bounds. My pastor was not only a spiritual father to me but also a father who filled in the gaps that my absentee father had left. Thus, I was trained in the nuts and bolts of manhood and life as well as in the things of the Spirit.

A regular session for me and others in the church revolved around Bible study. We would study entire books of the Bible over a long period of time. In my two years with the pastor, we studied the Gospel of John and the Epistle of Romans. Reading, interpreting, questioning, responding, and applying were standard practices with each pericope or chapter of Scripture that we studied. We would open our time together with prayer and hymn singing. Accountability, questioning, and soul care would follow, as he asked how it was with my soul that day. Accountability and soul care were also addressed during the time we interpreted and applied Scripture. Following Scripture study, we prayed for the issues I was facing and that the word of God would be fruitful in my life. *Repentance was a central theme and practice throughout the session.* I was grateful for this emphasis, which is often not stressed in many of our churches. Repentance was a gamechanger for me because it opened the door to deliverance from sin and growth into maturity.

Another dimension of that discipleship relationship that was highly impactful for me was our informal time together, when we ate, fellowshipped, had coffee, or worked outdoors together. The life-to-life exchange was transformative. I was a tough kid from the street and a wannabe gangster before coming to Christ. Much of that rugged edge remained with me even after conversion. I could be quite intimidating. But my pastor didn't fear me, which was unusual for me. He had no problem looking me in the eyes and speaking the truth in love to me. He confronted me with tough love and hard truth that I should have gotten at home but never did. I think in that time period, I not only grew as a disciple of Christ, but I became a man—a man of my word, a man of responsibility, honesty, commitment, self-awareness, humility, and true courage. Discipleship and training the brain need to take place in a safe, nurturing environment where development and growth can occur.

Later, I myself would become a spiritual father to many. I took that one-to-one model of discipleship and implemented it wherever God assigned me in ministry as a missionary, pastor, church-planter, revivalist, professor, and, most importantly, into my family with my wife, two children, and granddaughter. Through me, God raised and grew a family, several churches, church turnarounds, new church starts, new mission endeavors and ministries, and hundreds of men and women of God throughout the world. The key has been intentional, Spirit-filled discipleship. Some avoid or eschew a one-to-one or one-to-two or -three format of discipleship. They believe it is not the best stewardship of their time. However, I have found it to be the most efficient and fruitful use of God's time. Direct personal discipleship allows me to pour a deeper, more impactful investment in those I know will reproduce and be fruitful. It maximizes the quality and value of my input by directing my attention into receptive minds that are potentially highly productive. Nothing falls to the ground.[38]

My one-to-one discipling relationships have never returned void but have always reproduced to at least the fourth generation. On the other hand, my experience with larger discipleship groups rarely turns out the quantity and quality of fruit that I have observed with discipling three or less. The modeling, mirroring, interacting, and internalizing, all essential for deep learning, are maximized in smaller units. Granted, there is a place for larger groups of discipleship, but if one is discipling leaders or potential leaders, there is no substitute for the personal touch of one-to-one (or -two or -three) discipleship. Rarely are we discipleship minded in this particular way, yet it is our spiritual heritage revealed in Scripture and the church age.

Discipleship is God's method for building the Kingdom. Yet we have a nation of spiritual orphans who have never been spiritually parented and trained in Christlike maturity. The result is often a church rife with immaturity, brokenness, carnality, pride, and self-centeredness. Many have even abandoned the church and returned to the world. When the church has lost the holiness and power of God and is no longer firing on all cylinders, it cannot truly minister the hope and victory of the Kingdom to a lost and dying world. The cry from Malachi is for the hearts of the fathers and mothers to turn to the children, the orphan sons and daughters, and invest in their lives. Train them in the way that they should go, lest the land be stricken and left with a curse (Mal. 4:6), which seems to be occurring in America with the current pandemic of fatherlessness. God is Father to the fatherless and yearns not only to raise daughters and sons but to do so through us (Gen. 1:28; Ps. 68:5–6).

The Case of Mike Tyson

Boxing and boxers have always fascinated me from the time I received my first pair of Hutch gloves at age six. Today, as a side job, I am the owner of a free boxing club. We run it as an outreach ministry for young men and women. We teach life through the metaphor of boxing. I am the head coach at the club, but the students see me as their life coach, their spiritual father. I have witnessed many lives changed through the sport—fatherless, motherless, abused, abandoned, addicted, and some just searching for purpose, young people needing someone in their corner who cares and can teach them a useful skill and sport that symbolizes the larger fight of life. At times, life hits hard and often. It even knocks us down. But there are no losers, only

---

38. For a further rationale on the preference for smaller discipleship groups, see Greg Ogden, *Transforming Discipleship: Making Disciples a Few at a Time* (IVP, 2003).

quitters. As Rocky Balboa instructed, "Going that one more round when you don't think you can—that's what makes all the difference in your life."[39]

I stand by my fighters in the ring and in life to encourage them and let them know it's not over as long as they have breath, with God and me in their corner. We teach them how to have hope, how to endure, how to work hard, how to reach their goals, and how to enjoy what is good. Boxing (and sports in general) has redirected tens of thousands of young people that the devil had counted out, but God had another plan for their lives. Fighters like Jack Dempsey, Jim Braddock, Joe Louis, Sonny Liston, Joe Frazier, George Foreman, Larry Holmes, and many others were all taken off the streets and out of poverty and thrust into a life of sacrifice, meaning, and purpose through the sweet science. The Lord can use anything to reach anyone.

A spiritual father made all of the difference in my life, but I am clearly not the only one. Iron Mike Tyson, born in Brooklyn in 1966, was one of the most feared and powerful heavyweights in boxing history. He was the total package of thunder and lightning, power and speed. He had the hand speed of Ali matched with the power of George Foreman. Tyson could knock his opponents out with either hand at any time. Accompanying his physical tools and prowess was his looming, daunting, menacing presence. Fighters were paralyzed with fear when facing Iron Mike. Many had already lost the fight before ever entering into the ring. Ask Michael Spinks.

As a youth, Tyson was raised on the streets of a high-crime neighborhood. There was no father in his life, and his mother was busy attempting to earn a living and taking care of three children. Without direction and several untreated mental health issues, he learned to run with the wrong crowd. Inevitably, he was involved in all types of criminal activity, having been arrested thirty-eight times by the time he reached thirteen. He was eventually sentenced to Tryon School for Boys in Johnstown, New York, a medium-security residential facility. There he met Bobby Stewart, a counselor in the detention center and former boxer. Stewart noticed that the shy young man had skills and promise and contacted the legendary trainer Cus D'Amato, also a former boxer, who trained champions like Floyd Patterson and Jose Torres. D'Amato is considered to be one of the greatest boxing managers and trainers in history. The cerebral D'Amato had the mind of a philosopher, a psychologist, and a four-star general when working with his fighters.

D'Amato was what the young reckless Tyson needed: a man of tough love and discipline, someone who could show him care and compassion while building up his brain's executive function to learn self-control and focus on the positive goal of becoming a champ. Boxing was the perfect vehicle to channel Tyson's pain and rage, and D'Amato was the funnel to harness and hone that raw energy into a lethal, ring-wrecking machine. When Tyson's mother died when he was sixteen, D'Amato became his legal guardian and Tyson lived with him.[40] Tyson was not his first disciple. D'Amato regularly took socially maladjusted young men into his home to mentor and train. D'Amato taught Tyson how to fight but also how to grow up and be a

---

39. *Rocky IV*, directed by Sylvester Stallone (MGM/UA Entertainment Company, 1985).

40. For more on Tyson's relationship with D'Amato, see Mike Tyson and Larry Sloman, *Iron Ambition: My Life with Cus D'Amato* (Blue Rider Press, 2018).

man, from responsibility, commitment, and dedication to proper dress, speech, reading habits, to handling interviews with the press. D'Amato was not only his mentor and trainer but also his spiritual father. He trained and shaped Tyson in his formative years physically, mentally, and emotionally.

Under the tutelage of D'Amato and world-class trainer Teddy Atlas, and later Kevin Rooney, Tyson found not only the right winning combination to contend for the title, but he also found a family, belonging, and the emotional glue of resonance. Tyson found meaning, purpose, and confidence under the sagacity of the shrewd D'Amato. His brain was developing, his mind was maturing, and a champion was emerging. The quotable, winsome D'Amato was known for his wisdom and philosophical wit. He taught Tyson that "the hero and the coward both feel the same thing. But the hero uses his fear, projects it onto his opponent, while the coward runs. It's the same thing, fear, but it's what you do with it that matters."[41] D'Amato's training philosophy was more than teaching slips and punches. He addressed the inner person: "I never teach until I've spoken to the fighter. I have to first determine his emotional state, get his background, to find out what I have to do, how many layers I have to keep peeling off so that I get to the core of the person so that he can recognize, as well as I, what is there."[42]

He basically built Tyson from the inside out, dealing with his inner demons, hurts, fear, contradictions, and other character flaws. D'Amato taught Tyson to face his demons and fears and not be controlled by an overactive amygdala but override it with intention and purpose. He preached, "Boxing is a sport of self-control. You must understand fear so you can manipulate it. Fear is like fire. You can make it work for you: it can warm you in the winter, cook your food when you're hungry, give you light when you are in the dark, and produce energy. Let it go out of control and it can hurt you, even kill you. . . . Fear is a friend of exceptional people."[43]

After training a fighter to face their fears (exposure therapy), he built their will to overcome: "Boxing is a contest of character and ingenuity. The boxer with more will determination, desire, and intelligence is always the one who comes out the victor."[44]

D'Amato's plan was to build up his fighter's confidence and will and to convince him that he was a champion long before he would win the title: "When two men step into the ring, one and only one deserves to win. When you step into the ring, you gotta know you deserve to win. You gotta know destiny owes you victory, 'cause you trained harder than your opponent. You sparred harder. You ran farther."[45]

The pugilistic sage was at his best when he was able to discern the raw material of talent, gifting, and desire in his students and convert it into pugilistic success. D'Amato shared his passion: "A boy comes to me with a spark of interest, I feed the

---

41. "Cus D'Amato Quotes," Reemus, accessed April 25, 2024, https://reemusboxing.com/cus-damato-quotes/. (Reemus Boxing n.d.)

42. "Cus D'Amato Quotes." (Reemus Boxing n.d.)

43. "Cus D'Amato Quotes." (Reemus Boxing n.d.)

44. "Cus D'Amato Quotes." (Reemus Boxing n.d.)

45. "Cus D'Amato Quotes." (Reemus Boxing n.d.)

spark, and it becomes a flame. I feed the flame, and it becomes a fire. I feed the fire, and it becomes a roaring blaze."[46] The fire roared on November 22, 1986, when Tyson became the youngest heavyweight champion in history, at twenty years old, by knocking out Trevor Berbick in only two rounds. D'Amato prophesied that he would be champ but died in 1985, a year before Tyson became champ.

The mentoring lessons learned and applied by D'Amato are built into the natural order of things, like the falling rain and the shining sun. One does not even have to be in a Christian discipleship relationship to watch such wisdom produce astounding results in life. How much more does a discipleship relationship produce astounding results for eternal life? The lesson learned from the story of D'Amato and Tyson is that a spiritual father, a mentor, a disciplemaker can make all of the difference in the world between a criminal and a champion. No one is beyond hope and redemption. We all need someone in our corner who will speak the truth in love to us, care for us, and help us to see God's plan for our lives. We all need someone to train us to overcome in life and in death.

The difference D'Amato made in Tyson's life was more evident after he died. Without D'Amato's direction, Tyson began to regress and revert back to his former way of thinking. Later, in 1991, he would be arrested, tried, and incarcerated for the rape of eighteen-year-old Desiree Washington. It was reported that he was physically abusive with his first wife, actress Robin Givens. Tyson served three years of a six-year sentence and was released. He came out as a registered sex offender and a convert to Islam, with prison tattoos of Communist leaders Mao Zedong and Che Guevara branded on his body. Tyson would come back and win the title again, but he was never the same, nor was his career. Under the yoke of former criminal and slippery boxing promoter Don King, Tyson no longer had the esteem for the sport as before and fought just for money. Millions went through his hands on a luxurious, lavished, hedonistic lifestyle.

Tyson received $30 million alone on his second fight with Evander Holyfield, which ended in disqualification when Tyson bit Holyfield's ear not once but twice. He was fined $6 million and temporarily lost his boxing license. Later, he was fined $5,000 and sentenced to a year in prison, two years' probation, and community service for assaulting two people. He finished his career millions of dollars in debt. Only recently has Tyson seemed to settle down and adjust socially, launching a foundation for children yet still living off of his lucrative cannabis company Tyson 2.0 and occasional exhibition bouts.[47] What a difference a spiritual father makes!

The 7 Primary Practices of Discipleship

I have discovered that many would love to disciple or be discipled, but they do not know where to begin. Again, often this is because they have never been discipled. They have no experience on which to base their ideas of discipleship. They know discipleship is in the Bible. They know it is important and must be done, but they do

---

46. "Cus D'Amato Quotes." (Reemus Boxing n.d.)

47. For more details on the life of Mike Tyson, see Mike Tyson, *Undisputed Truth.* (Penguin, 2013)

not know how. Through studying Scripture, church history, the experiences of others, and my own experience, I identified what I believe to be the seven primary practices of a discipleship relationship. A discipleship relationship should provide for these seven functions: instruction, care, fellowship, accountability, spiritual disciplines, impartation, and service. These seven facets make up a well-rounded approach to a process that can often be unwieldly. These seven practices can be modeled and taught to spiritual sons and daughters following their profession of faith and baptism. Here is an overview of each practice.

Instruction (Catechesis)

This practice is as old as the Judeo-Christian tradition. From the Talmudic and Rabbinic traditions to the early Christian catechesis, to the apologists and the Alexandrian school, throughout the Patristic age into Scholasticism, the Reformation, and into the modern era, the people of God have employed intentional instruction to better interpret and understand the faith and to shape the minds of converts. Forming the mind in the Scriptures and the doctrine of the church (belief formation) is vital to strong discipleship. How can we know and follow Christ if we do not know the truth about God and his ways? Students of Christ are called to repent, stop following the world's misguided footsteps, unlearn its ways, and follow their Savior. Two processes are working simultaneously. *There is an unlearning of old destructive thoughts and ways and a learning of new thoughts and ways.* The neuroscience of belief begins in the prefrontal cortex with study.

Early Christian discipleship process (the catechumenate) can be viewed as a rite of passage taking the new student or catechumen through the traditional three stages of a rite to passage: separation, transition, and incorporation.[48] Separation occurs when a seeker is called to leave their nets, come out of the world, and follow Christ. They renounce their sin and their former way of living and are set apart to begin a new life in Christ by preparation and catechesis. As a catechumen, they are betwixt and between where they were as a sinner, one who followed themselves, and where they will be in the future, a baptized believer serving Christ. The place of betwixt and between is a place of transition or liminality where the identity of the person is being formed. Finally, the third stage is incorporation. Through baptism, the baptizand is incorporated into the body of Christ as a new creation.

In the early church, according to the *Apostolic Tradition* by Hippolytus, catechumens, or new disciples of Christ, spent three years under the tutelage of a spiritual mentor learning Scripture, the doctrine of the church, and the moral practices of the church. During those three years they spent arduous time in repentance and even exorcism to be set from sin and Satan. They were held strictly accountable in their quest to believe and receive the faith that the apostles delivered to the saints and to live a holy life. Central to a catechumen's learning of doctrine was a proto creed (e.g.,

---

48. For more on ritual theory and rite of passage, see Arnold van Gennep, *The Rites of Passage* (Chicago University Press, 1960); and Catherine Bell, *Ritual Theory, Ritual Practice.* (Oxford University Press, 1992).

Jesus is Lord) and later a creed, such as the Apostles' Creed and the Nicene Creed. Creeds are a symbol or confession of our faith. Catechumens were being prepared for baptism and the Christian life. Through baptism, they would be initiated into the Christian faith. It was imperative to understand what one was being baptized into, if one was expected to believe and live the Christian faith. Thus, doctrine, specifically our confession of faith, is *sacramental*, tied tightly to baptism and Holy Communion.

In baptism, we are immersed into a specific faith (Christianity) that consists of truth statements comprising a narrative that we are covenanting to believe with our whole hearts and lives. The confession of faith, like the Nicene Creed, is a prayer. We are praying an affirmation of what we believe to the one in whom we believe: Father, Son, and Holy Spirit. The ancient church put it this way: *lex orandi, lex credenda* (we pray what we believe). The law of prayer is the law of belief. We pray what we believe and live. Our doctrine shapes our prayer and life. Thus, it is paramount that we get our doctrine straight.

Disciples in training were not at liberty to believe whatever they wanted to believe, unlike in some progressive, pluralistic churches today, which claim that right doctrine is not imperative. Catechumens, or students of the faith, were expected to be taught and to believe a particular body of Christian knowledge that is derived from Scripture and was handed down by the apostles and the tradition of the church (Jude 3). Specific truths about the nature of God the Father, the Son, and the Holy Spirit are to be received by new believers. Specific truths were taught about creation, the Incarnation, the virgin birth of Christ, the forgiveness of sins, salvation, the second coming of Christ, eternal judgment, worship, prayer, the work of the Spirit, the sacraments, and the church. These precious truths have been protected by the Holy Spirit and passed on to the church and are to be safeguarded because they are eternal. They are not subject to change, vote, or pick and choose. No cafeteria- or buffet-style selective preferences. For the Christian, there are no options to reject or delete and reset. Jude indicates that they "were once delivered to the saints" and that we should "contend," fight for, and defend the doctrine of the church. And indeed, the early church fought and died for the faith.

Discipleship training must involve Spirit-filled instruction both deep and wide. Often, we avoid talking about or teaching doctrine because it is said that it can be divisive. The church has thousands of denominations and perspectives. Yes, we have many expressions of the Christian faith, but at the core, orthodox Christianity is basically in agreement. We agree on the tenets in the Apostles' Creed and in the Nicene Creed. The *filioque* ("and the Son") addition to the Nicene Creed held by Roman Catholics and Protestants and the original wording held by the Orthodox represent the only exception, though a major one. Yet the more these two parties are in dialogue about the meaning and intent of the wording, the more understanding and acceptance is found. In fact, both Pope Francis of the Roman Catholic Church and Patriarch Bartholomew of the Orthodox Church have confessed in public both versions of the Creed.

There is a doctrinal core of belief, represented by the Creed, that Christians have agreed upon "everywhere," "always," and "by all" throughout the centuries, that is called the Vincentian Canon, which was declared by *St. Vincent* of Lérins (400–450 CE).[49] The core of Christian Scriptural doctrine, which has developed and superintended by the Spirit through the church, safeguards truth necessary for our salvation. These truths are expressed within the larger Scriptural doctrines of the Trinity and the Incarnation. They are revealed in Scripture and have been discerned in the first seven ecumenical councils (at least) and confessed in their creeds, representatively by the Nicene Creed and the Chalcedonian Formula (Christ is fully God and fully human). God is one Divine being, in three distinct persons: Father, Son, and Holy Spirit. The second person of the Trinity—who is fully Divine, became fully human as well, two natures (Divine and human) in one person—is Jesus Christ, who died on the cross and was resurrected for the forgiveness of our sins. We are baptized in Christ by the grace and work of the Spirit and receive salvation and live it out in holiness through faith.

Not all truths and teaching in the Christian faith are *necessary* for salvation. But these truths that are creedal, and that we confess, are salvific. There may be other beliefs and practices that are adhered to by a particular group or denomination within Christianity that are not necessarily salvific. We call these beliefs and practices *adiaphora* (indifferent), meaning they do not carry salvific import. They are neither commanded nor condemned in Scripture. Such teachings may include modes of baptism (sprinkling, pouring, immersion), forms of church government (papal, episcopal, presbyterian, congregational), theories of eschatology (premillennial, postmillennial, amillennial), assurance of salvation (unconditional or conditional). Instruction may also include teaching that is doctrinally specific to one's tradition—for example, Catholicism or Orthodoxy (the liturgy and sacraments), Charismatics (the gifts of the Spirit), Pentecostalism (the baptism of the Holy Spirit), or Wesleyanism/Methodism (entire sanctification).

Curricula and plans of specific instruction beyond core Christian doctrine may vary depending on one's church tradition, the specific focus of discipleship, and even different learning styles. Discipleship can be used to train seekers, new converts, mature believers, new leaders, seasoned leaders, or in specific areas of ministry, such as worship, Scripture study, visitation, music, healing, gifts of the Spirit, church government, evangelism, discipleship, outreach, mission, preaching, or teaching. There should also be extensive teaching in practical areas, such as finances and giving, prayer and hearing God, as well as other spiritual disciplines, and mission and minis-

---

49. For a sound explanation of the Nicene Creed and its use for teaching, see Luke Timothy Johnson, *The Creed: What Christians Believe and Why it Matters* (Doubleday, 2004). For positions for and against the adequacy of the Vincentian Canon, see the following: Thomas Guarino, *Vincent of Lérins and the Development of Christian Doctrine* (Baker, 2014); Robert Arakaki, "Defending the Vincentian Canon: 'Everywhere, Always, and By All'—A Response to Outlaw Presbyterianism," OrthodoxBridge, July 10, 2012, https://orthodoxbridge.com/2012/07/10/defending-the-vincentian-canon-everywhere-always-and-by-all-a-response-to-outlaw-presbyterianism/ Kenneth J. Stewart, "Review: *Vincent of Lérins and the Development of Christian Doctrine*," *Themelios* 38, no. 3 (2013): https://www.thegospelcoalition.org/themelios/review/vincent-of-lerins-and-the-development-of-christian-doctrine/; Joe Heschmeyer, "Development of Doctrine and St. Vincent of Lerins," Catholic Answers, December 29, 2022, https://www.catholic.com/audio/sp/development-of-doctrine-and-st-vincent-of-lerins.

try. One area of instruction that will require considerable effort is ethics. We are faced with complex choices in our day. Christians need to be trained in the Scriptures and church doctrine in order to develop a worldview whereby they can critically think, approach, dialogue, decide, and act in a way that is consonant with the person and work of Jesus Christ.

Beliefs and ethical practices related to faithfulness and idolatry; virtue and vice; honesty and deception; marriage and divorce; wealth and poverty; human sexuality and gender; race and ethnicity; health and wholeness; life and death; law, order, and Scriptural justice; war and peace; crime and punishment; AI and human intelligence, and a host of other issues challenge the faith of Christians. Leaders need to instruct on how to think scripturally, theologically, and critically about the challenges we face in this world. Neither a thin legalism of dos and don'ts, nor a flimsy liberal license to do what feels good will suffice if we are to form virtue-driven believers with any real degree of substance and depth. Fearlessly expose disciples to the truth in love.

Care

Although in discipleship we are partnering with the Spirit to instruct seekers or new converts in the faith, our responsibilities are to the whole person—spirit, soul, and body. Years of urban ministry made this quite clear to me. We are in ministry with and to the whole community and the whole person. Few actions will demonstrate the love of Christ more effectively than care, especially in practical, everyday matters that address our physicality. Love and care are inseparable. We can't just work out of our rational brain and forsake our brain's resonance system of empathy and compassion. Caring for the needs of the poor, the homeless, the hungry, the naked, the incarcerated, and the oppressed are commanded of us by Christ and manifest the inbreaking of the Kingdom. If we want to be with Christ, we need to find him in his poverty, homelessness, hunger, incarceration, and oppression (Matthew 25). He is our neighbor wounded along the side of the road. He is the ostracized leper and the outcast at the well. He is the groping blind man. He is the widow with only two mites. What we do to the least of these, we have done unto him.

Those whom we disciple should be cared for and not go without the basic necessities. Whether a spiritual mother or father provides from their own pocket or a fund from the church, we cannot feed and bless the soul but leave the body cold and hungry (Jas. 2:14–19). When I was first discipled, I struggled financially. Upon receiving Christ, I was called to leave everything, including graduate school, where I was preparing for my future career. I took on various menial jobs while the Lord was redirecting and recalibrating my life. During my period of discipleship, I was a copy machine technician making just enough to pay the bills. My spiritual father, knowing the state of my soul and livelihood, often offered to help and even cooked for me at times. It was in such times that I was blessed to see the gospel truly embodied.

Love cares in concrete ways. We must make sure that we know the full state of those who are given to our care. We should do it in a proper and respectful way as to not be pushy or offensive or to trespass their dignity. Discipling the whole person means that we do not compartmentalize facets of one's life. What we neglect or impart to the spirit affects the soul and body. And what we do or not do to the body affects the mind and the spirit. Often in discipleship relationships, I have been directed to assist in vocational counseling that involved GED preparation, helping build a résumé and interviewing skills, job searches, and dressing for success. Areas where I was limited or unqualified, I would refer.

One urban church where I pastored was situated in the largest sexually oriented business district in Ohio and the fourth largest in the country. There were a couple dozen of highly trafficked strip clubs that also involved prostitution and drug use. The Lord led us to start a new ministry to reach the women trapped in the sex industry. As mentioned earlier, we created a women's center called Oasis House.[50] I was the CEO pastor, but ultimately the women in our church operated the ministry under the leadership of our associate pastor, who is a woman. One-to-one discipleship was the heart of the ministry. However, sharing Christ also involved caring. The women's center offered GED training, a food pantry, free counseling from an in-house therapist, a free clothing boutique, life skills and boundary training, and other services. We also deployed prayer teams to prayer walk the perimeters of the club, praying for salvation and the closing of the clubs. We witnessed many salvations and many transitions into productive citizens, and over a ten-year period of time, the Lord closed down every sex club on the strip!

Fellowship

Early Methodists stressed the need for social holiness. Wesley meant that we cannot grow as disciples by ourselves. We are social creatures with a social brain (the amygdala, the ventromedial prefrontal cortex, the orbitofrontal cortex, and the temporal poles).[51] Our brains, especially the frontal lobe, are larger than any other animal's. Biologists tell us its larger size is necessary to accommodate our complex social world in which we engage. We live, love, and work as social beings. We need each other and are wired for each other. Iron sharpens iron. Each part of the body edifies the others in love (1 Corinthians 12; Eph. 4:15–16).

Though the social brain has the capacity for community, it needs to be intentionally developed, or it does not occur. Christian fellowship (*koinonia*) is not merely coming together over a cup of coffee or a meal. Both our unity and communion are in the Spirit (Acts 2:42–47; 2 Cor. 13:14; Eph. 4:3). Believers are called to know each other by the Spirit and not according to the flesh (2 Cor. 5:16). Though we are diverse in so many aspects of our lives, we are one in Christ by the Holy Spirit. The Spirit is our common uniting factor; the unity of the Spirit defines the nature of the fellowship of the saints. Our time together in the Spirit brings joy and strengthens

---

50. See https://www.oasisforwomen.org/home/ for more information. (Oasis House n.d.)

51. For more on the social brain, social cognition, mirroring, and empathy, see Ralph Adolphs, "The Social Brain: Neural Basis of Social Knowledge," *Annual Review of Psychology* 2009;60 (2009): 593–716. https://doi.org/10.1146/annurev.psych.60.110707.163514.

us as we share the work of Christ in our lives. We are able to build each other up in the Spirit.

One of Satan's most effective strategies in the life of young believers is to isolate them and convince them that they are alone. He points to their temptations, sins, failures, and struggles and accuses them that only they are going through these experiences. He brings them to the place where they think, "I am alone. No one else has my problems." Satan accomplishes his purpose to bring the self-condemning soul to a place of discouragement and defeat. On the other hand, fellowship in the Spirit can provide discernment, direction, and drive that strengthens our faith and enables us to overcome our trials and temptations. When we hear the testimonies of others, we know that we are not alone in our struggles. Others have faced similar opposition and discovered that God is faithful. Fellow believers point us to the Scriptures that undergirded their faith. The Lord created a path in the wilderness and provided streams in the desert for saints of old and will do the same for us. We experience, learn, and improve empathy (in the anterior insulate cortex and amygdala) when we are actively involved in the lives of others and practice doing unto others as we would have them do unto us.[52]

During my season at spiritual bootcamp as a young disciple, I was surprised how God could work through simple things, like shared meals, everyday talk over a cup of coffee, or working on a project together. I was edified and blessed by the Holy Spirit, who molded me through life-to-life exchange in informal settings with my spiritual father. *Affirmation, acceptance, and approval were a given.* These essential building blocks of identify formation were our starting point and not the end goal. Too many times, we find ourselves striving and running endlessly on the moral treadmill, groping for the hanging carrots before us of affirmation, acceptance, and approval. Through Christ, we are gifted with those blessings at the start of the race. Likewise, any spiritual parent worth their weight in compassion and wisdom will grant the same.

Because affirmation was modeled before me, I was empowered to do likewise. I heard their words and witnessed their actions for myself. I knew what it looked like and felt like to belong unconditionally because of the pardoning love of Christ. Nothing excites me more than to speak words of life and hope into my spiritual (and natural) children. To watch the smile, the countenance, and the confidence emerge in others when releasing encouragement lights my candle as well. Disciplemakers need to learn to speak the language of encouragement as their primary ministry language if they do not already. *Encouragement* means to inject courage into another. We can accomplish this with our presence, words, and actions. We have the power to cata-

---

52. Abigail A. Marsh, Elizabeth C. Finger, Katherine A. Fowler, Christopher J. Adalio, Ilana T. N. Jurkowitz, Julia C. Schechter, Daniel S. Pine, Jean Decety, and R. J. R. Blair, "Empathic Responsiveness in Amygdala and Anterior Cingulate Cortex in Youths with Psychopathic Traits," Journal of Child Psychology and Psychiatry, and Allied Disciplines 54, no. 8 (2013): 900–910. https://doi.org/10.1111/jcpp.12063 (Marsh, et al. 2013).

pult people over the top with our support. And the good news is that it doesn't cost anything to lift up our neighbor.

Those whom I disciple are assured and certain that I am in their corner regardless of how the fight unfolds. I am there to wipe away the sweat from their eyes, to bind and clean up their cuts, to hydrate their souls with living water, and to speak words of wisdom and strength into their hearts so that they can overcome in the ring of life. Affirmation, acceptance, and approval in Christ Jesus enables us to do all things that we are called to do because of the power that works within us. Early in my Christian walk, these edifying practices changed me from being a "can't-do" person into a 'can-do" person. Their innate power gave me the breakthrough I needed to overcome in life. Tried, tested, and true! Upon seeing the results, I began to relay those blessings to others whom I was mentoring. Turning can't-doers into can-doers is one of my favorite pastimes. The world has enough can't-doer attitudes. Let us repopulate the world with never-say-die can-doers for Christ.

Encouragement and motivation have their correlates in the brain. The neuroscientific dynamics of motivation comprises three main areas and functions: "the motivation-related phenomena as functions of the ventral striatum involved in reinforcement learning, the orbitofrontal cortex (OFC) region linked to value judgment and decision-making, and the anterior cingulate cortex (ACC) and the dorsolateral prefrontal cortex (DLPFC) regions associated with executive function and cognitive control."[53] Motivation is *generated* by our brain's reward-driven system. The *maintenance* of motivation is sustained by our brain's value-based decision-making process (hierarchy of preferences), and the *regulation* of motivation is controlled by goal-directed control process.[54] We will discuss more about the neuroscience of motivation in Chapter 4 regarding the cognitive neuroscience of addiction and in Chapter 5 regarding the neuroscience of resistance. Simply put, the promises of God, spoken by others to us and we to ourselves, that we can enjoy pursuing and attaining heavenly goals is the fuel we need to achieve them. Jesus endured the anguish of the cross because he reminded himself of the joy that was awaiting him in heaven, to sit at the right hand of the Father (Heb. 12:2).

We notice this type of encouragement even in the relationship between the Father and his Son, Jesus Christ. Prior to Christ's earthly ministry and his temptation in the wilderness, Jesus, fulfilling all righteousness, was baptized. When Jesus came up out of the water, the Spirit of God, like a dove, descended on him. Then he heard his Father's voice from heaven: "This is my Son, whom I love; with him I am well pleased" (Matt. 3:15–17 NIV). Simply mind-blowing! Before Jesus resisted the devil, before he preached one sermon, before he taught one lesson in the synagogue, before he healed one sick person, before he cast out any demons, before he performed one miracle, before he did anything, his Father was *already* pleased with him. He was

---

53. Sung-il Kim, "Neuroscientific Model of Motivational Process," *Frontiers in Psychology* 4 (2013): 98. https://doi.org/10.3389/fpsyg.2013.00098. (Kim 2013)

54. Kim, "Neuroscientific Model of Motivational Process." (Kim 2013)

pleased with who he was *before* he was pleased with what he did. The Word was with the Father from all eternity as his Son, his beloved Son (John 1:1–3, 17). Through the Incarnation, the Word became human, the person Jesus Christ.

From all eternity and in time and space, the Father loved the Son, and the Son loved the Father. Their loving relationship preceded and empowered Christ's performance. He was loved as a Son long before he did any works to please the Father. Jesus' *being* came before his *doing*. He was loved, affirmed, approved, accepted based on who he was (Son) rather than on what he did (his works). From the solid base of a loving relationship with the Father, Christ was empowered and moved to do the work of a Son. Christ knew who he was, whose he was, where he came from, and where he was going. His identity was eternally settled. The bond between Christ and the Father was the source and the drive to fulfill the mission on the cross. Nothing, not even Satan, could stop him (John 13:3; 14:30). The power of *koinonia*!

Accountability

John Wesley, the founder of Methodism, organized the movement into discipleship groups. He was influenced by the *collegia pietatis* (small groups for piety or holiness) of pietism and similarly the *choirs* (a discipleship cell group, not for singing) of Moravianism under Count Zinzendorf. These groups were designed so that members could grow spiritually through prayer, Bible study, and accountability. In early Methodism, groups, such as societies, classes, bands, penitent bands, and select bands, were formed based on the level of maturity and commitment of the believer. Accountability was one of the main functions and strengths of Methodist small groups.[55]

Initially, Methodist societies were formed within Anglicanism for prayer and to help seekers "flee from the wrath to come and to be saved from their sins." They met weekly, usually on Thursdays. *Societies* were further divided into *classes*, comprising twelve members and a leader. The leader that would visit class members and inquire how their souls were prospering. Early monastics took three vows (poverty, chastity, and obedience) and had three rules (humility, silence, and obedience). Wesley, likewise, drew up three general rules for the Methodists. Members of a society were to be held accountable to the Methodist General Rules: (1) do no harm by avoiding evil of every kind; (2) do good to all people through works of mercy; and (3) attend upon all the ordinances of God, such as worship service, reading and studying Scripture, taking Holy Communion, praying, fasting, self-denial, and other acts of piety or means of grace (practices that convey the grace of God to us).[56] Early Methodist leaders and members took seriously the covenants formed in these groups: "If there be any

---

55. See Kevin Watson's works on discipleship groups within Methodism, including *The Class Meeting, the Band Meeting, a Blueprint for Discipleship: Wesley's General Rules as a Guide for Christian Living* (Discipleship Resources, 2009); and *Pursuing Social Holiness: The Band Meeting in Wesley's Thought and Popular Methodist Practice.* (Oxford University Press, 2014)

56. "The General Rules of the Methodist Church," United Methodist Communications, accessed May 7, 2024, https://www.umc.org/en/content/the-general-rules-of-the-methodist-church. (The United Methodist Church n.d.)

among us who observe them not, who habitually break any of them, let it be known unto them who watch over that soul as they who must give an account. We will admonish him of the error of his ways. We will bear with him for a season. But then, if he repent not, he hath no more place among us. We have delivered our own souls."[57]

The Methodist band meeting, for the more mature, usually had around five people of the same sex and marital status for the purpose of accountability, confessing sin, and prayer. They gathered to assist each other in living a holy and victorious life over temptation and sin. The select bands were for those seeking entire sanctification or Christian perfection. And the penitent bands were for those who had fallen back into sin and were being called to repent and return to Christ (in recovery).

Wesley's Rules for Band-Societies

Drawn up December 25, 1738.

The design of our meeting is, to obey that command of God, "Confess your faults one to another, and pray one for another, that ye may be healed . . ."

To this end, we intend.

1. To meet once a week, at the least.

2. To come punctually at the hour appointed, without some extraordinary reason.

3. To begin (those of us who are present) exactly at the hour, with singing or prayer.

4. To speak each of us in order, freely and plainly, the true state of our souls, with the faults we have committed in thought, word, or deed, and the temptations we have felt, since our last meeting.

5. To end every meeting with prayer, suited to the state of each person present.

6. To desire some person among us to speak his own state first, and then to ask the rest, in order, as many and as searching questions as may be, concerning their state, sins, and temptations.

Some of the questions proposed to everyone before he is admitted among us may be to this effect.

1. Have you the forgiveness of your sins?

2. Have you peace with God, through our Lord Jesus Christ?

3. Have you the witness of God's Spirit with your spirit, that you are a child of God?

4. Is the love of God shed abroad in your heart?

5. Has no sin, inward or outward, dominion over you?

6. Do you desire to be told of your faults?

---

57. "The General Rules of the Methodist Church." (The United Methodist Church n.d.)

7. Do you desire to be told of all your faults, and that plain and home?

8. Do you desire that every one of us should tell you, from time to time, whatsoever is in his heart concerning you?

9. Consider! Do you desire we should tell you whatsoever we think, whatsoever we fear, whatsoever we hear, concerning you?

10. Do you desire that, in doing this, we should come as close as possible, that we should cut to the quick, and search your heart to the bottom?

11. Is it your desire and design to be on this, and all other occasions, entirely open, so as to speak everything that is in your heart without exception, without disguise, and without reserve?

Any of the preceding questions may be asked as often as occasion others; the four following at every meeting.

1. What known sins have you committed since our last meeting?

2. What temptations have you met with?

3. How were you delivered?

4. What have you thought, said, or done, of which you doubt whether it be sin or not?[58]

Wesley also offered Methodists twenty-two questions for self-examination.

Wesley's 22 Questions for Self-Examination and Accountability

1. Am I consciously or unconsciously creating the impression that I am better than I really am? In other words, am I a hypocrite?

2. Am I honest in all my acts and words, or do I exaggerate?

3. Do I confidentially pass on to another what was told to me in confidence?

4. Can I be trusted?

5. Am I a slave to dress, friends, work, or habits?

6. Am I self-conscious, self-pitying, or self-justifying?

7. Did the Bible live in me today?

8. Do I give it time to speak to me every day?

9. Am I enjoying prayer?

10. When did I last speak to someone else about my faith?

11. Do I pray about the money I spend?

---

58. "Wesley's Rules for Band-Societies," House Church, accessed May 7, 2024, https://housechurch.org/miscellaneous/wesley_band-societies.html. (Wesley, Wesley's Rules for House Churches 1738)

12. Do I get to bed on time and get up on time?

13. Do I disobey God in anything?

14. Do I insist upon doing something about which my conscience is uneasy?

15. Am I defeated in any part of my life?

16. Am I jealous, impure, critical, irritable, touchy, or distrustful?

17. How do I spend my spare time?

18. Am I proud?

19. Do I thank God that I am not as other people, especially as the Pharisees who despised the publican?

20. Is there anyone whom I fear, dislike, disown, criticize, hold a resentment toward or disregard? If so, what am I doing about it?

21. Do I grumble or complain constantly?

22. Is Christ real to me?[59]

Some of Wesley's rules and questions tend to be dated and relevant for life in eighteenth-century English society. They would need to be updated and contextualized for our use today. Other rules seem to be more universal and hold their value across time and place. Their purpose is for self-examination (2 Cor. 13:5), cross-examination, and accountability in a group setting (Jas. 5:16). As the analytic psychologist Carl Jung taught us, the archetype of the shadow lurks hidden deep within each of us. In the raw, dark underground of our subconscious, our shadow side, "the hidden masked face of our inner, unwanted other," is lodged, waiting to arise.[60] Often, we cannot detect our own dark side. The prophet Jeremiah pointed out, "The human heart is the most deceitful of all things, and desperately wicked. Who really knows how bad it is?" (Jer. 17:9). The Apostle Paul poignantly describes how we fall short of our best attempts at being good and doing the right thing. He cries out, "For I do not do the good I want to do, but the evil I do not want to do—this I keep on doing" (Rom. 7:19 NIV). Satan blinds us, and sin deceives us from seeing the truth about the contradictions and hypocrisy in our own heart (Matt. 7:5; 2 Cor. 4:4; Heb. 3:13). We need the caring and keen eyes of another to help us spot our blind side. We also need the sword of the Lord and the Spirit to penetrate the depths of our soul and spirit in order to reveal the hidden motives, intentions, and thoughts of our hearts (Heb. 4:12).

---

59. "John Wesley's 22 Questions of Self Examination," United Methodist Communications, accessed May 7, 2024, https://www.umc.org/en/content/john-wesleys-22-questions-of-self-examination (Wesley, John Wesley's 22 Questions of Self Examination 2024)

60. Peter Bellini, *Artificial General Intelligence (AGI) and the Image of God: Can Machines Attain Consciousness and Receive Salvation?* (Wipf and Stock, 2023), 108. (P. J. Bellini, Artificial General Intelligence (AGI) and the Image of God 2023)

However, like King David, we also need to be humble and open to the light and conviction of the Spirit that exposes our sins and our secrets (Ps. 17:3; 26:2; 51; 139:23). Our flesh will fight us to the death to keep our sins hidden so that we can continue in them. Satan will fight us to the death to keep our sins hidden so that he can keep us bound and serve his purposes. Repentance and confession, though gifts from God's grace, do not come easy for us because we rebel and fight God, and our spirit and flesh war within us.

Thus, we are called to examine diligently our hearts and motives to discern if we are right with God and others. Examination and confession are enhanced when we are held graciously accountable by our brothers and sisters in Christ. Our brothers and sisters can see what we cannot. They can see what our blind side will not reveal. James commands us to confess our sins to each other, especially if we have sinned against another (Jas. 5:16; Matt. 5:23–25; 18:15–20; Luke 17:3). We are also promised that our sins will be forgiven, and we will be healed.

Accountability can be a powerful instrument of grace if it is used properly. It can also become a weapon for abuse if held improperly. Confession and accountability should be practiced with mature, safe persons who have demonstrated their ability to hold confidentiality, restore others in a spirit of meekness, and minister with grace and truth. Grace and truth constitute the gospel balance that prevents the poisoning polarity of both license and legalism from taking root.

We need a non-anxious presence who is filled with the fruit of the Spirit, especially love and gentleness, to hold us accountable. We need caring people, who, like Christ, "will not crush the weakest reed or put out a flickering candle" (Matt. 12:20 NLT). Their words are not careless but well thought out and measured before speaking and seasoned with salt (Prov. 15:28; Col. 4:6). We need truth-tellers who do not fear telling it like it is (Gal. 4:16). They can call it as they see it. A ball is a ball, and a strike is a strike (2 Sam. 12:7). Yet we need safe truth-tellers who can speak the truth in love (Eph. 4:15). The purpose of accountability is not gossip, evil-speaking, humiliation, condemnation, or destroying one's reputation. Accountability is opening one's heart before the Lord and a safe mature person so that they can cowork with the Spirit in grace and truth to assist one in the process of repentance and restoration and to encourage one with one's presence, words, and actions. Those who are called to hold us accountable are in our corner to help us overcome. I can attest to many spiritual sons being delivered of certain stubborn addictions with the help of godly accountability.

Spiritual Disciplines

We referenced early Methodism's "method" of accountability through small groups and "attending the means of grace," which is shorthand for practicing spiritual disciplines. The two—accountability and spiritual disciplines—are inexorably connected. They work as a dialectic, or they speak to each other. We are held accountable to practice spiritual disciplines. And we practice spiritual disciplines because they empower us to be held accountable. *Spiritual disciplines are grace-led practices that allow us to experience God*—for example, attending worship, Scripture reading and study, praying, fasting, abstinence, silence, solitude, accountability, self-denial in any area, confession, fellowship, rest (sabbath), giving, even disciple-making.[61] Christ, his disciples, and believers throughout the church age have used spiritual disciplines to build up the body of Christ.

Spiritual disciplines are for spiritual *exercise* to strengthen and shape us in the image of God in Christ. One of my hobbies is powerlifting. Even in my older age, I daily lift weights for strength and fitness. My daily routines throughout the week hit every muscle group and area of my body. I do not want to be imbalanced, as some lifters can be. They hit one muscle group hard, like the arms or the chest but neglect the legs or back. Their appearance becomes asymmetrical and their strength imbalanced.

When I was younger, my lifting and diet plan as a powerlifter was to lift as much as I could and eat as much as I could. I can no longer afford to overeat or eat the wrong foods at my age. Some people are picky eaters. That was never my problem. In terms of spiritual disciplines, we cannot afford to be picky. No one likes to fast. Personally, I run from it. Nonetheless, there is no substitute for fasting if one wants to break the power of a stubborn sin in one's life. When I need to get close to God to hear his voice concerning an important matter, I would be foolish not to couple prayer with fasting. *When our bodies are hungry and weak, our spirit becomes hungry and strong. A decrease in the flesh equates to an increase in the spirit.*

Whether we are studying Scripture, practicing silence or solitude, praying, or any of the other spiritual disciplines, we need to hit every area of our life with each spiritual practice if we are to grow. I never heard of a disciple who doesn't pray or study Scripture. Similarly, I never witnessed a believer walk in the authority and power of Christ who has never fasted, practiced solitude, or self-denial. We cannot partake of the spiritual disciplines via cafeteria-style, picking and choosing. A balanced spiritual diet of holy habits done right will enable us to grow in Christlikeness. Further, we recognize that we do not eat merely for eating's sake. Along with the satiating taste, we eat food for its nutrients that build a healthy body. I do not exercise for the sake of exercising but for fitness and strength. Likewise, spiritual disciplines are a blessing, and they are satisfying to our spirit. But ultimately, they are not an end in themselves. They lead us to God. God is the only end in himself. Spiritual disciplines appropriately and successfully practiced bring us closer to the Lord.

We learn to exercise the spiritual disciplines properly and effectively when they are modeled in a discipleship relationship. In such a learning environment, we move from abstract knowledge about prayer, fasting, or study to concrete experience lived before us. Whether as a powerlifter, boxer, baseball player, garage mechanic, or a

---

61. To read more on the spiritual disciplines, see the classic by Richard Foster, *Celebration of Discipline: The Path to Spiritual Growth* (HarperCollins, 2018).

three-chord, pentatonic scale guitarist, a sizeable portion of what I have learned was transferred to me through modeling. Sometimes, an explanation is not enough. We need to see what it looks like in real life and in real time.

The power of spiritual disciplines is that they are rhythmic and ritualistic in nature. When we practice spiritual disciplines, we often establish a routine and an order of implementation. We ritualize them. For example, monastics live by an order or a rule. Monks follow an order that functions ritualistically in their daily lives. Consider how monks pray. St. Benedict in 516 CE established canonical hours for daily prayer (Ps. 119:62): Matin or Vigils, Lauds, Prime, Terce, Sext, None, Vespers, and Compline.[62] The ritual of the Daily Office with Canonical Hours enables the monk or nun to incorporate prayer as a part of his or her life rather than seeing it as a detached practice. Ritual facilitates integration. When practices are ritualized, they significantly assist to integrate the content of the practice into our learning and our identity. When ritualized, spiritual disciplines become a part of who we are. Their rhythms are integrated into the song of our life. We are engineering neuroplasticity that is being reinforced with each repetition.

Also, through spiritual disciplines we are united not only with God but with other members of the body of Christ who participate in the same disciplines apart from us or together with us. Neuroscientist Andrew Newberg, referencing his colleague, anthropologist Eugene D'Aquili, writes, "Rituals act to synchronize affective, perceptual-cognitive, and motor processes within the central nervous system of individual participants. Rituals synchronize these processes among the various individual participants."[63] The disciplines as rituals join us with God and others and strengthen our own personal integration as beings of wholeness and wellness. Newberg claims spiritual rituals "not only helped connect people to each other but also to the basic beliefs of a given religious or spiritual tradition."[64] Effective rituals strengthen the impact of discipleship and Christian identity personally and with the body of Christ.

Finally, a healthy approach to spiritual disciplines recognizes that although they require "discipline," working them does not earn us salvation. God does not grant us his favor because we worked hard for it. The truth is that spiritual disciplines can be hard. They do require discipline. However, God's grace prompts us to exercise them and empowers us to practice and complete them. Though we work, God is working in us and gives us the desire and "the power to do what pleases him" (Phil. 2:13 NLT).

---

62. "Canonical Hours," Constitutions of Clarendon, April 22, 2014, https://conclarendon.blogspot.com/2014/04/canonical-hours.html. (Roberts 2014)

63. Newberg, *Neurotheology*, 184 (Newberg, Neurotheology: How Science Can Enlighten Us About Spirituality 2021); Eugene D'Aquili and Andrew Newberg, *The Mystical Mind: Probing the Biology of Religious Experience.* (Fortress Press, 1999) (D'Aquili and Newberg 1999)

64. Newberg, *Neurotheology*, 111 (Newberg, Neurotheology: How Science Can Enlighten Us About Spirituality 2021); D'Aquili and Newberg, *The Mystical Mind.* (D'Aquili and Newberg 1999)

Impartation

One of my favorite pastimes is to research genealogies. I have researched and put together a thorough family genealogy. On my mother's side of the family, I can trace our lineage to the 1500s with documentary evidence. I can loosely go back another three hundred years but without as much solid evidence. I am always elated to find a new piece of information, a new piece to the puzzle that fits in with the whole picture.

As an academic, I am also intrigued by genealogies of various thinkers and movements. Following the permeating, mastodonic influences of philosophers like Plato and Aristotle on major philosophical figures for over two thousand years is transfixing. Tracing the intricate, recondite genealogies of the Pentecostal-Charismatic movement through the scattered, unrenowned fire starters and prudent, modest messengers who are peculiarly pixilated together in a cacophonous web that in part eventually winds up at John Wesley is enthralling. Even seeming atom-like anonymities can influence an astronomical spiritual movement like Pentecostalism, not because of who they are but because of what they bear and to whom they are connected.

Consider the genealogy and genius of rock and roll music. It is a shimmering confluence of gesticulating, sonorous streams, protean and opulent with talent, form, and flair. Its rich, robust DNA of homespun beats is a double helix of gospel, jazz, blues, and rhythm and blues, wound together with swing, boogie-woogie, folk, country, and country blues, among others. The translation, transmission, and transference of sonics, moods, motion, reverie, and textures through a cadre of unlikely theatrical personae is nothing short of a chimeric miracle. The spirit of music!

That the dual harmony (diatonic thirds) of Don and Phil Everly was imprinted on the lips of John Lennon and Paul McCartney, that Chuck and Elvis taught them how to rock and roll, that Buddy Holly's Crickets likely influenced the name Beatles, that early on Brian Epstein taught the Beatles to dress in uniform like Cliff Richard and the Shadows, that Paul practically nicked Little Richard's vocal attack, that Dylan's nasal crooning rubbed off on John and a generation of folkies, and that George learned his guitar licks from Carl Perkin's records illustrates the contagion of impartation.

Speaking of impartation, when Ron Argent of the band Argent, and before that the Zombies, sang their hit "God Gave Rock and Roll to You" in 1973, he may not have been lying. Think about the gospel forerunners and foundations of rock and roll: Elvis Presley, Jerry Lee Lewis, Little Richard, Arizona Dranes, Bo Didley, Marvin Gaye, Mabel John, Carl Perkins, Rosetta Tharpe, and B. B. King were all raised Pentecostal. Hank Williams, Thomas Dorsey, Chuck Berry, James Brown, Aretha Franklin, Mahalia Jackson, Johnny Cash, Etta James, Sam Cooke, Al Green, Ray Charles, and Diana Ross were nurtured in the Baptist church. Merle Haggard, Pat Boone, and Loretta Lynn were brought up in the Church of Christ. Catholicism birthed Dion DiMucci and Fats Domino (later Baptist). The Everly Brothers were Methodist. Much later, the church gave popular music Bob Dylan, Van Morrison, Alice Cooper,

Tina Turner, Donna Summer, Whitney Houston, Amy Grant, U2, Katy Perry, John Legend, Justin Timberlake, Jack White, Faith Hill, Carrie Underwood, and others.[65]

This section is about impartation in discipleship. Few phenomena illustrate the contagion and power of influence and impartation like music. Simply ponder what the Beatles meant for the 1960s, nothing short of invention. Music is spiritual. Nothing transports us to the throne room and into the presence of God like anointed worship music—ask King David, the psalmist. Yet the music is just the form or the vehicle that God employs. The source and content of the contagion and the power of anointed music is the Holy Spirit. He is the impartation itself, the agent of Divine experience. As the spirit of music flowed through the various artists mentioned, each influencing and giving to the next generation and movement, so also the Spirit of God flows through and unites believers from movement to movement across generations.

We noted this generational transference from spiritual parents to their children throughout Scripture and the history of the church. The transfer and impartation of the giftings, anointings, and ministries of God are solidified and codified in the ancient Scriptural doctrine and practice of the laying on of hands (Num. 27:23; Deut. 34:9; Mark 8:23; 16:18; Acts 8:18; 19:6; 1 Tim. 4:14; 5:22; 2 Tim. 1:6; Heb. 6:2). Discipleship, like music, generates offspring and communicates its DNA to its spiritual children. If we are truly the disciples of Christ, we will bear much fruit, being fruitful and multiplying disciples (Gen. 1:22, 28; John 15:1–8). Believers are given the power and the expectancy to reproduce through the Holy Spirit. And when we reproduce, we impart spiritual genes, which includes ministries, giftings, anointings, and other spiritual traits and characteristics. Spiritual generation, transmission, and impartation are exemplified with Christ and his disciples and the subsequent generations of spiritual children throughout the church age. So lay hands on those whom you are training and pray for the impartation of the Holy Spirit.

What is transmitted when we lay on hands and pray? Surely, it is not the person's ability or his or her natural traits but the Holy Spirit and the Spirit's ability. Nonetheless, the Spirit does indwell our earthen vessels. He uses us and all that we are. We are the packaging that the Spirit comes in and through, but not the content. Our personhood and all of its distinctions, features, characteristics, and idiosyncrasies are the vehicle through which the Spirit is communicated. The spiritual DNA of our spiritual parents is deposited in us through discipleship (life-to-life transference), and it influences us and mixes with our own spiritual identity to help form and develop us into maturity. Christianity is not gnostic or a mere acquiring and transferring of information. Christianity is an embodied faith based on the bodily incarnation and resurrection of the Son of God. The Spirit of God and Christian beliefs are embodied in our lives and influence others through us, a holy contagion. We have been given

---

65. For connections between gospel music, Christianity, and rock and roll, see Greg Laurie, *Lennon, Dylan, Alice, and Jesus: The Spiritual Biography of Rock and Roll* (Regnery, 2022); J. Othello, *The Soul of Rock and Roll: A History of African Americans in Rock Music* (Regent, 2004); and Leah Payne, *God Gave Rock and Roll to You.* (Oxford University Press, 2024)

the grace and the gift to inject spiritual vitamin B12 in the lives of whom we disciple. What a blessing!

My spiritual father and other spiritual aunts and uncles have imparted wisdom, knowledge, discipline, and maturity in my life. They put dense muscle on my boney spiritual frame. Likewise, God has used me to jump-start, fire up, turbocharge, and accelerate the lives of so many of my students in the local church, in seminary, and in the ministry. You become the Cus D'Amato that a raw, unseasoned soul needed to take him or her over the top and become a champion for Christ.

As we draw the parallel between natural parenting and spiritual parenting, let us learn from the full extent of the analogy. As there are good, loving, wise, and mature parents who parent in a healthy manner, there are also not so good, loving, wise, and mature parents who parent in an unhealthy manner. Unfortunately, I have seen spiritual parenting and discipleship become legalistic and abusive when taken on by immature and misguided leaders. They exploited the discipleship process by using it as an occasion to attract followers to serve themselves.

In the late 1960s and early '70s, the Jesus Movement broke out among the flower power, hippie generation. Young people came to Christ in droves and were converted and baptized. The generation that experimented with free love, LSD, and transcendental meditation was now being called to repent and give their lives to Christ, and they came en masse. The "turn on, tune in, dropout" crowds that rebelled against parental, societal, and governmental authority were now being asked to follow the authority of Jesus as their Lord. Understandably, leaders realized that intentional discipleship would be required, as the new converts were called to unlearn sinful habits and learn holy ones

Seeking to correct the free-living hippie zeitgeist, often rigid and excessive forms of discipleship were implemented that were tantamount to spiritual abuse. One such case was the highly influential Shepherding Movement. It required its adherents to strictly submit to authoritarian overseers or "shepherds" and their rigid rules and direction concerning every area of life, including decisions about where to live and whom to marry.[66] The heavy-handed shepherds in the movement often appealed to the gifts of the Spirit and "hearing God's voice" to ground their authority and substantiate their dictates and control. However, Christ taught us that true leadership is humble, does not abuse authority, and does not lord its rule over others as the Gentile's sovereigns do. In contrast, Christ requires that leaders who want "to become great among you must be your servant, and whoever wants to be first must be slave of all" (Mark 10:43–44 NIV).

Broken, unhealed, toxic traits in people can be communicated to spiritual children from spiritual parents who should never have taken up the vocation and ministry. Hurt people hurt people. Broken people break people. Controlled people control people—and so on. Spiritual fathers and mothers are qualified by being spiritual sons and daughters of healthy spiritual parents. In our pawky, lethiferous depravity,

---

66. For a scholarly history and critique of the Shepherding Movement, see S. David Moore, *The Shepherding Movement: Controversy and Charismatic Ecclesiology* (Continuum, 2004).

111

it does not take much for an immature, maladjusted, or even a typical well-adjusted, individual to slip into control, manipulation, and abuse if left unaware, unguarded, and unaccountable. Like parenting, spiritual parenting is not to be entered into and taken up lightly. It's a call for the spiritual healthy and mature.

Service

Throughout Scripture, the people of God were called to care for and serve the well-being of others, especially the poor, the downtrodden, and the outcasts. Care for the poor and benevolence were mandated in the law and reinforced by the prophets. Christ's ministry was to take care of the least of these, and he commanded his disciples to do likewise (Matthew 25). Following Christ's example, the early church likewise cared for the needy among its sister churches (Acts 2:44; 6:1–7; 11:25–30; 24:17; Rom. 16:16; 1 Cor. 16:1–4; 2 Cor. 9:1–2; Gal. 2:10). Monasticism throughout its history, beginning in the fourth century, combined acts of service with their study and daily hours as a logical outcome of their discipleship. Monastic orders fed the poor; clothed the naked; housed the homeless; built hospitals, charities, and agencies to minister to those affected by poverty, disaster, or war.[67] Zinzendorf at Herrnhut provided for all of the social needs and livelihood for its inhabitants. Early Methodists under John Wesley opened schools, free clinics, pharmacies, and lending services to the poor.[68] Wesley's ministry with the poor continued with his spiritual sons and daughters in the holiness movements, evangelicalism, and mainline Methodism.[69] Simply put, the evangelical mandate to preach the gospel and the cultural mandate to serve the poor and the rest of society must work together.

In my experience discipling others, I have always been careful to assure that all forms of discipleship from one-to-one to small groups performed all seven of the practices that have been mentioned, even service. Compassionate service is the natural outcome of training disciples to be like Christ because we are called to imitate Christ and obey his commands to bring good news to the poor, declare freedom for the prisoners, healing to the blind and brokenhearted, and release the oppressed (Isa. 61:1–2; Luke 4:18). If we are teaching believers to follow Christ, they need to follow

---

67. See Alvin J .Schmidt, *How Christianity Changed the World* (Zondervan, 2004); Mike Aquilina and James L. Papandrea, *How Christianity Saved Civilization . . . and Must Do So Again* (Sophia Institute Press, 2019); Greg Peters, *The Story of Monasticism: Retrieving an Ancient Tradition for Contemporary Spirituality* (Baker, 2015).

68. See Theodore W. Jennings Jr., *Good News to the Poor: John Wesley's Evangelical Economics* (Abingdon, 1990) (Jennings 1990); Richard Heitzenrater, *The Poor and the People Called Methodists* (Abingdon, 2002).

69. Roger J. Green, *The Life and Ministry of William Booth: Founder of the Salvation Army* (Abingdon, 2006); David C. Kirkpatrick, *A Gospel for the Poor: Global Social Christianity and the Latin American Evangelical Left* (University of Pennsylvania Press, 2019) (Kirkpatrick 2019); Donald Dayton, *Rediscovering an Evangelical Heritage*, 2nd ed. (Baker, 2014) (Dayton 2014); Janine Giordano Drake, *The Gospel of Church: How Mainline Protestants Vilified Christian Socialism and Fractured the Labor Movement* (Oxford University Press, 2023) (Drake 2023).

him to the poor, the hungry, the naked, the homeless, and the incarcerated, for that is where he is waiting for us.

TEACHING OUTLINES: A STUDY GUIDE FOR DISCIPLESHIP

We have included a sample curriculum with various outlines that one can use for discipleship training. While some of these outlines reflect an explicit Wesleyan heritage, many of the ideas expressed are similar to discipleship models from other traditions.

Discipleship Basics

1. **Discipleship:** Definitions
   a. Disciple = *mathetes* = a student or a learner. In ancient learning, students sought out masters (rabbi) to live with them and learn from them by their words and life.
   b. Disciple = a disciplined learner and follower of Jesus Christ.
   c. Discipleship = the disciplined process of learning and following Jesus.

4. **Discipleship:** How to do it (Matt 28:18–20; 7:24–29; 11:28–30)
   a. Learn/teach Jesus' Word for obedience.
   b. Teach from the word of God. Teach what Jesus taught.
   c. Learn from the word. Learn to obey Jesus.
   d. Learn/teach from the word and life shared.

5. **Discipleship:** Qualities of a disciple
   a. Teachable and good listener (Matt 11:5, 29)
   b. Humble (Matt. 18:3)
   c. Spiritual hunger (Matt. 5:6)
   d. Availability and radical commitment (Matt. 4:19–20; 16:24–28)
   e. Faithful and loyal (Matt. 5:33–37; 7:21–23; 10:17–25, 37–39)

THE MATTHEW MODEL:
A FRAMEWORK FOR DISCIPLESHIP

1. **Our Purpose:** Make disciples of all nations (Matt. 28:16–20).
   a. The Master-Student Model: Jesus raise disciples. Goal - to learn from the Master and be like the Master.
   b. Disciples were appointed by Jesus (28:16).
   c. Now, we make disciples by his authority (28:19).
   d. We are called to make disciples of all people (28:19).
   e. We do this by teaching people God's word for the purpose of obedience. Teach people to obey God's word. **Jesus Is our Teacher:** Jesus is both our Teacher and our Lesson (11:25–30).
   f. The Truth is hidden from the proud. We must be humble to receive (11:25).
   g. We are called to *submit* to God's revelation, the Word (11:25–27).
   h. We submit by becoming like little children (11:25).
   i. Jesus is both the teacher and the lesson (11:29).

2. **The Character of a Disciple:** Sermon on the Mount, Chapters 5–7.
   a. The attitude and fruit of the heart (5:1–16).
   b. Inner attitudes of the heart and practices of life (5:17–48).
   c. A perfect heart (5:48).
   d. Warnings and wisdom for the disciple (7:1–29).

3. **The Call of the Disciple:** Equipping, Chapter 10.
   a. Power: To heal, cast out demons, preach (10:1, 7–8).
   b. Disciplined living (10:9–10).
   c. Sharing the word of God (10:11–15).
   d. Be wise and harmless (10:16).
   e. Facing opposition (10:17–36).
   f. The cost of discipleship (10:37–42).
   g. Being with and serving the poor and the oppressed (ch. 25).

SEVEN PRIMARY PRACTICES OF DISCIPLESHIP

Another outline that predates the Jesus Movement.

1. **Instruction**
   a. Teaching on the doctrine of the church.
   b. Teaching on the ethics of a disciple.
   c. Teaching on character and the attitudes of the heart from Scripture (spiritual formation).
   d. Teaching on the church's mission, vision, call, and purpose from Scripture.
   e. Teaching on spiritual gifts and skills for service.
   f. Teaching and practicing spiritual parenting or one-to-one discipleship.
   g. Modeling Christian life and ministry.
      i. I do, you watch➔I do, you assist➔You do, I assist➔You do, I watch.
      ii. Modeling prayer, teaching, ushering, outreach, laying on of hands, visitation, etc.

2. **Care**
   a. Internal care or in-reach.
   b. Making sure every need physical need is met within the group.
   c. Small group roles: Phone minister; letter or email writer; transporter; resource person for food, clothes, and other needs; prayer leader; counselor; visitation; treasurer; apprentice.
   d. Every member of the small group takes on a role and ministers it on a weekly basis.

3. **Fellowship**
   a. Enjoy the fellowship of the saints.
   b. Love each other and build each other up.
   c. Practice speaking the language of encouragement.

4. **Accountability**
   a. One-to-one and small group. Assign one-to-one partners.
   b. Take time to hold each other accountable to spiritual disciplines.
   c. In love, hold each other accountable to church doctrine and ethics.

    d. Hold each other accountable to church mission, vision, order, values, purpose and ministry.

    e. Practice speaking the language of encouragement.

5. **Impartation (Equipping)**

    a. Impartation of the Spirit: Mantle, anointing, gifts, prophet's reward.

    b. Life-to-life transference. Be a giver.

    c. Spend time together outside of church and church business.

    d. Retreat together.

    e. Recreational and rest time together.

    f. Life together outside of church.

    g. These outside occasions provide for effective bonding (glue events).

6. **Service**

    a. Outreach.

    b. Works of mercy: Serving the poor and the widow; outreach and evangelism; prison ministry; ministering to Jesus among the least, the last, and the lost. He is where the poor, marginalized, imprisoned, naked, and homeless are.

7. **Spiritual Disciplines**

    a. Worship,

    b. Works of piety: Prayer, fasting, self-denial, Scripture reading, Holy Communion, confession, warfare, etc.

    c. Works of mercy: feeding the hungry, clothing the naked, visiting the prisoner and the sick.

DISCIPLESHIP AND DISCERNMENT QUESTIONS

1. What is happening in your life?
2. Why is God allowing this in your life?
3. What is God trying to teach you or show you? What are you supposed to learn?
4. What has God said in prayer?
5. What do the Scriptures say about this?
6. What does God want you to do?

BECOMING A DISCIPLEMAKING CHURCH

1. **Models of the Church**
   a. Church as business or marketing
   b. Church as Starbucks
   c. Church as social club
   d. Church as institution
   e. Church as a mall or ChurchMart
   f. Church as family-discipleship model
      i. *Oikos*/family language (Eph 2:11–22; 1 Peter 2)
      ii. Organic language: Sheepfold, vineyard, body, bride, people of God, living stones, spiritual temple
      iii. Charismatic community (body): *Charis* is both grace for salvation and gift for service
      iv. Grace-constituted (body): a Spirit-filled body for salvation and service with a gift-based ministry

2. **Spiritual Parenting**
   a. The Jethro Principle: Exodus 18; Numbers 11:16–29
   b. The Elijah Principle: 1 Kings 19:19–21; 2 Kings 2
   c. Jesus' Master Plan: Selection, modeling, delegating, evaluating, and celebrating (Robert Coleman, *Master Plan of Evangelism*)
   d. Paul and Timothy: 1 Corinthians 4; 11:1; Philippians 1:1–7; 2:22; 3:17; 1 Thessalonians 1:6; 2:11, 14; 1 Timothy 1:2; 2; 2 Timothy 1:2
   e. E4-12 method of ministry: Ephesians 4:12
   f. Each person disciples at least one person. Begin with leaders, then begin with the second, third, and fourth generations of leaders, moving towards the goal of every lay person
   g. Reproducible leaders and discipleship relationships
   h. Discipleship relationships are the nucleus of every cell in the church

3. **Christian Discipleship Structures**
   a. Early house church
   b. Catechetical relationships with spiritual parent
   c. Monastic orders and Daily Offices
   d. *Collegia pietatis:* Small groups for holiness among Lutheran pietists
   e. Wesley and Methodist: Class (discipline), bands (confession and prayer), select bands (entire sanctification and maturity)

4. **Implementing Discipleship Structures**
   a. One-to-one, one-to-two or -three
   b. Small groups
   c. Tasks: Instruction, modeling, accountability, life-to-life transference
   d. For different purposes
      i. New believers: Informational, support, accountability, prep for baptism and membership
      ii. Maturing believers: Doctrine, practical living, service, spiritual disciplines
      iii. Leadership development: Ideological training, character training, call, giftedness, people skills, and mission
      iv. Ministry groups: Mission, vision, service, skills, gifts, etc

SPIRITUAL PARENTING AND DISCIPLESHIP IN THE ORDER OF ELIJAH

TEXT: 1 Corinthians 4:14–17
TERM: Spiritual Parenting (Mothering or Fathering) = Spiritual Mentoring/Discipling

1. **Background to Spiritual Mentoring**
   a. Occurred in the biological family
      i. In ancient cultures, including Israel; Proverbs is a lesson plan for mentoring in the biological family; a word from tribal fathers to their sons, preparing them for leadership.
      ii. Occurred with Abraham➜Isaac➜Jacob➜the Twelve Tribes. It was often father-to-son instruction and modeling.
      iii. Occurred in the Levitical priesthood as the office, ministry, anointing, craft, skills, roles, and teachings of the priesthood were passed down in the family.
      iv. Many cultures have such relationships and structures for this type of mentoring to occur; in ancient Greece we find this lineage of mentoring: (Socrates➜Plato➜Aristotle➜Alexander).

   b. Occurred in the spiritual family
      i. Moses➜Joshua: Moses passed his ministry and mantle on to Joshua.
      ii. Elijah➜Elisha and the School of the Prophets: They followed and served Elijah and each other in daily tasks, while he taught them the art and science of the office of prophet. They called Elijah their father, and they received the prophet's reward of an imparted anointing and office. Elisha received a double portion and did twice the miracles.
      iii. Eli➜Samuel.
      iv. Jesus➜the Twelve.
      v. Barnabas>Paul➜ Timothy.

   c. Lessons taught and imparted in biological and spiritual mentoring include
      i. Life lessons, skills, manhood, fatherhood, parenting, roles, etc.
      ii. Character, virtue, responsibility, the tradition, conduct, ritual, purpose, etc.
      iii. Ministry, office, and anointing.
      iv. The word and ways of God.

2. **Paul as Spiritual Father to the Church**
   a. Writes to the churches as sons. Timothy was a spiritual son (1 Cor. 4:14–17).
   b. Corinthians had information without relation (1 Cor. 4:15).
   c. Teacher as father or mother is beyond information but interaction, impartation, and transformation (1 Cor. 4:15).
   d. Disciple is to follow the mentor, meaning he sets a worthy example (1 Cor. 4:16).
   e. Timothy was his spiritual son, followed his mentor, and communicated to his mentees what he was taught (Phil. 4:9; 2 Tim. 2:2; 3:10).

3. **Mentor Imparts unto His or Her Son and Daughters**
   a. Be followers of me as I follow Christ. The person, life, and work of Christ is imparted to us by the Holy Spirit even through other people (especially leaders and teachers).
   b. Mentoring/discipling/spiritual parenting in the order of Elijah is a way, a structure, and a relationship by which learning, maturity, growth, reproduction, blessing, increase of anointing, ministry impartation, etc. occurs.
   c. We see this method used in eastern Christianity; in monasticism; among the Pietists, the Moravians, and the Methodists; among Pentecostals and Charismatics; and in Eastern Orthodoxy.
   d. There are many analogies for discipleship and spiritual mentoring, but parenting is the most accurate. You birth sons and daughters and train them in life through life by your life-modeling. Although books, strategies, and programs can be helpful, they in themselves are not parenting. Parenting uses but transcends these resources. Parenting is about imprinting both your DNA and your blood, sweat, and tears on your biological and spiritual offspring—reproduction, being fruitful and multiplying. Parenting is the best analogy in terms of describing what is required of the mentor–student relationship, its commitment, its intentionality, its love, its sacrifice, its longsuffering, its equipping and imparting, its prayer and dedication.
   e. See 1 Corinthians 11:1; Philippians 1:1–7; 2:22; 3:17; 1 Thessalonians 1:6; 2:11, 14; 1 Timothy 1:2; 2 Timothy 1:2.[70]

---

70. For more excellent texts on discipleship, see Hull, *The Complete Book of Discipleship*. Ogden, *Transforming Discipleship*; and Wilkins *Following the Master*.

121

FIVE AREAS OF TRAINING

1. **Salvation**
   a. Orthodox, Scriptural doctrine
   b. Teaching and practice of true repentance
   c. Full faith and obedience to Jesus Christ as Lord of all
   d. Teaching and experiencing: justification, regeneration (conversion), and sanctification
   e. Witness of the Spirit as our guide in all things: Our primary epistemic instrument—being led by the Spirit's witness
   f. Teaching and experiencing the benefits of salvation: Forgiveness and acquittal of sins, guilt, shame, justification, adoption, new birth, witness of Spirit, sanctification, eternal life, indwelling of the Spirit, participation in body, sacraments, power, ministry, etc
   g. Learning, receiving, teaching, and ministering in each area listed above

2. **Discipleship**
   a. Learning the theory and practice of daughtership and sonship
   b. God's method: Build people. People build the kingdom. Invest in people
   c. Teaching, living, and ministering the seven functions of discipleship and other teaching
   d. Learning, embodying, and teaching the biblical qualities and practices of a disciple
   e. Learning, receiving, living, teaching, and ministering in each of these areas of discipleship

3. **Sanctification/Holiness**
   a. Define Scriptural holiness
   b. Wesleyan teaching on entire sanctification: What it is and is not
   c. Repentance in believers and entire consecration (learn, receive, live, teach)
   d. Sanctification by faith (learn, receive, live, teach)
   e. God: Promised, is able, performs it now, done and witnessed in that moment
   f. Fruit of the Spirit
   g. Abiding and maintaining that participation in his holiness
   h. Daily self-examination
   i. Learning, receiving, living, teaching, and ministering holiness

4. **Power of the Spirit**
   a. What is the New Testament power of the Spirit?
   b. Gifts of the Spirit and inventory
   c. What is your charismatic language?
   d. Gifts of the Spirit involving perception and reception (e.g., hearing, seeing, feeling, word pictures, words, symbols, songs, feeling, burdens)
   e. Impartation, reception, activation, development, practice, and ministry of the gifts
   f. What is your charismatic office? What is your gift set given to accomplish that office's roles and work? What is your area of deployment and assignment?
   g. Learning, receiving, living, teaching, and ministering the power and gifts of the Spirit

5. **Prayer, Warfare, and Ministry**
   a. Define these terms biblically, theologically, and historically
   b. Learning and operating in a biblical theology of prayer
   c. Hearing God as mastered practice (learn, receive, live, teach, minister)
   d. Taking time to be holy
   e. Building a prayer chapel
   f. What are the weapons of our warfare?
   g. Prophetic declarations and decrees
   h. Informed, prophetic intercession
   i. Know your domain, jurisdiction, assignment, authority, strategies and tactics, metaphor; know who you are and who you are not
   j. Prophetic etiquette
   k. Ministering wisdom
   l. Learning, receiving, living, teaching, and ministering prayer, warfare, and ministry

SPIRITUAL DISCIPLINES FOR ACCOUNTABILITY

1. Daily prayer: Morning and evening, if possible, with family

2. Daily Scripture study: Morning and evening, if possible, with family

3. Daily repentance and confession of sin when needed

4. Weekly church attendance

5. Regular ten percent tithing of gross income (start where you can)

6. Holy Communion

7. Fellowship of the saints

8. Fasting when God calls

9. Hearing God's voice regularly

10. Daily self-denial: "No" to your will and "yes" to God's will

11. Daily renewing the mind with the Scriptures

12. Financial discipline: Practice living in simplicity

13. Physical exercise and diet: Care for your temple

14. Practicing God's order in every area of life

15. Time management: Holy use of time; serve in a ministry

16. Discipleship, small group accountability, or one-to-one

SPIRITUAL EXERCISE PLAN

1. **Things to cut out:**
   a. _____ Too much TV, movies, internet, video games, or other excesses.
   b. _____ Excessive and needless spending
   c. _____ Gossip or too much complaining or talking in general
   d. _____ Addictive habits
   e. _____ Anger outbursts
   f. _____ Spiritual laziness
   g. _____ Unforgiveness

2. **Areas to build up:**
   a. _____ More Scripture study (at least 15 minutes a day)
   b. _____ More prayer time (as in at least 30 minutes a day)
   c. _____ More edifying communication and appropriate silence
   d. _____ More love (family, neighbor, enemy, etc)
   e. _____ More family time
   f. _____ Rest and recreation

3. **Communion and community**
   a. _____ Regular church attendance
   b. _____ Service in ministry (serve in my gifted area)
   c. _____ Regular 10 percent tithing to your local church

4. **Discipleship**
   a. _____ Renewing the mind with truth
   b. _____ Other: _____

REPENTANCE: CHANGING THE MIND

What is repentance? It is a decisive change for the better, a breaking of the will, a turning from sin and a turning to God, or a kindling of the fire of zeal for exclusively God-pleasing things, with renunciation of the self and everything else. It is above all characterized by an extreme breaking of the will. If a person has acquired evil habits, he must now rend himself. . . .. Decisive and active resistance to sin comes only from hatred of it. Hatred of sin comes only from a sense of evil from it; the sense of evil from it is experienced in all its force in this painful break within repentance.[1]

—St. Theophan the Recluse

Introduction: True Repentance and Holiness

It took me decades of walking with Christ to realize experientially that repentance is one of the most powerful and least talked-about practices in the Christian life. Repentance and prayer are a double-barreled shotgun in my life. When I came to Christ nearly four decades ago, I was given the grace to turn from my sinful life and surrender completely to Christ. However, churches that I attended in my early walk did not preach on repentance. At that time, many Pentecostal and Charismatic churches were caught up in the health and wealth and Word of Faith movements. Preaching or teaching on the cross, sin, suffering, repentance, or holiness were virtually unheard of in those circles. I was never convinced that those aspects of those movements were biblical or orthodox. I soon left, looking for more biblical and theological substance.

As a former Catholic turned atheist, now newly converted, I was not terribly knowledgeable about Protestant history or theology. Following my conversion from atheism, I undertook a historical and theological journey in search of roots for my charismatic conversion experience. I devoured everything I could get my hands. Be-

---

1. St. Theophan the Recluse, *The Path of Salvation*, trans. Seraphim Rose (St. Paisius Monastery, 1996), 92. (Recluse 1996)

sides recovering some of my Catholic roots in Thomism (Thomas Aquinas), I discovered the Methodist and Holiness roots of my Pentecostal-Charismatic Christianity. Needless to say, I adopted John Wesley as my spiritual father and began to pursue Scriptural holiness, because without it no one will see God. It was then that I began to seek to understand true repentance—not repent and repeat but repent and release!

Repentance is an aspect of what Wesley called "convincing grace." The Holy Spirit begins to show us our sin. He convicts us of "sin, righteousness, and judgment" (John 16:8 CSB). He gives us the grace to see sin how God sees it, to hate it as God hates it (Ps. 45:7; Amos 5:15; Heb. 1:9). Because the church and the culture coddle and rationalize sin, it is no wonder repentance is rarely preached and less understood. Even among the faithful, we are taught that we can never be free from sin, that we sin in thought, word, and deed daily. To say otherwise is prideful and presumptuous. Thus, many do not even attempt to walk in holiness because they are convinced that it is not possible or legalistic.

For years, I read many great nineteenth-century Wesleyan Holiness writers wax eloquently on the doctrine of entire sanctification (deliverance from sin) and testify to its reality in their lives. I began to believe it was possible. The grace of God can really grant us true repentance and free us from the power and presence of sin so that we could love God and neighbor with our whole hearts. John Wesley defined entire sanctification in shorthand: "It is love excluding sin."[2] Holiness is possible because it comes from a holy God, and he makes us holy. We do not make ourselves holy. If we are willing, hungry, and thirsty for righteousness, he will purify our hearts as only he can (Matt. 5:6, 8; Acts 15:9; 26:18; 1 Thess. 5:23–24; 2 Thess. 2:13; 1 Pet. 1:2). I noted it plainly in Scripture and began to believe that God could do it. For the first time, entire sanctification became a realistic goal for me and not an abstract ideal to approach but never attain.

Like John Wesley claimed in his sermon "The Scripture Way of Salvation," "Exactly as we are justified by faith, so are we sanctified by faith."[3] Wesley sums up his theology for receiving entire sanctification in four statements: "First, that God has promised it in the Holy Scripture. . . . Secondly, that what God has promised he is able to perform. . . . Thirdly, a Divine evidence and conviction that he is able and willing to do it now. . . . [Fourthly,] a Divine evidence and conviction that he does it. In that hour it is done."[4] Theologically, Wesley sealed the deal for my faith. Subsequently, I received a few experiences of full salvation, but it never would stick. I failed to walk in entire sanctification consistently. For many years I wondered why, until I began to understand true repentance.

---

2.   Wesley, Sermon 43, "The Scripture Way of Salvation," in *Works of John Wesley*, 7:46. (Wesley, The Scripture Way of Salvation n.d.)

3.   Wesley, Sermon 43, "The Scripture Way of Salvation," in *Works of John Wesley*, 7:48. (Wesley, The Scripture Way of Salvation n.d.)

4.   Wesley, Sermon 43, "The Scripture Way of Salvation," in *Works of John Wesley*, 7:52–53. (Wesley, The Scripture Way of Salvation n.d.)

I believed God could deliver me from the power of sin, but I thought after the experience of sanctification that I would not have to *leave* my life on the altar of the cross—that somehow the experience of holiness would be the apex or the conclusion of my Christian walk, and I could coast to victory over sin. Later, I realized it would be just the beginning. Unless my heart *remained* decisive about sin, I would not be yielded to receive and maintain his sanctifying grace and continue to grow in it. Simply put, the decision to be entirely consecrated to God, so that he has my will fully yielded to him, is not a one-time offering. Like the old hymn commanded, "Leave it there. Leave it there."[5]

My heart was called to *remain* in a posture and lifestyle of true repentance (always turning from sin) and entire consecration (always surrendered to him) if I am to receive his grace to continue in sanctification and to walk in holiness. As I was humbled, broken, and dependent when I first truly repented, so I must *remain* and even *grow* in contrition and godly sorrow for sin so that I would never turn back again. If I will not abide in him, I will not be able to do anything (John 15:1–8). One cannot take off one's dirty clothes and then put on spotless, new white clothes and roll back in the mud. The clothes need to stay clean and white. One cannot muddy the new clothes or put on the old muddy ones again. Sanctification needs to be retained, sustained, and cultivated. When I learned this sobering lesson, I began to walk in consistent victory. In the same sermon, "The Scripture Way of Salvation," Wesley expounds on the repentance that precedes entire sanctification:

> It is properly a conviction wrought by the Holy Ghost, of the *sin* which still *remains* in our heart . . . It is a conviction of our proneness to evil, of an heart bent to backsliding, of the still continuing tendency of the flesh to lust against the spirit. . . . It is a conviction of the tendency of our heart to self-will, to Atheism, or idolatry; and above all, to unbelief . . . one thing more implied in this repentance; namely, a conviction of our helplessness, of our utter inability to think one good thought, or to form one good desire; and much more to speak one word aright, or to perform one good action, but through his free almighty grace, first preventing us, and then accompanying us every moment.[6]

True repentance, entire consecration, and entire sanctification are gifts of God's grace. However, one must be *willing* to cease from sin, *willing* to fully yield, and *willing* to believe and receive God's sanctifying grace. He will not perform these works without our absolute willingness. Moment by moment God will only work in our lives as we are freely willing and fully open (with no hindrances) to receive. Once this revelation became a lifestyle, I learned to overcome and walk as God desired of me. True repentance is to cease from sin and give no permission to the flesh—not an inch, no compromise. The flesh needs to stay dead on the cross. Clement of Alexandria defines true repentance: "He that repents of what he did, no longer does or says the

---

5. Tindley, Charles A, "Leave It There," 1916. (Wesley, The Scripture Way of Salvation n.d.)

6. Wesley, Sermon 43, "The Scripture Way of Salvation," in *Works of John Wesley*, 7:50–51. (Wesley, The Scripture Way of Salvation n.d.)

128

things he did . . . He, then, who has received forgiveness of sins should sin no more."[7] Let this be our goal!

When the Spirit cultivates such a heart in us, following much prayer, fasting, longing, hungering, and thirsting we learn to let go of the false promises of the devil, the flesh, and the world. We leave all of this world on the cross and faithfully and consistently yield our spirit, soul, mind, and body to Christ as instruments of righteousness and holiness (Rom. 6; Gal. 6:4). When we do not submit to the sanctifying grace of the Spirit, we "frustrate grace" (Gal. 2:21 KJV). We "receive God's grace in vain" (2 Cor. 6:1 NIV). Grace moves, and we must respond in rhythm, like a holy dance. If not, then we resist grace (1 Thess. 5:19; Eph. 4:30).

In order to go forward in Christ and grow in grace, two things must occur. First, we can never turn back for a moment for the rest of our journey. Our commitment needs to be resolute. This is true repentance, and it is a lifestyle. If we do fall, we go back to the point of failure and seek God's grace for repentance and forgiveness. Conviction and repentance call us to have godly sorrow for our sin. We pray for holy light to shine into the depths of the darkness of our heart. We pray that we may see our sin the way God sees it and fully confess our sin. Confession of sin (Grk, *homologia*) involves godly sorrow and saying the same thing that God says about our sin (2 Cor. 7:10; 1 John 1:7–9).

St. John the Theologian exhorts the church, "My dear children, I write this to you so that you will not sin. But if anybody does sin, we have an advocate with the Father—Jesus Christ, the Righteous One. He is the atoning sacrifice for our sins, and not only for ours but also for the sins of the whole world" (1 John 2:1–2 NIV). Victory over sin is the Scriptural norm expected of believers. However, if we sin by commission or omission, we are to seek Jesus Christ our High Priest and Helper for mercy, repentance, and forgiveness. Upon our confession and walking in the light of Christ, we are promised forgiveness, and the blood of Christ cleanses us from all unrighteousness (1 John 1:7–9).

Second, by grace, we must continually press forward without ceasing to possess what has possessed us. This is entire consecration, and it is a lifestyle (Phil. 3:12–14). God supplies the grace for both, but we must be willing. He gives us the power to cease from sinning if we desire to receive it. As we ceaselessly surrender to his will, the Spirit sanctifies us wholly and keeps us in his holiness by grace and power. Faithful is the one who calls us to be holy, who will also make us holy (1 Thess. 5:23–24). If we want real deliverance from our sin, no repent and repeat, praying and fasting earnestly and regularly for a willing heart and true repentance is a great place to begin.

Ultimately, repentance comes from God and is confirmed by God, through the witness of the Spirit. The Spirit lets us know when we have truly repented, as opposed to going through the motions or a perfunctory process and meaningless ritual to satisfy our conscience, or appease our guilt, or shame. Our repentance is not offered

---

7.   David W. Bercot, ed., *Dictionary of Early Christian Beliefs* (Hendrickson, 1998), 556. (David W. Bercot 1998)

to ourselves to appease our own feelings or because we have been caught in our sin. Repentance is our response to God's gracious call to believe on Christ for the forgiveness of sins.

Repentance: Changing Our Mind Changes Our Life

Christ has come to bring liberation, healing, and restoration to our mental well-being (Matt. 8:17; 1 Pet. 2:24). Through his atonement on the cross, he has finished the work for deliverance, healing, and victory. There he cried out, "It is finished" (John 19:30 NIV). He meant that sin was finished. Death was finished. Satan was finished. Forgiveness of sins is finished. And salvation is finished. Christ the Victor (*Christus Victor*) has defeated our enemies. As believers, we stand in Christ's finished work and execute and enforce his authority and victory against the enemy of our souls. Because of Christ the Overcomer, we occupy a position of victory (John 16:33). Because we are born of God, we inherit Christ's victory by faith (1 John 5:4). We are equipped to use the authority and power that Jesus gives us to implement the benefits of the cross (Luke 10:19–20). One benefit is victory over the enemy. Thus, when we truly submit to God and resist the devil in the name of Jesus, Satan flees (Jas. 4:7). We are more than conquerors against all of our foes (Rom. 8:31–39). The key, though, is consistent submission to God.

Our victory begins with repentance that is turning from our sins to God. Repentance is when we cease from living a self-centered life and turn to God to live a Christ-centered life. The sinner places him- or herself at the center of the world. Everything is seen, felt, experienced, and done through the perspective of self at the center. God, others, and the world are marginalized to the periphery with self at the center. With repentance and conversion, we exchange places with God. He is at the center, and we retreat to the margins. We decrease so that he can increase in our life. Perspectives are flipped. Everything is referenced from God's vantage point. Through prevailing prayer and Scripture meditation, God's light begins to shine in our hearts and minds and show us how God sees things. The Lord gives us his perspective and thoughts. We then see God, ourselves, others, and the world through his eyes. We see ourselves and everything in reference to God. The Lord becomes our metaphysical reference point for understanding all things. Although our decision to turn from a self-centered life to a God-centered life is an immediate decision, the implications and sustaining of our commitment is a lifelong journey.

The word for "repentance" in the New Testament Greek is *metanoia*, which means a change of mind that leads to a change of life. The mind is instrumental to governing the individual. Whatever controls the mind controls the person. As the mind goes, so goes the person. We become what we think about: "For as he thinks in his heart, so is he" (Prov. 23:7 NKJV). The mind is the throne of each individual. It is the place of rule, the control center. Who or what sits on the throne of the mind rules the person. Thus, St. Paul declares that we are "transformed by . . . renewing

[our] mind" (Rom. 12:1–2 NIV). A new mind will yield a new life. The mind is key, which is why Satan wants to control it, and Christ wants to rule over it. If the mind is singularly focused on the light that God shines, we will be flooded with the light of Christ and full of the goodness of God. But if the mind is singularly focused on the darkness of this present age, we will be inundated with darkness and full of the wickedness of hell.

What we think on is crucial. Our mind is ours. Thus, its choices are ours. If we do not approve of the thoughts that appear on the screen of our mind, our will, the remote, is in our hands. We can exercise our will and change the channel to something that pleases God (Phil. 4:4–9). Think on things that are holy and true. Change the channel. Click on something righteous. Set your sights above. Yes, change is difficult! Everyone says that they want to change, but what many really want is the *results* of change without going through the rigorous *requirements* of change. They want the *success* of change without the demanding *process* of change! When we decide truly to change our mind and see things how God sees them, we will begin to experience true change in our lives. True repentance is the gateway to a new mind and a new life in Christ. John the Baptist understood this as the only valid response to the coming of God's Kingdom and its King. That is why his message was "to repent; for the kingdom of God has come near" (Matt. 4:17 NIV). God wants our focus to be on the Kingdom of God, setting our mind on the things that are above and not below (Col. 3:1–3).

The Neuroscience of Change: Growing the Mind of Christ

We have been given the mind of Christ. It is a gift from God. Nevertheless, we need to open up that gift and begin to use it. Through learning, training, and applying, we begin to develop the mind of Christ, which is strategic for our discipleship. We become what we dwell on in our minds. Romans 12:1–2 is clear that change and transformation of our lives comes by renewing our mind. A new mind generates a new life. Unfortunately, most of us want the fruit and results of change without undergoing the discomfort, discipline, and pain of change. Absurdly, we want the change without changing.

In the denomination that I serve, the average age of a local church congregant is around sixty. The median local church worship attendance is thirty-eight.[8] And the denomination loses around 200,000 members every year.[9] Currently, it has lost over

---

8.   Liam Adams and Thao Nguyen. "Most United Methodist Church Disaffiliations Are in the South: Final Report Outlines Latest in Ongoing Split," *USA Today*, January 23, 2024, https://www.usatoday.com/story/news/nation/2024/01/23/methodist-church-rift-disaffiliations-report/72319658007/. (Adams and Nguyen 2024)

9.   Mark Tooley, "Exiting United Methodism Now," Juicy Ecumenism, August 5, 2022, https://juicyecumenism.com/2022/08/05/exiting-united-methodism-now/. (Tooley, Exiting United Methodism Now 2022)

one-fourth (7,631) of all of its churches and over 1.3 million members due to disaf-filiation over human sexuality.[10] I have pastored churches that fit this description. They were in decline, older, theologically liberal, and reticent to change. When I ar-rived at my first church as pastor, they said they were excited because I was young and enthusiastic. They claimed that they were ready for change and to grow the church.

It did not take long for me to figure out that they were delusional and in denial, bless their hearts. First, like so many churches, they were a church of learned helpless-ness. Their former pastors operated out of an Old Testament priestly model of pastor-ing. The Old Testament high priest in the tabernacle did all of the work of the min-istry, while the people camped around the tabernacle waiting to receive the fruit and the blessing of the high priest's sacrificial work. Churches that function with an Old Testament priestly model of pastoring put everything on the minister, and they learn to do nothing except sit on a council board but receive the benefits. Similarly, con-gregants in this new church did not know how to pray, study the Bible, evangelize, or do any of the work of the ministry besides controlling board meetings. Instead, they made the pastor do everything. "That is what we pay you for!" they would exclaim." Thus, they never learned how to serve in ministry—as I said, learned helplessness.

Second, although they claimed they wanted to change and grow the church, their de facto position was, "We are not going to change. We want the community to change and be like us." They had the same people governing the church since St. Paul installed them there. They run the worship service and all the other holy activities of the church, like potlucks, mother–daughter banquets, church bazaars, bake sales, card-playing, and white elephant bingo. The worship and music of the service had been the same for over 100 years. They wanted me to go out in the community and find people just like them who would love to come to their version of church. They were elderly, upper-middle-class, white people. The community had changed over the years. It was now predominantly made up of young, poor African Americans, Hispanics, and Palestinian Muslims. Nonetheless, I was expected to go out into the mix of this community and find a group of old white people who loved centuries-old pipe organ music, baking apple pies, living like it was still 1957, and playing canasta. That fish won't fry. Ain't gonna happen! They wanted the results of change without going through the pain of change.

As a recreational powerlifter, boxer, and owner of a boxing club, I learned early the motivational phrase, "No pain, no gain!" Real change is hard! It's painful! The neuroscience of change indicates that even the slightest change is difficult for our

---

10. Yonat Shimron, "The UMC Lost a Quarter of Its Churches—Most in the South," Religion News Service, January 26, 2024, https://religionnews.com/2024/01/26/the-umc-lost-a-quarter-of-its-churches-most-in-the-south-reflecting-political-patterns/ (Shimron and Miller 2023); Yonat Shimron and Emily McFarlan Miller, "United Methodists Lose 1,800 Churches in Split Over LGBT Stance," Christianity Today, January 24, 2023, https://www.christianitytoday.com/news/2023/january/umc-churches-leave-global-methodist-denomination-schism.html.

brains to process. The prefrontal cortex of the brain, which carries the heavy weight of the change process, is like a powerful high-horsepower drag-racing engine. It demands a ton of fuel (energy) for its high performance, but it can only run for a short distance. For example, a typical Top Fuel NHRA dragster with 11,000 horsepower can do a quarter mile in less than 3.7 seconds and can eclipse 330 miles per hour. They are "powered by a supercharged and fuel-injected 500-cubic-inch adaptation of the famed Chrysler Hemi engine. Top Fuel dragsters can burn up to 15 gallons of nitromethane fuel during a single run."[11] They run high and fast but cannot go very far.

Our brains run similarly. Most brain activity has to pass through the prefrontal cortex. Thus, it is an area with much activity, requires high energy, and is slow moving because so many signals pass through it, like a long line at the checkout.[12] In addition, the neural process of change and a sense of threat that come from a decision to change slow down prefrontal cortex activity even more. Further, security-minded persons, who feel threatened easily, including the elderly at my church, become more averse to change.

Our brain prefers to bypass the demanding activity of intentional reasoning that occurs in the prefrontal cortex and operate automatically out of routine and habit, which involves low-energy output. Being creatures of survival, our brains prefer safety and comfort over risk and threat. Our first instinct is survival and stasis to sustain survival. Change is too risky and psychologically painful. When confronted with change, our first response is somatic, including "threat response (fight or flight), increased anxiety and fear, reduced ability to focus and think clearly, impaired performance and increased emotion." Thus, we prefer the same old routine rather than facing any threat to our security.[13]

Encountering change can elicit indolence or resistance, even from the institutionally faithful. It is the reason we do the same old thing and get the same old results when faced with change. When faced with change, the brain demands an extraordinary amount of energy and incentive (positive and negative reinforcement) to override the powerful and well-supported neural networks of routinization and fear. Even if one decides to change, converting that decision to behavior is extremely taxing on the neural system. But if the change does not occur fairly quickly, the odds are that we will not change. The window closes quickly. Neuroscience indicates that "the longer

---

11. "Drag Racing Classes," NHRA, accessed April 12, 2024, https://www.nhra.com/nhra-101/drag-racing-classes#:~:text=They%20are%20capable%20of%20covering,fuel%20during%20a%20single%20run (NHRA n.d.).

12. "The Neuroscience of Change," CIPD, accessed April 11, 2024, https://www.cipd.org/ae/views-and-insights/thought-leadership/people-profession/neuroscience-change/.

13. Helena Boschi, "The Neuroscience of Change: Why Changing Course Is Painful for the Brain," Welldoing, September 24, 2020, https://welldoing.org/article/the-neuroscience-change-why-changing-course-painful-for-brain (Boschi 2017).

a decision stays in the brain, the harder it is to change it."[14] Hence, change is difficult and rare! The immortal Vince Lombardi wisely stated, "Fatigue makes cowards of us all."[15] Change can be risky, painful, and exhausting:

> Using functional magnetic resonance imaging (fMRI) researchers have found that reversing a decision involves rapid coordination between two specific zones, the *prefrontal cortex* and the *frontal eye field* (FEF). The FEF is a region situated just behind the prefrontal cortex that is involved in controlling eye movements and visual awareness. We can only successfully reverse our decision when we change our mind within 100 milliseconds of making it. If we wait any longer, it is less likely that we will be able to change.[16]

Well, then, how do we train our brain to change? Intention, attention, and consistency seem to be the neuroscientific recipe. First, realize that although it takes more energy and probability diminishes as we get older, the brain is *always* capable of growing new brain cells (neurogenesis) and changing even its structure (neuroplasticity). It's never too late! The brain is extremely resilient even when facing adversity such as age, trauma, or impairment. Neuroplasticity allows for the brain to learn, adapt, and change. The brain is also able to repair itself. We are quite neuroresilient. The main reason for the brain's adaptability is that it is continually changing structure over time because it possesses a high capacity for malleability, resilience, and healing. Neuroscientists call this "common progression of growing, changing and adapting," "synaptic potentiation—a process by which new connections between brain cells are made."[17]

The older we get, the harder it becomes to change due to our habits that correlate with the routinization of patterns in our neural circuitry. It takes much energy and effort to override them. Thus, we need to be intentional and pay attention to old habits in order intercept them. And we need to be intentional and focused on the desired new behavior. Intention and attention are functions of the prefrontal cortex of the brain. Whatever has our intention and attention will have us. With the prefrontal cortex, specifically the executive function, we are at the core of our neural control center. The desired new behavior needs to occupy our intentionality and focus. This takes energy and some neural sweat and pain, but the reward pays off.

As we have become aware, habits can take from a few weeks to several months to form.[18] Overriding our old routines and reprogramming our hippocampus, the part

---

14. Boschi, "The Neuroscience of Change." (Boschi 2017)

15. "Vince Lombardi Quotes," Brainy Quote, accessed April 14, 2024, https://www.brainyquote.com/quotes/vince_lombardi_380768 (Brainy Quote n.d.).

16. Boschi, "The Neuroscience of Change." (Boschi 2017)

17. Jessica Sieff, "The Neuroscience of Behavioral Change: Why Intention, Attention and Persistence Matter," University of Notre Dame, January 31, 2023, https://news.nd.edu/news/the-neuroscience-of-behavioral-change-why-intention-attention-and-persistence-matters/. (Sieff 2023)

18. Jocelyn Solis-Moreira, "How Long Does It Really Take to Form a Habit?," Scientific American, January 24, 2024, https://www.scientificamerican.com/article/how-long-does-it-really-take-to-form-a-habit/. (Solis-Moreira 2024)

of the brain responsible for learning and memory, takes time. Consistency and perseverance are required. Accountability partners or apps, journaling, reminder cues, positive and negative reinforcement (rewards gained or lost) all can be helpful to keep us on track. Ultimately, there are no crosscuts to healthy, holy change. Christlikeness is a work of God's grace, but it also involves our faithful participation and obedience.

Spiritual Exercise: No Pain, No Gain!

One way to exercise our spirit and our brain for change and growth is to practice what John Wesley, the founder of Methodism, called the "means of grace." The means of grace are "the ordinary channels whereby he [God] might convey to men preventing, justifying, or sanctifying grace."[19] They are the common ways that God has ordained to work grace in our lives. Today, we often call them *spiritual disciplines*. In order to receive the grace of God we need to position ourselves and be present in the places and practices where God is working. God commonly works through Scripture, prayer, worship services, Holy Communion, fasting, self-denial, and other channels. We do not always need a special supernatural revelation to receive a move from God. We need to exercise ordinary means of grace or spiritual disciplines. Exercising the means of grace for spiritual growth is like exercising with weights for physical growth. Wesley did not construe these means as human works to merit grace, but they were to be practiced in the power of the Spirit and by faith.[20] God's grace will actually meet us when we participate in these practices and make them fruitful for our lives.

However, he will not bless our sloth or lethargy. We have a responsible part to play in discipleship. The Spirit will not force us. As I referenced earlier, God does the heavy lifting, like the forklift, and we are the operator. He is the power behind the forklift, but you have to be seated in the forklift doing your part. He will not let the forklift operate by itself. We need to exercise fully our will and other faculties to operate the forklift. Spiritual diet, exercise, and growth are no different than physical exercise. They take time, dedication, and commitment.

Related to diet, I notice more and more people in my relational circles go out to eat and do not cook and eat at home. Many among the younger generations do not even know how to cook a simple meal. As a youth, I learned to cook by watching my mother and grandmother. Who do the children watch today to learn how to cook? The cooks at McDonald's are too far in the back of the kitchen to observe. Still, there are plenty of cooking shows available on cable to instruct the viewer. The problem is increasing heart disease. One study shows that "the age-adjusted death rate from cardiovascular disease increased to 233.3 per 100,000, up 4 0% from 224.4 per 100,000 reported last year, whereas the rate had increased 4.6% in the previous year. Last

---

19. John Wesley, "The Means of Grace," in *The Works of John Wesley's*, vol. 5, *Sermons*, vol. 1, ed. Thomas Jackson (Baker Books, 1978), 187. (Wesley and Jackson, The Means of Grace 1978)

20. John Wesley, "The Means of Grace," in *The Works of John Wesley's*, vol. 5, vol. 1, 188. (Wesley and Jackson, The Means of Grace 1978)

year's increase was the first increase in age-adjusted death rates seen in many years."[21] We are paying more than we think for fast food consumption.

Growing up in the 1960s and '70s, going out to eat on a regular basis was unheard of. We were lucky to go out and eat perhaps once a year, and it was a big deal. Now it's practically the norm. Only 64 percent of Americans cook and eat at home.[22] For many, the number one reason to cook and eat at home is to save money during economically challenging times. During and following the Covid-19 pandemic, people retrained themselves to return to the kitchen and DIY. Another study shows that 65 percent of American (two out of three) eat fast food at least once a week and spend an average of $148 per month on it.[23] We are a people that eat on the run out of convenience to accommodate our busy schedules.

Similarly, we consume our spiritual food on the run. About a quarter of us get our worship online or from some form of media rather than being in-person at church.[24] Many attend Christian conferences or seminars regularly, even following various high-profile Christian rock stars like they would their favorite music group, attending their concerts when they come to town. The idea is to soak up their anointing and receive quickly and freely what others have received through years of sacrifice. This drive-thru mentality satisfies our misguided search for quick fixes. But real spiritual growth and health do not work that way. If we go to a conference seeking a quick fix or easy solution, we will soon find that whatever is poured into us will not remain or sustain. We came to the conference with a hole. And the fresh experience will drain down that same hole. Unless the hole is repaired and the cracks fixed in our lives, we will not be able to contain someone else's anointing.

We have not paid the spiritual price and time required for the Lord to build within us the spiritual foundation or substructure to house and process profound teaching or costly anointing. Most of the deep lessons I have learned that have stuck

21. American Heart Association, "More Than Half of Americans Uninformed as Heart Disease Claims Top Spot Again," News-Medical.net, January 24, 2024, https://www.news-medical.net/news/20240124/More-than-half-of-Americans-uninformed-as-heart-disease-claims-top-spot-again.aspx#:~:text=The%20age%2Dadjusted%20death%20rate%20from%20cardiovascular%20disease%20increased%20to,rates%20seen%20in%20many%20years. Martin, Seth S., Aaron W. Aday, Zaid I. Almarzooq, Cheryl A.M. Anderson, Pankaj Arora, Christy L. Avery, Carissa M. Baker-Smith, et al. "2024 Heart Disease and Stroke Statistics: A Report of US and Global Data from the American Heart Association." *Circulation* 149, no. 8 (February 20, 2024). https://doi.org/10.1161/cir.0000000000001209.

22. "Survey reveals 81% of consumers now cook more than half of their meals at home," pr newswire, december 6, 2023, https://www.Prnewswire.Com/news-releases/survey-reveals-81-of-consumers-now-cook-more-than-half-of-their-meals-at-home-302007657.Html#:~:text=survey%20reveals%2081%25%20of%20consumers,of%20their%20meals%20at%20home. (National frozen & refrigerated foods association 2023)

23. Emily Rodgers, "75+ Fast Food Consumption Statistics," Drive Research, September 19, 2023, https://www.driveresearch.com/market-research-company-blog/fast-food-consumption-statistics/. (Rodgers 2023)

24. "Online Religious Services Appeal to Many Americans, but Going In Person Remains More Popular," Pew Research Center, June 2, 2023, https://www.pewresearch.org/religion/2023/06/02/online-religious-services-appeal-to-many-americans-but-going-in-person-remains-more-popular/. (Pew Research Center 2023)

to my ribs came with much time in prayer, seeking and wrestling with God. They were lessons that involved much sacrifice and suffering, as well as painful death to my own will. There are no shortcuts or quick fixes in building our souls for eternity. In my experience as a professor, revivalist, pastor, counselor, and mentor, one of the greatest deficiencies that I frequently detect in believers is the lack of ability and desire to seek, find, and be trained by the Holy Spirit. We look to bypass the toil and drudgery and get a speedy solution. The problem seems to be manifold, including a lack of desire, practical know-how, perseverance, and openness to hear and be taught by the Spirit.

Simply, many of us do not know how to pursue God with persistence until we find him and hear from him. It is easier to go to the pastor, seek a prophet for a word, or go to an anointed conference for an easy, effortless solution. Such quick-fix believers have fallen into a paralyzing learned helplessness. As we learn in the parable of the ten virgins, each one needs to seek the Spirit to have their vessels filled with oil (Matt. 25:1–13). One cannot rely on someone else's oil supply. I am not against going to your pastor or to a conference when needed and when God leads. We need the body of Christ to grow and confirm our faith. Nonetheless, sacerdotalism (overreliance on a priest or mediator) should never replace your own pursuit and relationship with God. Neglecting one's own personal faith commitment with undue reliance on someone else's can lead to a hollow and crippling nominalism, becoming a Christian in name only. Quality time needs to be spent alone with the Lord in the spiritual gym (the prayer closet) if we are going to grow healthily in Christ and sustain that growth.

St. Paul encourages Timothy to hit the spiritual gym. He exhorts, "Physical training is of some value, but godliness has value for all things, holding promise for both the present life and the life to come" (1 Tim. 4:8 NIV). If we want results, we have to put in the effort—intention, attention, and consistency. This three-rung ladder is needed to reach any goal, physical or spiritual. In both powerlifting and boxing, my training requires unwavering focus on my goals and my exercises. Going through the motions will do you no favors when you have 400-plus pounds on a bar over your chest. You need heartfelt, gut-busting intentionality to keep that weight from crashing down on you.

Same in the ring. One cannot be halfhearted when another 250-pound hungry heavyweight is trying to take your head off with piledriving punches. Intentionality! Keep your guard up. Not just for one round but your whole lifelong. If you drop your guard, Satan is waiting to counter and make you pay. So it is vital to give 100 percent, even in training, whether it is our body, mind, or spirit. I instruct my fighters that they will never be any better on fight night than they were in training. If they do not train in the gym with 100 percent intention, attention, and consistency, they cannot expect to magically be better once they step in the ring. No shortcuts. No easy way out. We are training the brain to reign!

The reader may be thinking, "That puts much onus on the individual." Well, we are responsible for our own decisions and actions. Thankfully, the neuroscience of change has been hardwired into us by our Creator. Since God calls us to repent, which is a change of mind involving a change of life, it stands to reason that he designed us with the inner equipment and capacity to change. When our desire is to change and be transformed into his image, we can expect that his grace will be at work in us by the power of the Holy Spirit. The indwelling Holy Spirit is God living inside of us and empowering us to overcome! Following prayer, the Spirit will infuse a holy desire in us for change and will move with his power on our brain circuitry. Scripture promises as much: "For God is working in you, giving you the desire and the power to do what pleases him" (Phil. 2:13 NLT). But you have to do your part.

Remember, God is the forklift moving the heavy weight, but you have to drive the lift and operate it. So spend quality time in your prayer gym. Build up your resistance to sin and temptation with regular practice of righteousness (right choices and right living). Listen to your coach, the Holy Spirit. Do your Scripture reps. Run your prayer laps. Resistance train against temptation. Deadlift that flesh and put it on the cross. You do what you can, and God will do what you can't. You do the possible, and God will do the impossible. Over time, this spiritual regimen will empower you to overcome evil and grow in godliness.

Garbage In, Garbage Out

One effective way to grow in Christ is to pay attention to our spiritual diet. Our mind consumes copious amounts of data during the day. Some of it may be toxic to our spiritual health. Are we monitoring our spiritual intake? Are we as meticulous about examining our spiritual diet as we are our physical diet? If one is a diabetic, that person is duteous not to eat foods high in sugar or carbohydrates. Taking in excessive amounts of sugar is tantamount to ingesting poison. Yet many Christians have no problem ingesting heaps of spiritual junk food, leading to fear, worry, anxiety, vanity, anger, lust, judgmentalism, or hatred that are lethal to the soul. Other things that we may ingest, though not deadly, offer no spiritual nutrition and are devoid of edification—for example spending too much time on social media or obsessing over the news. Proper stewardship over our mind and our time is a responsibility that we often carelessly neglect.

In some ways our mind functions similarly to a computer. GIGO—"garbage in, garbage out"—was an expression used in early computer programming, indicating that illogical or invalid outputs are the results of illogical or invalid inputs. Simply, if we program nonsense or garbage into the computer, we will get garbage as a result. If we program junk in our mind, we will get junk coming out. Or as the Bible said two thousand years before, "You will reap what you sow" (Gal. 6:7).[25] If the eye is singularly focused on darkness, the mind will be filled with darkness. You will become what you focus on for better for worse. Time to take out the garbage! It's garbage day.

All of the blessed circuitry of the brain can be used for good, to achieve success, perform effectively, serve others, love your neighbor, and worship God. On the other hand, the same wonderful neural cognitive system can be used as a synaptic and

---

25. Author's translation.

logistical highway to hell. The choice is ours. We become the programmers of our own mind. We are also the operators, downloading and uploading content regularly. What are you downloading into your memory? Is it corrupt? Does it contain cognitive malware or other spiritual viruses? What is infecting the files and system of your mind and copying itself and attaching itself to other files in your system and infecting areas in your life? Delete the trash! It's time to choose God.

The Cognitive Neuroscience of Addiction

The viral hijacking of a computer is similar to the basic dynamic that occurs with addiction of most types. The neurocircuitry (brain wiring) of reward that controls the mesolimbic system (reward and motivation) can be hacked and hijacked by addiction. The gratification or reward system in our brain works with the executive function to regulate and prioritize self-sacrificial investments with long-term benefits over short-term immediate gratification. The reward system (the mesolimbic pathway) and the executive function work together with the hippocampus and amygdala (emotional and arousal memory), which are responsible for memory and learning. Thus, the executive function chooses a rational, long-term goal with long-term rewards and gratification, and the hippocampus learns and remembers the sacrifice and work involved in these long-term decisions, helping to strengthen one's commitment to delay gratification for the long-term reward. A feedback loop is created that reinforces the learned behavior. In other words, we choose to play the long game over the short game.

Here is how the reward system is supposed to work. For example, if we go to college, we realize that we will be making many sacrifices. The financial cost is exorbitant. In order to keep up with the workload, many extracurricular and leisurely activities will have to be cut out of our schedule. We will spend intellectual fuel paying attention in class and burning the midnight oil to complete our studies. We realize that we cannot indulge in a lifestyle that will interfere with this deep commitment. We cannot afford the consequences of short-term gratification, binges, and habits that will impede and interfere with our education and long-term goals. We sacrifice the immediate, short-lived, and negatively consequential gratification and benefits, and we make a long-term sacrifice to study hard in order to achieve long-term gratification, like graduation and a career. The reward system is regulated to prioritize *long-term* benefits over *short-term* gratification.

The executive function and other neurocircuits monitor and moderate the reward system, making sure proper priorities are considered and implemented. However, genetic, epigenetic, environmental, behavioral, and stress conditions can predispose someone to impulsive, risky behavior, which, if unchecked, can become abuse and then addiction. Many types of abuse lead to addiction, including alcohol, illegal and legal substances, internet use, and sexual addictions. Some people are more predisposed to these indulgences than others.

The addiction cycle begins with trial (experimenting), then moves into repetitive use, followed by abuse and addiction. The addiction cycle can be perpetuated into binge mode, negative withdrawal, and anticipation for the next high. Addiction literally changes the structure of one's brain. Under addiction the brain changes, adapts (neuroadaptation), and learns to override and hijack its own system. The desire and drive for the reward (the dopamine and the high) increases (increased incentive salience). The rewards are not enough, and the executive function (the brain's defense) is compromised. The person under addiction wants more, better, faster, and stronger rewards. Harder stuff is needed. The old stuff doesn't work anymore. Our incentive salience (the motivation and desire for reward) controlled by the nucleus accumbens becomes pathological. The desire increases, while the pleasure decreases, because of increased tolerance.

With addiction, the process of regulating gratification is compromised, and dopamine levels are increased.[26] One gets high merely from pursuing the high. Dopamine is released upon anticipation of the reward to come. Dopamine release in the reward system (nucleus accumbens and dorsal striatum) can occur in exorbitant amounts in a short period of time. Because the reward system has been hijacked, something toxic like fentanyl or porn are misinterpreted as positive reinforcement. The brain conditions itself (teaches itself) and remembers the stimulus–reward dynamic that attained the high (affecting memory in the hippocampus). Then a feedback loop is created to repeat the process, as one spirals down a vortex of devastation. One becomes doped up on dopamine. The "drug," whether it is substances, inappropriate internet content, sex, or alcohol, is never enough. One needs more and harder.

Some studies indicate that dopamine does "not signal pleasure" but signals "the anticipation of pleasure."[27] It is like the anticipating, savoring, and salivating that comes before one eats a meal. Some get high off the pursuit more than the thing itself. Dopamine is released into the nucleus accumbens that generates the motivation, desire, and craving to pursue (incentive salience) the reward (the rewarding stimulus). The incentive salience or the craving for a pleasing reward can replace the reward itself. "Liking something" and "craving something" often go together, but they can be separated.[28] Thus, with addiction it is possible to crave something and *not* like it or get pleasure from it anymore; increased tolerance can cause an increase in desire but a decrease in pleasure. Through addiction, the brain is hijacked and manipulated to want something that is destructive as if it were constructive or positive. Furthermore, it manipulates the brain to want what it no longer likes.

---

26. Dopamine is a neurotransmitter responsible for mood, feeling, and motivation affecting our reward and gratification system, among other functions. Some call dopamine the feel-good brain chemical.

27. Judith Grisel, *Never Enough: The Neuroscience and Experience of Addiction* (Penguin Random House, 2019), 27. (Grisel 2019) Stefano Puglisi-Allegra and Rossella Ventura, "Prefrontal/Accumbal Catecholamine System Processes High Motivational Salience," *Frontiers in Behavioral Neuroscience* 6 (2012): 31. https://doi.org/10.3389/fnbeh.2012.00031. (Puglisi-Allegra and Ventura 2012)

28. Puglisi-Allegra and Ventura, "Prefrontal/Accumbal Catecholamine System Processes High Motivational Salience."

Through addiction, the brain experiences faulty programming. Addiction wrongly teaches a person that they do not have to spend years of sacrifice for a reward. Why work hard and long and wait for the good feeling of satisfaction from a reward that comes with graduating college, waiting for marriage, or saving and investing money, when one can get the same high and greater in a moment by pursuing one's addiction of choice? Bypass sacrifice and suffering and get immediate gratification and pleasure! But there is a price to pay. Many don't read the small print that comes with addiction: "If you allow addiction to hijack your system, you will sell your soul and everything else for this short-term destructive high."

The hijacking that occurs with addiction is like a virus entering your computer. The virus will flood the system, take it over, corrupt it, and destroy it. Addiction is destructive to the spirit, mind, and body. With addiction, in the end, a person will sacrifice their soul and *everything* they love for the *one* thing that will destroy them. Recovery is giving up the *one* thing that is destroying them to gain back *everything* that they love. Addiction cannot heal the hurt that lies underneath. It only exacerbates it. It is said that with addiction one loses their entire life for one false pleasure, but in recovery one gains their entire life by simply losing one false pleasure. The key to recovery is to recover the mind and the agency of the one in addiction, which means to gain the mind of Christ by surrendering to God.

Forty-year-old Cory had been a user of pornography since his youth. Over the years he attempted to quit with minimal success. The addiction opened the door to bizarre fetishes and temptations to act out on them. He became more serious about quitting when his wife discovered his secret. Desperate, he sought out local deliverance ministers and contacted me. I connected him with an addiction specialist, introduced him to Truth Therapy (see Chap. 6), set up an accountability system for him, and ministered deliverance sessions with him. Over a period of time, he had some minor relapses but was finally set free. Whereas in the past he was powerless to resist, today he is able to live in victory and in peace. I have seen this regimen work countless times over the years in the lives of persons with all types of addictions. The power of the Spirit working through Truth Therapy and deliverance were key.

In deliverance, prayer and fasting are "legal" spiritual steroids without the destructive side effects. Deliverance from addiction is not an easy task. Habits that did not occur overnight often are not broken overnight. Beyond seeking professional help, seekers need to hunger and thirst for true repentance. Ask the Lord to cultivate a holy hatred in your heart for that sin and a holy hunger in that area for righteousness. Meditate day and night on God's word for that area of your life so that the sharpness of the sword's truth and conviction may penetrate, touch, and uproot the sin that is deeply entrenched in your heart and mind. Once the gratification system (mesolimbic system), memory (hippocampus and amygdala), and learning in the hippocampus are hijacked due to addiction, the cycle loops effortlessly on automatic pilot. The biological neural networks are deeply entrenched in this destructive pattern and downward spiral. Reversing this process is almost impossible without the grace of God and proper intervention from professionals, including substance abuse specialists, counselors, a spiritual director, and a seasoned deliverance team.

Seeking true repentance through prayer and fasting is key. Having intercessors in your life who understand deliverance is essential, especially if you cannot break free from the addiction. Freedom is the ability to do otherwise. If you cannot stop, you are most likely addicted. Through behavioral psychology, we know that addiction or any practice is strengthened over duration, frequency, and intensity, plus the factor of any genetic predispositions (generational sin or proclivity). Intercessors also need to pray and fast to prepare for a session of deliverance. If one is truly repentant and open to deliverance, in the right season at the right time, God will set them free because he is merciful as well as powerful.[29]

---

29. For an exhaustive theological and practical treatment of deliverance from sin and demons, see Bellini, *The X-Manual*.

THE WAR FOR THE MIND

"I found more and more undeniable proofs, that the Christian state is a continual warfare; and that we have need every moment to watch and pray lest we enter into temptation."

—John Wesley's journal entry for May 17, 1740[1]

A Mighty Fortress Is Our Mind

Concerning the war for the soul, as the mind goes, so goes the person. As the battle of the mind goes, so goes the war. *If the enemy can capture the mind, he can capture the soul.* The mind is the strategic battle site for the war of our soul. Throughout military history, key battles have determined the outcome of an entire war. Marathon (490 BCE), Ravenna (476 CE), Tours (732 CE), Hastings (1066 CE), Constantinople (1453 CE), Waterloo (1815 CE), Gettysburg (1863 CE), Stalingrad (1942 CE), and Okinawa (1945 CE) were pivotal battles that turned the tide of the war and decided the winner. Similarly, the battle for the mind is the crucial site that determines the victor. Therefore, it is imperative that we fortify our mind with the word of God. The wise person builds their house on the Rock!

The mature Christian's mind is like a strategic, well-armed fortress that is surrounded by towering walls for its defense. However, before Christ, we did not know how to fight. Our feeble defenses were easily penetrated. The walls around our fortress were scaled, and the doors of our fortress breached. Our mind soon became a bastion of strongholds for the devil. Although Christ vanquished the enemy and set us free, our fortress had been decimated and is in need of major repair. The holes and cracks in our walls need to be filled and patched up, lest the enemy return and intrude again through the open accesses that have not been restored. Our gates were broken down and need repair. The truths of God's word are the stones that the Spirit uses to repair the breach and rebuild the fortress (Isa. 58:12). Our thought life is restored and fortified with the word of God. The stronghold of our gates (authority and access) is refortified and restored, as Christ is made Lord over every entrance into our lives (Ps. 24:7–9; Isa. 60:18; Rev. 21:12). We learn who we are in Christ and what we can do through Christ.

---

1. John Wesley, journal entry for May 17, 1740, in *Works of John Wesley*, vol. 1, *Journals I*, ed. Jackson. (Wesleyan Conference Office, 1872), 272. (Wesley, Journal Entry for May 17, 1740 1872)

After the Babylonian captivity, the Israelites returned home to restore the devastation and rebuild the city. The Babylonians had demolished the city and razed the temple. Ezra led the reconstruction of Jerusalem. Zerubbabel directed the rebuilding of the temple (Hag. 1:1; Ezra 1–6). Following, Nehemiah rebuilt the walls and the gates (Neh. 2:11–20). However, not everyone was in favor of this new building project. Many opposed these leaders and their workers (Ezra 3; 4:1–23; Neh. 2:19; 4). Nehemiah and his men were forced to build the walls while fighting off their enemies (Neh. 4:16–18). One group fought, while another group built. Some had a hammer in one hand and a sword in the other, fighting while building. As the Spirit restores our mind, he has furnished us with the truth to rebuild the walls of our defense and with the sword of the Lord to fend off the enemy's attack, diligently building and vigilantly battling.

Spiritual Warfare 101 in One Verse: James 4:7[2]

Submit to God and Resist the Devil

Often, I write and teach on the subject of spiritual warfare and am frequently requested to share on it at conferences and local churches. There is an abundance of information out there on the topic, some not as trustworthy as others. It seems some tribes are more versed in the subject than others. Many of my fellow Methodists and Wesleyans admit that they have had minimal teaching on spiritual warfare in their upbringing and training and are looking for something that is entry-level. While that does not describe everyone in our tribe, both novice and seasoned alike appreciate complex and cryptic subject matter such as spiritual warfare or demonology broken down and served up with simplicity, clarity, and concision.

In an attempt to be Wesleyan and offer "plain truth for plain people," I believe I can sum up the whole of spiritual warfare in one verse, James 4:7: "Therefore submit yourselves to God. Resist the devil and he will flee from you."[3] *Submit (to God) and resist (the devil)!* Of course, the entirety of Scripture is available to us to draw from as we study the matter of spiritual warfare. But if any one verse captures the warp and woof of spiritual warfare from identifying its combatants to its winning strategy and its effective execution, it is this verse in James. Simply put, *submit and resist!*

The greater context surrounding verse 7 identifies the particular conflict that the apostle James is addressing. He writes that there are quarrels *between* believers because there are quarrels *within* believers. Verse 1 reads, "What is causing the quarrels and fights among you? Don't they come from the evil desires at war within you?" (NLT).

---

2. This section is adapted from my article, "James 4:7—Spiritual Warfare Made Simple," *Firebrand Magazine*, December 19, 2023, https://firebrandmag.com/articles/james-47-spiritual-warfare-made-simple?rq=bellini. (P. J. Bellini, James 4:7—Spiritual Warfare Made Simple 2023)

3. Author's translation.

James identifies lust, jealousy, contentiousness, manipulation, wrong motives, and even murder rising up within unchecked hearts that wage war against one's soul and one's neighbor. In 4:2–3 he writes, "You want what you don't have, so you scheme and kill to get it. You are jealous of what others have, but you can't get it, so you fight and wage war to take it away from them. Yet you don't have what you want because you don't ask God for it. And even when you ask, you don't get it because your motives are all wrong—you want only what will give you pleasure" (NLT). War raging on the inside of us eventually erupts into war against our neighbor.

External conflicts often reflect deeper, unresolved internal ones. Often, we find that if we do not win the inner battle against self and its desire to sit on the throne of our hearts, we are led by the flesh and not the Spirit. Temptations to lust, deceive, judge, rage, and the like, if not resisted and crucified, will assail and overcome our will. Earthly, carnal drives will saturate our souls and leak out into our social interactions, infecting our relationships. As a result, we find ourselves saying and doing things that do not reflect our better spiritual selves. We are not walking in the Spirit and no longer reflect the character of Christ.

God Opposes the Proud

In verse 4, the apostle goes deeper in his analysis of the battle, characterizing such behavior as explicitly unfaithfulness to God: "You adulterers! Don't you realize that friendship with the world makes you an enemy of God? I say it again: If you want to be a friend of the world, you make yourself an enemy of God" (NLT). Our sin is always *first* against God and then *second* against others. During and after sin, our focus is on ourselves, *our* will, and *our* wants. Then afterwards, we may be consumed with *our* guilt, *our* shame, and *our* misery. Rarely do we humbly gaze up and consider that above all, our transgression is against *our* holy, loving Father. In fact, the nature of sin is so oppositional, violent, and unruly, it sets us *against* the one who loves us. When we act on our own distorted passions, we decree our own autonomy. However, our decree is also a declaration of war against God and his righteousness. Unthinkably, we become "enemies of God," as Scripture clearly claims.

"God opposes the proud but gives grace to the humble" (4:6 NLT). Battling against God, this is a war that we cannot win! Ask Satan! When we choose to walk in sin, our confrontation is actually against God. We are resisting his Spirit and his righteousness and are claiming our own will and its wants over those of the Lord's. When our pride resists the grace of God, we are fighting God, and he will fight back. He will oppose us. Ask the Israelites in the wilderness! Needless to say, that is not a good place to be. Banging our heads against the will of God is a no-win, hopeless situation. When sinning, long before we have a problem with Satan or even self, we have a problem with God. Sin is primarily against God and then an issue with self and the devil.

God has a holy jealousy toward those whom he died for and loves. He wants us to be wholly devoted to him. "God is passionate that the spirit he has placed within us should be faithful to him" (4:5 NLT). But to our surprise, for our rebellion he returns grace. He exhorts us not to fight him any longer, not to resist his gift: "And he gives grace generously. As the Scriptures say, 'God opposes the proud but gives grace to the humble'" (4:6 NLT). The remedy James prescribes in verse 8 is to repent, "purify our hearts," and humbly "draw close to God."[4]

Humility: The Secret to Receiving Grace

James plays off the word *resist* in this passage. We are called to *resist* Satan and sin, but if we walk in pride, God *resists* us. If God *resists* us, we cannot *receive* grace to *resist* Satan. How do we break the cycle? Humility! Repentance begins by decapitating our pride through humility (4:6). Humility is the chief virtue. In one of his letters St. Augustine expounded on the essence of the Christian life: "The way to Christ is first through humility, second through humility, third through humility."[5] Every blessing we have comes from the grace of God—repentance, forgiveness, salvation, assurance, healing, sanctification, and every spiritual and material blessing. If grace holds such primacy in our lives and is the wellspring of all blessings, how vital is humility that God only gives grace to the humble but resists the prideful? God gives grace freely; such is the nature of grace. However, humility is the *prerequisite* to *receiving* grace. Without humility, we can receive nothing from God but find ourselves opposing him. But *with* humility, we receive all of the riches of grace upon grace and are able to overcome temptation and live victoriously. "He gives grace to the humble" (James 4:6 NIV).

Not only is humility to be our predominant posture toward the grace of our Lord, but it is also the antidote to neutralizing the venom of the enemy. Humility deactivates Satanic pride in our life. Ironically, humility is the optimal response to both our Lord and the devil. Humility is both the proper response to God's grace and to Satan's temptation of pride. Humility is our prime virtue *and* weapon. Humility positions us to receive all that we need from God to live a holy life and overcome sin. His grace gives us power to resist the onslaught of the flesh, the devil, and the world. James 4:7 (NKJV) exhorts, "Therefore submit yourselves to God. Resist the devil and he will flee from you." Note, only once we are submitted to God in humility and full of his grace can we resist the devil. Otherwise, we are no match for Satan and his demons. Satan was cursed to crawl on the earth and consume the dust of our flesh. He will eat us for breakfast! He lives off of our uncrucified flesh. Only when we humbly yield to the grace and power of the Spirit of God can we combat Satan, because only then do we have access to God's authority over the enemy. At that point, Satan is no longer fighting us. He is fighting God.

---

4.   Author's translation.

5.   St. Augustine, Letters (83-130), ed. Roy Joseph Deferrari, trans. Wilfrid Parsons, vol.18, The Fathers of the Church (Washington, DC: The Catholic University of America Press, 1953), 282. (Augustine 1953)

Resist!

Remarkably then, in warfare our preoccupation is not first with the devil but with God. And only when we are submitted humbly before him and indwelt by his grace are we able to face and oppose the enemy of our soul with triumphant victory. In a position of humility and grace, we do not battle on our own and in our own strength. It is no longer I but Christ who then battles for me and for you. We are clothed with *his* armor and authority and are able to resist or oppose the devil categorically and conclusively. Resistance means to hold the line, not to give in, but to push back with all of your resources. We have been given God's grace and power, but *we* need to choose to resist. It is a command. Grammatically, *resist* is an understood second-person singular command, meaning "you resist." When we resist, or say no to Satan, we are promised that he will run from us (Christ in us). Jesus has already defeated Satan on the cross, but now his victory is ours. When you stand in Christ, Satan cannot stand before you. He must flee! At whatever level spiritual warfare may occur—personal, social, physical, mental, emotional, denominational, political—the battle plan is the same: "Submit yourselves to God and resist the devil, then he will flee from you."

The Neuroscience of Resistance

How does this dynamic of resistance translate over into neuroscience? Our desire as disciples is to train the brain. How do we train the brain to resist according to neuroscience and neuropsychology? What is the neuroscience of resistance? What are the neural correlates of resistance? What is the neuropsychology of resistance? Resistance, in terms of cognitive neuroscience, is a product of self-regulation:

> Self-regulatory failure is a core feature of many social and mental health problems. Self-regulation can be undermined by failures to transcend overwhelming temptations, negative moods, resource depletion, and when minor lapses in self-control snowball into self-regulatory collapse. Cognitive neuroscience research suggests that successful self-regulation is dependent on top-down control from the prefrontal cortex over subcortical regions involved in reward and emotion. We highlight recent neuroimaging research on self-regulatory failure, the findings of which support a balance model of self-regulation whereby self-regulatory failure occurs whenever the balance is tipped in favor of subcortical areas, either due to particularly strong impulses, or when prefrontal function itself is impaired. Such a model is consistent with recent findings in the cognitive neuroscience of addictive behavior, emotion regulation, and decision making.[6]

Due to our innate weaknesses, mental health susceptibilities, temptations, and sinful proclivities, we often fail to self-regulate (control ourselves) sufficiently or at all. Our self-regulatory resources are also limited and are depleted easily through

---

6. Todd F. Heatherton and Dylan D. Wagner, "Cognitive Neuroscience of Self-Regulation Failure," *Trends in Cognitive Sciences* 15, no. 3 (2011): 132–39. https://doi.org/10.1016/j.tics.2010.12.005. (Heatherton and Wagner, Cognitive Neuroscience of Self-Regulation Failure 2011)

fatigue.[7] Scripture states that even the young grow weary and weak, but when they wait on the Lord, their energy is renewed. God never grows tired or weary. He gives power to the powerless and strength to the weak (Isa. 40:28–31). Strong self-regulatory functioning enables us to resist defeat, temptation, and sin and overcome in life.[8] Energized by the Spirit of God, our victory begins in the prefrontal cortex (executive function) and ends with regulation in the gratification or reward system of the subcortical regions of the brain, a top-down process.[9] In the first chapter, we learned that the executive function is responsible for self-control, reasoning, planning, self-monitoring, working memory, strategizing, organizing, prioritizing, time management, emotional self-regulating, goal setting and achieving, focus and attention, cognitive flexibility, adapting, and more. We need a battle plan that activates the higher purpose of our executive functions over the lower purpose of capitulating to our immediate desires of the flesh.

In order to accomplish this goal in our brains, we need to implement a strategy that maximizes agency and the power of our executive function to override impulses and compulsions for destructive thoughts and actions. God created us with the cerebral hardware to overcome, if we would use it properly. We pray for the Spirit of God to align our executive functions with his will and for the grace of God to give us the guidance, power, desire, and focus to construct and implement a plan to use properly his neurological resources so that we can submit to God, resist Satan, and overcome in battle. Now, we also believe that if God chooses, he can work a miracle of instantaneous deliverance and victory, bypassing any of our plans to use the neuroscience and neuropsychology of resistance. When I was converted, the Lord graciously delivered me instantly of many besetting sins, strongholds, and bad habits. However, God chooses how he will work. Until we receive such a miracle, we will seek God for a battle plan.

When engaging in spiritual warfare and resisting temptation, it is vital that we have a long- and short-term battle plan and a coordinated strategy that is aligned with it. The plan should involve goal setting and a strategy to achieve our spiritual goals. The short-term plan is to renounce the desire to succumb to the tyrannical immediacy of impulses that Satan wants to use to hijack our gratification system (mesolimbic system of motivation and reward), amygdala (emotional and arousal memory), and hippocampus (learning and memory). Tempting the flesh to yield to desire, Satan wants us to remember and learn how to do it again and again, so he hijacks memory in the hippocampus. The more that we yield to the temptation, the easier it becomes to do it again, like on automatic pilot. Repetition creates a well-routed pattern in

---

7. Heatherton and Wagner, "Cognitive Neuroscience of Self-Regulation Failure." (Heatherton and Wagner, Cognitive Neuroscience of Self-Regulation Failure 2011)

8. Simple exercises such as using your nondominant hand in daily activities can increase the capacity for self-regulation. For more, see Heatherton and Wagner, "Cognitive Neuroscience of Self-Regulation Failure." (Heatherton and Wagner, Cognitive Neuroscience of Self-Regulation Failure 2011)

9. Puglisi-Allegra and Ventura, "Prefrontal/Accumbal Catecholamine System Processes High Motivational Salience." (Puglisi-Allegra and Ventura 2012)

our brain circuitry. We learned earlier about the Hebbian theory: Neurons that fire together, wire together! The enemy wants to create a neural autobahn (infrastructure) that allows for the free flow of traffic so that sinful impulses will speedily and regularly arrive at their destination—sinful behavior. We cut this off by renouncing sinful impulses in Jesus' name.

Of course, resisting impulses is not always so easy. Thus, the long-term plan must take advantage of the executive function's power and ability to control the reward system. But we need to fuel the executive function to get maximum drive out of its engines. We do this through long-term goal setting that will delay gratification and put the brakes on the immediacy of impulses. We set high-value, high-yielding rewards as our goals over instant self-gratification. We activate the hippocampus (memory and learning) by applying negative reinforcement, a common principle of behavioral psychology that trains us to avoid certain thoughts and behaviors because of their negative outcome.

Through negative reinforcement, we remind ourselves that short-lived pleasure and acts of instant self-satisfaction are thin and without substantial and lasting value. They are often condemned by God's word and also result in feelings of unwanted, gut-wrenching guilt and even shame. In other words, the rewarding stimulus of sin (its pleasure) is temporary and comes with a high cost. Finally, when we regularly do not resist sin and resist repentance, we will find that the long-term reward for sin is death (Rom. 6:23). As Pascal's wager taught us centuries ago, giving up eternal life for temporal pleasure and eternal torment is a bad bet. A true believer does not want to grieve the Spirit nor displease the Father who loves them so much that he sent his Son to die for them.

Together, the negative reinforcement of these unpleasant outcomes, distasteful stimuli, and operant punishment that we have identified produce an aversive salience or motivation to avoid certain thinking and behavior and even the cues or triggers for those sinful "rewards."[10] Satan seduces us by offering "rewards" personally designed for our liking and taste. Satan knows how to bait each one of us specifically based on his past experiments (temptations) on our souls and our past performances. Of course, these rewards are ultimately not rewards. He lies. However, the deception regarding the sinful reward gives it an illusory veneer of attractiveness, a mirage, like the forbidden fruit, which appeared delicious and gratifying. The attraction seduces our senses and builds a desire or an appetite in us for the coveted reward. The desire for the attractive reward draws us to approach and pursue it.

Become aware of your own strong impulses that lead to destructive thinking and behavior. Also, become aware of your own personal cues or triggers that set off those impulses. The cues may be certain times of the year or times of the day, being around certain people, particular stress levels, certain internet use, seeing certain images, hearing certain sounds, feeling certain feelings, and so on. The negative rein-

---

10. George F. Koob and Michel Le Moal, *Neurobiology of Addiction*, 415. (Koob and Le Moal 2006)

forcement of gaining the world, losing our soul, and displeasing the one we love is a strong enough incentive to resist evil cues and impulses.

After establishing the power of negative reinforcement and aversive salience, we supplement it with positive reinforcement and incentive salience. The long-term reward must be greater in value than the short-term reward, which will produce a greater desire for it. Thus, it becomes an easy rational choice to opt for the greater reward. We may not want to think of our spiritual choices in these terms, but it is how the neuropsychology of our brain operates when making decisions. We create a hierarchy of preference based on reward. Thus, it is imperative that we train ourselves to appreciate the value of the eternal over the temporal, the spirit over the self-centered flesh, and the holy or transcendent over the corruptibility of materialism. So what are the rewards of greater, even infinite value that come from submitting to God and resisting the evil? What are the spiritual riches that trump the rewards of immediate gratification? God himself is our reward, and yet he adds blessings as well. They are manifold, such as experiencing more intimacy with Christ, pleasing the Father, greater spiritual growth, more Christlikeness, deeper sanctification, perfect peace and joy, increased spiritual authority and power, obtaining an eternal crown, and other heavenly rewards and blessings that will never fade away.

We then rehearse in our minds over and again the rewards or blessings that come from submitting to God until they are encoded in our memory. Then we activate the function of attention and focus that we learned about in the cognitive neuroscience of attention in Chapter 1 and in the cognitive neuroscience of addiction in Chapter 5. Our fixed, unwavering attention on the long-term goal of submitting to God and receiving his favor and blessings fuels and empowers the executive function to control the gratification system by signaling "no" to our immediate impulses and "yes" to delaying gratification for the greater good and blessing. As a result of learning and implementing God's battle plan with intensity, passion, and consistency, the task of submitting to God and resisting the devil becomes easier to achieve and sustain. Neurons that fire together wire together. The brain makes a way for itself.

Furthermore, this pattern of reward predicting, reward seeking, and reward experiencing runs in a feedback loop to sustain the process. Reward-predictive cues, like believing and experiencing the promise of a reward that comes from submitting to God, generate the neural signaling of the dopaminergic pathways (from the ventral tegmental area [VTA]). These signals release the feel-good hormone of dopamine (dopamine neurons) into the nucleus accumbens that motivates and impels us to seek after the reward or blessing, which comes from submitting to God (the reward-seeking behavioral response).[11] This motivational function of the nucleus accumbens

11. S. M. Nicola, S. A. Taha, S. W. Kim, and H. L. Fields, "Nucleus Accumbens Dopamine Release Is Necessary and Sufficient to Promote the Behavioral Response to Reward-Predictive Cues," *Neuroscience* 135, no. 4 (2005): 1025–33. https://doi.org/10.1016/j.neuroscience.2005.06.088 (Nicola, et al. 2005); Puglisi-Allegra and Ventura, "Prefrontal/Accumbal Catecholamine System Processes High Motivational Salience" (Puglisi-Allegra and Ventura 2012); Anna M. Klawonn and Robert C. Malenka, "Nucleus Accumbens Modulation in Reward and Aversion," *Cold Spring Harbor Symposia on Quantitative Biology* 83 (2018): 119–29. (Klawonn and Malenka 2018) https://doi.org/10.1101/sqb.2018.83.037457.

is called *incentive salience*. Incentive salience is a cognitive function that provides us with motivation and the want—the desire, hunger, and thirst—to pursue an attractive reward.

And, of course, the greatest of these rewards or blessings that we pursue is God himself (Num. 18:20; Job 22:25; Ps. 16:5; Heb. 11:6; Rev. 21:1–7; 22:1–5, 12–13). God told Abraham, "I am your shield, your very great reward" (Gen. 15:1; 17:1–8 NIV). When we submit to God, we receive the greatest reward: God! Incentive salience released by the nucleus accumbens fuels the insatiable, passionate drive forward and chase after God with all of our spirit, soul, and body. Let God above all others be the object of our incentive salience. No other gods! Pray that the brain and its various functions align with God's original intention at creation. Specifically, name the various parts and functions of the brain and pray that they fall into Divine order and perform according to God's original intentions.

In conclusion, let us summarize this passage on spiritual warfare in chapter 4 of the epistle. The apostle James instructs us that warfare begins in our hearts as we fight against sin, which prevents us from loving God and our neighbor. Sanctification needs to be our first line of defense in spiritual warfare. But if we succumb to sin, we find ourselves resisting the grace of God and opposing his will. At this point, it is imperative to repent. We begin by resisting our pride and humbling ourselves before God so that we can receive more grace to overcome ourselves. In turn, once we submit to God, *then* we can resist the devil and his temptations, which are the lust of flesh, the lust of the eyes, and the pride of life. The summation of spiritual warfare made simple is this: Submit and resist!

Boxing as a Metaphor for Life and Spiritual Warfare

My full-time gig is teaching. I am a professor at a mainline denominational seminary where I train master's and doctoral students in theology. On the side, I run a free boxing club that functions as an outreach ministry. We train people from all walks of life, young and old, male and female, black and white, poor and rich and everything in between. One of the draws is the rigorous training, which is second to none for burning stress, losing weight, getting fit, and aligning your numbers in the healthy zone. Among the many other features that also attract people to the boxing gym is that it serves as a classroom for life. Yes, boxing is an effective metaphor for life that teaches you about setting and attaining goals, hard work, discipline, facing tough opposition, and overcoming. In boxing, a fighter sets a goal to succeed in some area of their training. They focus and work hard to attain that goal.

Often there are many obstacles that would prevent them from success, such as inadequate training, deficiency of skill, insufficient confidence, a muddled mind, a weakened will, cloudy judgment, the wrong game plan, incorrect strategy, poor health, debilitating injuries, a shortage of finances, lack of support, an ineffective corner, and unbeatable opponents. A boxer must successfully face each of these battles

151

inside and outside of the ring. If they fail to do so, they may be denied their goal to succeed. Life is very similar.

We face those same battles in the ring of life. There are so many factors to overcoming in life and achieving our goals. The variables, challenges, and circumstances that a boxer faces in the ring, we also face in the ring of life. Likewise, we also need adequate training, proper skills, a clear mind, a will to win, sound judgment, the right game plan, correct strategies, good health, appropriate funding, strong support, and faithful people in our corner in order to win our battles in life and attain our goals. Life, like boxing, is not a cakewalk. It takes the heart of a lion and an iron will to face the battle with a winning attitude. Attitude is 90 percent of the battle!

The great undefeated heavyweight Rocky Marciano won his fights due to two factors: conditioning and heart-attitude. He was not a tremendously skilled fighter. In fact, he was not very graceful but somewhat awkward in the ring. He was short in stature, not very heavy by today's standards, and had the smallest reach of any heavyweight champion. Yet in spite of adversity, he compensated by training as hard or harder than any fighter, and he had the right attitude. He had made up his mind before entering the ring that he would fight his fight and win. He won many of his fights on conditioning and attitude alone. Indeed, life can really throw some hard shots at us at times, but we win or lose in our minds before we win or lose in life. "Fight or Die" is our motto at Big Bang Southside Boxing Club.

Though he called himself the greatest, Muhammad Ali took some thunderous punches in the ring, like when Ken Norton broke his jaw in the second round. Ali did not throw in the towel but grunted it out for the remaining ten rounds. Ali, "The Greatest," was not exempt from getting tagged, and neither are we. We attempt to duck, slip, block, or roll with the punches, but sometimes, in spite of our best efforts, they land. And they land hard. Life's punches may even knock us down to the canvas, taking our wind from us and even our desire to get up and keep fighting. It is there on the canvas with the life knocked out of the boxer that they have to decide if they to want to win or lose. I always tell my fighters, there are no losers except the ones who quit. The great Jack Dempsey is credited with asserting that "a champion is someone who gets up when he can't." Don't let life count you out!

Fighters train their minds to push past any inner suggestion of throwing in the towel and quitting. They fortify their wills to press on and knock down every wall that the body and mind erect to stop them from overcoming. Getting counted out on the canvas of disappointment in the ring of life is never an option. Real fighters know that the battle is won in the mind long before it is ever fought in the ring. In fact, the mind is the real ring, and the only actual opponent is us. In our mind, we are battling with our will. Will we be counted out or go one more round? The decision is ours. No one makes us stay on the canvas of life and get counted out but us. No one makes us rise to our feet for one more round but us (by the grace of God). The amiable but tough-nosed Rocky Balboa put it best: "Going that one more round when you don't think you can, that's what makes all the difference in your life."

We will fight many hard rounds in the battle of life. Life does not pull any punches. It's live and real. Life is also undefeated. No one can fight it and ultimately win. For life has a famous, formidable punch. It's a real killer. It's called death. In the end, life deals a death blow to each of us. No one can slip this punch. It lands every time and has taken out the best. The brightest and best have gone toe to toe with life but have succumbed to its final deadly blow. But there is one undefeated champion who defeated the previously unbeaten champion, death. No one has survived their battle in the ring with death except one: Jesus Christ, the resurrection and the life. On our behalf, he took on life, sin, death, and hell and came up victorious. Through death (and resurrection) he conquered death. We share in that victory because Christ died and rose again for us. His cross is our cross, and his victory is our victory.

Demons Are Real

Not only is life a battle with everyday challenges, but it is also a battle with spiritual challenges. We are faced with temptations and opposition from our perennial enemy, the devil. He purposes to keep us away from God and his plan of salvation for our lives. He separates us from God by seducing us through the power of his lies and deceit. Deception is his only power, but it has proven very useful and effective for him for thousands of years. He lures us into the lie that we can create a world where we are our own god and we can live by our own desires and have whatever we choose. As usual, Satan writes a check to us that we cannot cash. His promises are false. The devil never delivers. Well, he does deliver sin and death. He comes to separate us from God and destroy our lives and God's dream for us. John 10:9 declares Satan's mission statement is "to steal, kill, and destroy." The devil, our adversary, is looking to devour us, like a roaring, hungry lion. He sets wiles, or strategic traps, to snare us.

Yes, the Bible reveals that we are in a spiritual war against invisible foes (demons). The modern mind has a tough time believing that there is a spiritual, supernatural world inhabited by spiritual, supernatural angelic beings both good and evil (fallen). However, Scripture and the tradition of the church have always recognized this reality. The modern mind puts much trust in the ability of science, and we should. It has made astounding discoveries, invented game-breaking technology and resources, created our modern conveniences, and offered satisfying explanations for much of our universe. However, it cannot explain everything, including God, the cause of the universe, and what is beyond the universe. When we put our faith in science to explain everything, we are making science our god or theology, which is called *scientism*.

Physics, for example, has made titanic leaps in the last couple hundred years to explain the empirical and phenomenal world. Einstein's theory of relativity, mass-energy equivalence, quantum mechanics, Hubble's expanding universe, the standard model, the Higgs boson, and others are among the many astounding discoveries. However, many mysteries remain unresolved, such as the definitive origin of the universe, unifying the quantum and gravity in one theory, quantum entanglement, understanding the nature of dark energy and dark matter, matter–antimatter asymmetry, and many others. Also, science is not designed to resolve existential and metaphysical questions such as the following: Is there a God? Why am I here? What is the meaning of life? Though I am an avid student of the sciences and earnestly appreciate all of the advances and accomplishments they have made for the good of the modern world, it does not take much effort to deduce that science cannot explain everything. Merely consider the recent Covid-19 crisis and our misguided faith in science that attempted to explain and treat it.[12] As believers, when considering spiritual truths, we put our faith ultimately in God and his Word, who "created all things in existence both visible and invisible" (Col. 1:16).[13]

There is an *invisible* creation. God made heaven, hell, angels, and fallen angels (demons). These are part of the invisible created order. Scripture informs us that there was a war in heaven (Revelation 12). Lucifer, meaning "bearer of light," was a powerful angel that chose to rebel against God (Isaiah 14; Ezekiel 28). He deceived himself into thinking he could overthrow God. Because of the beauty and power that God had given him, he worshipped himself instead of thanking and worshipping God. He coaxed one-third of the angels to rebel with him. But as we know, Michael the Archangel and his angelic armies defeated the rebel angels and cast them out of heaven to the earth. The fallen angels, due to their wickedness, have been transformed into demons. They lost their place and power in heaven. However, even in their fallen state, a vestige of their knowledge and power remains. In this age, they roam the earth to and fro, tempting, stealing, killing, and destroying (Job 1; Matthew 4; John 10:9; 1 Pet. 5:8). Beginning in the garden, their main target has been humanity, God's greatest creation.

The devil came in the form of a serpent and seduced Adam and Eve to disobey God and eat from the forbidden tree of the knowledge of good and evil. The enemy promised the couple that they could be like god, though they already were, being made in his image. They were seduced to believe that the fruit of sin and death would actually make them wise and would satisfy them. From the moment humanity's parents succumbed to sin, Satan placed his foot in the door of human hearts. We have been in a spiritual war for our souls ever since. Remember, the serpent's punishment was to crawl on the ground and eat the dust of the earth (Gen. 3:14), and humanity was made from the dust of the earth (Gen. 2:7; 3:19). Demons eat flesh, so keep yours crucified (Gal. 5:24). Starve the devil by not feeding him your flesh. Like reading the signs at the zoo that say "Don't feed the animals," don't feed the demons. They will only get stronger, while you get weaker. Feeding is breeding! Satan is our enemy, but greater, we are our own worst enemy. Satan cannot use what we don't give him. Keep your flesh on the cross. A dead believer is a victorious believer (Romans 6–8; Gal. 2:20; 5:23; Eph. 4:12–14; Colossians 2–3).

---

12. We will not discuss the shortcomings of science and proofs for the existence of God in this book. I refer the reader to Bellini, *Through the Threshold*; and Jerry Walls and Trent Dougherty, eds., *Two Dozen (or so) Arguments for God: The Plantinga Project* (Oxford University Press, 2018).

13. Author's translation.

The enemy's goal is to keep our flesh active and to enslave us in sin, keeping us from God's purpose that he has for our lives. He is envious that God created humanity and gave them this special purpose in the world to bear his image and likeness and represent his Kingdom on the Earth. The enemy of our soul is angry that Christ died for our sins and set us free from the power of sin, death, and Satan. Satan is jealous that God has made a covenant with us through Christ that we should have an eternal loving relationship with him and experience all of his blessings for every area of our lives. He wants to steal those blessings and our relationship with the Father. He wants to kill our souls and destroy God's plan for us. Satan aims to destroy our lives, families, friends, and churches. He intends to destroy our call and ministries. The devil aspires to destroy our peace, joy, faith, and hope in heaven and have us punished eternally in hell. Although Christ has defeated Satan at the cross, many do not realize this finished fact. Neither do they realize that we have been given authority and power over all of the enemy (Luke 10:19–20; 1 John. 3:8). Countless times I have watched my spiritual children and young believers come to life and find great joy once they learned how to battle and defeat the enemy. They were tired of being bullied and living in bondage. They hungered for freedom and became freedom fighters. We have not been taught how to fight (Ps. 144:1). Disciples need to be taught the art and science of spiritual warfare.

The Art of War

Sun Tzu (544–496 BCE), the eminent Chinese general and military strategist, wrote the classic manual on warfare that has been the gold standard of warfare wisdom for ages.[14] Upfront, the author strongly asserts, "All warfare is based on deception."[15] That statement is clearly true for the enemy of our souls as well. Deception is his sole weapon. He is a liar and the father of all lies. Mendacity is woven intricately into all of his machinations, devices, and wiles. Hence, we need to be aware of his schemes (2 Cor. 2:11; 10:4–5; Eph. 6:11–12). He is an opportunist, a dirty fighter. He waits for an opening in our life when we are vulnerable to attack (Luke 4:13). He rarely throws one punch at a time. We can usually defend against those attacks. No, he throws a barrage of punches at a time. Punches in bunches! They are harder to defend. He throws multiple temptations, trials, and tragedies at a time; he throws them when we are helpless; and he attacks those in our life who are most vulnerable. He hits your spouse with a cancer while he decimates your finances and leads your children into rebellion, drugs, porn, and promiscuity, all at the same time. I have been there for sure.

He attacks us personally. He attacks our family, friends, spiritual life, prayer, health, finances, church, ministry, work, reputation, possessions, our faith in God and the Scriptures, and everything pertaining to God's covenant with us. Most im-

---

14. Although authorship of the book has traditionally been attributed to Sun Tzu, uncertainty has been expressed as to authorship and even the existence of Sun Tzu.

15. Tzu, *The Art of War*, 3. (Tzu 2000)

portantly, be aware that most of his vicious insidious assaults are against our mind. The mind is the central, key battlefield. Remember, as the mind goes, so we go! Psychological warfare! The battlefield is seven to nine inches between your two ears. The enemy indirectly (through the flesh) or directly shoots lies into our minds 25/8—twenty-five hours a day, eight days a week. That is why we are commanded to cast down and destroy every vain thought that exalts itself against Christ (2 Cor. 10:4). We are further commanded to capture each of our "rebellious thoughts and teach them to obey Christ." How do we accomplish that? Change the channel on evil thinking. Replace rebellious thoughts with the word of God. In doing so, we align our minds with the mind of Christ.

At times, victory may seem difficult. Satan and his evil angels have known and fought against the heart and mind of humanity for centuries. They know what works and brings our defeat. They also know our lives thoroughly. They have military intelligence on each of us. They are familiar with our fight record. They have all of the fight films that they study. They know our weaknesses, susceptibilities, soft spots, and desires. Demons are also relentless in their persistence to defeat us. They have all the time in the world until Christ returns to wear us down and then come in for the kill. Therefore, we need to be well-trained in the art of spiritual warfare and be prepared. Pastors, teach your people how to fight!

As we have stated throughout, Christ already defeated Satan on the cross (John 19:30; 1 John 3:8). We are merely enforcing the finished work of the cross. We have already won the battle. We need to go into battle knowing that our foe has already been defeated, and, ultimately, we are guaranteed the victory. We need to encode and imprint this crucial truth into our brain's circuitry. Even Sun Tzu assuredly declared, "Victorious warriors win first and then go to war, while defeated warriors go to war first and then seek to win."[16] We are fighting and resisting Satan in Jesus' name. The name of Jesus is one of our most potent weapons. Demons run with their tail between their legs at the name of Jesus (Jas. 4:7; Mark 16:17; Luke 10:19–20; Phil. 2:10). God has equipped us with all that we need to win the battle over our mind and the war with Satan.

"The best defense is a good offense" is an invaluable piece of wisdom that has been claimed by savvy strategists from George Washington to Vince Lombardi. I train the boxers in my gym to fighter smarter and not harder, and that includes an impenetrable defense. Your opponent can't hurt what they can't hit! I teach them to keep their guard up at all times. Don't drop the hands. And keep your eyes wide open and awake to see the punches coming long before they make contact so that you can make your defensive adjustment and counterattack.

God has also provided us with an airtight defense. When we learn to use it properly, we will find ourselves victorious. The Lord has given us the "armor of God" to suit ourselves for the battle (Eph. 6:11). In the Greek New Testament, "the armor of God" is in the genitive case. The phrase can mean the armor that *belongs* to God,

---

16. Paraphrased from Sun Tzu, *The Art of War*, 4. (Tzu 2000)

but, further, it can also mean the armor that *is* God. In that sense, God himself is our armor. He is our defense. Each piece of the armor is an attribute or work of God. We are grounded and girded with God's truth (Eph. 6:14). Our heart is covered by his righteousness (Eph. 6:14). Stand firmly in his good news of peace (Eph. 6:15). Our bodies are protected by the faith that God gives us to trust him (Eph. 6:16). Our minds are protected by his salvation (Eph. 6:17).

These pieces of God's armor are all mainly for defensive purposes. There is no armor or protection for the warrior's back because the Roman soldier was never to turn in battle. All of their wounds were found to be in front. Our courage and strength for the battle is not our own but comes from God. We are "strong in the Lord," not in ourselves, "and in his mighty power," which never grows weary or weak (Eph. 6:10). Finally, there is one piece of equipment that was fashioned for offensive purposes, the double-edged, flaming sword of the Spirit, which is the word of God (Eph. 6:17). It is the same sword that proceeds from Christ, the warrior's mouth whereby he slays the evil armies of this world (Rev. 19:15). He has given us his own sword (Word) to wield skillfully against the enemy. His weapons are sufficiently mighty to throttle and thrash the enemy (2 Cor. 10:3–4).

God has thoroughly equipped us with other spiritual weapons for this spiritual war (2 Cor. 1:3–4), including the blood of Christ (Rev. 12:11), praise and worship (1 Sam 16:14, 23; 18:10; Ps. 18:1; 2 Chron. 20:15–22), intercessory prayer (Eph. 6:18), the cross (Heb. 2:14), humility (Jas. 4:7), the keys of the kingdom to bind and loose (Matt. 16:19), a hedge of protection (Job 1:10), thanksgiving (2 Chron. 20:21), fasting (Matt. 17:21), and spiritual gifts (2 Chron. 20:14–17), among others. Like any skilled fighter, we need to be trained to use effectively both our defensive and offensive weapons. Know how to use the armor of God and the sword of the Spirit to fight against stubborn, harassing, personal sins, such as anger (wrath), lust, pride (vanity), laziness (sloth), jealousy (envy), gluttony (covetousness), and greed (avarice), which are traditionally known as *the seven deadly sins*. Later, "sadness" (despondency, acedia, misery or dejection) was added as the eighth deadly sin. And of course, "unbelief," which opens the door to all of the others, is to be avoided.

Like a vigilant fighter who knows the tactics of his opponent and is prepared to defend, be aware of these personal sins. Be aware what, when, where, why, and how Satan strategizes to implement these weapons against you. Keep track of strategies, tactics, defeats, and victories in a journal. Record them for your memory and future learning. Know your triggers, and, as much as possible, don't put yourself in a place of temptation mentally or physically. Often Satan does not need to provoke or tempt us; we do a good job working for him on our own. We remember that our chief enemies are the devil, the flesh (sinful), and the world (world's evil system).

Here is a list of some of the enemy's favorite, more frequently used personal, psychological warfare tactics:

- **Condemnation:** A false guilt imposed on us by Satan or ourselves for a wrongdoing, even though we may have repented and been forgiven or even though it was an imaginary wrongdoing. The *voice of condemnation* from Satan or self-condemnation accuses, bullies, oppresses, is forceful, disregards mercy and forgiveness, is never satisfied, keeps one bound and guilty, and knows no peace. The *voice of conviction* from the Spirit is meek, gentle, a still small voice. It leads; woos; is satisfied with mercy, repentance, and forgiveness; liberates; and gives peace.

- **Disqualification:** The voice from Satan or self that says that no matter what we do, we are wrong, unforgiven, guilty, not enough, not saved, not loved, and so on. This voice is never satisfied; it is the voice of fault-finding; it relentlessly points out why we don't qualify for any of God's blessings. The voice of qualification is full of grace, affirmation, acceptance, and approval based on the blood of Jesus; it encourages us in who we are in Christ and what we can do through Christ, who strengthens us; it assures us that all of the promises of God are yes and amen in Christ (2 Cor. 1:10). The voice of disqualification has the same characteristics as the voice of condemnation previously mentioned. The voice of qualification is encouraging, hopeful, affirming, empowering, faith building, and assuring.

- **Doublemindedness:** James speaks of having two minds: a mind that says yes to God and not to the devil, the flesh, and the world, and a mind that says no to God and yes to the devil, the flesh, and the world (1:8; 4:8). We are called to be single-minded (Matt. 6:22–24), a mind controlled by the Spirit and not by the sinful flesh (Rom. 8:5–6). A double mind is a doubting mind filled with unbelief. At times we can have doubts and questions about God that may arise naturally (e.g., during a tragedy or when studying). A heart filled with unbelief is a rebellious mindset that refuses to submit and believe God's word. Satan will take whatever he can get. Thus, if he cannot get us to condemn or disqualify ourselves, throw in the towel, give in to sin, or quit the Christian life, he is content to let us live miserably, flip-flopping back and forth from faith to doubt in doublemindedness. In this way, we are paralyzed and ineffective in our walk because we are weighed down and trapped between two minds. Pray against doublemindedness and ask for a single-hearted commitment to Christ. Be resolved and willing to have a mind fixed on God regardless of the temptation to doubt and waver (Isa. 26:1–3).

- **Legalism:** Can occur when we begin to rely on our own knowledge, power, or morality to save us from sin. We are saved by the finished work of Jesus Christ on the cross (John 19:30; Rom. 3:21–31), and we receive salvation by grace through faith and not of our own works (Matt. 7:15–23; 12:33; Eph. 2:8), which naturally results in the fruit of the Spirit (Gal. 5:22–23) and wrought works (Rom. 13:8–10; Jas.

2:14–25). Satan tempts us to add to what Christ has already done for us in order to be saved. The blood of Christ alone has the power to save. Christ completed the work of salvation at Calvary. However, salvation is received in our lives by grace through faith and not by our own works. Yet true salvation will, by its very nature, produce fruit and godly works in and through us, through the power and work of the Holy Spirit as a witness and confirmation of what Christ has accomplished for us (Rom. 8:14–16; Phil. 2:13; Jas. 2:18–19, 22). Legalism convinces many that they can be saved by a specific mode or formula of baptism, by only attending a particular church, by keeping the Sabbath, by performing the full Old Testament law, by only using a particular translation of the Bible, by paying tithes and offerings, by praying or fasting enough, by sitting under the covering or authority of a particular minister, and so on (Gal. 3:3). These are false doctrines.

- **License:** The opposite of legalism. License claims that because we are saved by grace, we are allowed to continue in sin (Rom. 6:1–7; 14). By grace (true grace), we have died to sin and are no longer under sin's dominion. License, theologically termed *antinomianism*, declares that because we are under grace and forgiven, the moral law of God is obsolete or nullified. St. Paul addresses this mindset through question and answer: "Do we, then, nullify the law by this faith? Certainly not! Instead, we uphold the law" (Rom. 3:31 BSB). We are called to walk by the Spirit that will allow us by faith to fulfill the righteous requirements of the law (Rom. 8:4), which is love (Rom. 13:8–10), not just with our words but with our deeds (1 John 3:18). Satan convinces many believers that because they are forgiven and saved, they can continue in sin and do whatever they please. However, Scripture strongly condemns this false doctrine and rebellious attitude (Matt. 7:15–23; 10:22; Heb. 6:4–11; 10:19–39; 1 John 3:1–10). A true believer wants to do the will of the Father, and the Father will empower him or her with the Holy Spirit, who makes us holy and empowers us to his works. The Spirit keeps us balanced in our walk to not tilt toward legalism nor license.

- **Sin-sampling:** Similar to license. It is a spirit and mindset of permission. Sin-sampling occurs when Satan convinces us that just a little taste from the forbidden fruit won't hurt. He coaxes us because it is just a peccadillo (a tiny sin or mistake) that we can give ourselves permission to indulge. He persuades us that because God will forgive us if we taste, why not try it and see what we have been missing? There is a big, luscious party at the tree of the knowledge of good and evil, and God has excluded us. He didn't invite us, and we are missing out on all of the fun. Just take a taste. God won't mind. There are several problems with sin-sampling. First, God does not lead us to sample sin. Our flesh, the flesh of others, or the devil is swaying us to sample sin. Second, it is true that God does forgive sin, but when we sin knowingly and willingly, we are putting God to the test, which is a sin (Deut. 6:16; Ps. 78:18–56; Matt. 4:7; Gal. 6:7). The Spirit of God will not always strive and contend with a rebellious soul. So don't count on a blank check or a free lifetime pass from God (Gen. 6:3).

Third, the devil will *always* take you further than you wanted to go with him. You wanted just a taste of one sin, but years later, you ended up devoured by a mass of sin. Some want just a puff, a sip, a look, a sniff, a feel, a thought, a word, a part, or whatever the temptation minimally requires. Satan always allows a free sample at his fruit market. But once you make a transaction with the devil, you will receive more than you bargained for, my friend. As a minister, I have heard hundreds of tragic stories about dealings with the devil. Virtually, they all started and ended the same. The person said that their curiosity started out small and innocent and ended with more than they could handle. Satan took their soul and everything in it. There is no such thing as sin management with the devil. You can't manage sin; sin manages you.

- **Offense:** Satan gets a lot of mileage out of offense. Granted there are legitimate reasons to be offended, and we all can become offended at times when we experience an injustice. I am not referring to that type of offense but more so the pathological, chronic type that is experienced whether slight or projected. When we walk with wounds that have not been healed, sins that have not been forgiven, ego that has not been crucified, eyes gazing at our navel, self that is pitied, and feelings overly fixated and sensitive to hurt, perceived or projected, we are open to be controlled by a spirit of offense. Dead people do not get easily or wrongly offended. An uncrucified ego coupled with a self-pitying spirit are an easy target for offense. Such people are always offended no matter what you do to assuage them. It's either too much or too little, too sweet or too sour, too heavy or too light, too long or too short, too loud or too soft, *ad infinitum.*

  Offense happens everywhere, but for those who are offense-friendly or pathologically offended, it happens most often with the family, marriage, or church. The offended at church are the easiest to spot. They are always complaining about something—the music, the sermon, the color of the carpet, the children, the meeting, the pastoral visit, or the way congregants treat them. And of course, they are always extorting the church. "If such and such occurs or doesn't occur again, I am leaving the church" is their mantra. Satan loves to get us offended by either real or imagined offenses. Some are even offended by the unalloyed truth of the gospel (Matt. 13:57; 18:7; Rom. 9:33; Gal. 5:11; 1 Pet. 2:8). Its unsanded edges of truth are too rough for the offended to handle. Thus, the preacher has to feed the people milk and itch their ears with what they want to hear, lest they get offended.

Offense keeps people imprisoned in bitterness, blame, resentment, jealousy, anger, and unforgiveness. Offense keeps people from being blessed and productive in their Christian walk and service. Pathologically offended people blame everyone for their problems and faults except themselves. "If it wasn't for so and so, I would be such and such. If so and so wouldn't have done such and such to me, I could have been doing this and that." The offended are rarely responsible, and they see themselves as victims. The psychology of offense and blames "affords the blamer a sense of mastery and control—even feelings of omnipotence—over their surroundings. Exhilaration infuses blamers as they accuse another and claim the entitlement to justice or payback for the supposed wrongdoing." Though the offended seems to get a high from the sensation, "the blamer is often someone prone to internal fragmentation and shame, followed by storms of narcissistic rage. The act of dispensing blame serves to reconsolidate the self. It is the glue that keeps the personality from becoming disorganized. Surprising though it may be, the angry person shaking a pointer finger is often falling apart on the inside."[17] Offense and blame trigger the amygdala and the fight, flight, or freeze mechanism. When triggered frequently, offense and blame become an automatic response. Crucifixion, putting on the helmet of salvation, good CBT/Truth Therapy practices, and forgiveness are the best remedy for offense.

The Need for Deliverance

In some cases a person can no longer resist the devil, perpetually falling into sin in one or more area of his or her life and needing deliverance from a demonic stronghold and sin. They are no longer free and need help. *One shorthand definition of moral freedom is the ability to do otherwise.* If someone is bound in a sin and cannot stop if he or she wanted to, he or she most likely is a slave to it and cannot find freedom. In this case, he or she should call on the assistance of the church for help. Although many churches are not knowledgeable and seasoned in deliverance, it is an increasingly needed ministry in an age when the presence and working of evil is mounting. Churches need to catch up and begin to train those called in healing and deliverance and deploy them in the church and in the world. They serve as intercessors who are

---

17. Molly S. Castelloe, "Needing a Target for Blame" *Psychology Today*, June 30, 2023. https://www.psychologytoday.com/us/blog/the-me-in-we/202306/needing-a-target-for-blame. (Castelloe 2023)

equipped by Christ to stand in the gap for those who are bound in sin by the devil and can no longer walk in victory.

Repentant persons desiring freedom do not have to remain enchained by the devil. Nor should we be fearful of the demonic. Popular depictions of deliverance and exorcism from horror movies are deceiving and have given the wrong impression of the power dynamic between God and the devil. In these films, such as *The Exorcist*, the devil is portrayed as greater and more powerful than God and the church. Usually, some innocent child is victimized by the demonic, and the priest or other church official is powerless to set them free. This scenario is a blatant lie. Satan is a defeated foe. Christ defeated him on the cross. Further, Christ has given the church, each of us, power and authority over the devil (Luke 10:19–20). If we know who we are in Christ and our authority in Christ, Satan cannot harm us. In fact, demons actually fear the Spirit-filled believer who knows the power of the name of Jesus. In the name of Jesus, we can bind, rebuke, and drive out demons—as simple as that (Mark 16:17).

Deliverance, along with preaching, teaching, and healing, was a staple in Christ's earthly ministry. He extended that same ministry, power, and authority to the disciples, and it is extended to us (Matt. 10:1–8). The early church practiced deliverance (e.g., Acts 16:16–34). The renunciation and exorcism of devils was also a vital component of the catechumenate and the baptismal liturgy.[18] Many baptismal rites today still include the renunciation vows from the early church. The monastics (e.g., St. Francis of Assisi, Martin Luther), the Puritans (e.g., William Gurnall), John Wesley and the early Methodists, Pentecostals and Charismatics, modern Catholics (e.g., Francis MacNutt and Neil Lozano), and the majority of global Christians have practiced deliverance and exorcism. Every disciple should know how to fight and be ready, willing, and able to cast out demons if necessary.

Consider Tina. She was a twenty-three-year-old woman who called the church in desperation needing help. She came into the pastor's office and shared her story—and what a story! She was dedicated to Satan as an infant. Her mother was a practicing witch who cursed her and used witchcraft on her. A family sexually abused her as a child. She became addicted to meth in her teens and prostituted herself to support her habit. She birthed three children but also had several abortions. She was in an abusive relationship with her boyfriend, who pimped her out to make money off of her. Child Protective Services took her kids away from her. She was starting to hear voices and see demonic manifestations that she could not control. Could you help her? Would your church know how to minister to her? That afternoon, when she came into the church, we ministered deliverance on her and led her to the Lord. She left that office free, in her right mind, born again, and speaking in other tongues because we knew how to minister to her.

For a comprehensive treatment of the theology and practice of deliverance, I recommend the book *The X-Manual*.[19] One segment of the text that is worth sharing here is the Four Laws of Deliverance. These laws provide the theoretical and practical basis to exercise deliverance. An abridged version appears here:

---

18. See *The Apostolic Tradition* of Hippolytus.

19. Bellini, *The X-Manual*.

1. **The Law of the Cross:** The basis for our victory over demons and sin comes from the finished work of the cross. When Jesus died, he defeated sin, death, and the devil. The power of sin, death, and the devil were broken and defeated at the cross. From the cross, Christ cried out, "It is finished" (John 19:30). The work needed to defeat Satan and sin was finished at the cross. The cross is our theological and practical foundation for deliverance from the demonic and victory over the devil. Believers do not need to strive to attain victory over Satan. He has already been defeated. We just need to implement the finished work of the cross and exercise and enforce the authority that Christ gave us.

    *   **Romans 6; Ephesians 1:20; 2:6:** At the cross the power of sin is broken. When Christ died, we died. When Christ was buried, we were buried. When Christ resurrected, we resurrected. When Christ ascended, we ascended.
    *   **Romans 8:3:** At the cross Jesus condemned sin in his body. He judged and destroyed sin and Satan through his death.
    *   **John 12:31; 16:8-11:** Satan was cast out and defeated.
    *   **John 19:30:** It is finished!
    *   **Colossians 2:12-15:** Satan was defeated. Demons mocked. Keys were taken!
    *   **Hebrews 2:14-15:** Through his death, Jesus defeated Satan, who had the power of death.
    *   **Revelation 1:18; 20:10:** Jesus has the keys of hell and death. Satan awaits his sentence in the lake of fire. We war from a position of victory. We merely execute the finished work of the cross.

2. **The Law of the Will:** The law of the will applies to our God-given agency and power to will and choose. Neither God nor the devil will override our will. The will is key to enslaving the soul. Satan seduces and tempts the will to yield to sin. When we yield to sin and Satan, our will to a degree becomes bound to that sin and the enemy. Through deliverance, our will needs to be freed and agency restored so that we can submit to God and resist sin. The target is the will. Satan targets the will. God targets the will, and in deliverance, we target the will. To the degree a person submits to sin/the demonic or Christ, to that degree sin/the demonic or Christ has authority over the person. Degree of submission determines the degree of authority proportionate to the number of generations, duration, frequency, and intensity of the practice. Deliverance occurs by the grace of God through the power of the Spirit. It is a gift from God, but it requires one's repentance, full surrender, and willingness to die to sin to receive it. The Spirit bears witness immediately to the person's spirit and over time through

the fruit of the Spirit if the deliverance was successful. "Demonization" (*daimonizomai*) is a better translation than "possession." The word implies degrees of influence versus possession. It is not all or nothing but in degrees and in areas of the soul.

- **Mark 8:32–33:** Attachments in an area rather than full possession. St. Peter struggled with fear of man and people pleasing, and even though he was a believer, he was demonized in this area. He didn't want Christ to be rejected and die but hoped for an earthly kingdom on earth.
- **Romans 6:13, 16, 19:** You are a slave to whatever you obey or submit to.
- **2 Peter 2:19:** For you are a slave to whatever controls you.
- **John 5:6:** Do you really want to be healed? One must be willing. Recovering the will and agency are key to deliverance and healing.
- **Mark 9:14–29:** I believe; help my unbelief. He expressed a willingness to believe.

3. **The Law of True Repentance:** True repentance is the condition for breaking with sin and Satan. Repentance breaks the legal ground and bonds with both. By the grace of God, when one is *willing* to cease from sin and no longer permit it to have a place in one's life, the power and authority of Christ through the cross is free to work fully in one's life. If one is not willing to cease from the sinful practice and falls into repent and repeat, sin and the enemy will bring the person into bondage once again. One's willingness does not free one from sin and Satan. It merely gives God permission to do the work necessary for deliverance and no longer gives consent to the flesh to resist God's grace and continue to sin. A bound person cannot will themselves free, but a person can be willing to be set free and willing to cease from sin. Repentance is a gift. It is a gracious work of the Spirit. Yet the Spirit will work on our desire and will to allow him to work. He will not override our will. The person chained in sin must use the prevenient grace afforded to them to be willing to repent, to turn from a self-centered life to a God-centered life, to turn from a sinful practice to practicing righteousness. Ultimately, repentance comes from God and is confirmed by God through the witness of the Spirit. The Spirit lets us know when we have truly repented, as opposed to going through the motions or a perfunctory process and meaningless ritual to satisfy our conscience or appease our guilt, or shame. Repentance is not offered to us to appease our own feelings or because we have been caught in our sin. Repentance is our response to God's gracious call to believe on Christ for the forgiveness of sins.

- **Matthew 3:** Lay the axe at the roots. Scripture requires us to have fruit that is fit for repentance, which means if our repentance is true, then there will be right action. "(You) repent" is a commandment.
- **2 Corinthians 7:8–12:** True repentance that does not need its own repentance.
- **Romans 12:1:** Offer yourself as a holy, living sacrifice. It is your reasonable service.
- **1 John 2:1, 3:** I write these things, so you do not sin.

4. **The Law of Authority:** Christ gives us power of attorney to act in his behalf, and use his name, authority, and power to defeat and cast out devils. God gives you the authority to exercise deliverance. You have been given the keys of the Kingdom to bind and loose, open and close. These keys of authority can loose heaven and bind the demonic on earth. The name of Jesus is the name of authority. In the name of Jesus, we have the power to drive out demons.

- **Luke 19:18-21:** Christ has given us his authority.
- **Matt. 16-19; 18:18:** We have been given the keys to the Kingdom.
- **Mark 16:17: Phil.2:10:** Even demons submit to the power of Jesus' name.

Psychological Warfare

From 1953 to 1973, the Central Intelligence Agency (CIA) operated an illegal top-secret human experimentation project called MK Ultra.[20] MK Ultra tested various procedures and drugs to induce mind control that would weaken wills, force confessions, produce amnesia, and program subjects to commit assassinations.[21] Some of the methods included psychedelic drugs, electroshock treatment, biochemical weapons, sensory deprivation, physical abuse, hypnosis, and other forms of torture. It has been argued that some of the scientists recruited to work in the United States under *Operation Paperclip* after World War II were former Nazi scientists who brought with them tactics that they had employed on World War II prisoners of war. The object

---

20. U. S. Congress, Senate Select Committee on Intelligence, *Project MKUProject MKULTRA, the CIA's Program of Research in Behavioral Modification*, 94th Cong., 2 sess. (U.S. Government Printing Office, 1977), 70; *Book 1: Final Report of the Select Committee to Study Governmental Operations with Respect to Intelligence Activities, United States Senate Together with Additional, Supplemental, and Separate Views* (U.S. Government Printing Office, April 26, 1976), 391. (U.S. Congress, Senate Select Committee to Study Governmental Operations with Respect to Intelligence Activities 1976) Terry Gross, "The CIA's Secret Quest for Mind Control: Torture, LSD and a 'Poisoner in Chief,' NPR, September 9, 2019. (Gross 2019)

21. Some have suggested that Lee Harvey Oswald may have been a test subject in the CIA project. Ryan Grim, "Lee Harvey Oswald, the CIA, and LSD: New Clues in Newly Declassified Documents," *The Intercept*, December 18, 2022, https://theintercept.com/2022/12/19/lee-harvey-oswald-cia-lsd-jfk/. (Grim 2022)

of the psychological warfare inflicted on the human subjects was to incapacitate the will in order to control the mind. Thankfully, following Watergate, the program was discontinued and later investigated by the Church Committee, the Rockefeller Commission, and the Senate Select Committee on Intelligence. The committees and the public could not conceive that the American government, *their* government, would be involved in terror such as this.

The horrors that were discovered in this government program were unspeakable, but even worse has been the psychological warfare program operated by Satan and his legions since the fall of humanity. The devil's goal has been terror and mind control. The enemy has injected the most deadly lies into the minds of individuals, institutions, corporations, systems, political parties, militaries, populations, and nations throughout history to control us and to get us to destroy ourselves and each other. His psychological warfare has been gravely successful in controlling minds with blinding deception, venomous ideologies, enslaving systems, and voracious passion for wickedness.

For example, one toxic sociopolitical ideology that the enemy has reinjected into the mind of various cultures time and again is the seductive system of totalitarianism. Today, it seems that people, whether it is the left or the right, want it *all*. The political arena is rapidly becoming a zero-sum game of totalization. We need to refresh our memory and recall the cycles of totalitarianism and oppression that stained the twentieth century with the blood of the masses, between the Nazism of Germany (the right) and the communism of the Soviet Union, China, and other regimes (the left).

I wonder how much emphasis is placed on twentieth-century history in the schools. In light of recent politically charged curricula that seem to have subverted every other classroom subject, there is a concern that the basics are not being taught. And for those of us who remember the events of twentieth-century history, we have readily forgotten those lessons that arguably more persons were killed under totalitarian left and authoritarian right regimes in that century than in all of human history; modest estimates are around 262 to 360 million people.[22] "Democide" is the genocide, mass murder, systemic torture and killing, politicide, executions, systemic starvation, forced labor, imprisonment, massacres, and extermination of innocent people under totalitarian regimes and dictators, such as Lenin and Stalin (62 million), Hitler (21 million), Mao Zedong (35 million), Tito (1.1 million), Ho Chi Minh (1.6 million), Pol Pot (2.3 million), and others. Of all the types of totalitarian and authoritarian regimes, communist states have killed the most.[23]

History teaches us that in order to conquer and control a people effectively and totally, first control their minds and their language (the primary carrier of culture), and then their heritage, culture, systems, and institutions will fall, including their systems of communication, education, economy, and military. Then the deed is done.

---

22. Rudolf Rummel, *Statistics of Democide* (Rutgers University Press, 1997), https://www.hawaii.edu/powerkills/DBG.CHAP1.HTM.

23. G. W. Scully, *Murder by the State* (National Center for Policy Analysis, 1997), https://www.ncpa-thinktank.org/pdfs/st211.pdf; (Scully 1997) Rummel, *Death by Government*.

So let us beware of attempts at controlled thought and speech in our day, especially in schools and universities, historical bastions of free speech and the soil where seeds are planted. On the other hand, there can be a fine line between free speech and hate speech that demonizes, hurts, threatens, and leads to violence.

Rudolf Rummel's thesis on democide is that power kills because it *can*. When injustice, oppression, and violence are not opposed, power kills. We find power unbridled mainly in totalitarian regimes as opposed to democracies, which are *basically* nonviolent and peacekeeping. In his epic research, Rummel states, "My overall aim was to test the theoretical hypothesis that the more democratic a regime, the less democide; the less democratic and more totalitarian a regime, the more democide. . . . Power kills, power kills absolutely." Rummel's monumental work calculates the democide from totalitarian regimes throughout history and compares those statistics with those of democracies to show the immense disparity and provide evidence for his hypothesis.

Satan employs an array of strategies in a multifront attack on the mind. At the macro level, he uses faulty metaphysical systems, false grand narratives, erroneous worldviews, and their devastating effects. Examples of these can be located in certain religions, philosophies, scientific claims, or political and sociocultural ideologies that are purposed to enslave the collective mind of a people. In addition, at the micro level, he unleashes personal ground-level campaigns with deception and works of the flesh against the individual at all points of interrelational contact with self, others, the world, and God.

Psychological Warfare in the Culture

Jesus Christ Is Lord!

Different scholars give their own takes on the demonology revealed in Scripture. Not much detail is provided within its pages, so the ranking and defining of demonic offices can be highly speculative. The Bible does not provide all of the inside information on 'the hordes of hell' because they are not the most important characters in the narrative of Scripture. My take is that the devil is fighting a multifront war against humanity on the ground and in the air. Boots on the ground, the enemy is warring against the soul of every believer in hand-to-hand combat. In the air, the enemy is warring in "heavenly places," (Eph. 6:12), which means not on the earth but in places of high spiritual authority and power in the heavenly realms—that is, more likely against angels and not humans. These high-ranking demons are called the "evil rulers and authorities of the unseen world" (Eph. 6:12 NLT). They call the shots, pull the levers, press the buttons, and rule over the rulers and "mighty powers of this dark world" (Eph. 6:12 NLT).

The "rulers and mighty powers of this dark world" take their orders from authorities in the heavenly realms and carry them out in the world. Demons battle strategically over this world, meaning over nations, regions, systems, governments, and power structures that govern the world's system. For this reason, Satan is called "the god of this world" and "the prince of the power of the air" (2 Cor. 4:4 NLT; Eph. 2:2 ESV), and one ruling demon is called the "Prince of Persia" (Dan. 10:13–20). Below this level of demonic regiments are the principalities and powers that work more directly with an assigned jurisdiction and their targeted area. Many theologians in their demonology, like Thomas Aquinas, have provided classifications, jurisdictions, and assignments for Satan's hosts. Because Scripture does not specifically lay out a detailed demonology, these "job descriptions" are speculative.

Spiritual warfare is against the individual and against collective groups, like institutions or governments, against the world as a whole, and against angels in this realm and the heavenly realm. Spiritual combat directed at us takes place primarily in the mind of the believer, most prominently in the form of temptation. The battlefield of the mind is extended to the culture. The psychological warfare that takes place at the level of society and culture is ideological—that is, ideological warfare. A war of ideologies has polarized the West and other parts of the world. The parties in this war are manifold, yet they generally fall into two camps. I am reluctant to overgeneralize and rehash tired, meaningless, and unnecessary categories. Nonetheless, it seems that the current iteration of left (liberal and progressive) versus right (conservative) has not resolved itself or gone away. My task in this section is not to enlist and be positioned on frontlines of the current culture war or the extreme politicization of American life. Such an endeavor would require an entire volume that I am not called to undertake, nor would I take any pleasure in such morbid, masochistic self-affliction.

We are all casualties of this war, and yet we live another day to die again. Drawing the battlelines, inspecting the field, analyzing the two sides and their strategies, and broadcasting the score has been rehearsed ad nauseum. The left seems eternally obsessed with enforcing whatever shards of Marxism have survived the twentieth century and piece them back together into whatever social activist, revolutionary iteration will catch on with our institutions and companies, regardless of its disastrous track record and millions of casualties that lie in its wake. The right is eternally obsessed with countering the red specter at all costs by propping up any messianic demagogue who can promise to bring deliverance out of the left's captivity. 'Nuff said!

Every culture in every society from time immemorial has had ideological battles, some at times more polarizing and volatile than others, though that is a challenge to believe. What exacerbates our culture war is technology and all that it delivers, which adds fuel to the fire. Opinions are no longer kept in one's mind or at home but are sent throughout the world on the Web. Technocracy has created a platform for everyone's fifteen minutes of fame. Every individual becomes a self-appointed judge, jury, journalist, legislator, politician, scientist, and overall universal expert. Many of us are included in those prestigious ranks. We have drafted ourselves into the seedy, sordid culture wars and are battling for the left or right or trying to hold the ever-vanishing ground in the center. Though many of us have suited up for battle in full regalia for the culture war, we cannot disregard our higher commitment to the Most High God.

In the early church, baptized believers made a dangerous confession when they professed, "Jesus Christ is Lord!" They were swearing full allegiance to the resurrected Son of God. With this confession. Christians became enemies of Rome. The Roman Empire demanded sole and full allegiance to Caesar. Its confession was "Caesar is Lord!" For both Rome and Christians, two lords could not coexist. Christ's Lordship was declared over Christians' entire lives, including cultural and political fidelities. Many early Christians were put to the test and even martyred for their faith. They refused to pay loyalty to anyone or anything but Christ. "Jesus is Lord" was not a flippant assertion or taken lightly. Today, in our politically charged environment, believers would do well to be reminded of the meaning of Christ's Lordship. Our hope is in a King who carries the government (the Kingdom of God) on his shoulders (Isa. 9:6), and the kingdoms of this world will become his kingdom (Rev. 11:15). We scripturally, intelligently, prayerfully, and faithfully perform our civic duties as good citizens, but our ultimate trust is in Jesus Christ the Lord.

Worldview, Church, and Culture

In the first chapter, we discussed the concept of worldview and specifically a "Christian" or "Scriptural" worldview. We noted that Christians need to think differently than non-Christians about God and the world. We are inhabitants of the world. We live and function in the world. Yet we do not walk in the moral darkness of this world nor do we follow its god, Satan (John 18:36; 1 John 2:15–17). Scripture is quite clear that if we are friends with the world, we are enemies of God, even adulterers (Jas. 4:4). We are called to be spiritually and morally separate from the world (2 Cor. 6:17), to be holy as God is holy (1 Pet. 1:16). Holiness includes a holy or godly worldview. In Chapter 3, we examined the nature of discipleship. One major mark of a disciple of Christ is studying, confessing, and obeying orthodox Christian doctrine. Christian doctrine and ethics are two of the chief components that comprise a Christian worldview or a worldview informed by Scripture. How does God see the world? How did Christ see the world? The Spirit leads us to view the world in a Christlike manner, and Scripture is our touchstone that reveals the content of that worldview.

Scripture normatively informs Christian doctrine and ethics; the Bible is our basis for what we believe and do. The historic Christian tradition also provides us a hermeneutical framework to interpret Scripture. It enables us to interpret Scripture, doctrines, ethics, and moral decisions in light of the wisdom of the one, holy, universal, apostolic church throughout the ages as guided by the Holy Spirit. The tradition consists of the councils, creeds, confessors, martyrs, saints, liturgy, theology, and other treasures of the church. Believers have a storehouse of riches to draw from when constructing a worldview and applying it to making decisions about issues in philosophy, science, politics, culture, and the like (Matt. 13:52). Evidently, not every organization, idea, or practice that comes from the world's system is of God.

There are many institutions, ideologies, systems, positions, and practices that are in diametric opposition to the precepts of Scripture and the principles of the Kingdom. Christians need to be well-studied, astute, and discerning of the ways of the world that Satan uses to assail the mind of believers. Currently, numerous, hot issues have been embraced in some part by the world and the church. The church has been divided on these positions, such as abortion, evolution, LGBTQ+ issues, the criminal justice system, immigration, stem cell use, and others. Many of these topics are quite complex and beyond the goals and scope of this book to resolve. Nonetheless, we can follow some useful frameworks to assist us in understanding the bigger picture in which these issues are situated and to facilitate a means to construct Scriptural positions on weighty issues.

Theologian H. Richard Niebuhr (1894–1962) did a service to the church in giving us the classic *Christ and Culture*. The text provides a theological framework of perspectives on the relationship between Christ/church and culture.[24] His framework illustrates not only the possible options between Christ/Church and culture, but also what is at stake with each position. His taxonomy is neither perfect nor clear cut. The categories can be limiting, insufficient, imprecise, or even overlapping. Nonetheless, his work is as good of a place as any to start examining the relationship between Christ and culture.

Christ/Church and Culture[25]

- **Christ of Culture:** A cultural model. The relationship between Christ and Culture is amicable and accommodating. The church looks favorably and basically uncritically at culture, identifying it as fundamentally good. In fact, where Christian truth may be in conflict with the culture, the church may have to adjust to adapt to the culture. This is the position often taken by mainline cultural Protestantism. Upon outside observation, one may conclude that there is not much difference between the church and culture. Eminent evolutionary biologist Richard Dawkins, an atheist, claimed that he is a "cultural Christian."[26]

- **Christ above Culture:** A synthesist model. Culture is seen as basically good but needs to be improved and perfected by the revelation of Christ through the church. The church critically examines culture for its good and builds on it with the gospel. Thus, Christ rules over the church and through the church influences and rules the culture. This view is usually associated with Roman Catholicism and Eastern Orthodoxy.

---

24. H. Richard Niebuhr, *Christ and Culture*. (Harper Row, 1976) (Niebuhr 1976) D. A. Carson and Timothy Keller each have given their own updated versions of the Niebuhr classic.

25. David Naugle, "H. Richard Niebuhr, *Christ and Culture*" (lecture, Dallas Baptist University), https://www3.dbu.edu/naugle/pdf/3304_handouts/Christ%20and%20Culture-Five%20Models.pdf. (Naugle n.d.)

26. Leading Britain's Conversation, "If I had to choose between Christianity and Islam, I'd choose Christianity every single time," X, March 31, 2024, 1:54 p.m., https://x.com/LBC/status/1774510715975368778. (Leading Britain's Conversation (@LBC) 2024)

- **Christ and Culture:** A dualist model. Christ and culture are held together in paradox. Culture is radically fallen and tainted by sin, but we are called to live in it and not separate from it. Thus, we live in two worlds, this fallen world and the Kingdom of God. We have commitments to both realms, but we perform our duties in the culture as faithful followers of Christ. The goal is not to separate, transform, or rule over culture. Change occurs in the church and not in the culture. It is often connected with the Reformed tradition's "two kingdoms" view. There is a Kingdom of God and a Kingdom of humanity, and we are called to give to God what belongs to God and give to Caesar what belongs to Caesar. One is called to do one's duties in both.

- **Christ transforming Culture:** A conversionist model. This model, like "Christ *and* Culture," notes that creation was made good, but it is fallen from sin. Christ came to redeem and transform culture. Thus, the gospel is to have a leavening effect on people and society. Salvation should affect and transform the world. This model is usually associated with reforming and revivalist traditions (Evangelicalism, Methodism, Holiness, Pentecostal, and Charismatic churches)

- **Christ against Culture:** A radical model. This model also understands creation to be good but fallen and in need of salvation. The church is called to be separate from the sinful culture and not follow its ways. Culture itself is corrupt and irredeemable. So God has created an alternative: the church. The church is called to be a salt and light example to the world that draws people to its witness of Christ. This model is usually associated with early monasticism; Anabaptist, pacifist, and separatist traditions; and some radical holiness sects.

Christians should critically examine these and other categories in light of Scripture and Christian tradition and ask what the nature of the relationship between Christ and culture is. Following, a theological position is formulated that becomes the lens through which one examines and draws inferences about various scientific issues that confront the believer's faith. These guiding questions may help one to discern.

Five Questions for Interpretation and Application

1. **Scripture Questions:** What does Scripture say about this issue? What do the Christian tradition, commentaries, and lexical resources say about the passage and the issue?

2. **Timeless Truth Culture Questions:** Is the Scriptural truth concerning this issue a timeless truth or bound and valid only in the time and culture in which it was written? How do we know it is timeless or strictly culture bound? Is the truth found elsewhere in Scripture? A timeless truth is true at all times and in all places. Some truths were bound to a particular time, place, and culture but are no longer valid or binding.

171

3. **Critical Contextualization Questions:** If it is a timeless truth, does it need to be critically contextualized for our time and place?

4. **Seed-Truth Questions:** Is it a seed of truth? Perhaps there is a truth in Scripture that appears to be for the place and time in which it was written, but it also seems to have some relevance today. Was it a seed of truth planted in Scripture that was intended to grow and bear fruit in the future that may look different over time? A seed-truth means there is a grain of truth regarding that issue in the Scriptures. Was it expected to grow to its full realization after the canonization of Scripture over time? What are the other Scriptural indicators that it is a seed-truth on a moral trajectory to be realized in a fuller way? For example, the Old Testament "an eye for an eye" was mean to prevent national bloodshed over an issue that involved an entire nation. Going to war with a nation over one person's infraction is not equal justice, but an eye for an eye is. Forgiveness and justice from the Old Testament are seed-truths that would grow into a greater realization of forgiveness and justice through Christ's sacrifice on the cross. He took all of our infractions on himself, and thus justice means to forgive and love your neighbor and your enemy.

5. **Position Questions:** Which of the models is the most Scriptural and why? What positions has the Christian tradition taken on this issue? Has it been Scriptural? What is my position?

Similarly, we can offer a framework of perspectives for the problem of the relationship between *religion/theology and science*. This framework can aid our approach to critically examine the theories and claims of the sciences. Like Niebuhr, Ian Barbour, physicist and theologian, crafted a taxonomy for understanding possible relationships between religion and science (faith and reason). Religion's object of inquiry is ultimately God, while the universe is the object of inquiry for science. Faith is the primary epistemology for religion with reason supporting it secondarily. For science, rational empiricism is the primary epistemology, though it contains an aspect of faith or a fiduciary commitment. Although they differ in many ways, both religion and science attempt to answer the big questions around life, the origin and end of the universe, what is the nature of reality, and why we exist. Barbour's framework also has its limitations. The models may be insufficient, limiting, or overlapping in cases. Listed are Barbour's four models of the relationship between religion and science.

- **Conflict:** The object, methodology, goals, and language of religion and science are in opposition. The two fields claim opposing views of truth and reality. For example, religion knows God by faith. Science knows the universe through reason. The truth of Scripture undergirds Christian theology. The truth of math undergirds physics (science).

- **Independence:** The object, methodology, goals, and language of religion and science are independent and unrelated to each other. The two are incommensurable. They each stand alone, do not intersect, and are to be studied and participated in independently. Independence affirms and preserves the integrity of each discipline. The differences seen in the conflict model are not because the two fields are in opposition, but it is because they are two different approaches to two different truths. Religion seeks to know the truth of God and not the universe. Science seeks to know the truth about the universe and not God. For example, God creating the universe according to Genesis 1 is not necessarily attached to the big bang, and the big bang is not necessarily attached to God.

- **Dialogue:** The object, methodology, goals, and language of religion and science have some common denominators, some overlap. Dialogue acknowledges that the two fields are unique and have their own essence and integrity. However, they intersect at some points and share common concerns, warranting mutual conversation and exploration. One point of contact with some correlation is between the theological notion of creation and the scientific notion of the universe, specifically humanity. Both ask and attempt to resolve the big questions of life. For example, science, specifically psychiatry and psychology, is interested in human mental wellness and wholeness. Although it has a different take on mental well-being, religion clearly has an interest in humanity and its mental health. These types of boundaries where both fields come together are a site for dialogue.

- **Integration:** The object, methodology, goals, and language of religion and science have some overlap, and thus there needs to be dialogue at those places of intersection to investigate the possibility of critically combining the truth that do indeed intersect. In order to bring the two fields together there often needs to be a "causal joint," which is the place where God and the universe work together.[27] For example, some theologians and scientists identify quantum mechanics as a potential site where the two cohere. They speculate that perhaps Divine agency is what collapses the wave function, solving the randomness of quantum indeterminacy.

Christians should critically examine these and other categories in light of Scripture and Christian tradition and ask what the nature of the relationship between

---

27. Ian G. Barbour, *Religion and Science: Historical and Contemporary Issues* (HarperCollins Publishers, 1997), 77–103. (Barbour 1997) Other models besides Barbour's exist. See Robert J. Russell's article, "Dialogue Between Science and Theology" in the *Interdisciplinary Encyclopedia of Religion and Science*, ed. G. Tanzella-Nitti and A. Strauma, accessed May 22, 2024, http://inters.org/dialogue-science-theology.

religion and a science is. A theological position is formulated that becomes the lens through which one examines and draws inferences about various scientific issues that confront the believer's faith.

(Refer to Five Questions for Interpretation and Application on page 171)

Likewise, we can examine the problem of the relationship between *Christianity and other religions* through a helpful taxonomic framework. There are many ways to approach the problem of other religions. I find Paul Knitter's work helpful.[28] Are all Gods the same or one? Are all religions different but with basically the same message? Do all religions lead to heaven? If one religion is true, must all of the others be wrong? Is there truth in other religions? Is there salvation in other religions? *How should Christians view and engage other religions, including philosophy?* Knitter's models have their limitations. The models may be insufficient, constraining, or overlapping in cases. Nonetheless, Knitter offers five models for our discernment.

Five Models of Christianity and Other Religions (Including Philosophy)[29]

- **Total Replacement:** This model holds that only Christianity contains revelation of God and truth. Thus, only Christianity is salvific. Every religious and philosophical system needs to be totally replaced by Christianity. No other religion or philosophy has truth or saves. The two determining questions asked are, is there a possibility for truth in other religions or philosophy (*no*), and is there salvation in other religions or philosophy (*no*)? This view was held by Karl Barth, who had no place for any general revelation or natural theology that is claimed to be found in any other religion or philosophy. Some exclusive and fundamentalist type of denominations hold to this view.

- **Partial Replacement:** This model holds that other religions or philosophies may contain some general revelation of God, or a natural theology of God, or truths about God or truths in general. However, these truths are not salvific. Salvation is only found in Christianity. Thus, there needs to be some but not total replacement of a given system with the truth of Christianity. There may be a preparation of the gospel in other systems that can be used in Christianity and need not be discarded. For example, some version of the Golden Rule (do unto others as you would like done unto you) can be found in many other religions and philosophies. This truth does not have to be replaced in one's system, when one accepts Christianity. Is there a possibility for truth in other religions or philosophies (*yes*), and is there salvation in

---

28. Paul F. Knitter, *Introducing Theologies of Religions* (Orbis, 2014) (Knitter 2014).

29. Knitter, *Introducing Theologies of Religions.* (Knitter 2014)

other religions or philosophies (*no*)? I believe this view was held by John Wesley and many of his descendants.

- **Fulfillment:** This model focuses on what it claims to be the one message of all true religions and philosophies, which is to love God and neighbor, do good, and shun evil. This is their function or purpose. If a religion or philosophy fulfills this purpose, it is accepted as true and salvific. The Roman Catholic Karl Rahner was a proponent of this view and claimed that many followers of other religions and philosophies are "anonymous Christians." They believe and practice the essence of religion to love God and neighbor, do good, and shun evil, and are then accepted by God like the so-called Gentile God-fearers in Acts 10, who feared God and did right and were accepted by God. Each of these religions reflects a degree of revelatory and salvific light, but Christianity is the fullness of religion and fulfills the highest aspirations of every religion. Is there a possibility for truth in other religions and philosophy (*yes*), and is there salvation in other religions or philosophies (*yes*)? Many Roman Catholics and mainline Protestants hold to this view.

- **Mutuality:** The mutual model contends that all models of religion and philosophies lead to God or the Absolute. All religions and philosophies reflect the essence of religious truth that is belief in God or the Absolute, love God and neighbor, do good, and shun evil. In other words, all religious roads, though different and unique, lead to Rome. God or the Absolute is the unknowable *noumena* of Kant, and it can only be known through the phenomena of religion(s), though each different, yet all point to the Absolute. John Hick held to this view. Is there a possibility for truth in other religions and philosophy (*yes*) and is there salvation in other religions or philosophies, (*yes*)? Many in mainline liberal Protestantism hold to this model.

- **Acceptance:** The acceptance model draws from theories found in George Lindback and Ludwig Wittgenstein's works. It contends that systems like religions or philosophies are unique cultural-historical-linguistic entities that reflect their own context and thus cannot be compared to each other, like apples and oranges. They are incommensurable and untranslatable. Thus, one needs to accept each system on its own terms. Each offers its own truth. Each offers its own salvation, which are equally valid. Is there a possibility for truth in other religions and philosophy (*no* and *yes*), and is there salvation in other religions or philosophies (*no* and *yes*)? No, in that they do not all claim the same truth and same salvation. Yes, in that all have truth and salvation, but it is their own version. This view is held by radical pluralists in Christianity and other religions.

175

Christians should critically examine these models, religions, and philosophies in light of Scripture and Christian tradition and ask what the nature of the relationship between Christianity and other religions or philosophies is. Following, a theological position is formulated that becomes the lens through which one examines and draws inferences about various religious and philosophical issues that confront the believer's faith.

(Refer to Five Questions for Interpretation and Application on page 171)

Winning the Spiritual War or the Cultural War?

Culture wars, divisions, and polarization have always been issues for nations as far back as history records. The current striking discord in the United States is the most severe that I have observed in my six decades. We are divided religiously, politically, racially, ethnically, and economically; and each group is jockeying for power and influence. The culture war is real and somehow needs to find resolution if we are to live in a peaceful and just society. Each side has invested much to win this war at all costs, even taking strategies right out of the playbook of Machiavelli. I have taken the position that we need to be good citizens, live by the law of the land, and participate in the democratic process to make needed changes. When the law and authorities are not in line with God's word, it is better that we obey God rather than human institutions (Acts 5:29–32; Rom. 13:1–7).[30] *Ultimately, Jesus Christ is Lord over all potentates.*

However, as believers we also actively engage in the spiritual battles that often dictate the cultural war. The unjust systems, structures, and practices of the day often are the product of not only earthly institutions, rulers, or even the zeitgeist of the day but also of demonic powers that have wreaked havoc and waged war since the beginning of time. Scripture informs us that our battle is not against flesh and blood, Republicans or Democrats; white people, African Americans, or people of any racial or ethnic group; LGBTQ+ or straight people; the rich or the poor; or progressives, liberals, or conservatives. Our war is against spiritual powers that seek to destroy us all and will use our own factions to accomplish it. *We do our civic duty, but more importantly, we do our Kingdom duty.* The lion's share of our energy and elbow grease goes to advancing the reign of Christ and extinguishing the kingdom of darkness. We best accomplish this goal on our knees in prayer, then on our feet, by walking in righteousness in every sphere of life.

The ancient demons of Baal (idolatry), Molech (child sacrifice), and Ashtoreth/Ishtar (sexual perversion) are alive, well, and active in our day, waging war on the world, nations, communities, institutions, families, marriages, individuals, and

---

30. Some contend that the idea of government was established by God to maintain law and order in the temporal world. We are to submit to government when it is fulfilling God's purpose of implementing laws that reflect his moral and divine law. Others question the Pauline authorship of the text and its meaning. See Greg Herrick, "Paul and Civil Disobedience in Romans 13:1–7," Bible.org, June 24, 2004, https://bible.org/article/paul-and-civil-obedience-romans-131-7.

especially children. Their weapons are deception, vice, terrorism, murder, unbibli-cal ideologies, idolatry, pride, hatred, the love of money (covetousness), confusion, adultery, fornication, perversion, abuse, oppressing the poor, the occult, witchcraft, and anything that Scripture prohibits. Members of the church spend more time arguing on social media than they do praying and fasting against the forces of evil working behind the scenes in these areas of iniquity. The unity of the saints praying in the power of agreement with God's word can tear down demonic strongholds over our communities and put ten thousand demons to flight (Deut. 32:30; Josh. 23:10; Isa. 54:17). Christ has given us authority over evil. If we humble ourselves, pray, repent, and seek his face, he will save us and heal our land, which so desper-ately needs it (2 Chron. 7:14).

Revival history tells us how praying and fasting intercessors that have travailed and not grown weary have watched the Kingdom of God break through not just in Jerusalem at Pentecost but in Antioch, Alexandria, Rome, Constantinople, As-sisi, Wittenberg, Geneva, Hernnhut, Aldersgate, Northampton, Cane Ridge New York City, Moriah, Azusa, Toronto, Brownsville, and other locations. The fire was sparked in these sites and spread throughout the land. Crime rates went down. Addictions broken. Corruption dissipated. Sinners saved. The sick healed. The brokenhearted mended. Lives were pieced back together. Families restored. New songs sung and ideas birthed. Victory won. Christianity has had its problems, and even evils, but arguably no other force has had an influence for truth, goodness, righteousness, and beauty in the world than it.[31] This dark world needs to see the light of the truth and the salt of God's goodness once again, and we are that salt and light.

---

31. For similar arguments, see Justin Brierley, *The Surprising Rebirth of Belief in God: Why New Atheism Grew Old and Secular Thinkers are Considering Christianity Again* (Tyndale Elevate, 2023); Mike Aquilina and James L. Papandrea, *How Christianity Saved Civilization . . . And Must do So Again* (Sophia Institute Press, 2019); Kevin Schmidt, *How Christianity Changed the World* (Zondervan, 2004); Tom Holland, *Dominion: How the Christian Revolution Remade the World* (Hachette, 2019); Rodney Stark, *The Triumph of Christianity: How the Jesus Movement Became the World's Largest Religion* (HarperCollins: 2011); Sharon James, *How Christianity Transformed the World* (Christian Focus, 2021); among others.

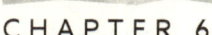

CHAPTER 6

TRUTH THERAPY

Lies bind. Truth frees.

—Peter J Bellini

Introduction

As we learned in Chapter 3, a disciple is a disciplined learner and follower of Jesus Christ. Our account of Jesus Christ is found in holy Scripture, which is inspired by the Holy Spirit. Thus, in order to learn about Christ and follow him, we need the Holy Spirit to teach us through the holy Scriptures. The Word of God is the alpha and omega, the beginning and end, of our discipleship. The Scriptures are our source for truth and are God's instructions to make us holy. The Word and Spirit of God are two sides of a double-edged sword that the Father uses to sculpt us in his image. Thus, Scripture enlightened by the Holy Spirit is our primary touchstone for truth and God's instrument to craft us into his disciples. We will not be seduced by postmodernism or any philosophy that denies the existence of absolute and objective truth (Col. 2:8; 2 Pet. 1:20). We are firmly convinced that Scripture is the Spirit-inspired word of God and is trustworthy for salvation. In this chapter, we will learn a way or method in which the Spirit works truth in our lives in order to transform us to be like Jesus.

Back in the 1990s when I was pastoring in the inner city, our church began to evangelize and disciple the neighborhood. Many came to Christ from diverse racial, ethnic, and socioeconomic backgrounds. Some came out of the occult and false religion. Many came out of addiction, and many struggled with mental health issues. This time period preceded the Affordable Care Act. A significant portion of people living in our community could not afford health care. Thus, many of those coming to Christ were underserviced, underdiagnosed, and undertreated in terms of mental health care.

We created an elaborate referral system and also housed a countywide health department office in our church. However, for practical discipleship, I created a curriculum called Truth Therapy, which later was published as a book.[1] By implementing

---

1. Peter Bellini, *Truth Therapy: Renewing Your Mind with the Word of God* (Wipf and Stock, 2014) (P. Bellini, Truth Therapy: Renewing Your Mind with the Word of God 2014).

Truth Therapy, we witnessed much healing, deliverance, transformation, and restoration. Truth Therapy can be used for personal devotions or for discipleship settings. It combines contemplative and Charismatic theology with strategies of identity and belief formation, which makes it ideal for discipleship. Embedded cognitive behavioral theory (CBT) adds a therapeutic component to the mix. You may remember that we introduced CBT back in Chapter 2. The Truth Therapy method is applied to *learning doctrine, contemplating the names of God, and rehearsing Scriptural affirmations.* These are thoroughly covered in the book *Truth Therapy.* Some of them we will touch on in this chapter.

Truth Therapy is a methodology for repentance and renewing our mind in discipleship. As our hearts and minds line up with God's word, so will our lives. Training our minds is a necessary discipline. Scripture declares that knowing the truth will set us free (John 8:31–44; 1 John 2:20–21). Well, if the truth sets us free, the opposite is true as well. Lies will enslave us. These two basic premises are threaded throughout my Truth Therapy model. *One, lies bind. Two, truth liberates.* The problem is the lies that we believe about ourselves, our past and future, others, the world, and God. These lies can come from us, others, or Satan, who is the father of all lies (John 3:44).

In any case, they contribute to a script (our self-talk) that has chained us and driven our lives by fear, anxiety, brokenness, inadequacy, confusion, insecurity, dysfunction, and sin. The solution is the truth that we believe about ourselves, our past and future, others, the world, and God. Though lies blind and bind, the truth sets us free and delivers us from bondage. Lies are enslaving. Truth is liberating. What lies have we believed and continue to believe that keep us bound? These foundational truths synthesize principles from Scripture and CBT to help us unlearn the lies and learn the truth.

Satan is the father of all lies. He is the chief purveyor of deception and distortion. In fact, deception is his sole power, and he injects a heavy, lethal dose in each temptation. Deception is the essence of sin. Similarly, CBT recognizes that thoughts shape emotions, and emotions shape behavior, and behavior influences thoughts, in a feedback loop. Thoughts that are characterized by deception, error, inaccuracy, or irrationality are called *cognitive distortions.* Satan is the father of lies, but God is the Father of truth! The remedy is in replacing those patterns with thoughts that are true, accurate, realistic, and rational. This process in CBT is called *cognitive restructuring.* Hence, Truth Therapy is a method for discipleship that targets the mind, specifically identity and belief formation in Christ. It involves replacing the lies that we believe with the truth or renewing our minds with the word of God. The truth is *therapeutic.* It delivers, heals, cleanses, saves, and sanctifies the sin-sick soul (Ps. 107:20; John 8:32; 17:17; Eph. 1:13; 2 Thess. 2:13; 1 Tim. 2:4; 1 Pet. 1:22). *Truth Therapy,* the book, uses Scripture, Scriptural reflection, basic doctrine or transforming truths, the names of God, affirmations, renunciations, and the best of CBT to help believers to be transformed by renewing their minds.

Truth Therapy Overview: Ten Principles

1. **Lies Bind:** John 8:31–32; 2 Corinthians 4:4

   Lies bind, and lies blind. We have been listening to lies for as long as we can remember. From Satan, ourselves, and others, we hear lies about ourselves, others, God, the world, the past, and the future. The lies that we subconsciously tell ourselves we often do not hear or recognize. They ruminate just below the surface of our awareness. They are part of our self-talk. Certain lies are self-scripts that have run through our minds on a feedback loop for years. They tell us that we are not loved, that we will not amount to anything, that we are unforgiveable, that we have no future, and so on. Unconsciously, we read these scripts endlessly to ourselves until we are paralyzed with doubt and fear. The lies that we believe bring us into bondage. We are chained and cannot free ourselves. The lies prevent us from knowing the truth about God, his love, and salvation. Lies keep us from knowing who we are in Christ and what we can do through Christ. We are tempted to believe lies in the Five Domains of Belief: What do we believe about God, ourselves, others, the world (space), and time (past, present, future)?

2. **Truth Delivers:** Psalm 107:20; John 8:31–32; 17:17

   If lies bind, the truth delivers. The truth liberates and sets us free from the lies that have enslaved us. The truth of God's word is a sword that pierces to the depths of our being and breaks the chain of lies that bind us. When we know the truth, it will set us free. Particularly, when we know Christ, who is the truth, and the Holy Spirit, who is the Spirit of truth, we are delivered from our sins. We are delivered from the lies and the bondage of sin and Satan. The task of the disciples is to cultivate the mind of Christ through the word of God. We have sinful and unhealthy thought patterns that need to be unlearned. They did not get there overnight, and most likely they will not leave overnight. Renewing the mind is a process that involves repentance of old thinking, forgiveness from past thoughts and actions, believing the word of God, and obeying it. Truth Therapy entails believing the truth in the Five Domains of Belief: What do we believe about God, ourselves, others, the world (space), and time (past, present, future)?

3. **We Cannot Control God, Others, or our Circumstances:** Proverbs 3:5–8; Matthew 6:25–34

   Humanity still believes the lie that Satan told Eve in the garden that we can be gods. And one of our first acts as false gods is to attempt to be in control, instead of God. Although we surely try, we cannot control

God, others, or our circumstances. Often, we struggle even controlling ourselves. At some point, we are all controlled by the desire to control. Controlled by control. Control offers us the illusion of absolute security. It is an illusion because only God can provide true security. The need to control is a stubborn habit to unlearn and break. Freedom begins with the truth. The truth is that we cannot control anything outside of ourselves. The truth is that God is in control. The truth is that we can experience freedom when we accept these truths and trust God with our lives, the lives of others, and circumstances. "Let go and let God" is simple, common wisdom. The aphorism is true, but it can be more challenging to implement than first imagined. The Lord allows us to experience our own weakness to humble us and depend on him and not on our sinful, limited human ability.

4. **We Can Control Our Thought Life:** 2 Corinthians 10:4–5; Galatians 5:23; 2 Timothy 1:7

Although we cannot control God, others, or circumstances, in a limited sense, we can control ourselves, especially through the power of the Spirit. Self-control is a fruit of the Spirit (Gal. 5:23). God gives us a spirit of self-control (2 Tim. 1:7). God created each person with moral agency and limited freedom to resist evil and choose good. Agency is a divinely bestowed power that is essential to being a human person, to being free, and to being responsible. Humanity's fall into sin defaced but did not erase the image of God. Our will is bound in sin, and our agency is bent toward choosing evil. Through salvation in Christ, we are freed from sin, and our will is restored with the power to resist evil and to choose the good. It is our responsibility to do so and become agents of righteousness. As rational, moral agents redeemed by Christ, we are responsible for what enters and cohabitates in our mind. Thoughts can come from God, the devil, self, or others. We are required to test the spirits and discern the source of those thoughts (1 John 5:1). A disciple is called to have the mind of Christ. Thus, only the thoughts from God should rule in our hearts and minds. Thoughts from Satan should be cast out. Faulty or sinful thoughts from us or others should be expelled and appropriately replaced with God's word that relates to the subject. We are responsible for what we watch on the screen of our minds. If the images are not of God, change the channel. Think on the truth. We are responsible for what we hear in the inner headphones of our mind. If the voice is not of God, change the station. Liberation and transformation begin when we recognize that we have the ability to choose life or death, truth or lies. Recovering our responsibility to choose and not to be passive about our thought life is the first step to repentance and deliverance. Freedom begins to be experienced when we begin to identify our power to choose, a recovery of agency (the will). Monitor daily thinking. The **M.E.E.T.** method is effective for monitoring daily thoughts and self-talk: **M**onitor thoughts. **E**valuate them. **E**xpel lies. **T**ruth replaces the lies.

5. **We Change by Changing our Stinking Thinking:** Romans 12:1–2; Ephesians 4:22–24; Colossians 3:10

St. Paul declares that we are "transformed by the renewing of our minds." Simply put, a changed life comes from a changed mind. *Metanoia* is the Greek New Testament word for repentance. *Metanoia* means change the mind so that the life is changed. In repentance, we turn from self to God, from sin to righteousness, from unbelief to faith. God gives us the grace to change, but he gives us the freedom to decide to make the choice. A changed mind results in a changed life. The mind and the heart have that power and influence over our lives. If we have thoughts of fear, we become fearful. If we have thoughts of anxiety, we become anxious. If we have thoughts of worry, we become worrisome. As a man or woman thinks in his or her heart, so is he or she. The same dynamic exists with the truth. If we have thoughts of peace, we become peaceful. If we have thoughts of joy, we become joyful. A true change of mind results in a change of life. As we monitor our thought life, it is imperative to identify, expel, and replace stinking thinking with truth-based thinking.

6. **We Cannot Change the Past, but We Can Change How We Think About the Past:** 2 Corinthians 7:9–11; Galatians 2:20; 1 John 1:7–9

Many have undesirable and regrettable pasts. The blood of Christ removes our sins, but often there is an ongoing consequence for our sins. There are also those who have been sinned against. They suffer from the trauma and pain of past hurt. Sadly, we cannot change the past. However, we can change how we think about the past. At times, our interpretation of a traumatic event does more and lasting damage than the event itself. The Spirit wants to override past negative neural circuitry and rewire our hippocampus to learn and remember what God says about our past. Through redemptive listening, we can pray for God to reveal what his heart and will were for us at the time of trauma. The Lord often gives us revelations that speak the truth into that harrowing situation that can begin to heal our brokenness.

Trauma experts indicate that more than the event itself, our interpretation of it is what is most distressing. We may think that we deserved it or it was our fault. We may interpret the event to mean that we are unlovable, worthless, or hopeless. If we committed a sin, we may interpret the act to signify that we are pure evil, unredeemable, unforgiveable, and lost forever. Our self-talk may say that our sin defines us. It is who we are. In all of these cases, as well as others, we cannot change the past, but we can change how we think about the past. These examples of self-talk express faulty reasoning. We are not to blame for trauma or abuse committed against us. We are not unlovable and worthless. We are not unpardonable. We are created in the image of God. God loves us. We need to pray and ask Christ to intervene at the moment of our abuse or sin and show us what he says about the situation and about us.

Through redemptive listening, we can pray for God's light to reveal what he thought of us at that moment of crisis. Then we need to meditate on what God is speaking and rehearse it regularly in our minds. Ask the Spirit to heal our broken hearts and replace the lies with the truth. Rewire our hippocampus! The Greek New Testament word for "confession" is *homologia* (1 John 1:7–9), which means to say the same thing. We need to say the same thing that God says about us, our trauma, or our sin in order to be healed or to be forgiven and healed. Replace faulty self-talk with God-talk, the truth. Countless times, I have seen the Lord heal hearts, minds, and identities in this manner. Once people know that their self-talk may have been deceiving them and that Christ loves them and was with them in their moment of crisis, they begin to experience immediate release and healing. *Metanoia* means that we can change our thinking. *Homologia* (confession—to say what God says) means that we can change our self-talk.

7. **Align Our Thoughts With the Truth. Emotions and Behaviors Will Follow:** Matthew 3; 2 Corinthians 10:4–5; Philippians 4:6–9; 1 John 5:1

Just as the steering and the four wheels of a car can be jolted out of alignment, so also our thoughts, emotions, and behaviors can be jolted out of alignment with the truth. Through repentance, we can turn from sinful thinking and align with the mind of Christ. Changing the mind through true repentance means that a change of life will follow. CBT concurs. Changing the thoughts of our heart will influence our emotions and then our behaviors. I call it the **TEB cycle** (thoughts, emotions, behaviors). One affects the other continually in a feedback loop. The cycle begins with our thinking. Thoughts produce feelings that in turn produce behavior that in turn produces thoughts and so on. It is a cycle that continues and feeds back into our system. This cycle works for better or worse, depending on the nature of our thoughts and whether they are aligned with truth or lies and errors. We have the remote to change the channel when encountering lies and other faulty thinking. We can change our thinking that will change our emotions and behaviors. Align TEBs with the truth.

8. **Christ Has Finished the Work of Salvation ("It Is Finished")**: John 19:30; Romans 8:1–3; 1 Corinthians 3:11; Hebrews 2:14–15; 1 John 3:8

Lies bind. Truth delivers, and Christ is our truth (John 14:6). He is the truth and our source for truth. Thus, our foundation is Christ Jesus alone. Our salvation is founded on Christ and his finished work on the cross. All of the blessings and promises in Christ are yes and amen (2 Cor. 1:20). Truth, existence, repentance, deliverance, forgiveness, justification, regeneration, assurance, sanctification, healing, power, authority, abundant fruit, and abundant life all come from Christ. At the cross, he declared, "It is finished" (John 19:30). He meant sin is finished! Death is finished! Satan is finished! Salvation is finished! All that we need to be disciples in Christ is finished or completed in him (Col. 2:10). Christ is the source for the saving and healing work of the truth (Truth Therapy). He is the eternal well from which we draw waters of life.

9. **We are New Creations in Christ. We have the mind of Christ**: John 3:1–6; 2 Corinthians 5:17; Galatians 2:20; Ephesians 4:22–24

Becoming a disciple of Christ necessitates an identity change. Today, in our cyber-controlled world, is it not difficult to undergo some measure of identity theft. Our names, records, passwords, credit cards, and social security numbers can be compromised from hackers and thieves. I had my identity stolen once, and the culprit attempted to file a fraudulent federal tax return with it. I had to go through a lengthy, knotty process to verify my identity with the IRS. The process took an entire grueling year. When we forfeit our life to sin and Satan, we lose our God-intended identity. We become children of the enemy and slaves to wickedness (Rom. 6:16, 20; 2 Cor. 4:4; Eph. 2:3, 5:8). At the cross, we are offered to participate in the great exchange. We give him our unrighteousness. He gives us his righteousness. We give him our sin and death. He gives us eternal life. We give him our past. He gives us his future. We give him our old life. He gives us his new life. Through redemption and restoration, the Father is calling us to become sons and daughters of the Most High. In Christ, we are made a new creation. The old has passed, and the new has come (2 Cor. 5:17). We possess a new identity in Christ. We are given the mind of Christ. We are heirs to all of the promises of God. The spiritual DNA of Christ becomes our inheritance. Through our covenant with God in Christ, we participate in his Divine nature and all of its blessings (Eph. 1:13–14; 2 Pet. 1:4). God is love, righteousness, peace, sanctification (Lev. 20:8; Judg. 6:24; Jer. 33:16; 1 Cor. 1:30; 1 John 4:16). His names reveal his nature. And through his covenant, he extends his attributes to us.

God loves us. God is our righteousness. God is our peace. God is our sanctification. Through Christ, we become identified by and with the Father. We share in his love and love others (John 17). *Believers are often defeated because they do not know who they are in Christ.* They believe who Satan says they are. They let lies and limitations define them. We are who God says we are, and not who are flesh, others, or the devil say that we are. We need to renew our minds with the word of God to be the disciples God has called us to be.

10. <u>**We Can Do All Things Through Christ:**</u> Philippians 4:13; Ephesians 6:10

In Christ, we are granted a new identity (Gal. 2:20). In Christ, we are given new power through the Holy Spirit. The Spirit of God enables us to do all that God requires of us (Acts 1:8; Eph. 3:20; 2 Tim. 1:14; 2 Pet. 1:3). The Spirit of God is the dynamite (*dunamis*), or the ability of God working within us. We are promised that we can *do all* things through Christ (Phil. 4:13). The early disciples receive the promises of the Spirit and were enabled to do the works of Christ (John 14:12). The same Holy Spirit is promised to us today (Acts 2:38). We are promised a personal Pentecost through the baptism of the Spirit (Matt. 3:11–12; Acts 2). Through Christ, we are overcomers and more than conquerors (John 16:33; Rom 8:37; 1 John 5:4). We can overcome temptation, defeat, sin, Satan, and death through Christ who strengthens us through the power of the Spirit. *Believers are often defeated because they do not know what they can do through Christ.* They believe their flesh, others, or the devil to determine what they can and cannot do. We need to renew our minds with the word of God to do the works that God has called disciples to do.

Briefly on CBT

Cognitive behavioral theory is an autodidactic, problem–solution, learning model of short-term mental health treatment that enables clients to test empirically the reality and rationality of their own thoughts and to modify thought patterns to be more adaptive, mindful, realistic, and hope filled.[2] The principles of CBT are not just for those struggling with mental disorders but for anyone interested in solid, logical, healthy thinking. CBT is a learner-based form of therapy that teaches clients how to identify their own cognitive distortions or faulty thinking and how to help them restructure their cognition with thinking patterns that are more healthy, flexible, and realistic. CBT is also a type of treatment that helps clients understand the causal connection between thoughts, feelings, and behavior. Rather than external factors

---

2. Peter Bellini, *The Cerulean Soul: A Relational Theology of Depression* (Baylor University Press, 2021), 122. (P. Bellini, The Cerulean Soul: A Relational Theology of Depression 2021)

such as people, situations, or events, our own thinking is responsible for how we feel an act. The benefit of this principle is that, regardless of our circumstances, we can change the way we think in order to feel and act in a healthier way. CBT is the most widely used psychotherapeutic method by clinicians.[3] It is also the most empirically supported method of psychotherapy and one of the leading methods for treating a variety of mental and behavioral disorders.[4] The National Mental Health Institute (NMHI) explains how CBT works:

> CBT helps a person focus on his or her current problems and how to solve them. Both patient and therapist need to be actively involved in this process. The therapist helps the patient learn how to identify distorted or unhelpful thinking patterns, recognize and change inaccurate beliefs, relate to others in more positive ways, and change behaviors accordingly. CBT can be applied and adapted to treat many specific mental disorders.[5]

Historically, CBT emerged as a result of blending two types of therapies: cognitive therapy and behavioral therapy. Cognitive therapy focuses on a person's beliefs and how they influence a person's emotions and aims to change a person's thinking to be more adaptive and healthier. Behavioral therapy focuses on a person's actions and aims to change unhealthy behavior patterns. CBT was developed in the 1950s by psychotherapist Dr. Aaron Beck, who made revolutionary discoveries. He found that the standard approach of Freudian psychotherapy was not resulting in any significant changes in his patients. However, Dr. Beck realized that in his treatments there was a nexus between a person's automatic negative thoughts (ANTs) and the subsequent feelings of anxiety or depression. These ANTs would quietly emerge before a crippling feeling, like anxiety. And the ANTs occurred outside of the radar of the person's awareness. The ANTs would be triggered by some immediate experience of the patient and would pop up as a response. The ANTs are learned mental behavior patterns (schemas) that can be traced to early-childhood core beliefs that were instrumental in forming one's worldview. The result is faulty thinking that elicits negative emotion and possibly acting out with impulsive, unwanted behavior.

Thus, the paralyzing and destructive feelings of anxiety and depression were caused by the ANTs. Since Beck ascertained that thoughts were causal to feelings and feelings to behaviors, then if one changed one's thoughts, the feelings of anxiety and depression would change as well. The problem was that the ANTs popped up undetected at first, just below the surface of consciousness. They seem to occur automatically because the client is not aware of them. Beck had to train his clients how to identify the ANTs by recalling the unwanted feeling they experienced and trace it

---

3. Michelle G. Craske, *Cognitive-Behavioral Therapy* (American Psychological Association, 2010), 4. (Craske 2010)

4. Craske, *Cognitive-Behavioral Therapy*, 115. (Craske 2010)

5. "Psychotherapies," NIMH, accessed May 14, 2024, http://www.nimh.nih.gov/health/topics/psychotherapies/index.shtml. (National Institute of Mental Health 2024)

back to what triggered it and what they were thinking in that moment as a result of the trigger. Usually, some experience triggered an ANT that resulted in a feeling of anxiety or depression. So Beck challenged his clients to identify the ANT, assess it for truth and reality, then change the ANT to a thought that was more truthful, realistic, or logical. A more hopeful, realistic, positive feeling should result. And over much testing, he found it to be the case.

The difficulty was to train the client to detect the ANTs, which is no easy task because they hide outside of our immediate awareness. We all have what we call *self-talk*. Self-talk is that inner dialogue that we have with ourselves below the surface of our awareness. It is an inner script or narrative that we read to ourselves about ourselves, others, and the world around us. Sometimes we are naturally aware of our self-talk without having to be intentional. Other times, we are not aware of it, unless we intentionally listen for it. In those times, self-talk is a smooth, quietly flowing stream of consciousness that meanders through our mind just below the radar of our awareness. When clients have a negative episode, they are not trained to identify the ANT that caused it.

Once clients are guided by the therapist to backtrack from their negative or harmful emotion to the experience that triggered it, they can often identify what they were thinking right after the trigger but before the feeling. That missing piece in between is the ANT. Capture it. Evaluate it for its contents. Is it real, accurate, true? Can there be other explanations for the experience? Is the thought faulty, wrong, deceptive, unrealistic, an exaggeration, a projection, or some other distortion of reality? If so, change it (cognitive restructuring). Replace it with a thought that is more realistic, hopeful, flexible, accurate, and healthy. This exercise is the heart of CBT. In Dr. Aaron Beck's Cognitive Theory of Depression, he lists the goals of CBT strategies:

1. To monitor automatic, negative thoughts (cognitions).
2. To recognize the connection between cognition, affect, and behavior.
3. To examine the evidence for and against one's distorted automatic thoughts.
4. To substitute more reality-oriented interpretations for those biased cognitions.
5. To learn to identify and alter the dysfunctional beliefs which predispose one to distort one's experiences.[6]

At the same time that Aaron Beck forged CBT,[7] another psychotherapist, Albert Ellis, created his version of basically the same practice. He called it REBT (Rational Emotive Behavioral Therapy).[8] REBT uses the ABC treatment model for mental disorders. *A* is the Activating or triggering event. *B* is for Belief (distorted belief).

6.   Aaron T. Beck et al., *Cognitive Therapy of Depression* (Guilford, 1979), 4. (Beck, et al. 1979)

7.   Beck et al., *Cognitive Therapy of Depression.* (Beck, et al. 1979)

8.   Albert Ellis, *Practice of Rational Emotive Therapy*, 2nd ed. (Springer, 2007). (Ellis 2007)

And *C* is for Consequences (negative emotions and behaviors). Similar to Beck's CBT model, REBT identifies two known variables, A and C, the activating or triggering event and the negative consequence. The B variable, the underlying belief (or ANT in Beck's terms), is missing. The goal is to identify B, which is under the radar of awareness. Assess it and change it. Both of these pioneers, Beck and Ellis, discovered in their research that one's thought life greatly influences one's emotions and behaviors. Thus, by changing faulty thinking (cognitive restructuring), one can change one's emotional and behavioral outcome. Thus, mental health, at least in part, is subject to one's thought life, which can be identified, changed, and learned. If we don't like what we are watching on the screen of our minds, we can change the channel with our remote (our will).

Beck realized that cognitive biases and distortions and negative schemas are projected in how one views oneself, the world or others, and the future. Becks calls this the *cognitive triad of depression* (Diagram 7). The triad is characterized by an inner dialogue in the three areas that may claim, "No one loves me. The world and other people do not love me. I will never be loved." Here, we see a bias about how one sees self, others, and the future. These conclusions are unrealistic and impossible to prove. They presuppose omniscience. They presuppose one can know everything about how everyone feels about you or will ever feel about you. This inner dialogue is typical of depressive thinking.

The content of depressive thinking is characterized in another triad: helplessness, hopelessness, and worthlessness. These and other distorted cognitive traits are lethal to a healthy mind. In my book *Truth Therapy*, borrowing from the recovery community, I call biased and distorted thinking "stinking thinking" because it is wrongheaded.[9] Stinking thinking that results in a mental disorder is quite common. Up to 20 percent of the population in the United States has experienced a mental disorder, most commonly depression or anxiety.[10] Here you will find the criteria from the *Diagnostic and Statistical Manual of Mental Disorders*, 5th edition (DSM-5) used by clinicians to diagnosis depression and anxiety, among other conditions.

DSM-5 on Major Depressive Disorder

If one has five of the following nine symptoms daily:

___ depressed mood or irritable most of the day, nearly every day, as indicated by either subjective report (e.g., feels sad or empty) or observation made by others (e.g., appears tearful)

---

9. For a full catalog and description on "stinking thinking," see Bellini, *Truth Therapy*, 47–67 (P. Bellini, Truth Therapy: Renewing Your Mind with the Word of God 2014).

10. Julio C. Tolentino and Sergio L. Schmidt, "DSM-5 Criteria and Depression Severity: Implications for Clinical Practice," *Frontiers in Psychiatry* 9 (2018): 450. https://doi.org/10.3389/fpsyt.2018.00450. "Adult Data 2022," Mental Health America, accessed May 14, 2024, https://mhanational.org/issues/2022/mental-health-america-adult-data#:~:text=Adult%20Prevalence%20of%20Mental%20Illness%20(AMI)%202022&text=19.86%25%20of%20adults%20are%20experiencing,experiencing%20a%20severe%20mental%20illness. (Tolentino and Schmidt 2018)

__ decreased interest or pleasure in most activities, most of each day

__ significant weight change (5 percent) or change in appetite

__ change in sleep: insomnia or hypersomnia

__ change in activity: psychomotor agitation or retardation

__ fatigue or loss of energy

__ guilt/worthlessness: feelings of worthlessness or excessive or inappropriate guilt

__ concentration: diminished ability to think or concentrate, or more indecisiveness

__ suicidality: thoughts of death or suicide, or has suicide plan[11]

DSM 5 on Anxiety

The presence of excessive anxiety and worry about a variety of topics, events, or activities. Worry occurs more often than not for at least six months and is clearly excessive.

The individual experiences at least three characteristic symptoms including:

__ restlessness or feeling keyed up or on edge

__ being easily fatigued; always tired

__ difficulty concentrating or mind going blank

__ difficulty focusing

__ irritability; easily disturbed

__ muscle tension

__ and sleep disturbance[12]

CBT provides resources for clients to learn to overcome. It offers a framework to identify and evaluate negative feelings and problematic thinking. CBT also provides strategies for change, including cognitive restructuring. Learning to think healthy thoughts that contribute to healthy thought patterns over time can result in neuroplasticity and even neurogenesis. *Neuroplasticity* is the mind's resilient ability to change itself and be reshaped to perform new operations (neuroresilience).[13] Structurally and operationally, the brain is not static and fixed but malleable and changing. In my book *Truth Therapy*, I explain how "through thinking, learning, and acting, the brain can re-map itself and create new motor maps by altering neural networks and

11. American Psychiatric Association, *Diagnostic and Statistical Manual of Disorders* (London: American Psychiatric Association Publishing, 2013), 160, 161. (American Psychiatric Association 2013)

12. American Psychiatric Association. DSM 5, 222. (American Psychiatric Association 2013)

13. Jeffrey Schwartz and Sharon Begley, *The Mind and the Brain: Neuroplasticity and the Power of Mental Force* (HarperCollins, 2002); Norman Doidge, *The Brain That Changes Itself* (Penguin, 2007). (Schwartz and Begley 2002) (Doidge 2007)

neural structures."[14] The brain is not only learning anew, but it is always "learning how to learn."[15]

The brain redesigns itself constantly to solve its own problems by creating new brain maps through restructuring and rerouting neural networks.[16] The brain makes a way for itself."[17] It can even generate new neurons and brain circuits, neurogenesis, needed to perform the tasks that are demanded of it.

Overall, CBT has been demonstrated to be one of the most clinically effective means to treat depression, anxiety, ADHD, mood disorders, addictions, chronic fatigue syndrome, migraines, other chronic pain disorders, eating disorders, and other disorders. Sometimes CBT is implemented in tandem with psychiatric medications such as SSRIs. Although CBT has proven to be quite effective in treating numerous mental and behavioral disorders and addictions, it is not without its critiques. I allude to some of these appraisals in my book *The Cerulean Soul*:

> The "triumph of the therapeutic" has seen the priesthood and the healing charisms of the church replaced by the modern-day Western therapist with "life, liberty and the pursuit of happiness," that being the salvation offered by the gospel according to the American dream.[18] Improvement in mental health conditions is to be applauded, though standards based on unrealistic premises may be detrimental in the long run. In fact, there is increasing research and literature that counters the claims of CBT's effectiveness and asserts contrarily a decline in its ability to treat symptoms long term.[19]

CBT Overview

- Developed by Aaron Beck.
- Most successful form of psychological treatment available based on tested results.
- Thinking causes emotion and behavior. Thought →Emotion → Behavior (see Diagram 6).
- We cannot change circumstances, but we can change ourselves.
- Depressive, anxious, and negative feeling and behavior comes from wrong thinking—cognitive distortion.

---

14. Doidge, *The Brain That Changes Itself*, 63. (Doidge 2007)

15. Doidge, *The Brain That Changes Itself*, 47. (Doidge 2007)

16. Doidge, *The Brain That Changes Itself*, 61. (Doidge 2007)

17. Bellini, *Truth Therapy*, 20. (P. Bellini, Truth Therapy: Renewing Your Mind with the Word of God 2014)

18. Rieff, Philip. *The Triumph of the Therapeutic: Uses of Faith after Freud*, 40th anniv. ed. (Intercollegiate Studies Institute, 2006). (Rieff 2006)

19. For critiques of CBT, see D. Lynch, K. R. Laws, and P. J. McKenna, "Cognitive Behavioral Therapy for Major Psychiatric Disorder: Does It Really Work? A Meta-analytical Review of Well-Controlled Trials," *Psychological Medicine* 40, no. 1 (2010): 9–24; and Tom J. Johnsen and Oddgeir Friborg, "The Effects of Cognitive Behavioral Therapy as an Anti-depressive Treatment Is Falling: A Meta-analysis," *Psychological Bulletin* 141, no. 4 (2015): 747–68.

- Cognitive distortion is faulty thinking that may be deceptive, erroneous, irrational, exaggerated, inflexible, projecting, personalizing, polarizing, aggrandizing, awfulizing, overgeneralizing, self-defeating, self-disqualifying, prejudiced, arbitrarily inferring, or selectively abstracting, among others.
- ANTs: **A**utomatic **N**egative **T**houghts are triggered by external stimuli acting on past core beliefs and are immediate impulsive harmful thoughts that popup from our stream of consciousness, under the radar, self-script, and self-talk that function as our inner dialogue.
- Recognize cognitive distortion beginning with automatic negative thoughts.
- Interpret and assess reality empirically and logically.
- Triadic perspectives of depression: Faulty thinking affects perspective of self, others (God, world), and the future (see Diagram 7).
- Triadic content of depression: Helplessness, hopelessness, and worthlessness.
- Cognitive restructuring: Changing thinking (*metanoia*) changes feeling and behavior.
- Neuroplasticity: Transforming neural networks for better, performance, healing and overcoming.
- Neurogenesis: Generating of new neurons (nerve cells)

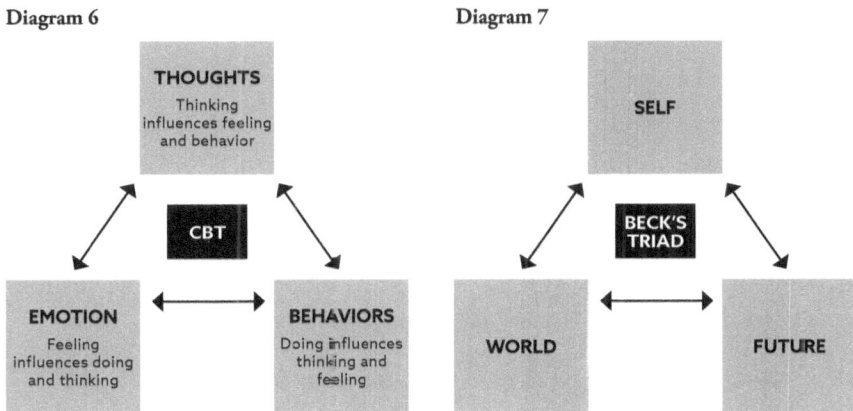

Diagram 6

Diagram 7

The Synergy:
Scriptural Principles + CBT = Truth Therapy

What does CBT, a theory of psychoanalysis, have to do with Truth Therapy or even discipleship? CBT is a strategy for better, logical, and healthier thinking. In some sense, Truth Therapy is as well, with its focus on lies and the truth. Learning and knowing the truth will assist in better, logical, and healthier thinking. However, my intention is not that Truth Therapy serves CBT, but that CBT serves Truth Therapy, discipleship, and Scripture. Even though CBT is not Scriptural or theological, *all truth is God's truth.* Whatever truth there is the sciences, philosophy, or other fields ultimately comes from the Lord of truth. God generously provides a general revelation of truth in the created order, demonstrating that he gives the sun and rain to everyone, the just and the unjust. Since all truth is God's truth, we need to learn to think in an interdisciplinary way. In our case, a theology of discipleship can dialogue with other relevant fields and critically integrate their insight and truth.

Thus, truths regarding the brain and the mind, such as neuroscience, cognitive sciences, or CBT, can be critically applied to our theological pursuit of truth. Science (and other fields) and religion can exist in contrast, independence (parallel), dialogue, or integration depending on the theory in question. It is my contention that CBT can be critically applied to discipleship and, in particular, to renewing the mind with the truth of God's Word. Both address the mind, truth, and transformation. My move is to embed and wed, where possible, the truths of CBT with Truth Therapy and the process of discipleship. Particularly, CBT functions as a psychological confirmation of a Scriptural perspective concerning lies, truth, renewing the mind, and discipleship. Lies are to be rejected, and the truth is to be received and obeyed. Discipleship begins in the mind, and we are called to renew our minds with the word of God (Rom. 12:1–2).

The truth in CBT is neither Scriptural nor salvific. However, it can be helpful because some of its principles regarding cognitive discernment are consonant with other Scriptural principles that call us to discern between lies and truth and good and evil. Some of the early desert fathers and mothers applied similar principles long before CBT was developed. Evagrius Ponticus (345–399 CE) was a third-generation anchorite and ascetic desert father. Evagrius was confronted with the problem of acedia (slothfulness, boredom) in his own life and in the lives of his disciple monks (novices), and he rightfully discerned that the problem originated in the thought life. Demonic attacks and fleshly temptations occurred in the mind through thoughts. Evagrius developed a sophisticated methodology for discerning flawed, deceptive, and sinful thinking (*logisimoi*) and a corresponding strategy to combat the problem, which resembles both CBT and charismatic spiritual warfare.

In CBT language, Evagrius cataloged various types of stinking thinking (*logisimoi*) so that his students could learn to be aware of their self-talk and to reject and replace unwanted thoughts. Following, he cataloged an extensive list of Scripture that disciples could implement to counteract stinking thinking and demonic attacks. Evagrius' work was revolutionary.[20] He influenced later Christian ascetics, quietists,

---

20. Evagrius of Pontus (Evagrius Ponticus), *The Praktikos and Chapters on Prayer*, 2nd ed., trans. John Eudes Bamberger (Cistercian, 1972) (Ponticus and Bamberger, The Practikos and Chapters on Prayer, 2nd ed 1972); Evagrius of Pontus, *Talking Back [Antirrhetikos]: A Monastic Handbook for Combating Demons*, trans. David Brakke (Cistercian, 2009) (Ponticus and Brakke, Talking Back [Antirrhetikos]: A Monastic Handbook for Combating Demons 2009); Gabriel Bunge, *Despondency: The Spiritual Teaching of Evagrius Ponticus on Acedia* (St. Vladimir's Seminary Press, 2011) (Bunge 2011); George Tsakiridis, *Evagrius Ponticus and Cognitive Science: A Look at Moral Evil and the Thoughts* (Wipf and Stock, 2010). (Tsakiridis 2010)

and mystics, such as John Cassian, Ignatius, St. John of the Cross, Molinos, Madame Guyon, and Bishop Fenelon, among others. Training the mind according to the word of God in order to overcome temptation, the flesh, and demonic attacks and to grow in the image of Christ was Evagrius' intention. It is also the purpose of Truth Therapy.

Truth Therapy, Belief Formation, and Discipleship

Earlier, we noted the importance of instruction as a mark of a disciple. Instruction includes teaching Scripture, theology, doctrine, church history, mission and evangelism, ministry, and other areas of the Christian life. The reader has his or her own doctrinal tradition with both common (e.g., Nicene Creed) and distinct creeds (e.g., The Creed of Alexander), confessions and articles of faith (e.g., Westminster Confession, Augsburg Confession, Methodist Articles of Religion), and doctrinal statements (e.g., Assemblies of God 16 Fundamental Truths). Integrating the doctrine of the church into one's faith and practice is essential for developing disciples. If we are committed to Christianity, we need to know what it teaches. Some denominations are indifferent and even hostile to doctrine. What are we, the global church, being asked to commit to? We cannot be committed to indifference. The historic, orthodox doctrine of the church has been laid down by the apostles and faithfully passed on throughout the ages. We are commanded to "contend" for the faith (our doctrinal beliefs) that has been delivered to us (Jude 3–4). If we do not know what faith is, we can hardly contend for it. Doctrine is paramount for a disciple's belief formation. A premise of Truth Therapy "is that truth-based belief formation contributes to effective discipleship, a healthy emotional life, quality decision-making, and productive, even virtuous, behavior."[21] When we know who we are and what we believe, we know who we are not and what we do not believe!

In *Truth Therapy*, I listed and expounded on thirty *practical* teachings to help form disciples. Here is an inexhaustive list of thirty biblical truths that transform:[22]

1. **New Creation:** I am a new creation in Christ.
2. **Image of God:** I am made in the image of God.
3. **Sin:** I have sinned and fallen short of the glory of God.
4. **Jesus Christ:** Jesus Christ is Lord of all.
5. **The Jesus Event:** It is finished.
6. **Repentance:** I turn away from my way and to God and God's way.
7. **Salvation by Grace through Faith:** I am saved by grace through faith.

21. Bellini, *Truth Therapy*, 287. (P. Bellini, Truth Therapy: Renewing Your Mind with the Word of God 2014)

22. Bellini, *Truth Therapy*, 69–70. (P. Bellini, Truth Therapy: Renewing Your Mind with the Word of God 2014)

8. **Forgiveness:** Forgiveness is complete in Christ but often realized over time. The forgiven forgive.
9. **Walk by Faith:** I walk by faith and not by sight.
10. **Holiness:** I am made holy by grace through faith.
11. **Spirit-Filled:** I will be filled with the Spirit and walk in the Spirit.
12. **Christian Identity:** I am complete in Christ.
13. **Self-Denial and Cross-Bearing:** I deny myself daily and take up my cross.
14. **Trust in the Lord:** I trust in the Lord and not in my own reason.
15. **Christian Life (the strength and ability):** I can do all things through Christ.
16. **Transformation:** Change begins with repentance by changing my thinking.
17. **Victory:** I am an overcomer and more than a conqueror in Christ.
18. **Spiritual Warfare:** Resist the devil, and he will flee from you.
19. **Overcoming Daily:** I overcome evil with good.
20. **Love Never Fails:** I love God and neighbor with my whole being.
21. **Resting in God:** It is finished.
22. **Servanthood:** The greatest will be a servant of all.
23. **The Future:** I have a blessed hope and future.
24. **Thanksgiving:** I will bless and give thanks at all times.
25. **Giving:** It is better to give than to receive.
26. **Divine Healing:** Go, your faith has made you whole.
27. **God's Purpose:** All things work for good.
28. **Our Daily Bread:** Abide in me and I in you. Without me you can do nothing.
29. **Prayer:** I will pray without ceasing.
30. **Mission:** Go and make disciples who can make disciples. The Spirit of the Lord is upon me to preach good news to the poor.

For each truth listed, the book *Truth Therapy* provides a related section on Scripture, a reflection, relevant names of God, repentance for stinking thinking, affirmations, applying the M.E.E.T. method, and further evening reflection for daily personal or group devotions.

Truth Therapy, Identity Formation, and Discipleship

As belief formation is critical for discipleship, so also is overall identify formation and formation of Christian practice. The *Truth Therapy* text uses a study on the various names of God and Scriptural affirmations to build believers up in their identity in Christ (identity formation). The two key principles, as cited earlier, are knowing

"Who I am in Christ" and "What I can do through Christ." We are new creations in Christ, and we can do all things through Christ, who strengthens us.

The various names of the Triune God point to God's character and actions. Simply put, the names of God reveal God's identity and acts—who God is and what God does. Through covenant, God's identity is related to our identity. We are his children. And God's acts are related to our acts. He works in and through us. More specifically, God's identity shapes our identity in Christ. And God's acts empower our acts in the Holy Spirit. God's holiness is my holiness. God's power is my power.

Paul summed up Christian identity formation best when he declared, "I have been crucified with Christ and I no longer live, but Christ lives in me. The life I now live in the body, I live by faith in the Son of God, who loved me and gave himself for me" (Gal. 2:20 NIV). The old identity is crucified on the cross. The new identity is raised from the dead with Christ. I am now defined by who I am in Christ. Similarly, Christian practice is best summed up again by Paul: "I can do all things through Christ who strengthens me" (Phil. 4:13 NKJV). He does not mean we can do whatever we want and claim this verse. The verse means that whatever God has called us to do, Christ will give us the strength to do. For a succinct overview of what we are called to do, see Christ's Sermon on the Mount (Matthew 5–7).

An Abridged List of the Names of God[23]

One way that our self-concept can begin to be transformed is by renewing our minds through appropriating the truth and power found in the names of God, which give us a right and healthy concept of God. The names of God are connected to God's nature and attributes. We can understand God through God's names, and we can understand how God envisions us as a new creation when we receive the attributes indicated by God's names. The desired result is a right and healthy self-concept that has been derived from a right and healthy concept of God.[24]

1. God (*Elohim*)
2. Lord (*Yahweh*)
3. Lord (*Adonai*)
4. Most High God (*El Elyon; Elyon*)
5. Eternal God (*El Olam*)
6. God who sees (*El Roi*)
7. God of Israel (*El Elohe Yisrael*)
8. The Lord who provides (*Adonai Yireh*)
9. The Lord our Banner (*Adonai Nissi*)
10. The Lord who strikes (*Adonai Nakeh*)
11. The Lord our Peace (*Adonai Shalom*)

---

23. The book has nearly 100 names of God listed. Bellini, *Truth Therapy*, chapter 6. (P. Bellini, Truth Therapy: Renewing Your Mind with the Word of God 2014)

24. Bellini, *Truth Therapy*, 255. (P. Bellini, Truth Therapy: Renewing Your Mind with the Word of God 2014)

12. The Lord our Sanctification (*Adonai Maccaddeshem*)
13. Jesus (Y'shua): *Savior*, Yeshua; Savior
14. Christ (*Christos*); Anointed One; Messiah
15. Lord (*Kurios*)
16. Savior (*Soter*)
17. Advocate (*parakletos)*
18. Spirit of God (*Ruah Elohim*)
19. Spirit of the Lord (*Ruah Adonai*)
20. Holy Spirit (*Ruah Ha Qodesh*)
21. The Spirit of Christ (*Pneuma Christou*)
22. Spirit of Truth (*Pneuma tes Altheias*)
23. Spirit of Life (*Pneumatos tes Zoes*)
24. Spirit of Holiness (*Pneuma Hagiosune*)
25. Holy Spirit (*Hagios Pneuma*)

In the book *Truth Therapy*, for each name of God there is a Scripture verse, a definition of the name, a reflection on the name, and an affirmation of the name's attribute in the life of the believer. For example:

Name: The Lord our Righteousness (Adonai Tsidkenu)

Scripture: Jeremiah 23:6

Definition: Truth about God: Righteousness—God is a God of Divine justice and righteousness.

Reflection: Righteousness. This compound name means "the Lord our righteousness." Righteousness means right or good standing, right relationship, of excellent moral quality of character. Righteousness as an attribute is distinct from human righteousness. Even the most righteous of persons falls short of the righteousness that belongs to God. Our most righteous deeds are like filthy rags compared to God's righteousness. The Lord's righteousness is a perfect standard. It demands a perfection that we cannot produce. Thus, God offers it to us as a free gift, and we accept it by faith. Jesus is our righteousness. He makes us acceptable in God's sight. By his blood we are forgiven, accepted, and made new. As we walk the Christian life, we are to stand in his righteousness and allow the Spirit to work Christ's righteousness through us in right action, action that reflects the character of God.

Affirmation: My righteousness falls short of the glory of God, but God is my righteousness, and God's righteousness in me leads me to live righteously. Jesus is my standard of righteousness and justice by which all actions are measured.[25]

---

25. Bellini, *Truth Therapy*, 266. (P. Bellini, Truth Therapy: Renewing Your Mind with the Word of God 2014)

An Abridged List of Affirmations

One way to be intentional and proactive in scripting our self-talk is to make regular confessions, affirmations, and declarations based on who we are in Christ, to tell ourselves what God's word says about us. Declare what God says about others and us. Affirm what God affirms. The psalmist David regularly found that he had to encourage himself in the Lord. He also would often ask his soul, "Why are you so discouraged and downcast?" He had to talk to himself in the Lord. In this next section, we are intentionally aligning our self-talk with God-talk. We are saying what God is saying.[26]

I am (we are) God's Creation.

1. I am created by God in the womb. (Ps. 139:13–16)
2. I am formed and set apart by God. (Jer. 1:5)
3. I am wonderfully made (Ps. 139:14)
4. I am created for his glory. (Isa. 43:7)
5. I have a purpose for living. (Jer. 29:11; Eph. 1:11–12)[27]

I am (we are) washed, forgiven, accepted, saved, and delivered through Christ Jesus.

1. I am forgiven. (Eph. 1:7)
2. I am forgiven and healed. (Ps. 103:3, 12)
3. I am accepted in Christ. (Eph. 1:6)
4. I am washed in the blood. (Rev. 1:5)
5. I am washed, justified, and sanctified. (1 Cor. 6:11)
6. I am purified, cleansed from sin by Jesus. (1 John 1:7–9)
7. I am reconciled to God. (2 Cor. 5:18)
8. I am redeemed from the curse of the law. (Gal. 3:13)
9. I am the righteousness of God through Christ. (2 Cor. 5:21)
10. I am free from condemnation. (Rom. 8:1)
11. I am free from sin and death. (Rom. 8:2)[28]

I am (we are) loved and victorious.

1. I am loved. (1 John 4:10, 19)
2. I have God's unfailing love. (Ps. 32:10)
3. I am loved with an everlasting love. (Jer. 31:3)
4. I am never forsaken. (Ps. 27:10)
5. I am comforted. (Isa. 66:13)
6. I am not afraid. (Heb. 13:6)

---

26. Bellini, *Truth Therapy*, 288. (P. Bellini, Truth Therapy: Renewing Your Mind with the Word of God 2014)

27. Bellini, *Truth Therapy*, 289. (F. Bellini, Truth Therapy: Renewing Your Mind with the Word of God 2014)

28. Bellini, *Truth Therapy*, 290. (F. Bellini, Truth Therapy: Renewing Your Mind with the Word of God 2014)

7. I am strong in the Lord. (Eph. 6:10)
8. I am victorious. (Rev. 21:7)
9. I am the head and not the tail. (Deut. 20:13)
10. I am above only and not beneath. (Deut. 28:13)
11. I am more than a conqueror. (Rom. 8:37)
12. I always triumph in Christ. (2 Cor. 2:14)
13. I can do all things through Christ. (Phil. 4:13)
14. I shall do even greater works than Jesus. (John 14:12)
15. I am an overcomer. (Rom. 8:9–11)
16. I have overcome the world. (1 John 5:4–5)
17. I possess the Greater One in me. (1 John 4:4)
18. I have authority over the devil and all evil. (Luke 10:19)
19. I have received the power of the Holy Ghost to heal the sick and to cast out demons. (Mark 16:17)
20. I have received the same power that raised Jesus from the dead. (Phil. 3:10)
21. I have the gifts of the Spirit. (1 Cor. 12:7)
22. God speaks to me, and I hear and know his voice. (John 10:3–4)[29]

I have received hundreds of testimonies over the years about the power of Truth Therapy, how it helped people overcome the battle in their minds and live a victorious life.

Truth in a Day of Deception

Aleksandr Solzhenitsyn (1918–2008) was a Russian writer and famous dissident from the former Soviet Union.[30] He was also a Christian, a devout member of the Russian Orthodox Church. However, at one point, under the hopeless, oppressive regime of communism, he became an atheist. While serving in the Red Army, he was arrested and sent to the gulag for sending a letter that criticized dictator Joseph Stalin. He experienced bitter, toiling labor and suffering in these godless work camps. During his imprisonment, he had time to reflect about Soviet society under communism. Later he was released and wrote of his experience in the gulag in *One Day in the Life of Ivan Denisovich* and *The Gulag Archipelago*.

Eventually, due to his penetrating analysis and criticism of the prison camps and life under Soviet communism, he was stripped of his Soviet citizenship and released to the West. His works became widely acclaimed in the United States and throughout the world, and Solzhenitsyn gave lectures throughout United States on the evil and terror of communism and the need to preserve freedom and human rights in the

---

29. Bellini, *Truth Therapy*, 291–92. (P. Bellini, Truth Therapy: Renewing Your Mind with the Word of God 2014)

30. For more on Solzhenitsyn, see Joseph Pearce, *Solzhenitsyn: A Soul in Exile*, revised and updated ed. (Ignatius, 2001).

West. He warned America that the fiber of its moral fabric as a society was eroding and that communism posed a potential threat even within its own borders. Though at times controversial even in the eyes of liberals in the States, Solzhenitsyn became emblematic for the need to tell the truth, regardless of whether one is being suffocated all around by the tyranny of lies. He wrote,

> To stand up for truth is nothing. For truth, you must sit in jail. You can resolve to live your life with integrity. Let your credo be this: Let the lie come into the world, let it even triumph. But not through me. The simple step of a courageous individual is not to take part in the lie. One word of truth outweighs the world. In keeping silent about evil, in burying it so deep within us that no sign of it appears on the surface, we are *implanting* it, and it will rise up a thousand fold in the future. When we neither punish nor reproach evildoers, we are not simply protecting their trivial old age, we are thereby ripping the foundations of justice from beneath new generations.[31]

And in his 1970 Nobel Lecture he proclaimed, "The simple act of an ordinary brave man is not to participate in lies, not to support false actions! His rule: Let *that* come into the world, let it even reign supreme—only not through me. But it is within the power of writers and artists to do much more: to *defeat* the lie! For in the struggle with lies art has always triumphed and shall always triumph! Visibly, irrefutably for all! Lies can prevail against much in this world, but never against art. . . . *One word of truth shall outweigh the whole world.*"[32]

We are bombed moment by moment with information due to the power of the internet and AI. We are connected to everyone's thoughts in a nanosecond. The democratization of knowledge is a blessing, but it can be a curse as well. So many sources of opinions. Where does one find truth? How does one discern truth? Many of the reliable sources that society has trusted for decades for credible information are now held suspect. Journalism, media, the White House, the government, the sciences, the medical community, higher educational institutions, even the church are at times questionable sources to deliver the truth. Some say that we are in a post-truth era, where the "real" truth does not matter. It is the optics of truth that matters. Worse, something is true if it lines up with our narrative or ideology. Everything else is dismissed.

We live in an age of fact-checking. However, fact-checkers check the facts based on their own ideology. So, we need to fact-check the fact-checkers, who also fact-check based on their ideology. Well, we need to fact-check the fact-checkers who fact-check the fact-checkers—and on and on. The truth and the road to it are rare commodities. Postmodernity has left us bleakly lost in a dark desert without a star

---

31. Alexander Solzhenitsyn, *The Gulag Archipelago* (Penguin Random House, 2018). (Solzhenitsyn 2018)

32. "The Nobel Prize in Literature 1970" n.d. ("The Nobel Prize in Literature 1970." n.d.) Nobelprize.org. Accessed December 30, 2024. https://www.nobelprize.org/prizes/literature/1970/solzhenitsyn/lecture/.

in the sky to guide us or a compass in hand to point us north. The culture offers no metanarrative or an absolute story to explain the other stories. No absolutes. No certainty of right or wrong, truth or lie. Like never before, we need the truth. Truth can heal a nation! For Christians, the truth is ultimately a person, not a formula, equation, theory, or idea. Our hope is in the Son of God, who has been sent for our salvation. Christ is our King, and we are citizens of his Kingdom. He is a ruler who cannot be elected or impeached. If Jesus is Lord, our ultimate hope cannot be in a nation, government, ruler, president, or any other for the *polis*. The city of (wo)man tends to corruption and is bound to fall. Only the City of God will prevail.

Disciples of Christ are called to be disciples of truth. Disciples seek the truth, believe the truth, and obey the truth. The Holy Spirit is truth (the Spirit of Truth). He is the truth, reveals the truth, and leads us in truth (John 14–16). The holy Scriptures are God's written revelation of truth, a sure word of prophecy by which we can test claims. Christians are called to love God not just with our hearts but with our minds. We are commanded to study so that our work may be approved by God, and we properly know and explain the "word of truth" (2 Tim. 2:15). The people of God should freely study Scripture, Greek, Hebrew, exegesis, hermeneutics, theology, Christology, pneumatology, ethics, history, and the like with every available scholarly tool we can find. If we worship God with all of our mind, that requires a certain rigor and even academic excellence when approaching Scripture and theology. The brain's power to reason, analyze, define, compare and contrast, memorize, concentrate, feel, experience, fear, enthrall, delight, imagine, recall, and implement are all engaged fully when we pursue the truth.

Although some brands of popular Christianity may eschew academic acumen and rigor and label it as "of the flesh" or the devil, the historic Christian faith has always used the fullness of our human ability to reason. From the apostle Paul to Athanasius and the Cappadocian Fathers, to Augustine and Aquinus, to Luther, Calvin, and Wesley, and to Barth, Brunner, and Balthasar, vital piety and vital knowledge have been wedded together. The heart and head work together in a needed dialectic of checks and balances with one ear to heaven and the other to the ground. We long to see once again that rare gem of sanctified reason radiating luminously in the minds of believers of this age. In our postmodern, post-truth era, sound doctrine and theology cannot be compromised for cultural correctness. We are participating in the mission of God (*missio Dei*), not the mission of culture (*missio culturae)* nor the mission of the state (*missio stati*). The mission does not belong to the culture, the state, or even the church (*mission ecclesiae*) but to God. Mission is the work of God that he permits us to participate in through his Spirit.[33] We are not called to cater to the mission of the culture or the state, and neither does the church invent its own mission. As there is one God, there is one mission of God (*missio Dei*) carried out by the Spirit (*missio Spiritus*). Our allegiance and service are to God's mission above every other agenda.

---

33. See Peter Bellini, "Origins and Early Development of *Missio Dei*: A Missional Hermeneutic for Today," in *Missio Dei in the United States* (GBHEM, 2018). (P. Bellini, Origins and Early Development of Missio Dei: A Missional Hermeneutic for Today 2018)

HOLY SPIRIT: THE SPIRIT-FILLED MIND

The Church has lost the note of authority, the secret of wisdom, and the gift of power through its persistent and willful neglect of the Holy Spirit of God. Confusion and impotence are inevitable when the wisdom and resources of the world are substituted for the presence and power of the Spirit of God.

—Samuel Chadwick[1]

The Holy Spirit: The Lord the Giver of Life

The Holy Spirit is the third person of the Trinity, one God in three persons (Father, Son, and Holy Spirit). As the Father is *Lord* and Christ is *Lord*, so also the Holy Spirit is *Lord* (2 Cor. 3:18; Eph. 4:5). There is only *one Lord* because there is only *one God*. The Nicene Creed declares that the Spirit is Lord, as the Father and Son, and receives worship and glory that are only due to God. The word *Lord* in the Hebrew Bible is a combination of the covenant name Yahweh (the great I AM THAT I AM) with the vowel pointing of Adonai. In the Septuagint (or LXX, the Greek translation of the Old Testament) "Lord" is translated "*Kurios*" as it is in the New Testament when referring to Christ. "Whoever calls on the name of the Lord shall be saved" refers to Yahweh (Joel 2:32 NKJV). The same verse is applied by Peter in Acts 2:21, but the reference to Lord is Christ. Jesus Christ is the Lord of salvation. Further, in 2 Corinthians 3:18, the Holy Spirit is called "Lord" (*Kuriou, Kurios*), the same word applied to the Father and the Son. The three who are called "Lord" are one God. We are also baptized in his one name, which is three: Father, Son, and Holy Spirit (Matt. 28:19).

The problem is that although the church confesses that the Spirit is Lord and God, it does not live like it. We run our lives and churches as if we are in control. If the Holy Spirit left our lives and churches, we would go about doing mostly what we normally do, because so much of what we do has nothing to do with the Holy Spirit. We can play-act in life and in church and go through all of the motions of the Christian life, as having the form but denying the power of the Spirit (2 Tim. 3:5). I have taught and ministered on the Holy Spirit for nearly four decades, and the great-

---

1. Samuel Chadwick, *The Way of Pentecost* (Christian Literature Crusade, 2001), 17. (Chadwick 2001)

est problem I find as to why people do not walk in the fullness of the Spirit's power and holiness is because we fear giving up total control and turning it over the Holy Spirit—simply, to make the Holy Spirit Lord. We are professionals at running our own lives and churches without the Lordship of the Spirit. We have gotten it down pat to a formula and a science, yet we do not experience consistent victory in our lives. We do not see the book of Acts–type of power in our churches and ministries. Signs and wonders are not following us, but we run from them.

The *missio Dei*, the mission of God, is not for *us* to grow churches. We cannot grow a church. It's impossible. "Unless the Lord builds the house, the builders labor in vain," is what my Bible says (Ps. 127:1 NIV). We can plant, and we can water, but only God can make things grow or give the increase (1 Cor. 3:7). No, we are commissioned to make disciples, another impossible task without the Holy Spirit (Matt. 28:19). All of our well-devised plans and strategies for growth and effectiveness cleverly concocted by our MBA-educated pastors and their business models of the church are capable of constructing remarkable institutions, structures, and companies of men and women, but they will not amount to one brick laid in the Kingdom of God without the Holy Spirit. The Spirit of Life who breathed life in the beginning is the only one who can give the church and the world true life. The body of Christ without the Spirit is dead (Jas. 2:26)!

The Holy Spirit: Another Counselor

Jesus did not leave us a vast sum of money, a government, an army, or even a book, since the Bible would not be fully canonized until nearly four centuries after Christ. He left the church what she truly needed: the Holy Spirit, another Counselor (*parakletos*). The church needed *another* Counselor, one just like Jesus, who was going to be with the Father. The word for "another" in the Greek New Testament is *allos*, meaning another of the *same* kind, not *heteros*, meaning another of a *different* kind. Christ would send one just like himself. As we know, the Son of God and the Holy Spirit are consubstantial, meaning of the one and same substance or essence. When the Spirit was sent at Pentecost to dwell in the hearts of believers, he came to reveal and bear witness to the person and work of Jesus Christ. Christ would live in believers through the Holy Spirit.

The Spirit would not reveal himself nor bear witness to himself. His role is to reveal and bear witness to the Son, whose role is to reveal and bear witness to the Father (John 14–16). The Spirit of Truth descended at Pentecost to minister salvation in the hearts of his followers. The Holy Spirit is the Divine agent of Christ's salvation in our lives. What Jesus finished objectively at the cross, the Holy Spirit applies subjectively in our lives. He is the agent of Divine experience. He is the Divine person, Divine presence, Divine purity, and Divine power in the heart of the Christian. The Spirit reveals, applies, and witnesses to the person and work of Jesus Christ in our lives. He is the *chief executor* of the salvation that Christ secured for us on the cross.

As another Counselor (Comforter, Advocate, Helper), or *allos parakletos*, he is Christ within us the hope of glory (John 14:16). As another Counselor, Christ is able to live and work in our lives. St. Paul explained this revelation when he declared, "I have been crucified with Christ and I no longer live, but Christ lives in me. The life I now live in the body, I live by faith in the Son of God, who loved me and gave himself for me" (Gal. 2:20 NIV). Christ through the Spirit is "his power that works within us" "to do immeasurably more than all we ask or imagine" (Eph. 3:20 NIV).

Over the years, I have coached many sports, from boxing and weightlifting to football, basketball, and baseball. An effective coach possesses the right combination of attributes and qualities, such as wisdom, encouraging or inspiring, cultivating, and an overcoming attitude. When I think of effective coaches, I think of John Wooden (wisdom), Jim Valvano (encouraging), Cus D'Amato (cultivating), and Vince Lombardi (overcoming attitude). Everyone needs at least one faithful coach in their life who helps them to overcome, whether it is a parent, a teacher, a sports coach, a mentor, or a friend. We are not alone. Christ has sent us the Holy Spirit to live inside of us. The Spirit of God is in our corner. In between grueling rounds, the battered fighter returns to their corner to regroup and be restored. His or her cornermen or -women wipe away the sweat from the fighter's face. They squeeze a sponge soaked with cold water over the fighter. They refresh him or her with water for his or her dry mouth. They tend to the cuts with salve and the bruises with an end swell bar. Most importantly, the coach instructs the boxer about what he or she has been doing right and wrong. The coach sees what the fighter cannot and gets him or her back on track with the fight plan, encouraging him or her to victory. *The Holy Spirit is in our corner for the battle of life*. He refreshes us with his presence. He also wipes away life's sweat, tends to our bruises, and heals our cuts. He convicts us when we get off track from God's plan. He instructs us with wisdom and truth for the battle of life and empowers us to victory. How little do we take advantage of this blessing.

When I am discipling someone, it is imperative that at some point following salvation I pray for the *baptism of the Holy Spirit for holiness and power*, a deeper work of the Spirit to live and minister an overcoming life (Matt. 3:11–12; Acts 1:8; Eph. 5:18). Believers *have* the Spirit at salvation; batteries are included (Rom. 8:9–16; 1 Cor. 12:3). However, those are rechargeable batteries. When the energy runs down, the batteries need to be recharged. We need to stay filled with the Spirit and his fruit and gifts to be and do what he has called us to be and do. There is more than one work or operation of the Spirit besides salvation (1 Cor. 12:4–5). The Spirit witnesses, sanctifies, empowers, and works miracles. We need to receive the full scope of the Spirit's work in and through us.

A few years ago, a vicious series of tornados hit our area in Ohio. The power went out everywhere. It was like living in the seventeenth century, walking by candlelight, heating the house with wood, and cooking over the fireplace. All of our amenities were gone. Life was rough and limited. After a week, the power came back, and modernity was restored. Today, there is a power outage in the church. Many are living the Christian life and doing ministry as if there were no spiritual electricity, no power. Many know there is electricity, but they fear it. We cannot afford to be pyrophobic. The fire will not burn the house down if you build and keep a safe fireplace. A safe fireplace means to disciple and train your people about the person and work of the

Spirit, train, certify, and publicly install gift ministers for the local church, and lay down a proper order for using them in the church (1 Corinthians 12–14). Such a method prevents both charisphobia and charismania! We cannot afford to have a carnal church, an unarmed spiritual army, and an unequipped ministry, or permit self-appointed spiritual terrorists and charismatic narcissists to take over the church. Over the years I have led hundreds into receiving more of the Spirit, and it has revolutionized every one of their lives and ministries. Never a regret. Pray for more!

The Work of the Holy Spirit

Coaches cultivate the potential that rests in their athletes. Christlikeness is our potential. It is the work of the Holy Spirit to inspire us to such a height. The Spirit reshapes our mind in the image of God. A disciple can not only have the mind of Christ and be pure as he is pure, but that he or she can walk as he walked. There can be no discipleship without the Holy Spirit, who is the ultimate disciplemaker. There can be no renewing of the mind without the Spirit of Life, who makes all things new. The Christian life and walk from grace to grace happens by the power of the Holy Spirit alone. There can be no substitute. Our own natural knowledge, ability, and morality will always fall short of his glory. Our best offerings can only be filthy rags. Our works don't work. Our goodness is not good enough. Our power fails. Our knowledge is idolatry. In the language of John Wesley, from prevenient grace to convincing grace to justifying grace and assurance, to sanctifying and glorifying grace, it is all the work of the blessed Holy Spirit. We will examine how when the Spirit governs our minds, we experience new life and peace: "Those who live according to the flesh have their minds set on what the flesh desires; but those who live in accordance with the Spirit have their minds set on what the Spirit desires. The mind governed by the flesh is death, but the mind governed by the Spirit is life and peace" (Rom. 8:5–6).

The Holy Spirit and the Way of Salvation

The Holy Spirit is the chief executor of the salvific work of Christ in our lives. The work of salvation from beginning to end is the work of the Spirit of God in the disciple. The Spirit of Truth commences by guiding our minds into all truth (John 16:13–15), beginning with conviction of sin (John 16:8–11). In John Wesley's way of salvation (*via salutis*), he broke these works down into *prevenient* and *convincing grace*. Prevenient grace is "the first wish to please God, the first dawn of light concerning his will, and the first slight, transient conviction of having sinned against him."[2] Prevenient grace is the Spirit going ahead of us to draw us to God. Convincing, or convicting, grace is the Spirit pointing out where we have deviated from following

---

2.   John Wesley, Sermon 85, "On Working Out Your Own Salvation," in *Works of John Wesley*, vol. 6, *Sermon II*, ed. Thomas Jackson (Wesleyan Conference Office, 1872), 509. (Wesley, Works of John Wesley 1872)

God and the call to repent. For Wesley, convincing grace is "in Scripture termed *repentance*."[3] By his grace, he gently but firmly touches on the areas in our life that are unlike Christ. His goal in convicting is not to condemn but to lead us to repentance, faith, and deliverance so that we can be free.

The Spirit brings us into *justifying grace*, where we "are saved by faith," "saved from the guilt of sin, and restored to the favour of God."[4] We are pardoned and brought into the family of God The Holy Spirit, in making us right with God, washes and regenerates our soul, giving us new life in Christ. Wesley defines the new birth as

> that great change which God works in the soul when he brings it into life; when he raises it from the death of sin to the life of righteousness. It is the change wrought in the whole soul by the almighty Spirit of God when it is "created anew in Christ Jesus;" when it is "renewed after the image of God in righteousness and true holiness;" when the love of the world is changed into the love of God; pride into humility; passion into meekness; hatred, envy, malice into a sincere, tender, disinterested love for all mankind. In a word, it is that change whereby the earthly, sensual, devilish mind is turned into the "mind which was in Christ Jesus."[5]

Following regeneration, or the new birth, the Spirit grants us assurance of our salvation that our sins are forgiven: "The Spirit bears witness with our spirit that we are the children of God" (Rom. 8:16 NKJV). John Wesley explained "that there is in every believer, both the testimony of God's Spirit, and the testimony of their own, that they are a child of God."[6] The Holy Spirit provides assurance inwardly, immediately, and directly in the heart of the Christian, and the Spirit provides assurance outwardly and indirectly by the fruit that he produces in the life of the Christian.[7] As we obey the grace of God, our assurance in Christ is strengthened by the witness of the Spirit.

One problem Wesley identified in believers is their struggle with inbred or birth sin. Inbred sin is simply the principle and power of sin that remains in Christians even after regeneration (Romans 7). Although they love God and neighbor and walk in the Spirit, they are still opposed on the inside by the flesh or the will to sin. When they want to do good, evil is present and seeks to oppose the good they want to do. This ongoing civil war inside Christians is described in Scripture: "For the flesh desires what is contrary to the Spirit, and the Spirit what is contrary to the flesh. They

---

3. Wesley, Sermon 85, "On Working Out Your Own Salvation," in *Works of John Wesley*, 6:509. (Wesley, Works of John Wesley 1872)

4. Wesley, Sermon 85, "On Working Out Your Own Salvation," in *Works of John Wesley*, 6:509. (Wesley, Works of John Wesley 1872)

5. Wesley, Sermon 45, "The New Birth," in *Works of John Wesley*, 6:71. (Wesley, Works of John Wesley 1872)

6. Wesley, Sermon 11, "The Witness of the Spirit," in *Works of John Wesley*, 5:113. (Wesley, Works of John Wesley 1872)

7. Wesley, Sermon 11, "The Witness of the Spirit," in *Works of John Wesley*, 5:122, 133. (Wesley, Works of John Wesley 1872)

are in conflict with each other, so that you are not to do whatever you want" (Gal. 5:17 NIV). Wesley simply called it "sin remaining in believers," which required believer's repentance, topics we discussed thoroughly in Chapter 4.

The purpose of being delivered from the presence and power of sin is so we can go onto "perfection" or maturity (Heb. 6:3), receive the full sanctifying work of the Spirit (1 Thess. 5:23), in order to love God and neighbor with a pure heart (Mark 12:30–31). The founder of Methodism proclaims, "By sanctification we are saved from the power and root of sin and restored to the image of God."[8] Without negotiation, disciples are called to holiness. Without it, we cannot see the Lord (Heb. 12:14). For Wesley, the distinct sanctifying work of the Spirit that empowers us to have victory over sin and to love God and neighbor is the essence and goal of Christianity. Christ understood it as the sum of the law and the prophets and the greatest command (Mark 12:29–31). Paul also concluded that "love was the fulfillment of the law" (Rom. 13:10). *Simply put, the Holy Spirit makes us holy because* Holy *is his first name.*

The Spirit's other dual role alongside sanctifier is empowerer (holiness and power). After Christ's resurrection, he instructed the disciples to pray in the upper room in preparation for the day of Pentecost. They were waiting for the promised gift of the baptism of the Holy Spirit (Luke 24:49; Acts 1:4–5, 8; 2:1). Jesus prophesies, "Do not leave Jerusalem, but wait for the gift my Father promised, which you have heard me speak about. For John baptized with water, but in a few days you will be baptized with the Holy Spirit" (Acts 1:4–5 NIV). The disciples' names were already written in the Book of Life (Luke 10:20). They knew Jesus was the Christ, the Son of the living God (Mark 8:29–30). They witnessed the resurrection (Matthew 28; Luke 24). They already received the Holy Spirit (John 20:22). Well, then, what is this baptism of the Holy Spirit? What is its purpose?[9] Jesus informs us, "But you will receive power when the Holy Spirit comes on you; and you will be my witnesses in

---

8. John Wesley, Sermon 85, "On Working Out Your Own Salvation," in *Works of John Wesley*, 6:509. (Wesley, Works of John Wesley 1872)

9. These questions are highly debated in diverse Christian circles. A variety of interpretations emerge. Some contend that the baptism of the Holy Spirit is the same as salvation. One receives the Spirit at salvation. Within that position, some hold that the Spirit is received for salvation at baptism (sacramental view), while others think that the Spirit is received on faith in Christ (evangelical view). The reason for the separation between the disciples believing in the resurrected Christ in the Gospels and receiving the baptism of the Spirit in Acts is a one-time-in-history event. Christ needed to resurrect, ascend, and be seated in glory for the Father to send the Holy Spirit through him on the disciples. Other groups contend that the disciples were saved in the Gospels and received the Spirit when they believed in the resurrection. The baptism of the Spirit in Acts thus represents a second experience or second work of grace (subsequence).

These groups are usually Keswick, Wesleyans, Pentecostals, and Charismatics. However, the purpose of the baptism of the Spirit is different for each group. Keswicks believe it is for living the overcoming, victorious life. Wesleyans (holiness) contend Spirit baptism is for entire sanctification. Most Pentecostals and Charismatics believe it is power for service to do the works that Christ did. Some Pentecostals, such as Wesleyan or Holiness Pentecostals, believe in three works of grace: salvation, sanctification, and the baptism of the Spirit for power. Ultimately, I do not contend for X number of works, as long as one receives all of what the Spirit has to offer, including salvation, holiness, and power; however many works that may take for one to receive.

See Ralph Del Colle, H. Ray Dunning, Larry Hart, Stanley M. Horton, and Walter C. Kaiser, *Perspectives on Spirit Baptism*, ed. Chad Brand (Broadman and Holman, 2004).

Jerusalem, and in all Judea and Samaria, and to the ends of the earth" (Acts 1:8 NIV). Tongues of fire fell on the disciples, and they began to preach the gospel and minister salvation. Fire in Scripture often represents the sanctifying work of the Spirit (Mal. 3:3; Matt. 3:11–12). John the Baptist called it a "baptism of fire" that would burn up the chaff (the flesh), a sanctifying or purging fire.

The descending flames were shaped like "tongues," as fire often appears as a "lick of fire." Their mouths, or witness, would be empowered by the Spirit to preach Christ. And they did at Pentecost. The message was from Joel 2 that the Spirit would fall on all people. Every human and social boundary that separates us would be broken down: women and men, old and young, Gentile and Jew, slave and free. Everyone would be touched by the Spirit and given gifts, such as signs and wonders, prophecy, dreams, and visions (Acts 2:17–21; 1 Corinthians 12). The fruit of Pentecost is observed throughout the book of Acts. The Spirit moves from "Jerusalem, Judea, Samaria, and to the ends of the earth" (Rome). The disciples notably walk in the exact same anointing and power that Christ did. What we witness in terms of ministry, salvation, and signs and wonders in Luke, we see manifested in the book of Acts; the continuity is striking. The reason is simple. The disciples were filled with the *same* Spirit as Jesus Christ to do what he did (John 14:12; Acts 4:13; Rom. 8:11). Disciples today need to be baptized in the Spirit for sanctification (Acts 15:8–9) and power (Acts 1:8; 3:12).

Pray and fast and seek the Lord for more. If you already are preaching the Word with signs and wonders following, if you have already been sanctified and are walking in holiness of heart and life, if you already are casting out demons and healing the sick, then pray for more. If you are *not* walking in these supernatural works of the Spirit, *then pray for more.* What harm or difficulty is there in praying for more? What theological issue can one find in praying for more? Where is the stumbling block or unbelief in praying for more? It is a simple request. Ask the Lord humbly for more— more holiness and power for his service and glory.

Do not be surprised if God empties you before he fills you, takes the flesh away to make room for the Spirit, subtracts before he adds, sanctifies before he empowers. Too often we teach young Christians to be filled with the power before they are crucified, emptied of self-will, and sanctified. We have immature Christians with the gifts packing heat, but they can't handle it. It is like giving a five-year-old an M-16. The old timers would say that person has the fire, the kind with a lot of heat but not much light. Immature, unsanctified believers operating as prophets and apostles can become spiritual terrorists. They become top-heavy with gifts and have no substructure to uphold the weight. Eventually, like a roof collapsing, so will a novice or immature person in a fivefold office eventually implode and cave in under the weight and pressure of life and ministry (Eph. 4:11; 1 Tim. 3:6). They were not taught holiness over power, character over charisma, and fruit over gifts.

Any disciple sitting under the ministry of a mature spiritual parent will be taught to be faithful with little before they are given more responsibility (Matt. 25:21–23; Luke 16:10). Granted, some mainline churches have a form of godliness but lack the power of the Spirit. On the other hand, many of our so-called Spirit-filled churches have too much spiritual granola (fruits, nuts, and flakes). Many are driving without a license. There are way too many lone rangers out there roaming the wild west, twirling their spiritual guns around their fingers looking for a gunfight. We have too many self appointed super apostles—three clicks and you're a bishop, ordained and graduated through a mail-order diploma mill—who do not know the difference between the book of Lamentations and the book of Hesitations. Empty titles puff us up in pride and are a form of malpractice. So seek the fire, absolutely, but build a solid, safe fireplace first that can contain the fire, or you will burn the house down. I recommend balanced teaching on the Holy Spirit (holiness and power) and taking a gifts inventory that reflects such a balance. Pray for and learn about the gifts of the Spirit so you can receive what the Spirit has for you and be employed for the Kingdom.[10]

"Smoke on the Water": A Case Study for the Importance of the Spirit's Gifts

As a newly converted radical Christian, I promised the Lord that I would obey his voice to the best of my ability, regardless of the circumstance. It did not take long for the Lord to test my commitment. One night I felt the Spirit of God wake me up around 3:00 a.m. I am not a morning person. He spoke to my heart clearly. He wanted me to get out of bed and follow him. In my mind, I began to debate with him, "Why, Lord? Why at this hour? For what?" The Lord replied, "You are on a need-to-know basis, and you do not need to know." I said to myself, "You promised the Lord that you would obey his voice, regardless of the circumstance." I got out of bed. He instructed me to grab my guitar. I paused and reluctantly picked up my guitar. "Grab your car keys," he directed me. I thought, *Why?* Then, I felt the conviction of the Spirit, and I grabbed my keys and headed out the door.

"Where are we going, Lord?" "Drive south on High Street. I will let you know," said the Lord. I drove south heading toward downtown. He reminded me of a small park on the side of the road near the bridge and the river. I drove toward it. He directed me where to park and to get out of the car. He showed me which picnic table to sit at. I eagerly went to the table and sat on top of it. Mind you, it's 3:15 a.m. He said, "Play!" I thought to myself, *What am I going to play? I don't know. Should I just start pounding out the chords to Deep Purple's "Smoke on the Water" or some other song?* Now, I play guitar, but I am not a guitar player. I have a good, deep bass speaking voice, but I am a prison singer, behind a few bars, looking for the right key. Regardless, the Spirit responded, "Just play." I felt the presence of the Holy Spirit fill and overwhelm me. I began to strum and sing.

---

10. For a balanced treatment of the Holy Spirit and an inventory of the gifts of the Spirit, see Peter Bellini, *Thunderstruck!: The Deliverance Ministry of John Wesley* (Wipf and Stock, 2023). See also Randy Clark, *There Is More: The Secret to Experiencing God's Power to Change Your Life* (Baker, 2013).

The words flowed from my heart through my lips. I sang the story of an elderly man who had everything and lost it. He had a beautiful wife, a lovely family, a great job, his sanity. He had everything, but instead, he gave his life to alcohol. It consumed his life. Over a period of time, he lost everything, his job, his family, his wife, and his life. I sang this sad song of this desperate man who wanted to end his life. As I concluded the song, I felt a presence behind me. I slowly turned and saw an elderly African American man behind me seated at the table. He began to weep. He cried, "You don't know me. You don't know who I am or anything about me. I heard you playing from down the street and came to listen. You don't know me, but you sang my life. That song you were singing was about me. I am that man. I had everything and lost it. I lost it and can't get it back. I came here last night to end my life. I was going to jump off that bridge over there, but I heard something inside say, 'Just wait one more day. Wait!' So I waited exactly twenty-four hours. Nothing changed. So I came back here to jump off that bridge and end it all, but then I heard you singing, and I came closer. That was me."

By that point, we were both in tears. I shared Christ with him, and how his life is not over, but it could be just beginning, if he would let Christ have his life. I let him know that the Lord can heal him and reverse his situation. The final chapter of his life has not been written and he should let the Lord finish writing it. God's miraculous intervention and prophetic song rocked him. He was weeping profusely. He was very open to the good news and was willing to give Christ a try. We prayed, and he asked Christ to save him and grant him a new beginning. I gave him my phone number and told him I would pick him up for church.

God's love is beyond words. He sees everyone and everything. Every tiny sparrow and every hair on our heads are on his radar. He sees us suffering. He weeps when we weep. The Lord is looking for faithful people who are radically committed and will respond to his call, even if it sounds insane, even if it is at 3:00 a.m., even if you don't know what song to play. The Lord saw this man and his plight, and he sent a gift to a willing vessel to be delivered to a desperate, lonely soul. If it were not for the gifts of the Holy Spirit, my elderly friend may not have survived the night and may not have received Christ. Thank you, Jesus!

Renewing the Mind: Healing and Restoring the Image of God

The Spirit of God is not only the primary evangelist but also the primary disciplemaker. Throughout the process of salvation, the Holy Spirit is renewing our mind with the word of God, crafting it into the image of Christ (the mind of Christ). Like a master sculptor or a potter spinning his wheel and forming the clay, the Spirit chisels away at our rough and raw edges and shapes us with his own hands. He is carefully fashioning us into vessels of honor, ripe and ready for the Master's use. We cannot form ourselves. Formation is the work of God alone. We are his masterpiece, "For we are God's handiwork, created in Christ Jesus to do good works, which God prepared in advance for us to do" (Eph. 2:10 NIV). The Greek word for "handiwork" is *poema*, from which we derive our word *poem*. We are a work of art, or God's poem written with the engraving of the Holy Spirit, whose colors will never fade and words never grow old. We are being fashioned for eternity.

One vital operation of the Spirit's handiwork in fitting us for heaven is to trade our ashes for beauty, our sorrow for the oil of joy, despair for a garment of praise (Isa. 61:3). The Holy Spirit heals the brokenhearted (Ps. 147:3; Is. 61:1). He heals our identity, the image of God within us. Many come to Christ with abuse, trauma, and pain. As we stated earlier, the past cannot be changed, but we can change how we think about the past. The Holy Spirit can guide us through the healing of our past that is needed to make us whole. He can speak words of healing to our past pains and renew our souls (image healing). The Spirit begins with regeneration. He restores us into a new creation, a new person in Christ with the capacity for a renewed mind: "Therefore we do not lose heart. Though outwardly we are wasting away, yet inwardly we are being renewed day by day" (2 Cor. 4:16 NIV).

As believers, we are truly a new creation in Christ, and *by faith*, the old life has departed and new life has emerged. Nonetheless, the "new you" still lives in your old body. After coming to Christ and being born again of the Spirit, the fact is that we remain in the same body with the same brain and basically the same mind. Our hippocampus contains the same memories of our old life without Christ. Our neural networks (brain circuits) remain the same, performing the same operations and enabling the same behaviors. Our personalities remain the same. All of our internal hardware and software are basically the same. We still live with a brain and mind that have been wired and trained to sin and need to unlearn past patterns of evil and learn patterns of righteousness. Our brains need to be rewired in reverse. God wants to undo what Satan has done and more so to do a new thing in us.

Prior to Christ, we followed our own will and not God's will. We did as we wanted. We walked in the flesh and not after the Spirit. Now we need to walk in the Spirit and not after the flesh. We are called to obey God's will and not our own. Basically, our life, beginning with our brain, needs reverse engineering. Our minds need to unlearn their old sinful ways and learn new ways of righteousness through the word of God. Reverse engineering is the work of the Holy Spirit. Sanctification is reverse engineering. Sanctification takes the unholy and makes us holy. Through salvation, we are allowed to begin again. Being born again is the beginning. When we are born again, the seed of salvation has been planted in us and must grow to fruition and completion. Reverse engineering occurs when we are led by the Spirit and obey his voice and not led by the sinful self and its old ways. The past way of life and its curse are being reversed. The Spirit is rewiring our brains through neuroplasticity and synaptogenesis.

We have salvation in Christ, yet we have minds that still need to be saved. One way to look at this reverse engineering and rewiring is that we are betwixt and between salvation now and not yet. In one sense we *were* saved 2,000 years ago when Christ died for our sins. Yet we only received that salvation personally when we accepted Christ, however many years ago that decision occurred. However, we are still *being* saved daily from sin, and finally, on the last day, at the resurrection, we *will be* fully saved in our new bodies. Thus, we *were* saved when we received Christ. Yet in one sense we are currently *being* saved, and in another sense, we *will* be saved.

How are we *being* saved? What does that mean? It means that every day, every moment, we are appropriating more and more the salvation that the Lord has purchased for us. We are growing in grace and in our faith. Every day we are still tempted because we live in these human, temptable bodies. In order to walk out our salvation, we need to continue to walk in the Spirit and not in the flesh. We need to live a lifestyle of repentance that turns away from sin and turns toward God. As we resist sin, walk in the Spirit, and grow in grace and Christlikeness, we are maturing in our salvation. We are living and experiencing more of it every day. We are advancing more in the Kingdom, receiving more of his Spirit, walking in more victory, and obeying God's plan for our life. We are tasting more of the fruit of salvation daily. We are being renewed in our minds daily, being more spiritually minded (Rom. 8:5–6). We are being reverse engineered by the Spirit.

During this process, we pray for God's light to illuminate our hearts and show us his will. At times, the light of the Spirit will shine in dark recesses of our hearts, showing us areas and issues that he wants to touch and do a work. The areas may involve past or present sin, wrong mindsets, past or present pain and trauma, or anything that is preventing us from growing in Christ. When the Lord convicts us about these matters, it is a call to surrender and draw near to his loving arms and gentle hands that long to remove our harassing sin or heal our broken hearts and traumatized minds. Through his holy light, he wants to expose those troubling areas, not to shame us but to reveal the sin or wound so that the soul may be healed.

This delicate process can be painful like surgery. We may feel tempted to not yield to the Spirit and to put up our usual defenses, close up, and go back into hiding. Our hiding place where we retreat and cope in a dysfunctional way is a place of self-deception where we do not have to face and work through the pain. It is easier to remain in our shell of security. We procrastinate. However, every moment we put off spiritual surgery and the hard work of transformation, we are permitting the sin, hurt, or pain to continue to devastate our lives. It is only when the pain of not changing becomes greater than the pain of going through the change do we decide to face and go through the necessary change. If the issue is sin, we allow the Spirit to convict us fully and we seek repentance until the Lord grants it and delivers us from sin's stronghold, guilt, and shame. In other cases, we may need healing from past hurt or trauma.

The Neuroscience of Trauma

Adverse Childhood Experiences (ACEs) are potentially traumatic events that can occur between birth and seventeen years of age. ACEs can negatively affect one's physical and mental health and require immediate and often lifelong treatment and management. Those affected by at least one ACE, when properly treated, can still lead a successful and flourishing life. Some examples of ACEs include the following:

- Experiencing violence, abuse, or neglect
- Witnessing violence in the home or community
- Having a family member attempt or die by suicide[11]

Also, a child's home environment can have an adverse effect on their mental well-being in cases where the following occur:

- Substance use problems
- Mental health problems
- Instability due to parental separation
- Instability due to household members being in jail or prison[12]

Sixty-four percent of adults have reported an ACE, with 17.3 percent (one in six) reporting at least four types of ACEs.[13] Long-term effects of ACEs can affect every area of one's life including physical and mental health, educational and job success, relationships, risk of injury, teen pregnancy and complications, STDs, sex trafficking, cancer, heart disease, diabetes, and suicide.[14] In terms of direct impact on physical and mental health, ACEs can negatively affect "brain development, immune systems, and stress-response systems."[15] ACEs can also contribute to ongoing poverty and racial discrimination.

Often ACEs are traumatic events and can result in post-traumatic stress disorder (PTSD), which affects around 8 percent of Americans.[16] PTSD can be accompanied by other ailments, such as depression, anxiety, personality disorders, dissociative identity disorders, and other health problems.[17] PTSD "is characterized by specific symptoms, including intrusive thoughts, hyperarousal, flashbacks, nightmares, and sleep disturbances, changes in memory and concentration, and startle responses."[18] Traumatic "stress results in acute and chronic changes in neurochemical systems and

---

11. "About Adverse Childhood Experiences," CDC, accessed May 29, 2024, https://www.cdc.gov/aces/about/index.html. (U.S. Centers for Disease Control and Prevention 2024)

12. "About Adverse Childhood Experiences." (U.S. Centers for Disease Control and Prevention 2024)

13. "About Adverse Childhood Experiences." (U.S. Centers for Disease Control and Prevention 2024)

14. "About Adverse Childhood Experiences." (U.S. Centers for Disease Control and Prevention 2024)

15. "About Adverse Childhood Experiences." (U.S. Centers for Disease Control and Prevention 2024)

16. J. Douglas Bremner, "Traumatic Stress: Effects on the Brain," *Dialogues in Clinical Neuroscience* 8, no. 4 (2006): 445–61. https://doi.org/10.31887/DCNS.2006.8.4/jbremner. (Bremner 2006)

17. Bremner, "Traumatic Stress: Effects on the Brain." (Bremner 2006)

18. Bremner, "Traumatic Stress: Effects on the Brain." (Bremner 2006)

specific brain regions, which result in long-term changes in brain 'circuits,' involved in the stress response."[19]

PTSD can adversely affect the prefrontal cortex, the hippocampus, and the amygdala. Capacities of the prefrontal cortex (anterior cingulate) and the hippocampus are diminished or made smaller, affecting their ability to function properly. This means memory and executive function can be adversely affected. Also, PTSD can inhibit neurogenesis (i.e., the production of new brain cells).[20] And amygdala functions increase in terms of *overactive* stress responses, an internal alarm system that is always going off when no danger is present but merely "perceived." The amygdala triggers the adrenal gland production (HPA axis) of cortisol and norepinephrine (both stress response hormones). These work together as the alarm system (the sympathetic nervous system) for your body, the fight-flight-freeze mechanism. The reactor system or acute stress response system in your body elevates certain functions and diminishes other systems to prepare for an emergency and survival.[21]

At times, those with PTSD cannot distinguish between a real danger and a falsely perceived one, which can trigger the acute stress response system unnecessarily, including the release of cortisol and norepinephrine. Too much unresolved stress becomes toxic. Unanswered or maladaptive stress can become a psychological cancer to our system. Too much cortisol in the bloodstream due to stress responses from the HPA axis can result in weight gain, headaches, increased blood pressure, an impaired nervous system, and increased blood sugar resulting in type 2 diabetes.[22] Stress is also connected to other deadly diseases such as heart disease and cancer.[23]

Current treatments for PTSD include CBT, EMDR (eye movement desensitization and reprocessing), prolonged exposure therapy, psychiatric medication (e.g., SSRIs), and intentional diaphragmatic (deep) breathing to control panic anxiety, a scientifically proven practice that I highly recommend for relaxing and recalibrating your systems.[24] I also recommend reading and applying *Truth Therapy* as a supple-

---

19. Bremner, "Traumatic Stress: Effects on the Brain." (Bremner 2006)

20. Bremner, "Traumatic Stress: Effects on the Brain." (Bremner 2006)

21. Bremner, "Traumatic Stress: Effects on the Brain." (Bremner 2006)

22. The HPA axis is the hypothalamic-pituitary-adrenal connection and communication in the neuroendocrine system that controls the body's stress response, specifically the release and regulation of cortisol.

23. Mahmut Cay, Cihat Ucar, Deniz Senol, Furkan Cevirgen, Davut Ozbag, Zuhal Altay, Sedat Yildiz, "Effect of Increase in Cortisol Level Due to Stress in Healthy Young Individuals on Dynamic and Static Balance Scores," *Northern Clinics of Istanbul* 5, no. 4 (2018): 295–301. https://doi.org/10.14744/nci.2017.42103. "Stress and Cancer," National Cancer Institute, October 21, 2022, https://www.cancer.gov/about-cancer/coping/feelings/stress-fact-sheet#:~:text=Although%20the%20fight%2Dor%2Dflight,and%20a%20weakened%20immune%20system. (Cay, et al. 2018) (National Cancer Institute 2022)

24. Xiao Ma, Zi-Qi Yue, Zhu-Qing Gong, Hong Zhang, Nai-Yue Duan, Yu-Tong Shi, Gao-Xia Wei, and You-Fa Li, "The Effect of Diaphragmatic Breathing on Attention, Negative Affect and Stress in Healthy Adults," *Frontiers in Psychology* 8 (2017): 874. https://doi.org/10.3389/fpsyg.2017.00874. "Diaphragmatic Breathing," Cleveland Clinic, last reviewed March 30, 2022, https://my.clevelandclinic.org/health/articles/9445-diaphragmatic-breathing. (Ma, et al. 2017) (Cleveland Clinic 2022)

ment to treatment offered by medical professionals. *Truth Therapy* provides the spiritual treatment needed in a holistic, integrated approach that addresses spirit, soul, mind, and body. The Spirit rewires our minds through the regular meditation on and practice of the word of God.

Many have had ACEs involving rejection and detachment wounds due to abandonment, abuse, divorce, or others fractures within the family. One salutary aspect of salvation is our adoption into the family of God. God begins to heal the lacerations in our resonance and memory systems by making us daughters and sons. We are no longer orphans. The Lord wants to break the spirit of rejection and orphanism that shrouds us in our relationships like a dark, fatal, looming shadow. Christ has bonded with us in our brokenness and lowest place where we have been rejected so that we can know the overcoming power of eternal sonship or daughtership flowing from our loving Father. Finally, above all, we can pray into our neuroanatomy, which I suggest one do regularly and for various needs such as memory, attention, concentration, and healing from trauma. Pray that the brain and its various functions align with God's original intention at creation. Specifically, name the various parts and functions of the brain and pray that they fall into Divine order and perform as God originally intended.

The Testimony of Tamela, Trauma, and Inner Healing

One of the most compelling cases of healing and overcoming trauma comes from Tamela, a young woman I ministered to over the years. Tamela was raised in a good Christian home and was raised in a Bible-believing, Christ-centered, Spirit-filled church. However, much of her trauma occurred early in life at church. She went through sexual abuse and trauma as a child and due to fear and guilt did not let her parents know until her mid-teens. By that time, the Christ-loving, good-natured, well-mannered, straight-A student had become another person. She began acting out at home and at school. She was rebellious to her parents, teachers, and other authority figures. Tamela began to hang out with other youth who came from broken homes, received poor grades at school, flirted with alcohol and drugs, and were in constant trouble at home, school, and on the streets. Soon after, Tamela started to dress differently, goth from head to toe. She was cutting, drinking with her friends, and smoking, and her grades dropped.

Her parents tried everything, including grounding and taking away privileges. They had interventions with her led by school counselors. They took her to several therapists. She was being treated with rotating cocktails of meds for depression, anxiety, oppositional defiance disorder, and mood disorder. None of them seemed to be working, as she became progressively worse and more rebellious. She began experimenting with, then using and even selling, illegal substances. As a result, her life became entangled with dangerous people who were abusive toward her and even threatened her life. Living a rebellious lifestyle and being involved in illegal activity, she came into trouble with the law. Her loving and praying parents were beside them-selves not knowing what to do or where to turn. They prayed and fasted. Kept doors of communications open with her. Loved her but tried to uphold boundaries. Be-cause of her radical defiance at home and at school, they would have to press charges on her with the juvenile courts, who put her on probation including drug testing.

In high school, Tamela began to hang out with teens who were sampling the occult, especially witchcraft, which I learned was a way for girls and young woman who have been violated to cope. Due to their trauma, they felt powerless and saw witchcraft as a way to regain power and protection against boys and men and to not feel vulnerable and helpless. As Tamela began to investigate and experiment with witchcraft, she found that it worked. Satan allowed her, and others, to see enough results and experience a taste of power to get her hooked. Seeing results, she delved into black magic more deeply and regularly. She claimed to have regularly cast incan-tations on the lives of those around her, family, friends, enemies, and teachers.

As Tamela's life was spiraling downward from one circle of hell to the next and her parents were wrought with unspeakable warfare and despair, I regularly attempted to minister to Tamela and the family for over a ten-year period, seeing very little re-sults for the first eight years. She had rejected Christ, became an avid witch, and es-pecially wanted nothing to do with the church, which was understandable. It was in the eighth year that we began to see a turn. Prayers were starting to be answered. She started opening up to other ideas and religions, even to the God of Judaism, which was better than atheism. She suddenly quit using and selling drugs out of paranoia and fear of being caught. She realized her circle of friends were not real friends. Some wanted to kill her. Others to traffic her. Others turned on her. God started slowly removing her from destructive influences.

She went to college and met new people, even some campus Christian preach-ers. I noticed our conversations began to change. She was more open to know about Christ and asked some tough but good questions. Another turning point was when she was in an accident, which resulted in total paralysis in her left leg and foot. I told her I would pray for her, and the next day she began to experience feeling and movement, which led to a gradual healing over the next month. Doctors origi-nally predicted that she would never have feeling or control again in that leg due to nerve damage, but God had something else in mind. This miraculous healing sparked Tamela's faith. She knew it was Christ who did it. Tamela began to witness other an-swers to prayer. Following in the tenth year, under heavy conviction that Jesus Christ is Savior and Lord, she surrendered her life fully to Christ. She experienced immedi-ate deliverance and transformation. She burned all of her occult paraphernalia and cut off all of her toxic friends. She started to go to church regularly and read her Bible.

I led her through several years of deliverance, Truth Therapy, inner healing, and discipleship. She was soon baptized in the Holy Spirit and later felt the call to min-istry. Eventually, Tamela attended seminary and received her Master of Divinity and went through further training to be ordained as a minister. She has since successfully pastored and grown four churches. She is not without her trials and struggles present and past, but she has passed through the fire and come out stronger. Christ has walked her through years of painful yet fruitful healing. Again, there are occasions when Satan tries to remind her of the past, but the Spirit has done an indelible work of forgiveness and healing in her life that has strengthened her to overcome. She attributes her miraculous turnaround to the power of Christ's love and the Holy Spirit's presence in her life. I am reminded of a saying rumored to come from Mike Tyson, "You never lose until you actually give up." Or from Rocky Balboa's, "It ain't about how hard you can hit. It's about how hard you can get hit and keep moving forward."[25]

Curing Versus Healing Versus Relief

I have ministered to hundreds of souls who experienced the Spirit of God heal them from the inside out of abuse and trauma. Trauma is complex, and thus healing can be complex. Healing is not always immediate and instantaneous, though it can be. Many get discouraged when they do not receive complete healing immediately. Healing is not always so cut and dry. It can be nuanced, and so we need to nuance our understanding lest we become discouraged or weary in well doing. "Hope deferred makes the heart sick" (Prov. 13:12 NIV).

There are many distinctions, types, and concepts to define in healing. First, there is a difference between curing, healing, and relief. Curing is an immediate or over time *cessation* of symptoms (physical and/or mental). Through treatment and time, the ailment has gone into remission and is no longer. Healing, or *therapeia*, in terms of *soteria* (salvation) is to be restored in the image of Christ—spirit, soul, and body. Relief is a temporary suspension of symptoms (physical and/or mental). One can be cured (of cancer) and not healed (of their sin sickness). One can be healed in part (spiritually and mentally) and not be cured of cancer but die, go to heaven, and receive their ultimate healing, a resurrected body. One can experience relief of symptoms and not be healed of a broken heart. One can have relief from lower back pain, be healed of rejection and pride, and not cured of scoliosis.

In the end, all curing, healing, or relief comes by the grace of God through doctors, medication, counseling, diet, sleep, exercise, or the supernatural power of the Spirit. God causes the sun to shine on the just and on the unjust. In his prevenient or common grace, the Lord blesses us with restoration and healing through a variety of means. The same God who created the universe, the elements in the universe that are synthesized for medication, and the gift of practicing medicine is the same God who heals by the stripes of Christ on the cross (Isa. 53:5; Matt. 5:45; 8:17; Jas. 5:15–16; 1 Pet. 2:24). The Lord has also built within our bodies a sophisticated immune system, indicating that he wants us to be healed and restored.

Thus, we should receive curing, healing, and relief from the best science that the Spirit has to offer. Ultimately, though, we will not live forever in this body. Thus, the ultimate healing is the resurrection. It is the alpha, omega, source, and goal of all of

---

25. *Rocky Balboa*, directed by Sylvester Stallone (MGM, 2006). (Stallone, Rocky Balboa 2006)

our healing in this life and in the life to come, immediate or gradual. Finally, there are what I call the 4T Factors in Healing: *type* (spirit, mind, body), *treatment* (medical, spiritual, natural), *timing* (total and immediate, gradual), and *trust* (total trust in God). Human trust in the medical system, yes. We should trust *but* verify. Human institutions are not perfect. These four factors add to the complexity of the nature and reception of healing. Thus, in light of these factors and variables, I believe an integrative holistic approach to healing is best, receiving the best gifts from God, the medical profession, and the natural order and expecting curing, healing, and relief immediately or over time, as God wills it. And through it all, we should keep our eyes on Christ and our hope in the resurrection, now and for eternity.

Hearing the Spirit's Voice

Hearing, When It's a Matter of Life or Death

One of the most indispensable tools on the disciple's utility belt is the ability to hear the voice of God consistently and effectively. When hell and high water come against us, when nothing else seems to work, just hearing one word from God can give us the breakthrough of victory. I was in such a place and can surely testify. Our world seemed to come to an abrupt end that dark fateful afternoon when the doctor informed my wife, Mariuccia, that she had cancer. We walked out of the doctor's office, and I looked straight up and felt the blackened, iron sky precipitously crash down on our heads and on our world. The feeling is inexplicable, and the warp and dissonance created from entering into the "cancer world" cannot be understood or put into words unless you have been there. I call it the *cancer world* because it is indeed a totally different world than any other. It is a world in which everything triggers the worst in your mind. The real world that one leaves, but one's body remains in, is far away, detached, and viewed as if underwater. One feels like an outsider, as the whole world is moving on with life but you cannot. You are trapped in the cancer world with unruly, raging, ruminating thoughts storming violently through your mind, a thousand per nanosecond. Every scenario of doom and death, the entire perilous permutation, runs incessantly on a loop day and night.

With my wife overnight in the hospital, I laid alone on my bed exhausted and physically numb. While lying there I heard the Holy Spirit speak softly and assuredly through the tumultuous tempest of my thoughts. He whispered four statements to my soul that I can never forget: "*One*, I love her more than you. *Two*, I will heal her. *Three*, I will heal her my way and not yours. *Four*, the doctors will be surprised, and all will be surprised." I was smitten. I meditated deeply on the first statement. The second one brought me a hint of hope and joy. The third statement almost took away all of the hope and joy from the second one. And the fourth statement left me confounded. Yet I knew that the Lord had spoken. I know the voice of my Shepherd. I know the one who called me into salvation and had led me for decades to green pastures, by still waters, and now through the valley of the shadow of death. My faith began to increase, and I was able to accept the second statement and be open to whatever surprise the Lord would bring with the fourth statement.

I shared with my wife and family the four revelations from God. I laid them down on the ground of my heart as a foundation and before me as a pathway through this indefinite journey into cancer world. Her colonoscopy and CT seemed to indicate to the doctors that it was a small, localized, stage 1 tumor with a 90 to 95 percent survival rate. That was the report on which we were betting the farm. My close friend who was a leading researcher in oncology at UCLA informed me that it was at most a two-hour procedure, and if it was taking longer, that meant there were further problems. My children and I were restless in the waiting room. Two hours had passed, then two and half and three, then three and half and four. I received a call from the operating room. I had an ominous feeling in my gut. The surgical oncologist was reviewing how she cut out the tumor with excellent margins, but I knew it was coming. The tumor was successfully removed from the colon, but they found a small spot in her liver. The cancer was metastatic. It had spread to a major organ. Stage 4. I swallowed my heart and hung up the phone.

I did the impossible. I informed my kids what the doctor had told me. With one hand I held onto the despairing news of stage 4 cancer, and with the other hand I tightly clenched the four revelations until I was sweating. At the conclusion of the surgery, the doctor met us in the waiting room and informed us that both tumors were resected with excellent margins. I pushed her for numbers. I am a logical, scientifically minded person. I needed to know quantitatively what we had to work with. An 11 percent chance was what we were given. Ugh! I clutched the four revelations more tightly.

We did what was expected—received multiple medical opinions and went for more visits and tests. I spend five to seven hours a night for several months reading medical journals on Mariuccia's type of cancer so I could be better informed as we took her health into our own hands. In fact, the oncologist recommended to treat her with three types of chemotherapy. I contested and retorted that she only needed two. We traveled to Cleveland Clinic to receive their expert advice. They agreed with me and gave us hope of a treatable outcome. Their good report was confirmed when we received the biopsy on twenty-seven lymph nodes that came back negative, a miracle in itself. The four revelations began to lighten up and glow in my hand as I gazed upon them again. They anchored us all through the next eight months of chemo, blood tests, CTs, MRIs, and PET scans, and through the next five years of the same, minus the chemotherapy.

We prayed, fasted, and trusted God through that five-year period, but above all we held onto the four promises of hope that he gave us. They all came to pass. God did it his way and not our way. We were all surprised by the discovery in surgery that she was metastatic. However, that surprise was overcome by the surprise that, eight years later, she beat the 11 percent prognosis. Long story short, we are approaching year nine, and my precious wife is with us, strong and healthy. Our children are married and successful, and she is the *nonna* of a beautiful, intelligent granddaughter named Costanza. Sometimes, hearing God makes all of the difference!

God Speaks! Listen!

God is a communicator. The universe and all of its detailed content are all the result of God speaking. In the beginning, God spoke, and everything came into being: "Through him all things were made; without him nothing was made that has been made" (John 1:3 NIV). If God did not speak but remained silent, nothing would have existed besides God. Nonetheless, God spoke. He is a speaking God. From quantum particles to single-cell organisms to black holes and supergalaxies, God has declared the existence of all things small and great. God has spoken over 8.75 million species on the Earth (hypothetically), including 7.8 million animal species, 293,000 plants, 611,000 fungi, 63,900 protists, 10,000 bacteria, and 500 archaea. Of these species, 1.75 million have been identified.[26]

God not only speaks entities into being, but he also speaks to entities, including humans. He has spoken to people from Adam and Eve to Noah, Abraham, Isaac, Jacob, Joseph, Moses, Joshua, Samuel, David, Elijah, Elisha, Isaiah and all of the major prophets, Daniel and all of the minor prophets, John the Baptist, Christ, the Twelve, and all of the saints throughout history. Speaking seems to be God's primary way of communicating, and hearing, our primary way of "perceiving" God through our senses.

> You came near and stood at the foot of the mountain while it blazed with fire to the very heavens, with black clouds and deep darkness. Then the LORD spoke to you out of the fire. You heard the sound of words but saw no form; there was only a voice. He declared to you his covenant, the Ten Commandments, which he commanded you to follow and then wrote them on two stone tablets. And the LORD directed me at that time to teach you the decrees and laws you are to follow in the land that you are crossing the Jordan to possess.
>
> You saw no form of any kind the day the LORD spoke to you at Horeb out of the fire. Therefore, watch yourselves very carefully, so that you do not become corrupt and make for yourselves an idol, an image of any shape, whether formed like a man or a woman, or like any animal on earth or any bird that flies in the air, or like any creature that moves along the ground or any fish in the waters below. And when you look up to the sky and see the sun, the moon and the stars—all the heavenly array—do not be enticed into bowing down to them and worshiping things the LORD your God has apportioned to all the nations under heaven. (Deut. 4:11–19 NIV)

In the Old Testament, the I AM commanded the people to hear and obey: "*Shema, Israel, Adonai Eloheinu, Adonai echad!*" ("Hear, O Israel: The LORD our God, the LORD is One" [Deut. 6:4 NIV]). Hear, obey, and live was the three-part command

---

26. John J. Wiens, "How Many Species Are There on Earth? Progress and Problems," *PLoS Biology* 21 (11): e3002388. https://doi.org/10.1271/journal.pbio.3002388. (Wiens 2023)

(Deut. 4:1; 31:12–13). God is invisible. We cannot see him. Thus, we are commanded to walk by faith and hear. We do not live by bread alone but by (hearing) every word that is continually proceeding from God's mouth (Matt. 4:4). Hearing God is our manna in the desert. We live by hearing, hearing the words from God's mouth and obeying them. We walk by faith, not by sight, and faith requires hearing, and hearing requires the word of God (Rom. 10:17).

As James 1:22 exhorts, "Do not merely listen to the word, and so deceive yourselves. Do what it says." We fall into self-deception when we merely hear God's word and assume we have obeyed it, when we have not. The trajectory of hearing leads to obeying. *Shema*, in the Hebrew, signifies *hearing* with the intention of *obeying*. Obeying is the intention and purpose of hearing. Jesus prophesied to each of the churches in Asia Minor and ended each prophecy with the exhortation, "Whoever has ears, let them hear what the Spirit says to the churches" (Revelation 2–3 NIV). Jesus was not asking if members of the church actually had two ears attached to their heads. No! He was questioning their motive and intentions. I paraphrase like this: "Are you willing to hear and obey my words?" Obedience is the fruition of hearing, lest we be like the false disciples who claim to know God, but he retorts, "Not everyone who says to me, 'Lord, Lord,' will enter the kingdom of heaven, but only the one who does the will of my Father who is in heaven" (Matt. 7:21 NIV). For true disciples, hearing must involve doing.

How Does God Speak?

We have identified the importance of the spiritual faculty of hearing and its vital connection with obeying. But what is the voice of God? Where do we hear it? How do we know and discern that we have heard it? The voice of God is clearly God's speaking. However, since God is invisible, where and how can we hear him? I believe God speaks through many channels, such as creation, conscience, circumstances, providence, or God's normative working through the natural order of things, and other people. These means are forms of what is often called *general revelation*, God revealing general aspects of himself to everyone in a general way. For me, creation, such as the sunrise, the sunset, the ocean, mountains, birds singing at dawn, and other expressions, is a frequent and powerful means through which the Lord speaks to me. However, I believe God's *special revelation* is even a greater and more specific way in which God speaks to us, specifically because special revelation speaks to his plan of salvation for us in Christ Jesus.

Thus, the primary means by which the Lord reveals Christ and his work of salvation for us is through the holy Scriptures and through the Holy Spirit, who illuminates the Scriptures to us. Yet he also speaks directly to our spirits through the inward witness and the gifts of the Spirit. When we hear the voice of the Spirit it must be tested and align with the written word of God (Isa. 8:20; John 5:39; 2 Tim. 3:16; Heb. 10:7; 2 Pet. 1:19; 1 John 4:1). Just because we are Christians, it does not mean that everything we hear is from God. When we attempt to hear from God, there are three possible sources: God, self, or the devil. It is imperative that we can discern when it is God and when it is self or the devil. Here are my top four criteria to discern the voice of the Spirit:

1. **Scripture Test:** The content lines up with Scripture, preferably two or more verses (Deut. 19:15; Isa. 8:20; Matt. 18:16; John 5:39; 2 Tim. 3:16; Heb. 10:7; 2 Pet. 1:19; 1 John 4:1). Be aware that Satan at times uses and twists the Scriptures for his benefit. So check the fruit (#2) and your motive (#3).

2. **Fruit Test:** The content, delivery, and intonation line up with God's character represented by the fruit of the Spirit (Matt. 7:20; 12:33; Luke 6:44; Gal. 5:22–23; Col. 3:15). God woos. Satan bullies. God gently leads. Satan pushes. God convicts. Satan condemns. God gives peace. Satan brings turmoil and confusion. God's voice is a still, small voice of peace. Satan's voice is loud, angry, and imposing like the roaring of a lion (1 Kgs. 19:12; Ps. 46:10; 1 Pet. 5:8). God's voice is in the stillness and not in the earthquake or the thunderstorm. Let peace rule or act as an umpire in our hearts (Col. 3:15). Let the presence of peace determine if it's God's will.

3. **Motive Test:** While praying, ask your conscience why you are praying for such and such. Ask your conscience why or what is your motive for wanting such and such. The Spirit will use your conscience to convict you of the truth and what is right. The conscience will excuse you (give a green light) or accuse you of a wrong or selfish motive (red light) (Rom. 2:15).

4. **Self Test:** The hearer has crucified their own will and prayed not my will but yours be done (Luke 9:23; 22:42; John 14:13–14; 15:7; 16:24). When we come to the bottom of our self-will, peeling it back like an onion one layer are a time, we will find what remains is of the selfless will of God. When white noise and static from the day's clamor and self are tuned out, we will hear the still, small voice of the Spirit. The word of God is the tuning fork or pitch that our spirits must be tuned to in order to be on the same frequency of the Spirit and hear God. Remember that although we must get past self in order to hear God, the Lord usually speaks in a way that is familiar to us, in a language we can understand, and using relevant images and dates in our brains and minds. Remember Samuel.

If God is a speaking God, we should enter our prayer closets expecting him to speak without hesitancy. Expectancy is the doorway to faith. Prayer, like all communication, is a dialogue, and God has more important things to say than we do. We have two ears and one mouth, so hearing God should be doubly important. Martin Luther was rumored to say that he prayed four hours a day. When asked how he could afford to spend so much time prayer, he allegedly responded that he couldn't afford not to pray for four hours a day. If we are not already taking at least thirty minutes a day and at night to commune quietly with the Lord in prayer, we need to repent and start a routine today. We cannot afford not to do so. We live off of every word that proceeds from the mouth of God. Hearing God is our daily spiritual bread. Hearing God is a matter of spiritual survival. Begin to take the time to develop the most critical skill needed for the Christian life: hearing God. I encourage every disciple to create a prayer chapel or corner in your home, a quiet place to find peace with God. We have a prayer chapel in our home, and we faithfully use it day and night. It is our safe space of refuge and a place where we encounter the living God.

We recall the story of the young Samuel who was being trained as a prophet-priest under Eli, the high priest (1 Sam. 3:1–21). As a spiritual son to the priest, Samuel wore his miniature ephod and he ministered in the Tabernacle under Eli. In a dark time when the Lord was not speaking much to the leadership of Israel, Samuel heard a voice calling him in the night, "Samuel," and he ran to Eli and responded, "Here I am" (1 Sam. 3:1–4). But it was not Eli calling him. This happened three times, and on the third time, Eli recognized that it must have been the voice of the Lord. So Eli instructed Samuel if the Lord calls him again to respond, "Speak, for your servant is listening" (1 Sam. 3:10 NIV). Samuel at first did not recognize the voice of God because it sounded familiar. He thought it was Eli. But often the Lord will speak to us relative to what we have deposited or programmed in our brain. He speaks to us in a familiar way or at least in a way that we can understand. He speaks to be understood.

The Spirit will give us remembrance of all things (John 14:26), which implies we have to program it in our brain first or the Spirit cannot bring it to our memory. Now, of course, the Holy Spirit can do anything, but it makes it easier for us if we deposit first so that we can make a withdrawal later. Hearing the voice of the Lord is vital because we are hearing the very word from the mouth of God that feeds us with spiritual manna. Think of when Peter was asked by Christ, "Who do you say that I am?" Peter responded, "You are the Christ, the Son of the living God." Jesus commented, "Blessed are you, Simon son of Jonah, for this was not revealed to you by flesh and blood, but by my Father in heaven" (Matt. 16:13–19 NIV). Peter received a revelation. He heard from God. Jesus informed him that his testimony to God's revelation would be the rock of revelation on which Christ would build the church.

The Revelation Revolution

What is that revelation? The faith and confession that Jesus is the "Messiah, the Christ, the Son of the living God." Christ will build his church on this rock, these living stones, and their testimony about Jesus the Christ. Thus, Peter experienced a revolutionary revelation, one that revolutionized his life and the lives of all of the saints who would follow him. Hearing one anointed word from the Spirit can heal, deliver, and transform your life in an instant. I am a strong supporter of medical science, doctors, medication, and counseling, but I have also seen hundreds of people's lives changed with one revelation, where years of medication and counseling did not help.

While in graduate school, I was radically converted through hearing God. God spoke to this self-destructive, self-avowed atheist and turned my life around forever. On the night that I came to Christ, I received three staggering and startling revelations from God that penetrated directly through my intellectual fig leaves that I propped over my spiritual nakedness. They pierced my unbelief, cynicism, anxiety, and despair and struck my heart like a lightning bolt. Using John Wesley's term, I was "thunderstruck." God's voice broke through the barriers, rationalizations, and defenses of my closed universe that defied the witness of many campus preachers and suffering circumstances.

The word of God revealed to the deepest part of a person can accomplish what no other property, power, or prescription can do. And clearly, God does not favor just those with the name of Peter. We recall. St. Paul's experience and those of St. Augustine, St. Francis, Martin Luther, John Wesley, and others who heard from God and the revelation revolutionized their life. When God speaks to our heart, the resonance, imprint, and echo are indelible. The Spirit is able to speak to our spirit, as if we had an "inner ear," or as John Wesley and others termed "spiritual senses," that see, hear, touch, smell, and taste in the spiritual world as our natural senses do in the empirical world.[27] The Spirit whispers to our spiritual ears that supernaturally transduces the Spirit's sound waves to electrical signals that are coded to our auditory nerve and travel to the brainstem and to our auditory cortex, which is responsible for processing electrical signals into intelligible sound such as language.[28] The auditory pathway also continues to the thalamus and hippocampus to process auditory information. We hear the Spirit's voice and are revolutionized.[29]

This explanation is oversimplified but sufficient for our purposes. Our compelling, evocative auditory experience of the Spirit's voice is registered in the limbic system releasing and attaching emotions to our experience that can even change the shape and function of our brain. Powerful experiences, such as a revelation from

---

27. John Wesley, Sermon 19, "The Great Privilege of those Born of God," in *Works of John Wesley*, 5:225–26. John Wesley, Essays, "Earnest Appeal to Men of Reason and Religion," in *Works of John Wesley*, vol. 8, *Addresses, Essays, Letters*, ed. Thomas Jackson (Wesleyan Conference Office, 1872), 4–14. For a history of spiritual senses, see Paul L. Gavrilyuk and Sarah Coakley, *Spiritual Senses: Perceiving God in Western Christianity* (Cambridge University Press, 2011). (Wesley, Sermon 19 The Great Privilege of those Born of God 1872) (Wesley, Earnest Appeal to Men of Reason and Religion 1872) (Gavrilyuk and Coakley 2011)

28. National Research Council (US) Committee on Disability Determination for Individuals with Hearing Impairments, "Basics of Sound, the Ear, and Hearing," in *Hearing Loss: Determining Eligibility for Social Security Benefits*, ed. Robert A. Dobie and Susan Van Hemel (National Academies Press, 2004), Chap. 2. Diane C. Peterson, Vamsi Reddy, Marjorie V. Launico, and Renee N. Hamel, *Neuroanatomy, Auditory Pathway* (StatPearls Publishing, 2023). (Dobie and Hemel 2004) (Peterson, et al. 2023)

29. Alexander J. Billig, Meher Lad, William Sedley, and Timothy D. Griffiths, "The Hearing Hippocampus," *Progress in Neurobiology* 218 (2022): 102326. https://doi.org/10.1016/j.pneurobio.2022.102326. (Billig, et al. 2022)

God, unleash the power of neuroplasticity. Hearing the voice of the Spirit is indeed an experience that can indelibly inscribe God's word on our brains, a revelation that can revolutionize our lives. The fiery British revivalist Leonard Ravenhill resolutely declared, "A person with an experience of God is never at the mercy of a person with an argument."[30] There are not enough devils in hell to take away what the Spirit has branded and emblazoned on your heart. "The gates of hell will not prevail against the church" or anyone whose life is established on the revelation of God in Christ.

Conclusion: The Spirit-Crafted Life

The Holy Spirit is our disciplemaker. He crafts us into the image of God in Christ, beginning with our brain and our thinking. We are his masterpiece that he carefully builds with his own delicate and secure hands. He shakes us, breaks us, and makes us into worthy vessels of honor able to receive and pour out his anointing to a hurting, broken world. God has fearfully and wonderfully fashioned our universe and likewise our minds to be icons and reflections of his glory. He has wired us for Christlikeness and holiness to shine his light from our oil-filled vessels into the darkness, as we walk this journey, as wise virgins, in the eleventh hour, seeking his coming. The journey can be lingering and grueling. We can easily feel spent, deflated, and defeated as we walk through the parched valley and gaze at the mountains ahead of us.

The Spirit renews our strength. God never grows weary. He, who is our strength, carries us on his wings and restores us with the breath of his sweet presence. He keeps our vessels filled so our lamps will burn brightly, even when our wick is burned to its end. The Spirit is a stream of refreshing water running through the desert and into our soul. Rivers of living water spring from the oasis of the Spirit's reservoir deep within our heart, when we offer the sacrifice of worship in spirit and in truth.

The sweet aroma of his anointing draws us to ascend his holy mountain with our offering of clean hands and pure hearts. The Lord then inhabits the pure praises of his people and tabernacles with us (Ps. 22:3; 24:3–4; Rev. 21:3). Discipleship may involve a program, but it is not a program. Being a daughter or a son is a covenant relationship with our eternal, loving Father that is expressed in spirit and truth through worship, praise, communion, and service. We learn Christ through the Spirit at the Father's feet and at the feet of others. As our Counselor, Comforter, Advocate, Coach, and Helper, the Holy Spirit is the chief disciplemaker who walks alongside of us in times of trouble, temptation, and triumph to make us into little christs.

Ten Next Steps

1. Pray that God would send you a spiritual mother or father to disciple you.
2. Pray that God would send you a spiritual daughter or son to disciple.
3. Meet weekly or biweekly for discipleship with your spiritual mother or father and your spiritual daughter or son.

30. Leonard Ravenhill, *Why Revival Tarries* (Bethany House, 2004), 117. (Ravenhill 2004)

4. Implement the Timothy 222 Principle: Make disciples who make disciples who make disciples.
5. Find and join a small discipleship group that implements the seven primary practices of discipleship.
6. Begin practicing daily spiritual disciplines, especially Scripture reading and prayer. As you learn more about the discipleship–brain connection, incorporate prayers and practices that exercise and activate various dimensions of the brain so that your soul will grow in Christlikeness. Follow up by reading a basic book on the brain and its functions, such as Rita Carter's *The Human Brain Book: An Illustrated Guide to its Structure, Function, and Disorders* (Penguin Random House, 2019).
7. Meet weekly or biweekly with a spiritual parent or accountability partner to be held responsible to uphold Scriptural principles, practices, and virtues in your daily life.
8. Incorporate Truth Therapy into your daily thinking.
9. Every morning put on the whole armor of God to fight the daily battle against evil.
10. Deny yourself, take up your cross daily, and follow Jesus.

BIBLIOGRAPHY

AbuHasan, Qais, Vamsi Reddy, and Waquar Siddiqui. 2023. "Neuroanatomy, Amygdala." *National Library of Medicine.* July 17. Accessed December 24, 2024. https://www.ncbi.nlm.nih.gov/books/NBK537102/.

Acharya, Sourya, and Samarth Shukla. 2012. "Mirror Neurons: Enigma of the Metaphysical Modular Brain." *Journal of Natural Science, Biology and Medicine* 3 (2): 118-124.

Adams, Liam, and Thao Nguyen. 2024. "Most United Methodist Church Disaffiliations Are in the South: Final Report Outlines Latest in Ongoing Split." *USA Today*, January 23.

Adler, Jonathan H. 2023. *Is Support for "From the River to the Sea" Based Upon Ignorance?* December 10. https://reason.com/volokh/2023/12/10/is-support-for-from-the-river-to-the-sea-based-upon-ignorance/#.

Adolphs, R. 2009. "The Social Brain: Neural Basis of Social Knowledge." *Annual Review of Psychology* 60: 693-716.

American Psychiatric Association. 2013. *Diagnostic and Statistical Manual of Disorders, Fifth Edition.* London: American Psychiatric Association Publishing.

American Psychological Association. 2017. "What Is Cognitive Behavioral Therapy?" *Clinical Practice Guidelines for the Treatment of Posttraumatic Stress Disorder.* Accessed April 8, 2024. https://www.apa.org/ptsd-guideline/patients-and-families/cognitive-behavioral.

Augustine, St. 1953. *Letters.* Vol. 18, in *The Fathers of the Church*, by ed. Roy Joseph Deferrari and Wilfrid, trans. Parsons. Washington, DC: The Catholic University of America Press.

Baily, Reemus. 2017. *The Cus D'Amato Mind.* Reemus Boxing.

Balthasar, Hans Urs von. 2003. *Cosmic Liturgy: The Universe According to Maximus the Confessor.* San Francisco: Ignatius Press.

Barbour, Ian G. 1997. *Religion and Science: Historical and Contemporary Issues.* HarperCollins Publishers.

Barna Group. 2016. *Porn in the Digital Age: New Research Reveals 10 Trends.* April 6. Accessed December 2024. https://www.barna.com/research/porn-in-the-digital-age-new-research-reveals-10-trends/.

Basinger, Hayden, and Jeffrey P. Hogg. 2023. "Neuroanatomy, Brainstem." *National Library of Medicine.* July 4. https://www.ncbi.nlm.nih.gov/books/NBK544297/.

Beck, Aaron T., A John Rush, Brian F. Shaw, and Gary Emery. 1979. *Cognitive Therapy of Depression.* Guilford Press.

Bell, Rob. 2019. *What is the Bible? How an Ancient Library of Poems, Letters, and Stories Can Transform the Way You Think and Feel About Everything.* San Francisco: HarperOne.

Bellini, Peter J. 2023. *Artificial General Intelligence (AGI) and the Image of God.* Eugene, OR: Wipf and Stock.

—. 2023. "James 4:7—Spiritual Warfare Made Simple." *Firebrand Magazine,* December 19.

Bellini, Peter. 2021. *The Cerulean Soul: A Relational Theology of Depression.* Baylor University Press.

—. 2014. *Truth Therapy: Renewing Your Mind with the Word of God.* Wipf and Stock.

Bercot, David W., ed. 1998. *Dictionary of Early Christian Beliefs.* Hendrickson

Bergland, Christopher. 2021. *Is the 'God Spot' Rooted Far Below Our Brain's Thinking Cap?* July 3. Accessed December 2024. https://www.psychologytoday.com/us/blog/the-athletes-way/202107/is-the-god-spot-rooted-far-below-our-brain-s-thinking-cap.

Biello, David. 2007. "Searching for God in the Brain." *SA Mind,* October: 38.

Bonhoeffer, Dietrich. 1963. *The Cost of Discipleship.* Macmillan.

Boschi, Helena. 2017. *The Neuroscience of Change.* June. Accessed December 2024. https://www.cipd.org/ae/views-and-insights/thought-leadership/people-profession/neuroscience-change/.

Brainy Quote. n.d. *Brainy Quote: Vince Lombardi.* Accessed December 29, 2024. https://www.brainyquote.com/quotes/vince_lombardi_380768.

Bunge, Gabriel. 2011. *Despondency: The Spiritual Teaching of Evagrius Ponticus on Acedia.* St. Vladimir's Seminary Press.

Burns, David D. 1999. *Feeling Good: The New Mood Therapy (Revised Edition).* New York: Plume.

Cady, Nick. 2020. *The Statistical Probability of Jesus Fulfilling the Messianic Prophecies.* February 20. Accessed April 9, 2024. https://nickcady.org/2020/02/18/the-statistical-probability-of-jesus-fulfilling-the-messianic-prophecies/.

Calvin, John. 2008. *Institutes of the Christian Religion.* Edited by trans. Henry Beveridge. Hendrickson.

Camina, Eduardo, and Francisco Güell. 2017. "The Neuroanatomical, Neurophysiological and Psychological Basis of Memory: Current Models and Their Origins." *Frontiers in Pharmacology* 8.

Caruso, Catherine. 2023. *New Field Neuroscience Aims to Map Connections in the Brain.* January 19. https://hms.harvard.edu/news/new-field-neuroscience-aims-map-connections-brain.

Castelloe, Molly S. 2023. "Needing a Target for Blame." *Psychology Today,* June 30.

Chadwick, Samuel. 2001. *The Way of Pentecost.* Christian Literature Crusade.

Cleveland Clinic. 2022. "Cognitive Behavioral Therapy (CBT)." *Cleveland Clinic.* August 4. https://my.clevelandclinic.org/health/treatments/21208-cognitive-behavioral-therapy-cbt.

—. 2022. "Hypothalamus." March 16. https://my.clevelandclinic.org/health/body/22566-hypothalamus.

—. 2023. "Parietal Lobe." *Cleveland Clinic.* January 8. Accessed December 2024. https://my.clevelandclinic.org/health/body/24628-parietal-lobe.

—. 2022. "Pituitary Gland." April 4. https://my.clevelandclinic.org/health/body/21459-pituitary-gland.

Clewett, David, Ringo Huang, Rico Velasco, Tae-Ho Lee, and Mara Mather. 2018. "Locus Coeruleus Activity Strengthens Prioritized Memories Under Arousal." *Journal of Neuroscience* 38 (6).

Cognifit. n.d. *Focused Attention.* Accessed January 2, 2024. https://www.cognifit.com/focused-attention.

Committee on the Judiciary, Republican Staff. n.d. "FBI Whistleblowers: What Their Disclosures Indicate About the Politicization of the FBI and Justice Department." U.S. House of Representatives.

Connors, Michael H., and Peter W Halligan. 2022. "Revealing the Cognitive Neuroscience of Belief." *Frontiers in Behavioral Neuroscience* 16.

Craske, Michelle G. 2010. *Cognitive-Behavioral Therapy.* American Psychological Association.

Damasio, Antonio R. 1994. *Descartes' Error: Emotion, Reason, and the Human Brain.* Avon Books.

D'Aquili, Eugene, and Andrew Newberg. 1999. *The Mystical Mind: Probing the Biology of Religious Experience.* Fortress Press.

1998. In *Dictionary of Early Christian Beliefs*, by ed. David W. Bercot. Hendrickson.

Dayton, Donald. 2014. *Rediscovering an Evangelical Heritage, 2nd ed.* Baker.

Dehaene, Stanislas. 2020. *How We Pay Attention Changes Things.* January 30. https://lithub.com/how-we-pay-attention-changes-the-very-shape-of-our-brains/.

Diamond, Adele. 2013. "Executive Functions." *Annual Review of Psychology.* January. Accessed December 2024. https://www.annualreviews.org/content/journals/10.1146/annurev-psych-113011-143750.

Doidge, Norman. 2007. *The Brain That Changes Itself.* Penguin.

Drake, Janine Giordano. 2023. *The Gospel of Church: How Mainline Protestants Vilified Christian Socialism and Fractured the Labor Movement.* Oxford University Press.

Ellis, Albert. 2007. *Practice of Rational Emotive Therapy.* Springer.

Fénelon, François. 1975. *Christian Perfection.* Bethany Fellowship.

Ferguson, Michael A, Frederick L.W.V.J. Schaper, Alexander Cohen, Shan Siddiqi, Sarah M. Merrill, Jared A. Nielson, Jordan Grafman, Cosimo Urgesi, Franko Fabbro, and Michael D. Fox. 2022. "A Neural Circuit for Spirituality and Religiosity Derived from Patients with Brain Lesions." *Biological Psychiatry* 91 (4): 380-388.

Fernandez-Espejo, E. 2000. "Cómo funciona el nucleus accumbens? [How Does the Nucleus Accumbens Function?]." *Revista de Neurologia* 30: 845-849.

Fight the New Drug. n.d. *How Does the Porn Industry Make It's Money Today?* Accessed January 9, 2024. https://fightthenewdrug.org/how-does-the-porn-industry-actually-make-money-today/.

Focus for Health Foundation. n.d. *How Pornography Impacts Violence Against Women and Child Sex Abuse.* Accessed March 28, 2024. https://www.focusforhealth.org/how-pornography-impacts-violence-against-women-and-child-sex-abuse.

Francis, Leslie J, and Mandy Robbins. 2003. "Personality and Glossolalia: A Study Among Male Evangelical Clergy." *Pastoral Psychology* (Springer Nature) 51 (5): 391-396.

Franklin, Tamara B, Bianca A Silva, and Zinaida Perova. 2017. "Prefrontal Cortical Control of a Brainstem Social Behavior Circuit." *Nature Neuroscience* 20 (7): 260-70.

Frith, Christopher D. 2007. "The Social Brain?" *Philosophical Transactions of the Royal Society B* (The Royal Society of Biological Sciences) 362 (1480).

Got Questions Ministries. n.d. *How Many Prophesies Did Jesus Fulfill?* Accessed April 9, 2024. https://www.gotquestions.org/prophecies-of-Jesus.html.

Goto, Yukiori, and Anthony A. Grace. 2008. "Limbic and Cortical Information Processing in the Nucleus Accumbens." *Trends in Neurosciences* 31 (11): 552-338.

Grim, Ryan. 2022. "Lee Harvey Oswald, The CIA, and LSD: New Clues in Newly Declassified Documents." *The Intercept.* December 19. https://theintercept.com/2022/12/19/lee-harvey-oswald-cia-lsd-jfk/.

Grisel, Judith. 2019. *Never Enough: The Neuroscience and Experience of Drug Addiction.* Penguin Random House.

Gross, Terry. 2019. "The CIA's Secret Quest for Mind Control: Torture, LSD, And A 'Poisoner in Chief'." *NPR.* September 9. https://www.npr.org/2019/09/09/758939641/the-cias-secret-quest-for-mind-control-torture-lsd-and-a-poisoner-in-chief.

Grossberg, Stephen. 2019. "The Resonant Brain: How Attentive Conscious Seeing Reguates Action Sequences That Interact with Attentive Cognitive Learning, Recognition, and Prediction." *Attention, Perception, and Psychophysics* 81 (7): 2237-64.

Hassner, Ron E. 2023. "From Which River to Which Sea?" *Wall Street Journal,* December 5.

Heatherton, Todd F., and Dylan D. Wagner. 2011. "Cognitive Neuroscience of Self-Regulation Failure." *Trends in Cognitive Sciences* 15 (3).

Heatherton, Todd F. 2011. "Neuroscience of Self and Self-Regulation." *Annual Review of Psychology* 62.

Hiebert, Paul. 2008. *Transforming Worldviews: An Anthropological Understanding of How People Change.* Ada: Baker.

Hogg, Hayden Basinger and Jeffrey P. 2023. "Neuroanatomy, Brainstem." *National Library of Medicine.* July 4. Accessed December 24, 2024. https://www. ncbi.nlm.nih.gov/books/NBK544297/.

Jennings, Theodore W. 1990. *Good News to the Poor: John Wesley's Evangelical Economics.* Abingdon.

Jerusalem Post Staff. 2023. *'From the River to the Sea' - Students chant but don't know which river or sea.* December 7. https://www.jpost.com/diaspora/article-776987.

Keener, Craig S. 2016. *The Mind of the Spirit: Paul's Approach to Transformed Thinking.* Ada, Michigan: Baker Academic.

Kempis, Thomas à. 2004. *The Imitation of Christ.* Hendrickson.

Kierkegaard, Søren. 1956. *Purity of Heart is to Will One Thing.* New York: Harper Torchbooks.

Kiernan, J. A. 2012. "Anatomy of the Temporal Lobe." *Epilepsy Research Treatment.* March 29. Accessed December 24, 2024. https://doi. org/10.1155/2012/176157.

Kim, Sung-il. 2013. "Neuroscientific Model of Motivational Process." *Frontiers in Psychology* 98.

Kirkpatrick, David C. 2019. *A Gospel for the Poor: Global Social Christianity and the Latin American Evangelical Left.* University of Pennsylvania Press.

Klawonn, Anna M., and Robert C. Malenka. 2018. "Nucleus Accumbens Modulation in Reward and Aversion." *Cold Spring Harbor Symposia on Quantitative Biology* 83.

Knitter, Paul F. 2014. *Introducing Theologies of Religions.* Orbis.

Koob, George F., and Michel Le Moal. 2006. *Neurobiology of Addiction.* Elsevier.

Leading Britain's Conversation (@LBC). 2024. *"If I had to choose between Christianity and Islam, I'd choose Christianity every single time.* March 31. Accessed December 30, 2024. https://x.com/LBC/status/1774510715975368778?mx=2.

Lindsay, Grace W. 2020. "Attention in Psychology, Neuroscience, and Machine Learning." *Frontiers in Computational Neuroscience* 14.

Liu, Taosheng, and Youyang Hou. 2013. "A Hierarchy of Attentional Priority Signals in Human Frontoparietal Cortex." *Journal of Neuroscience* 14.

Lopez-Persem, Alizée, Philippe Domenech, and Mathias Pessigione. 2016. "How Prior Preferences Determine Decision-Making Frames and Biases in the Human Brain." *eLife* 19 (5).

Luther, Martin. 1955. *Church and Ministry II, Luther's Works.* Fortress.

Marsh, Abigail A., Elizabeth C. Finger, Katherine A. Fowler, Christopher J. Adalio, Ilana T.N. Jurkowitz, Julia C. Schecchter, Daniel S. Pine, Jean Decety, and R.J.R. Blair. 2013. "Empathic Responsiveness in Amygdala and Anterior Cingulate Cortex in Youths with Psychopathic Traits." *Journal of Child Psychology and Psychiatry, and Allied Disciplines* 54 (8): 900-910.

Max Planck Institute. 2022. *How the Brain Helps Us Focus Our Attention.* January 7. https://www.mpg.de/18108721/0106-bild-how-the-brain-s-blue-spot-helps-us-focus-our-attention-149835-x.

Mayo Clinic. 2024. *SPECT.* January 5. https://www.mayoclinic.org/tests-procedures/spect-scan/about/pac-20384925.

Mehta, Kumar. 2023. *Parenting: Instinctive or Learned? How to Ace Parenting.* October 31. Accessed December 2024. https://www.forbes.com/sites/kmehta/2023/10/31/parenting-instinctive-or-learned-how-to-ace-parenting/?sh=540a430773b3.

Molapour, Tanaz, Cindy C. Hagan, Brian Silston, Haiyan Wu, Maxwell Ramstead, Karl Friston, and Dean Mobbs. 2021. "Seven Computations of the Social Brain." *Social Cognitive and Affective Neuroscience* 16 (8): 745-760.

National Frozen & Refrigerated Foods Association. 2023. *2023 Report: Shifting Consumer Eating and Grocery Shopping Habits .* December 4. Accessed December 30, 2024. https://interactive.4media-group.com/nfra-eat-at-home-report-2023.

233

National Institute for Mental Health. n.d. "Mental Illness." *National Institute for Mental Illness.* Accessed March 9, 2015. http://www.nimh.nih.gov/health/statistics/prevalence/any-mental-illness-ami-among-adults.shtml.

National Institute of Mental Health. n.d. "Any Anxiety Disorder." *National Institute of Mental Health.* Accessed March 9, 2015. http://www.nimh.nih.gov/health/statistics/prevalence/any-anxiety-disorder-among-adults.shtml.

—. 2024. "Psychotherapies." *National Institute of Mental Health.* February. http://www.nimh.nih.gov/health/topics/psychotherapies/index.shtml. .

—. 2024. *Suicide.* December. Accessed December 2024. https://www.nimh.nih.gov/health/statistics/suicide.

—. n.d. "Suicide in America: Frequently Asked Questions." *National Institute of Mental Health.* Accessed March 9, 2015. http://www.nimh.nih.gov/health/topics/suicide-prevention/index.shtml.

—. n.d. "U.S. Leading Categories of Diseases/Disorders." *National Institute of Mental Health.* Accessed March 9, 2015. http://www.nimh.nih.gov/health/statistics/disability/us-leading-categories-of-diseases-disorders.shtml.

Naugle, David. n.d. "H. Richard Niebuhr." *Dallas Baptist University.* Accessed December 30, 2024. https://www3.dbu.edu/naugle/pdf/3304_handouts/Christ%20and%20Culture-Five%20Models.pdf.

Newberg, Andrew. 2021. *Neurotheology: How Science Can Enlighten Us About Spirituality.* New York: Columbia University Press.

Newberg, Andrew, Eugene D'Aquilli, and Vince Rause. 2022. *Why God Won't Go Away: Brain Science and the Biology of Belief.* New York: Random House.

NHRA. n.d. *Drag Racing Classes.* Accessed December 2024. https://www.nhra.com/nhra-101/drag-racing-classes#:~:text=They%20are%20capable%20of%20covering,fuel%20during%20a%20single%20run.

Nicola, S.M., S.A. Taha, S.W. Kim, and H.L. Fields. 2005. "Nucleus Accumbens Dopamine Release Is Necessary and Sufficient to Promote the Behavioral Response to Reward-Predictive Cues." *Neuroscience* 135 (4).

Niebuhr, H. Richard. 1976. *Christ and Culture.* Harper Row.

NIH: National Institute of Neurological Disorders and Strokes. 2024. July 17. https://www.ninds.nih.gov/health-information/public-education/brain-basics/brain-basics-know-your-brain.

Oasis House. n.d. *Oasis House: About.* Accessed December 2024. http://oasisfor-women.org/about/.

Owens, Melinda T., and Kimberly D. Tanner. 2017. "Teaching as Brain Changing: Exploring Connections Between Neuroscience and Innovative Teaching." *CBE: Life Sciences Education* 16 (2).

Pew Research Center. 2023. *Online Religious Services Appeal to Many Americans but Going in Person Remains More Popular.* June 2. Accessed December 2024. https://www.pewresearch.org/religion/2023/06/02/online-religious-services-appeal-to-many-americans-but-going-in-person-remains-more-popular/.

Ponticus, Evagrius, and David, trans. Brakke. 2009. *Talking Back [Antirrhetikos]: A Monastic Handbook for Combating Demons.* Cistercian.

Ponticus, Evagrius, and John Eudes, trans. Bamberger. 1972. *The Practikos and Chapters on Prayer, 2nd ed.* Cistercian.

Psychology Today. n.d. "Cognitive Behavioral Therapy." *Psychology Today.* Accessed April 8, 2024. https://www.psychologytoday.com/us/basics/cognitive-behavioral-therapy.

Puglisi-Allegra, Stefano, and Rossella Ventura. 2012. "Prefrontal/Accumbal Catecholamine System Processes High Motivational Salinece." *Frontiers in Behavioral Neuroscience* 6.

Puiu, Tibi. 2019. *ZME Science.* November 28. Accessed December 2024. https://www.zmescience.com/feature-post/space-astronomy/astronomy-articles/how-many-planets-universe/.

Rao, T.S. Sathyanarayana, M.R. Asha, K.S. Jagannatha Rao, and P. Vasudevaraju. 2009. "The Biochemistry of Belief." *Indian Journal of Psychiatry* 51 (4): 239-41.

Recluse, St. Theophan the. 1996. *The Path of Salvation.* Edited by trans. Seraphim Rose. St. Paisius Monastery.

Reemus Boxing. n.d. *Cus D'Amato Quotes.* Accessed April 25, 2024. https://reemus-boxing.com/cus-damato-quotes/.

Rehman, Amna, and Yasir Al Khalili. 2023. "Neuroanatomy, Occipital Lobe." *Nih.gov.* July 24. Accessed December 2024. https://www.ncbi.nlm.nih.gov/books/NBK544320/.

Relevant . 2022. "Gallup: Only 20 Percent of Americans Believe the Bible Is the Actual Word of God." *Relevant* , July 11.

Rieff, Philip. 2006. *The Triumph of the Therapeutic: Uses of Faith after Freud.* Intercollegiate Studies Institute.

Rocky IV. 1985. Directed by Sylvester Stallone. Produced by MGM/UA Entertainment Company.

Roberts, CJD (Jim). 2014. *Canonical Hours.* April 22. Accessed December 29, 2024. https://conclarendon.blogspot.com/2014/04/canonical-hours.html.

Robinson, Robert. 1758. "Come Thou Fount of Every Blessing."

Rodgers, Emiy. 2023. *Fast Food Consumption Statistics.* September 19. Accessed December 2024. https://www.driveresearch.com/market-research-company-blog/fast-food-consumption-statistics/.

Schwartz, Jeffrey, and Sharon Begley. 2002. *The Mind and the Brain: Neuroplasticity and the Power of Mental Force.* Harper Collins.

Science Daily. 2022. *How the Brain's Blue Spot Helps Us Focus Our Attention.* January 7. https://www.sciencedaily.com/releases/2022/01/220107121453.htm.

Science First. n.d. "Ten Interesting Facts About the Human Brain." *Science First.* Accessed November 1, 2024. https://www.sciencefirst.com/10-interesting-facts-about-the-human-brain/.

Scully, Gerald W. 1997. *Murder by the State.* Policy Report, Dallas: National Center for Policy Analysis.

Segar, Carol A., and Earl K. Miller. 2010. "Category Learning in the Brain." *Annual Review of Neurosciences* 33.

Shimron, Yonat, and Emily McFarlan Miller. 2023. *The UMC Lost a Quarter of Its Churches–Most in the South.* January. Accessed December 2024. https://www.christianitytoday.com/news/2023/january/umc-churches-leave-global-methodist-denomination-schism.html.

Sieff, Jessica. 2023. *The Neuroscience of Behavioral Change: Why Intention, Attention, and Persistence Matter.* January 31. Accessed December 2024. https://news.nd.edu/news/the-neuroscience-of-behavioral-change-why-intention-attention-and-persistence-matters/.

Siegel, Daniel J. 2010. *Mindsight: The New Science of Personal Transformation.* New York: Random House.

Siegel, Ethan. 2023. *Ask Ethan: How Can We Comprehend the Size of the Universe?* January 13. Accessed November 2024. https://bigthink.com/starts-with-a-bang/comprehend-size-universe/.

Smietana, Bob. 2014. *Mental Illness Remains Taboo Topic for Many Pastors.* September 22. http://www.lifewayresearch.com/2014/09/22/mental-illness-remains-taboo-topic-for-many-pastors/.

Solano, Ingrid, Nicholas R. Eaton, and K. Daniel O'Leary. 2020. "Pornography Consumption, Modality and Fuction in a Large Internet Sample." *Journal of Sex Research* 57 (1): 92-103.

Solis-Moreira, Jocelyn. 2024. "How Long Does It Really Take to Form a Habit?" *Scientific American*, January 24.

Solzhenitsyn, Alexander. 2018. *The Gulag Archipelago.* Penguin Random House.

Sutton, Jeremy. 2023. *Mirror Neurons and the Neuroscience of Empathy.* September 7. Accessed December 2024. https://positivepsychology.com/mirror-neurons/.

The Global Methodist Church. 2022. "The Transitional Book of Doctrines and Discipline: The Global Methodist Church`." *The Global Methodist Church.* April 12. Accessed December 2024. https://globalmethodist.org/wp-content/uploads/2022/04/Transitional-Discipline.2022041257.pdf.

The United Methodist Church. n.d. "The Book of Discipline of the United Methodist Church 2016." *The General Rules of the Methodist Church.* Accessed May 7, 2024. https://www.umc.org/en/content/the-general-rules-of-the-methodist-church.

Tolentino, Julio C., and Sergio L. Schmidt. 2018. "DSM-5 Criteria and Depression Severity: Implications for Clinical Practice." *Frontiers in Psychiatry* 9.

Tooley, Mark. 2022. *Existing United Methodism Now.* August 5. Accessed December 2024. https://juicyecumenism.com/2022/08/05/exiting-united-methodism-now/.

—. 2017. *Methodist Bishops and False Doctrine.* May 19. https://juicyecumenism.com/2017/05/19/methodist-bishops-false-doctrine/.

Torrico, Tyler J., and Sunil Munakomi. 2023. "Neuroanatomy, Thalamus." *National Library of Medicine.* July 24. https://www.ncbi.nlm.nih.gov/books/NBK542184/#:~:text=The%20thalamus%20is%20a%20paired,other%20via%20the%20interthalamic%20adhesion.

Trafton, Anne. 2022. *How the Brain Responds to Surprising Events.* June 1. https://news.mit.edu/2022/noradrenaline-brain-surprise-0601.

Tsakiridis, George. 2010. *Evagrius Ponticus and Cognitive Science: A Look at Moral Evil and the Thoughts.* Wipf and Stock.

Tzu, Sun, trans Lionel Giles. 2000. *The Art of War.* Allandale Online Publishing.

U.S. Centers for Disease Control and Prevention, U.S. Centers for Disease Control and. 2024. *About Adverse Childhood Experiences.* October 8. https://www.cdc.gov/aces/about/index.html.

U.S. Congress, Senate Select Committee to Study Governmental Operations with Respect to Intelligence Activities. 1976. *Book 1: Final Report of the Select Committee to Study Governmental Operations with Respect to Intellegence Activities, United States Senate Together with Additional, Supplemental, and Separate Views.* Government Report, U.S. Senate, 94th Cong., 2d sess., Washington, D.C.: US Government Printing Office.

University of Maryland Rehabilitation and Orthopaedic Institute. n.d. *Pay Attention!! Attention and Attention Process Training in Brain Injury.*

van-Hasselt, Michelle Cosio, Julio C. Penagos-Corzo, Daniela Escobar, Rúben A. Vázquez-Roque, and Gonzalo Flores. 2022. "Mirror Neurons and Empathy-Related Regions in Psychopathy: Systemic Review, Meta-Analysis, and a Working Model." *Social Neuroscience* 17 (5): 462-479.

Voigt, Katharina. 2022. "Where Do Our Preferences Come From? How Hard Decisions Shape Our Preferences." *Frontiers in Behavioral Neuroscience* 16.

von Leibniz, Gottfried Wilhelm. 1951. *Leibniz Selections.* Edited by Philip P. Wiener. New York: Charles Scribner's Sons.

von Leibniz, Gottfried Wilhelm. 1985. *Theodicy.* Open Court Press.

Ward, Mark. 2013. *Web Porn: Just How Much Is There?* July 1. https://www.bbc.com/news/technology-23030090.amp.

WebRoot. n.d. *Internet Pornography by the Numbers: A Significant Threat to Society.* Accessed January 9, 2024. https://www.webroot.com/us/en/resources/tips-articles/internet-pornography-by-the-numbers#:~:text=Internet%20Pornography%20Statistics%20in%20the%20United%20States,the%20word%20%22adult%22%20into%20a%20search%20engine.

Wesley, John. 2024. *John Wesley's 22 Questions of Self Examination.* Accessed December 29, 2024. https://www.umc.org/en/content/john-wesleys-22-questions-of-self-examination.

Wesley, John. 1872. *Journal Entry for May 17, 1740.* Vols. 1, Journals 1, in *Works of John Wesley,* by ed. Thomas Jackson. Wesleyan Conference Office.

Wesley, John. n.d. *The Scripture Way of Salvation.* Vol. 7, in *Works of John Wesley,* by John Wesley.

—. 1738. *Wesley's Rules for House Churches.* December 25. Accessed December 2024. https://housechurch.org/miscellaneous/wesley_band-societies.html.

—. 1872. *Works of John Wesley.* Edited by Thomas Jackson. London: Wesleyan Conference Office.

Wesley, John, and Thomas, ed. Jackson. 1978. *The Means of Grace.* Vol. 5, in *The Work's of John Wesley's,* by John Wesley. Baker Books.

—. 1978. *The Works of Rev. John Wesley.* Edited by Thomas Jackson. Vol. 3. Wesleyan Methodist Book Room; repr., Baker Books.

Wiens, John J. 2023. "How Many Species Are There on Earth? Progress and Problems." *PLOS Biology.*

Willmington, Harold. November. "Old Testament Passages Quoted by Jesus." *Liberty University Scholars Crossing.* 2017. https://digitalcommons.liberty.edu/cgi/viewcontent.cgi?article=1060&context=second_person.

World Health Organization. n.d. "Depression: A Global Public Health Concern." *World Health Organization.* Accessed January 20, 2016. http://www.who.int/mental_health/management/depression/en.

SUGGESTED ADDITIONAL WORKS

Abraham, Eyal, and Ruth Feldman. 2022. "The Neurobiology of Fatherhood." *Current Opinion in Psychology.*

Abraham, William. 1989. *The Logic of Evangelism.* Eerdmans.

Adolphs, Ralph. 2009. "The Social Brain: Neural Basis of Social Knowledge." *Annual Review of Psychology* 793-716.

Albright, Carol Rausch, and James B. Ashbrook. 2001. *Where God Lives in the Brain.* Sourcebooks.

Aquilina, Mike, and James L. Papandrea. 2019. *How Christianity Saved Civilization ... and Must Do So Again.* Sophia Institute Press.

Arakaki, Robert. 2012. *Defending the Vincentian Canon: 'Everywhere, Always, and By All'—A Response to Outlaw Presbyterianism.* July 10. Accessed January 2025. https://orthodoxbridge.com/2012/07/10/defending-the-vincentian-canon-everywhere-always-and-by-all-a-response-to-outlaw-presbyterianism/.

Barton, William. 2013. *The Oxford Bible Commentary.* Oxford University Press.

Bauer, David R, and Robert A. Traina. n.d. *Inductive Bible Study: A Comprehensive Guide to the Practice of Hermeneutics .* Baker Academic.

Bauer, Walter, and Frederick William Danker. 2001. *A Greek-English Lexicon of the New Testament, 3rd Edition.* University of Chicago Press.

Beauregard, Mario, and Denyse O'Leary. 2008. *The Spiritual Brain: A Neuroscientist's Case for the Existence of the Soul.* HarperCollins.

Beauregard, Mario, and V. Paquette. 2006. "Neural Correlates of a Mystical Experience in Carmelite Nuns." *Neuroscience Letters* 405 (3): 186-90.

Bell, Catherine. 1992. *Ritual Theory, Ritual Practice.* Oxford University Press.

Bellini, Peter J. 2021. *The Cerulean Soul.* Baylor University Press.

Bellini, Peter. 2022. *The X-Manual: A Comprehensive Handbook on Deliverance and Exorcism*. Wipf and Stock.

—. 2023. *Thunderstruck! The Deliverance Ministry of John Wesley*. Wipf and Stock.

—. 2014. *Truth Therapy: Renewing Your Mind with the Word of God*. Wipf and Stock.

—. 2018. *Unleashed*. Wipf and Stock.

Bellini, Petey. 2024. *Through the Threshold: Breaking the Barrier of a Closed Universe*. Self Published (Kindle).

Brierley, Justin. 2023. *The Surprising Rebirth of Belief in God: Why New Atheism Grew Old and Secular Thinkers are Considering Christianity*. Tyndale Elevate.

Chen, Isaac, and Forshing Lui. 2023. "Neuroanatomy, Neuron Action." *Library of Medicine*. August 14. https://www.ncbi.nlm.nih.gov/books/NBK546639/.

Clark, Randy. 2013. *There Is More: The Secret to Experiencing God's Power to Change Your Life*. Baker.

Coleman, Robert. 2006. *The Master Plan of Evangelism*. Revell.

Damasio, Antonio. 1999. *The Feeling of What Happens: Body and Emotion in the Making of Consciousness*. Harcourt.

Del Colle, Ralph, H. Ray Dunning, Stanley M. Horton, and Walter C. Kaiser. 2004. *Perspectives on Spirit Baptism, ed. Chad Brand*. Broadman and Holman.

Fee, Gordon. 2014. *How to Read the Bible for All It's Worth, 4th edition*. Zondervan Academic.

Foster, Richard. 2018. *Celebration of Discipline: The Path to Spiritual Growth*. HarperCollins.

Fuhr, Richard Alan, and Andreas J. Köstenberger Ph.D. 2016. *Inductive Bible Study: Observation, Interpretation, and Application through the Lenses of History, Literature, and Theology*. B&H Academic.

Guarino, Thomas. 2014. *Vincent of Lérins and the Development of Christian Doctrine*. Baker.

Heitzenrater, Richard. 2002. *The Poor and the People Called Methodists*. Abingdon.

Herrick, Greg. 2004. *Paul and Civil Disobedience in Romans 13:1-7.* June 24. https://bible.org/article/paul-and-civil-obedience-romans-131-7.

Heschmeyer, Joe. 2022. "Development of Doctrine and St. Vincent of Lérins." *Shameless Popery.* Catholic Answers. Podcast, December 29.

Holland, Tom. 2019. *Dominion: How the Christian Revolution Remade the World.* Hachette.

Horrell, Nathan D., Melina C. Acosta, and Wendy Saltzman. 2021. "Plasticity of the Paternal Brain: Effects of Fatherhood on Neural Structure and Function." *Developmental Psychobiology.*

Hull, Bill. 2006. *The Complete Book of Discipleship.* NavPress.

Hunter, George. 2010. *The Celtic Way of Evangelism.* Abingdon.

Inglis, Holly J. 2014. *Sticky Learning: How Neuroscience Supports Teaching That's Remembered.* Fortress.

James, Sharon. 2021. *How Christianity Transformed the World.* Christian Focus.

Johnsen, Tom J., and Oddgeir Friborg. 2015. "The Effects of Cognitive Behavioral Therapy as an Anti-Depressive Treatment Is Falling: A Meta-analysis." *Psychological Bulletin* 141 (4): 747-68.

Johnson, Luke Timothy. 2004. *The Creed: What Christians Believe and Why it Matters.* Doubleday.

Keener, Craig S. 2016. *The Mind of the Spirit: Paul's Approach to Transformed Thinking.* Ada, Michigan: Baker Academic.

Keener, Craig. 2014. *The Bible Background Commentary of the New Testament.* InterVarsity Press.

Khammissa, Razia A. G., Simon Nemutandani, Gal Feller, Johan Lemmer, and Liviu Feller. 2022. "Burnout Phenomenon: Neurophysiological Factors, Clinical Features, and Aspects of Management." *Journal of International Medical Research* 50 (9).

Klemm, W.R. 2020. ""God Spots in the Brain: Nine Categories of Unasked. Unanswered Questions." *Religions* 11 (9): 468.

Kolb, David. 2015. *Experiential Learning: Experience as the Source of Learning and Development.* Pearson Education.

Laurie, Greg. 2022. *Lennon, Dylan, Alice, and Jesus: The Spiritual Biography of Rock and Roll.* Regnery.

Levering, Matthew. 2016. *Proofs of God: Classical Arguments from Tertullian to Barth.* Baker.

Lindsay, Grace W. 2020. "Attention in Psychology: Neuroscience, and Machine Learning." *Frontiers in Computational Neuroscience.*

Lynch, D., K.R. Laws, and P.J. McKenna. 2010. "Cognitive Behavioral Therapy for Major Psychiatric Disorder: Does it Really Work? A Meta-analytical Review of Well-Controlled Trials." *Psychological Medicine* 40 (1): 9-24.

Montazeribarforoushi, Saba, Abolfazl Keshavarzsaleh, and Thomas Zoëga Ramsøy. 2017. "On the Hierarchy of Choice: An Applied Neuroscience Perspective on the AIDA Model." *Cogent Psychology* 4 (1).

Moore, S. David. 2004. *The Shepherding Movement: Controversy and Charismatic Ecclesiology.* Continuum.

Mounce, William. 1993. *The Analytic Lexicon to the Greek New Testament.*

—. 2021. *Why I Trust the Bible.* Zondervan.

MSc, Olivia Guy-Evans. 2023. "13 Cognitive Distortions Identified in CBT." *Simply Psychology*, November 9.

Newberg, Andrew. 2008. *Born to Believe: God, Science, and the Origin of Ordinary and Extraordinary Beliefs.* Simon and Schuster.

—. 2021. *Neurotheology: How Science Can Enlighten Us About Spirituality.* Columbia University Press.

Newberg, Andrew, Eugene D'Aquilli, and Vince Rause. 2022. *Why God Won't Go Away: Brain Science and the Biology of Belief.* Random House.

Ogden, Greg. 2003. *Transforming Discipleship: Making Disciples a Few at a Time.* IVP.

Othello, J. 2004. *The Soul of Rock and Roll: A History of African Americans in Rock Music.* Regent.

Payne, Leah. 2024. *God Gave Rock and Roll to You.* Oxford University Press.

Pearce, Joseph. 2001. *Solzhenitsyn: A Soul in Exile, revised and updated edition.* Ignatius.

Persinger, Michael. 1987. *Neuropsychological Bases of God Beliefs*. Praeger.

Peters, Greg. 2015. *The Story of Monasticism: Retrieving an Ancient Tradition for Contemporary Spirituality*. Baker.

Russell, Robert J. 2002. "Dialogue Between Science and Theology." *Interdisciplinary Encyclopedia of Religion and Science*.

Schmidt, Alvin J. 2004. *How Christianity Changed the World*. Zondervan.

1985. *Rocky IV*. Directed by Sylvester Stallone. Produced by MGM/UA Entertainment Company.

Stark, Rodney. 2011. *The Triumph of Christianity: How the Jesus Movement Became the World's Largest Religion*. Harper Collins.

Stewart, Kenneth J. 2013. "Review: "Vincent of Lérins and the Development of Christian Doctrine" Themelios 38, no 3." *Themelios*.

n.d. *Strong's Exhaustive Concordance*.

n.d. *Thayer's Greek-English Lexicon of the New Testament: Coded with Strong's Concordance Numbers*.

Theodore W. Jennings, Jr. 1999. *Good News to the Poor: John Wesley's Evangelical Economics*. Abingdon.

Tyson, Mike. 2013. *Undisputed Truth*. Penguin.

Tyson, Mike, and Larry Sloman. 2018. *Iron Ambition: My Life with Cus D'Amato*. Blue Rider Press.

van Gennep, Arnold. 1960. *The Rites of Passage*. Chicago University Press.

n.d. *Vine's Expository Dictionary*.

Vygotsky, Lev. 1978. *The Development of Higher Psychological Processes*. Harvard University Press.

Walls, Jerry, and Trent Dougherty. 2018. *Two Dozen (or So) Arguments for God: The Plantinga Project*. Oxford Univerity Press.

Watson, Kevin. 2009. *A Blueprint for Discipleship: Wesley's General Rules as a Guide for Christian Living*. Discipleship Resources.

—. 2015. *Pursuing Social Holiness: The Band Meeting in Wesley's Thought and Popular Methodist Practice*. Oxford University Press.

—. 2017. *The Band Meeting: Rediscovering Relational Discipleship in Transformational Community.* Seedbed.

—. 2013. *The Class Meeting: Reclaiming a Forgotten (and Essential) Small Group Experience.* Seedbed.

Wiebe, Phillip. 2004. *God and Other Spirits: Imitations of Transcendence in Christian Experience.* Oxford University Press.

—. 2015. *Intuitive Knowing as Spiritual Experience.* Palgrave Macmillan.

—. 2023. *Religious Experience: Implications for What is Real.* Cambridge University Press.

—. 1997. *Visions of Jesus.* Oxford University Press.

Wilkins, Michael. 1992. *Following the Master: A Biblical Theology of Discipleship.* Zondervan.

—. 1988. *The Concept of Disciple in Matthew's Gospel, As Reflected in the Use of the Term "Mathetes".* Brill.

Witherington, Ben III. 2000. *Jesus the Sage: The Pilgrimage of Wisdom.* Fortress Press.

—. 1999. *John's Gospel: A Commentary on the Fourth Gospel.* Westminster John Knox Press.

SCAN HERE to learn more about
Invite Ministries—created to invite people to a deeper
faith and living relationship with Jesus Christ

www.ingramcontent.com/pod-product-compliance
Lightning Source LLC
Chambersburg PA
CBHW030412130626
46549CB00004B/1733